THE ECONOMICS OF UNDERDEVELOPMENT

A SERIES OF ARTICLES
AND PAPERS
SELECTED AND EDITED BY

A. N. AGARWALA
and S. P. SINGH

OXFORD UNIVERSITY PRESS
London Oxford New York

First published by Oxford University Press, Bombay, 1958
First issued as an Oxford University Press paperback, 1963

This reprint, 1969

Printed in the United States of America

CONTENTS

INTRODUCTION

THE PROBLEM of the economic development of underdeveloped countries has received worldwide attention, mainly since the end of the Second World War. This is a late beginning, indeed; but it has been marked with great intellectual activity and keen academic enthusiasm. In the last few years, the stream of fresh literature on the subject has assumed enormous proportions, and much of it is not easily accessible. While some of this literature represents real advancement of knowledge a large part of it is of only secondary importance, being policy-oriented in character, based on concepts which are not always carefully defined, and generally lacking in scientific analysis and mature treatment. But it would perhaps be unjust to censure such literature too harshly, as it has had a historic role to play, being inherent in the formative stages of new doctrines. It should also be remembered that this literature has not only succeeded in focusing attention on the economics of underdevelopment but has led in fact to the creation of a separate branch of economic studies. This process has been accompanied and stimulated by the appearance of some remarkable works of scientific analysis and construction, which have become the nucleus of it. The economics of underdevelopment is a subject of growing importance to the developed as well as to the underdeveloped nations of the world.

Although many useful ideas on the economics of underdevelopment can be found in the works of the great economists of the past, as a serious subject of study it began to emerge only during the 'forties of the present century. The contributions of the 'forties played a highly useful and educative role. They attracted the attention of other economists to the subject as well as themselves assisting in its advancement. Some brilliant work of great and lasting value was also done in this period, e.g. an article by Rosenstein-Rodan and three celebrated monographs by Eugene Staley, A. J. Brown and K. (now M.) Mandelbaum. Since 1950, there has been in evidence a marked trend towards specialization in study and rigour and depth in analysis. Moreover, it is now realized that the subject can no longer be confined within the bounds of articles, monographs and reports, and scientific treatises have begun to appear. The works of Ragnar Nurkse and W. Arthur Lewis have initiated this trend and have served to raise the standard of analysis, discussion and contemplation.

Even so, most of the contributions of basic significance are still scattered in a number of journals and periodicals, access to which is not easy, especially in India. Also it is our experience that students and researchers in many centres of learning in the underdeveloped countries often lack facilities of reference and remain unaware of the more important articles and of the relative worth and significance of each of them. We thought, therefore, that we could help to overcome these difficulties by bringing together reprints of certain articles which can be said to have given a direction to, or raised the level of, economic studies in this particular sphere in recent years. The present volume is therefore designed to assist research students and those reading for the separate paper now devoted in many universities to the subject of underdevelopment.

We should like to emphasize the importance of fostering the study of this new subject in underdeveloped countries themselves. Understanding depends not only on a familiarity with the outer form of underdeveloped economies, which is a superficial affair at best, but on an emotional appreciation of the spirit, culture and aspirations of the peoples of the underdeveloped areas. Such an appreciation, although not beyond the capacity of those who belong to industrially advanced economies, must, in their case, be the result of conscious effort, and there is therefore the risk of faulty appreciation with its concomitant dangers of mistaken conclusion and unsound theory. Thus it is necessary for economists belonging to underdeveloped countries to participate actively in this field and to formulate doctrines which are based on an inherent understanding of the forces and conditions existing around them. They should not be content with modifications or special applications of existing doctrines. And economic science can be a basis of economic policy only if it carefully promotes and jealously preserves an intimate relationship with the actualities of fact.

The work of the economists of underdeveloped areas may not by itself be sufficient for the full development of the subject, nor can anybody claim monopoly rights in any domain of knowledge; but help can be given in providing the point of view of the underdeveloped peoples and in offering verification of the theories and ideas propounded in other parts of the world. It has been a standing criticism of the economics taught in underdeveloped countries that it is a carbon copy of the economics taught in and appropriate to industrially advanced countries. It is hoped that the studies presented in this volume will stimulate those in the underdeveloped countries to think further for themselves.

This volume includes only those contributions which make a general and overall approach to the various aspects of the economics of underdevelopment. We have not included any article which pertains either to specific policy-issues, or to descriptions or analyses of economic conditions and institutions. The articles comprise reprints of a chapter from a book, two papers read at conferences and eighteen papers published in various economic journals. These twenty-one items have been classified into six sections.

The first section, entitled 'Approaches to the Problem of Underdevelopment', contains five contributions — by Jacob Viner, Colin Clark, G. M. Meier, Paul A. Baran and H. Myint. It is hoped that they will acquaint the reader with the criteria that can be adopted in defining underdevelopment, the causes and factors contributing to the phenomenon of underdevelopment, and the varied approaches that are generally made in analysing and discovering solutions to the problems of underdevelopment.

The second section contains only two papers — by Simon Kuznets and W. W. Rostow — which examine the problem of underdevelopment in an historical context. While Kuznets draws a highly illustrative comparison between the present-day underdeveloped countries and the pre-industrial phase in advanced countries, Rostow launches his well-known 'take-off into self-sustained growth' approach which, it is believed, is pregnant with possibilities for the future.

The third section contains three papers — by Henry C. Wallich, V. K. R. V. Rao and H. J. Bruton — which seek to analyse the problem of underdevelopment in the light of three important economic theories. Wallich analyses in the light of Schumpeter's theory of economic development, Rao in the context of Keynes's general theory of employment, and Bruton in the light of the currently developing growth economics of Harrod, Domar, Joan Robinson, Fellner and others.

The fourth section, entitled 'External Economies and Balanced Growth', contains five papers. The first is a contribution by P. N. Rosenstein-Rodan in which the celebrated 'balanced development' approach based on Young's ideas of external economies found its first expression as early as 1943. A similar but more far-reaching 'balanced growth' approach has been developed by Ragnar Nurkse during recent years. It has been elucidated by him at several places and finds fullest expression in his 1953 treatise on capital formation. The article which we have included in the present volume represents an early but perhaps the shortest expression of the theme. These ideas are examined critically by J. Marcus Fleming in the third paper of this section. The fourth paper, by Tibor Scitovsky, is short but serves to remove much of the fog that has gathered round the concept of external economies and the appropriateness of its use in the economics of underdevelopment. The fifth paper, by Celso Furtado, is a detailed, critical and useful commentary on the Nurksian thesis of balanced growth.

The fifth section contains only two papers. The first paper by Alfredo and Ifigenia Navarrete presents a succinct and useful analysis of underemployment in relation to underdevelopment. The second paper, by R. S. Eckaus, contains an instructive and thorough analysis of the factor-proportions problem and affords a useful perspective for understanding factor-disequilibrium, which is widely recognized to be a corollary of underdevelopment in the contemporary world.

The last section presents four models of economic development of an underdeveloped country, by H. W. Singer, W. A. Lewis, Hollis B. Chenery and M. Bronfenbrenner. The first two models (we hope we are correct in calling Lewis's paper a model) have already earned a place of repute and need no introduction. Their treatment of industrialization, savings and investment, and surplus labour is well-articulated and sufficiently realistic. Moreover, Lewis's paper deserves special attention because it is written in the classical tradition. Chenery's contribution is of comparatively recent origin but contains a useful exercise in model-building in that it provides scope for the treatment of factor-disequilibrium, of the foreign exchange gap, and the interconnectedness of productive sectors. Bronfenbrenner's triplets, though analytically very simple, are important because they contain an exploration into the communistic line of thinking. He provides an interesting analysis of the role of confiscation in economic development.

It should be mentioned that the articles in this volume are reproduced as originally published, with only slight modification to regularize style. We do not claim any special virtue for the contents or arrangement and we are conscious that some other method might be preferred by some of our readers. The task of planning and editing such a volume is rendered difficult by the many lines of approach open to us. For instance, a plausible case could be made for the inclusion of more items in this volume, though not perhaps for excluding any of those which have been included. In fact, so many varied and sometimes inconsistent considerations are involved that it is difficult to justify all editorial decisions. The appropriateness of each article from the editors' point of view, the necessity of covering a wide range of authors and topics, the limitations imposed by space and the requirements dictated by the need for commercial success are some of the conflicting considerations involved in the venture. There are certain topics on which appropriate articles are not available, while many excellent articles which are available do not fit into the general scheme of things. Moreover, the personal prejudices of the editors play, inevitably, a decisive part. This, however, neither explains nor justifies the blemishes and shortcomings of this volume, for which the responsibility is clearly the editors'. We are sorry we have not been able to include in this volume the contributions of Duesenberry and Spengler. Other important contributions were omitted either because they are readily available in other edited volumes or because they are not relevant to the scope of this volume.

The reader will understand that this volume contains papers on only certain aspects of the economics of underdevelopment, and that other important aspects have been left out. We really have an extended plan of work, and hope, if this volume is well received, to prepare two further volumes containing contributions on the remaining aspects of the subject, to be followed by a detailed bibliography.

The editors have pleasure in acknowledging a heavy debt of gratitude to all the authors whose contributions comprise this volume and who so promptly and generously allowed us to reprint them; in fact, their kindness has been overwhelming. The editors are also indebted to all the original publishers who helped in a similar manner; individual acknowledgements are to be found in footnotes to the various chapters and this explains the omission of individual names here. But particular assistance was extended by Mr H. W. Singer of the United Nations, Mrs Elizabeth Henderson of the *International Economic Papers,* Rome, Mr A. O. Reynal of *Fondo de Cultura Economica,* Mexico, the Secretary to the Delegates of the Clarendon Press, Oxford, and by Professor W. W. Rostow, to each of whom special thanks are due.

I. APPROACHES TO THE PROBLEM OF UNDERDEVELOPMENT

THE ECONOMICS OF DEVELOPMENT*

by **Jacob Viner**

THE OUTPUT OF LITERATURE ON 'ECONOMIC' DEVELOPMENT HAS in recent years reached massive proportions. The literature, however, is extraordinarily lacking in explicit definition of the basic terms it employs, and if one attempts to find from the context what definitions are implicit one discovers that a wide range of different and often conflicting concepts is being covered by a single verbal label. What, for instance, is an 'underdeveloped country'? Let me examine the most common criteria of 'underdevelopment' as they appear in the current literature.

1. A country is often labelled as underdeveloped merely or mainly because it has a low ratio of population to area. Since the term 'underdeveloped' always carries with it the implication that development is feasible and desirable, this usage overrates the importance of mere space, whether for economic or any other significant purpose. There are 'empty spaces' which it is not in anyone's interest to have filled. In the present state of knowledge, the Arctic and the Antarctic, the Sahara Desert, and even the great tropical jungles, are not properly to be regarded as underdeveloped areas unless 'underdeveloped' is to be used as synonymous with undeveloped.

It is a different matter if the sparsely settled area is 'rich' in natural resources in an economically significant sense. In the ordinary geography and travel books, and in the official handbooks of most countries, however, all areas tend to be labelled rich in resources, even when the 'resources' are unproven, or are of low quality, or are inaccessible, or are of a kind which has low economic value per unit of volume even at the point of consumption so that they are valuable assets only when located near important centres of population. The technique of discovery of hidden mineral resources is constantly improving, and new uses are constantly being found for organic

* *International Trade and Economic Development*—Lectures delivered at the National University of Brazil, 1953, Chapter VI. Reprinted with the permission of the Clarendon Press, Oxford, and the author.

and mineral materials which previously had no or limited serviceability. It is proper therefore to regard any extensive area as having potential value even if to date no one has found a way of making a decent living in it or from it. It nevertheless seems to be true that in the entire past century the only 'empty spaces' of any size which have been settled by a population which has succeeded in earning therein even a moderately high *per capita* income have been areas with good soil and good climate, and no more of such large empty spaces seem to exist. There is no sense in wasting scarce resources in 'developing' areas which cannot provide a decent living for human beings, but a good deal of effort and wealth, and even a greater deal of talk, are being wasted on such areas.

2. Scarcity of capital as shown by the prevalence of high interest rates is often used as a sign that there is underdevelopment. This is not a decisive test, however. Until tight national controls on the export of capital became common, there was a high degree of international mobility of capital, with the consequence that borrowers of equal creditworthiness were able to borrow at not greatly dissimilar rates of interest regardless of their location. Before 1914, India, Canada, the United States, the Argentine, and Australia borrowed long-term capital in the London money-market at substantially similar rates of interest. Where debtors were charged high rates, it was not because they operated in underdeveloped countries but because their past records showed them to be uncreditworthy or because the prospects that they would be able to meet their debt obligations were unfavourable.

High interest rates, moreover, are an ambiguous test as to the kind of 'scarcity' of capital which is prevailing. Interest rates may be high because the risk premium is high, or because the marginal productivity function of capital is high and has high elasticity, or because capital has so far been available only for the most urgent purposes but would have low marginal productivity if more abundantly used. All three would ordinarily be regarded as instances of capital scarcity, but there would be important economic differences between them. It can be taken for granted that for substantial economic expansion increase of capital is always a necessary condition. But only in the second case would it be clear that substantially increased investment would be economically justifiable, that is, would add sufficiently to the national output to meet depreciation and reasonable interest costs.

Another type of criterion of scarcity of capital is often used, namely, the ratio of capital supply to the supplies of other categories of factors of production. As a practical test, this probably has a substantial measure of validity, although abstract theory gives only qualified support to the proposition that where the ratio of capital to other resources is low, the marginal productivity of capital will be high. Cases are conceivable, because of, let us say, an unfavourable climate, or of bad government, where the marginal productivity functions of all the factors taken seriatim, and therefore the overall productivity of the combined factors whatever the proportions in which they are combined, are low. The factors of production, moreover, are in some degree rival or competitive even if it is true that in general they are more complementary or co-operative than rival. It is for this and other reasons at least theoretically conceivable, therefore, that there may be national economies where the marginal productivity function of capital is low beyond a fairly early stage of investment even though natural resources are abundant and good in quality and even though the marginal productivity function of labour is high and has high elasticity, provided the marginal productivity function of labour is high even at low levels of investment. If such cases exit, increase in the amount of capital investment per unit of labour employed, or per acre, would not result in an appreciable increase in *per capita* output after allowance for the costs of the capital itself and its maintenance. These capital costs must not be neglected. Even if the capital came from abroad as a free grant, there would be the costs of maintenance, and of defraying time-depreciation, use-depreciation, product-obsolescence, and process-obsolescence. And when the capital is the result of domestic accumulation, or is borrowed from abroad, the interest charges have to be met, either as payments to the lenders, or as opportunity-costs reflecting the sacrifice of alternative uses of the capital.

3. The most commonly used criterion for classification of countries as developed or underdeveloped is the ratio of industrial output to total output or of industrial population to total

population. In an earlier lecture, I pointed out that while it is true that the ratio of non-agricultural to total population tends to be highly correlated positively with *per capita* income, the degree of industrialization may be and often is a consequence rather than a cause of the level of prosperity, and that where agriculture is prosperous not only do tertiary or service industries tend spontaneously to grow, but there is widespread tendency to use disposable surplus income derived from agricultural prosperity to subsidize uneconomic urban industry, with the consequence that the overall level of *per capita* income, while still comparatively high, is lower than it would be if urban industry were not artificially stimulated.

I do not challenge the semantic sovereignty of economists or of anyone else, and if there is determination to continue to use 'underdevelopment' and 'non-industrialization' as synonymous terms, I must reconcile myself to the fact even if I do not approve of it. What I do have a right and a professional duty to insist upon, however, is that the practice is either arbitrary, or is more or less conscious question-begging, having as its consequence, and sometimes as its deliberate intention, the evasion of analysis which would lead to unwelcome conclusions.

4. I would question also the expediency of identifying 'underdeveloped' countries with 'young countries'. There are no satisfactory criteria for the 'age' of a country, and if, as is common, date of settlement by people of European stock is taken as the test of age, Brazil is an older country than the United States, and China and India have not been born yet. Except for the United States, the countries outside Europe with the highest levels of *per capita* income are countries which were 'empty spaces' until fairly late in the nineteenth century, and some of the 'oldest' countries are the poorest. Time brings all things, but not to the same country. To some it brings prosperity; to others persistent poverty.

5. A more useful definition of an underdeveloped country is that it is a country which has good potential prospects for using more capital or more labour or more available natural resources, or all of these, to support its present population on a higher level of living, or, if its *per capita* income level is already fairly high, to support a larger population on a not lower level of living. This definition puts the primary emphasis where I

would think it properly belongs, on *per capita* levels of living, on the issue of poverty and prosperity, although it leaves room for secondary emphasis on quantity of population. On the basis of this definition, a country may be underdeveloped whether it is densely or sparsely populated, whether it is a capital-rich or a capital-poor country, whether it is a high-income *per capita* or low-income *per capita* country, or whether it is an industrialized or an agricultural country. The basic criterion then becomes whether the country has good potential prospects of raising *per capita* incomes, or of maintaining an existing high level of *per capita* income for an increased population.

This definition, I am aware, would not be universally acceptable. It is not only that it would be objectionable to those who want 'economic development' even at the cost of a lowering of *per capita* income levels provided it brings the filling up of empty spaces, or urbanization, or industrialization. Patriotic citizens may want their national economies to grow in size of aggregate income or of aggregate output because of prestige considerations or strategic considerations even if this involves a lowering of average living standards. To others, living standards may be a weighty consideration, but in terms of the living standards—and conceivably also the size—of a particular class or a particular regional category of the population, rather than and perhaps to the total disregard of the average standard of living of the people as a whole. A colonial power may be interested in the economic development of a possession as an incident to its becoming an enlarged market for the mother country's export products or an enlarged source of supply of cheap foodstuffs, or raw materials, or military manpower, without regard to the economic welfare of the colonial population. All of these considerations have at one time or another been associated with the term 'economic development'. I do not question their claims to attention.

While the supplementing of data as to economic aggregates by *per capita* averages provides additional and often essential information, however, even this does not suffice for some purposes. Let us suppose, for instance, that a country which has embarked on a programme of economic development engages in periodic stock-taking of its progress, and finds not only that aggregate wealth, aggregate income, total population, total production, are all increasing, but that *per capita* wealth, income, production, are also all increasing. All of these are favourable indices, but even in combination do they suffice to show that there has been 'economic progress', an increase in economic 'welfare', rather than retrogression?

Suppose that someone should argue that the one great economic evil is the prevalence of a great mass of crushing poverty, and that it is a paradox to claim that a country is achieving economic progress as long as the absolute extent of such poverty prevailing in that country has not lessened or has even increased? Such a country, nevertheless, might be able to meet all the tests of economic development which I have just enumerated. If its population has undergone substantial increase, the numbers of those living at the margin of subsistence or below, illiterate, diseased, undernourished, may have grown steadily consistently with a rise in the average income of the population as a whole.

Not only this, but if immigration is a significant factor, these statistical tests are consistent with no native having undergone an improvement in his economic status beyond having more children survive to their teens instead of dying in infancy, and with no adult descendant of native parents having a higher level of income than did his parents or grandparents. It requires only one additional condition, that the immigrants shall not be as well off as they would have been if they had stayed in their native land, to make these statistical indexes of 'successful' economic development be consistent with no single individual being better off than or even as well off as his parents were.

Were I to insist, however, that the reduction of mass poverty be made a crucial test of the realization of economic development, I would be separating myself from the whole body of literature in this field. In all the literature on economic development I have seen, I have not found a single instance where statistical data in terms of aggregates and of averages have not been treated as providing adequate tests of the degree of achievement of economic development. I know, moreover, of no country which regards itself as underdeveloped which provides itself with the statistical data necessary for the discovery of whether or not growth in aggregate national wealth and in *per capita* income are associated with decrease in the absolute or even relative extent to which crushing poverty prevails.

There is a school of thought with respect to economic development which is aware of the point I have been discussing, but believes that to subject a national programme of economic development to the requirement that it shall prevent an increase in the absolute extent of severe poverty may doom the programme to failure without lasting benefit to any sector of the population. They hold that in many cases all that is practicable, at least for some time, is to increase the national area of economic health and strength, perhaps relatively but at least absolutely, without preventing or even retarding, and possibly even while stimulating, the growth of the area of desperate poverty. Eventually, they contend, the prosperity will trickle down to the lower levels of the population, and the national resources will become abundant enough to make possible large-scale programmes to rescue them from their poverty, whereas a direct and immediate attack on mass poverty would result only in the squandering of the limited national resources on temporary palliatives, with increases in the number of the desperately poor as the only important result.

This school is unaware, I suspect, that the views it holds are very close to one of Malthus's doctrines. Malthus was deeply concerned about the difficulty of raising the masses of the English poor from their level of desperate poverty, because of their tendency, as he believed, to absorb any increase in productivity in an increase in their numbers instead of using it to raise their standard of living. The remedy which he most emphasized was the limitation of births through postponement of marriage, with or without 'moral restraint', but without births, before marriage. He obviously did not have much confidence, however, in the practicality of this remedy, and he supported as an alternative or supplementary remedy the promotion within the English economy of what might be termed enclaves of economic privilege, whose members would be recruited from those sections of the population which could be relied upon not to absorb increases in income wholly in natural increase of population. It was largely on this ground that Malthus supported tariff protection for English agriculture as a means of increasing the prosperity of the landed classes and thus increasing the numbers of those who could be relied upon to use increased income either to raise their standard of living or for investment instead of to increase the size of their families. It is not an attractive doctrine. I am not aware, however, that where the population problem as Malthus envisaged it is a fact, and capital is scarce, patently superior alternatives are readily discoverable and applicable.

I proceed to an attempt at a schematic presentation of the obstacles to economic development, with the reminder that I use the term to signify not merely economic growth, but economic growth with which is associated either rising *per capita* levels of income or the maintenance of existing high levels of income. The classification of these obstacles about to be presented is admittedly a somewhat artificial one, since the categories of obstacles distinguished are not only not independent of each other but overlap and in some cases may represent the same factors looked at from different points of view rather than different factors.

First come low productivity functions. Foremost in responsibility for these are qualitative factors, physical or human. In the first lecture, I used, as an illustration of a type of assumption in the construction of economic models for theoretical analysis which was peculiarly destructive of the practical usefulness of economic theory, the assumption that each of the factors of production was universally homogeneous, so that the productivity functions were everywhere identical. Adherence to such a model would prevent consideration of the responsibility of international differences in the economic quality of factors, in their 'effectiveness', to use Taussig's term, for differences in the levels of *per capita* income as between countries. What follows is an amplification of the comments in the first lecture.

Much obviously depends on the character of the physical environment, or the 'quality', in my terminology, of the natural resources considered as factors of production. Here are involved such things as the character of the soil, the forest resources, topography as favouring or hindering cheap transportation, mineral resources, the availability of water-power, and rainfall and temperatures. The geographical situation of a country is also significant with respect to its opportunities for profitable foreign trade, since proximity to foreign markets and sources of supply can be of great importance.

An unfavourable physical environment can be a major obstacle to economic development. That it need not be a fatal obstacle, however, that it can be overcome by high quality in its human resources, is demonstrated *inter alia* by the case of Switzerland. Except for the one advantage of its strategic location across some major trade routes, Switzerland has scarcely a single physical advantage for economic development; taking all physical factors into account, it is one of the most poorly endowed countries in the world. Nevertheless, in wealth *per capita* it ranks at or near the top, and it ranks high also in *per capita* income.

Of great importance also is the 'quality' of the working population, including the rank-and-file of industrial and agricultural labour, the entrepreneurial and managerial *élite*, and the skilled engineers and technicians. I have in mind here not biological or 'racial' differences, which authoritative scientific opinion overwhelmingly holds to be undetectable or of minor importance, but the differences which result from historical and cultural factors, from environment, quality of health, nutrition, and education, and from the quality of the leadership provided by government and the social *élite*.

The first requirements for high labour productivity under modern conditions are that the masses of the population shall be literate, healthy, and sufficiently well fed to be strong and energetic. In many countries, I feel sure, if this were achieved all else necessary for rapid economic development would come readily and easily of itself. I also feel sure that whenever this has not been accomplished and is not being strongly promoted to the utmost limits which the national resources permit, it is not necessary to look for the other factors, although they are certain to exist, to explain pervasive poverty and slow economic growth.

Where there is a traditional agriculture, there is often a strong resistance to technical education, and to change in working processes. Aside from this, however, it seems to be common experience that it is not difficult to train peoples to new methods, to the use of machinery, to new products, once it is made clear that acceptance of the training brings substantial and prompt economic reward.

The real bottleneck is likely to be not the lack of adequate responsiveness of the masses to the new teaching, but the scarcity of the teaching and of teachers able to impart it. The process can be greatly speeded, however, if there is initiative in importing teachers to train teachers, or in sending abroad selected nationals to learn how to train teachers. It is fortunate that modern industry is not as much dependent on the skills of the rank-and-file workers which can be learnt only slowly as was industry in the past or as agriculture in some of its phases continues to be. The difficult skills tend nowadays to be built into the machine, or to be concentrated in a relatively small number of supervisors and mechanics, and where these are not initially available locally, they can be readily imported through selective immigration. The higher levels of designing, engineering, and scientific 'know-how' are often needed only in small quantities. High-grade managerial and technological skill is always on sale at a competitive price, and provided it can adapt itself to local conditions, local materials, and the requirements of local markets, is cheap almost regardless of its price. Managerial and engineering 'know-how' are the most mobile internationally of economic goods, and where they are lacking it is because of the absence of genuine local demand, or unwillingness to import them, rather than because of unavailability.

As far as lower-grade skills are concerned, however, it is probably not sound policy for any country which is not sparsely populated to plan to meet its needs for them by general immigration instead of by training its own people, with the aid perhaps of imported teachers. I am assuming, as before, that the national objective is a growth in *per capita* income and not merely in aggregate income, and that its concern is primarily with the prosperity of its own people rather than of the world at large.

Scarcity of capital is the second type of obstacle to economic development which I will consider. Capital-scarcity may be absolute, or may be relative only to the opportunities for profitable investment. The United States was a relatively high interest-rate country and a borrower of capital until shortly before the First World War, but it probably even then had more capital per industrial worker than some of the countries from whom it borrowed. The amount of capital *per capita* in use within a country is probably more significant for present purposes than the amount of capital *per capita* owned within the country, since capital often, and probably usually, promotes the economic development of the country using it more than that of the country supplying it where these are not the same country. Canada provides an apt illustration. But the significance of international payments and receipts of interest and dividends on the economic growth of a country is not to be disregarded.

The domestic accumulation of capital in a poor country is bound to be slow. Income is the source of savings, and where income *per capita* is low, the annual rate of voluntary saving *per capita* will also tend to be low. It is generally agreed, however, that, in a given population at a given time, the percentage of income annually saved will be greater for higher-income than for lower-income groups, so that the greater the inequality in the distribution of income the greater will be the percentage of the aggregate income which will be saved. It may also be true that as average income through time increases, the percentage of the national income which will be annually saved will also increase. But empirical evidence in support of this is lacking, and there are some *a priori* reasons for being sceptical about it. What can be said with more confidence, however, is that as average income rises through time, the absolute amount of annual savings *per capita* will also rise. It is also to be considered that the greater the amount of *per capita* wealth and income, the better will be the credit status of a population, and the more therefore will it be able to borrow from abroad *per capita* if it wishes to. To him that hath more is available on loan.

I have been referring to general tendencies, and these may in particular countries or at particular times be offset or counteracted by special institutional or other factors. Before the Industrial Revolution in western Europe, and up to the present day in non-industrialized countries, the bulk of accumulated wealth has consisted of landed property. Keynes in his *General Theory* presents an argument, which I am not sure that I understand, that in the past landed property, like money, was regarded as a liquid asset, that money was therefore borrowed at low rates of interest on the security of land, that this operated to retard the growth of wealth from current real investment, and that this explains why the world is as poor as it is today in accumulated capital. What Keynes may have had in mind was that landowners borrowed for spendthrift purposes, and that if land had not been regarded as good security for loans, capitalists, instead of lending to landlords, would have invested directly or indirectly, in productive enterprises. If this is what Keynes meant, it comes close to the proposition often encountered that in countries which are predominantly agricultural and where land is held in large estates, the rich, who should do the saving and investment, commonly are non-savers and spend their incomes in luxurious living, with the result that economic development of these countries is retarded.

I am sceptical as to the validity historically of Keynes's proposition. The English and Scottish landowners of the eighteenth century were 'improving' landowners, that is, they developed their estates by investing in them not only their own incomes but additional capital borrowed from the 'moneyed-men', and the resultant agricultural revolution was a more important contribution to the growth of British wealth than was in its early stages the partially simultaneous industrial revolution.

Wealthy landowners have greater opportunity to invest their savings in the improvement and embellishment of their own properties than does the ordinary urban saver. Peasant proprietors have notoriously been the greatest savers of all. For rural landowners spending and investing may be hard to distinguish, since improvement of an estate can be at the same time the most conspicuous way of displaying wealth and the most effective way of adding to it. As long as a country has a comparative advantage in the expansion of agriculture over the expansion of manufacturing, the investment in their own estates of their savings by rural landowners may be the most productive and the most efficient investment under way in the national economy.

The rate of savings, outside of Keynesian economics, depends, of course, on many factors in addition to the size of income, but we really have very little reliable knowledge about the psychological and other determinants of the volume of savings. It is generally held that inflation is an obstacle to private saving. This is probably true where the alternative to inflation is not mass unemployment. It is probably true also, under all conditions, for persons of middle incomes who are not able to find what they regard as effective hedges against the depreciation of the real value of their liquid assets and therefore flee from money and from assets having fixed money-values to consumable goods.

In past experience, however, the inflationary process has generally involved a shift of income and wealth from wage-earners, the salaried class, the holders of small pensions, savings accounts, government bonds, and life insurance policies, to the more wealthy classes, the landowners, entrepreneurs, middlemen, who automatically or by the exploitation of superior skill and opportunity were able to derive profit from the rise in prices which for the poorer classes brought only loss. Since those who profited from inflation were as a class those who saved larger fractions of their current incomes, it is conceivable, therefore, that in the net inflation as it has usually operated in the past has tended to increase rather than to decrease the proportion of national savings to national income.

Inflation, however, also operates arbitrarily to distort the direction of investment and also otherwise to generate economic waste. It brings profits to entrepreneurs even if they are inefficient, and thus dulls the incentives to efficiency. It artificially enlarges the field of operation of the middleman and the broker, and diverts talent and personnel from production to non-productive speculation. It puts a premium on investment in urban real estate and in idle inventories, and makes difficult the financing of enterprises whose prices because of regulation are not easily raised or which commonly obtain capital through the issue of bonds, largely regardless of the real productivity for the national economy of such enterprises.

If a government draws off from its citizens in taxes a part of what they otherwise would have spent for current consumption, and uses the proceeds in useful public works, the government is performing the saving function for the community. I do not think, however, that many well-authenticated instances of such procedures can be cited. In any case, it is much easier to cite instances where governments have either taxed away or borrowed private savings and used them to defray current expenditures of a non-investment, and often of a spendthrift, character. It is always incumbent on government in private-enterprise countries to create a favourable setting for saving and for private investment not only by providing a good example in its own financial housekeeping, but also by establishing an atmosphere of political and legal security for private investment, and by providing efficient and honest administration of the ordinary functions of government. The contributions which governments can make to sound economic development are often undoubtedly greater in these prosaic and old-fashioned fields than in the now fashionable 'plans' which have as their goals the diversion of private savings from the financing of routine private investment to the financing of spectacular and grandiose programmes of public investment not subject to the tests of profit-and-loss accounting.

In countries where the marginal productivity function of capital is high and elastic, capital scarcity can be a major brake on economic development, and its pace can be greatly speeded if capital can be borrowed abroad at moderate rates of interest. The obstacles to international investment, however, both on the creditor and the debtor side, have grown formidably in recent years, and while there has been no previous period in which as much reliance has been put on international investment as prevails today, it is long since the actual prospects for large-scale international investment have been as unfavourable as they now seem to be.

Main reliance is being placed today on governmental rather than on private international lending, both because debtor countries prefer to borrow from governments and because private capital shows great reluctance to go abroad except when it is fleeing from domestic perils. Through war losses, heavy taxation, and socialization, the fund of disposable private capital potentially available for foreign investment has been drastically reduced in some at least of the countries which formerly were important exporters of capital. The special hazards of foreign investment have increased and are increasing further by all appearances. Many capital-poor countries gave a grudging welcome to the private foreign investor, but if he nevertheless ventures his capital they give him cause to regret it. The popular prejudice which has always existed in all countries against the export of capital has become more effective in recent years with the decline in the political power of the propertied classes, the evaporation of *laissez-faire* objections to governmental regulation of capital flows, and the growth in the scale and the effectiveness of regulatory machinery.

There is no justification for more than very modest expectations as to the scale on which governmental foreign investment will take place, in the absence of pressure from political and strategic considerations which may tend to operate as much to make the potential borrowers unwilling to borrow as they do to convert otherwise reluctant lenders to willingness to lend. National economic planning has become general, and planning governments, as I have already found occasion to point out, tend always to get themselves into financial difficulties which foreign lending would alleviate in the short-run but augment in the long-run. The universal growth of national debts, moreover, makes all governments feel poor. Few governments have had substantial experience in foreign lending and most of such experience as they have had has been unhappy. The loans in the past have commonly brought neither lasting goodwill nor repayment. It is too early as yet for confident judgement that present-day governmental lending will have more gratifying results for the lenders. The number of potential lenders on a large scale is very small, scarcely larger than one, while the actual and potential seekers of credit number at least fifty. It would be easy to extend this list of reasons why it is not realistic for underdeveloped countries to place major reliance on foreign investment in their territories as an aid to their economic development.

To capital-poor countries, for reasons good and bad, borrowing from governments seems preferable to borrowing from private capitalists, and borrowing from multinational agencies to be preferable to borrowing from individual governments. So far, however, despite the establishment of new multinational lending agencies, there are no obvious grounds for expectation or hope that either existing multinational agencies or new agencies still to be established will make quantitatively important contributions to the international flow of capital. Such agencies, to recruit capital subscriptions, must accept limitations on their range of activities and on the terms which they are permitted to offer which force them to be, on debtors' standards, exacting creditors. The debtor countries find these limitations galling, and press continuously and strongly for relaxations of their severity. The result is that in their operations these agencies fail to satisfy the borrowing countries while impressing the potential lenders with the advantages of retaining national autonomy with respect to the extent of their foreign lending, the selection of the debtors, and the conditions on which they shall make loans available to prospective borrowers.

If it is accepted that interest and dividends must be paid on foreign borrowings and that it will always be a contingent possibility that some day, not necessarily a convenient day for the debtor, there will have to be repayment of principal, it should be recognized that there are economic limits to the profitability of borrowing, and that if the borrowing is by governments and for public expenditure programmes the limits are likely to be narrow. Unremunerative investment is possible, and has been common, even in countries starved for capital. Relative provision of capital in comparison with the technical opportunities for its productive investment is so unequal internationally, however, that it is difficult to overestimate the service to world prosperity that a free and abundant international flow of capital is capable of rendering if it is wisely conducted. In the light of the factors I have been discussing which make the prospects of large-scale international lending seem dim, I am regretfully forced to the conclusion that foreign capital, in the absence of major changes in the international scene, will make but a marginal contribution to the capital needs of underdeveloped countries. This makes all the more urgent the fostering of such internal conditions by these countries as will encourage domestic saving and the prudent use of the proceeds in the development of productive facilities, material and human.

The third category of obstacles to economic development which I will examine consists of conditions in foreign trade which have or are alleged to have peculiarly unfavourable impacts on relatively poor countries and on countries whose exports consist predominantly of primary products and whose imports consist largely of the products of industrially advanced countries.

It has been claimed by some of my professional colleagues, on the strength both of theoretical analysis and of statistical records, that the terms of trade of countries exporting primary products with countries exporting manufactures are generally adverse to the former and have a secular tendency to become worse, and from this proposition they derive the conclusion that such countries should strive to industrialize, and, I presume, either to become substantially self-sufficing, or to become exporters of manufactures and importers of foodstuffs and raw materials. In so far as the argument rests on an inherent inferiority in productivity of resources engaged in primary industries over similar resources engaged in manufacturing, I have in an earlier lecture stated with some fullness my reasons for rejecting the doctrine. I will now examine the phase of the doctrine which maintains that in trade between primarily agricultural countries and primarily industrialized countries the gains from trade go predominantly to the latter. It should be noted, however, that an adverse movement of the commodity terms of trade, although always in itself an unfavourable factor, is not necessarily associated with an adverse movement in the material gains from or the profitability of foreign trade. Other factors which are favourable, such as growth in the volume of trade, or a decline in the real costs of the exports more rapid than the decline in their prices, may more than counterbalance the loss from the adverse movement of the terms of trade.

The terms on which a country trades depend on the scale on which it unloads its products on export markets as compared to the world demand for these products. The greater the increase in a country's population, other things equal, the greater will tend to be the volume of its staple export products which it will attempt to market abroad, provided these are not also its staple articles of domestic consumption, and therefore the worse will its terms of trade tend to be. But this will apply equally, as a tendency, to countries whether they are predominantly agricultural or predominantly industrial, and the appropriate remedy in either case would be to check the rate of growth of population. In a predominantly agricultural country rapid growth of population unaccompanied by proportionate growth in demand for its agricultural products will under free-market conditions bring spontaneously into action forces tending to industrialize the country, by making agricultural production relatively less remunerative. In industrialized countries it will have the reverse effect.

Primary commodities generally have a wider amplitude of fluctuation in their prices during the business cycle than do manufactured commodities. Countries exporting primary commodities are consequently squeezed during a depression by a greater drop in their export than in their import prices. This is true, and regrettable. But the obverse side of the shield should also be looked at. During booms, primary products rise more in price than do manufactures. The profits of the fat years should be balanced against the losses of the lean years. With good fiscal and monetary management, it would even be feasible—it has occurred without being planned in the past, notably in New Zealand—to conserve some of the boom-time profits in foreign trade to meet the deficits of the depression years. Still better, of course, would be, by international action, to iron out the cycles.

It is claimed that statistical data show a secular trend in the terms of trade between agricultural and manufactured products adverse to the former. As far as the data go, no such uniform trend can be shown. English economists have, indeed, often claimed to have found the reverse trend to have been operating in the past, and on the invalid assumption that the law of diminishing returns is peculiar to agriculture have often forecast the continuance of an adverse trend for the future for manufactures as against agricultural products. They are, in fact, making such forecasts now. For comparisons over long periods, moreover, the available data are largely irrelevant. The primary commodities whose average prices for broad categories are used in the computations of the terms of trade are for the most part, for averages so computed, not superior in quality, and in some cases are perhaps inferior, to the corresponding commodities of earlier years. The articles whose prices are used are always a much smaller sample of the total exports of manufactures than of agricultural products, and no weight is given to the gain in utility from the new commodities which have become available, such as the automobile, the tractor, and penicillin. Where the manufactures are nominally the same, moreover, they have over the years become incomparably superior in quality. It may perhaps take more pounds of coffee, or of cotton, to buy a lamp today than it did in 1900, but today's coffee and cotton are, I presume, not appreciably better in quality than those of 1900, whereas today's electric lamp is incomparably superior to the kerosene lamp of 1900. The decline in transportation costs, moreover, has made possible the seeming paradox of the commodity terms of trade improving simultaneously for both sets of countries.

It is claimed also that there is an historical 'law' of more rapid technological progress in manufacturing than in agriculture. If this were true, and manifested itself in a more rapid rate of improvement of the *quality* of manufactures than of agricultural commodities, it would operate to deprive an adverse trend of the terms of trade for agricultural products of its significance, for the adverse trend in prices would be offset by a reverse trend in quality. If this were true, and manifested itself in a relative decline in real cost of production of manufactures, it would tend to result in a favourable and not in an unfavourable movement in relative prices for agricultural products.

I know of no grounds, however, which justify acceptance of the proposition that there is any tendency for technological progress to be more rapid in manufacturing than in agriculture, except as such tendency is a consequence—not a cause—of countries which are more advanced technologically being often more industrial than agricultural. There is not, as far as I know, any marked backwardness in technology of the agriculture of Denmark, of England, of New Zealand, or of Iowa.

I will grant, however, that where agriculture is primitive in its methods it will tend to be resistant to more efficient procedures involving change in long-established practices and habits, and that this will not be equally true of manufactures, which are less susceptible to conservative adherence to obsolete methods. The more backward a country is in its procedures, however, the greater is the field for technological progress. A country with the most modern processes can advance farther only by new inventions and discoveries. A country which is backward technologically can make great advances merely by borrowing from the already existing stock of knowledge. For countries which have a comparative advantage in agriculture despite their failure to use advanced techniques, it is not a subsidized industrialization at the expense of agriculture which is the appropriate remedy, but education and training for a modernized agriculture. This will require capital, and capital is scarce, but industrialization will generally require even more capital per worker, or per unit of product. It is an important consideration, moreover, that whereas in international trade in manufactures the product of obsolete methods or styling is often absolutely unsaleable in a competitive market, so that for a country dependent to an important extent on exports of manufactures to finance its essential imports any lag in technological progress can be fatal, this is not true to anything like the same degree, if true at all, for a country which exports mainly primary products.

The claim has also been made, invoking Engel's law, that as *per capita* income rises the proportion of the income spent on primary products shrinks, so that there results, with rising *per capita* incomes, a relative trend of demand unfavourable to agriculture. I do not dispute this, nor that it would be better for agricultural countries if Engel's law did not hold. But the relative decline in demand for agricultural products will not be a positive decline, and therefore will not prevent but will only lessen the rate of progress in *per capita* agricultural incomes, if agriculture does not increase disproportionately—which is again mainly a question of population growth. Even the relative decline in demand for agricultural products, moreover, is mainly a loss to services, and the provision of services is always predominantly a local industry, not directly affected by commercial policy. All that the most extreme free trader contends for, in any case, is that resources should not be prevented from being applied to their most productive uses. If a relative shift in demand makes employment in agriculture less productive than other employment, resources should be guided out of agriculture to these superior uses.

The opportunities open to an underdeveloped country in the foreign trade field are certain to be a vital factor in determining the rate at which it can make economic progress. No country except the United States has attained a high level of *per capita* income which has not maintained a high ratio of imports to total national product, and no country, except possibly Russia, can in this respect make the United States its model without courting perpetual poverty. The high degree of self-sufficiency of the United States was due in part to a deliberate national policy of high tariff protection. But it was the continental character of the United States, its richness and variety of natural resources and the great obstacle which internal transportation costs presented to international trade, as well as the technical skills of its people, which enabled the American to dispense with foreign products without having to pay a heavy cost in terms of either deprivation of products of any important kind or of extreme expensiveness of domestic substitutes, and which thus enabled the United States to achieve economic prosperity despite its commercial policy and its low ratio of foreign to domestic trade.

The individual country has, as a rule, little control over the treatment its exports shall receive in foreign markets or over the terms on which it can obtain its imports. What it has full control of, however, is the extent to which imports shall be hindered from entering by its own artificial barriers. There is no underdeveloped country which has not a great stake in the removal or reduction of foreign trade barriers, however, and in the past few years these countries have had an opportunity, which they have cast away, to bring about a lasting and substantial reduction in the world network of trade restriction by giving genuine and strong support to the American proposals in this direction. The Havana Charter, even if ratified, will, for the reasons I have given in an earlier lecture, constitute only a modest first step in this direction, and the underdeveloped countries must acknowledge their great share of responsibility for its failure to achieve more radical progress in removing the barriers to mutually profitable international division of labour. If the Havana Charter is not ratified, a second opportunity is not likely to come soon, and retrogression is the most likely prospect. Even the American conversion to freer trade was only superficial, and failure to exploit it when the opportunity was available may result in making it only a transitory conversion.

The fourth and final category of obstacles to economic development, as I prefer to define the term, is associated with a rapid rate of increase of population. I have found it necessary already to refer to this factor as an obstacle to the attainment of economic prosperity in the sense of a high level of *per capita* income and the absence of mass poverty. Population increase hovers like a menacing dark cloud over all poor countries. It can offset, and more than offset, the contribution to economic prosperity which all other factors can make. Whatever the opportunities for economic betterment created by technological progress, by the discovery of new natural resources, by economic aid from abroad, and by the removal of foreign trade barriers, they can have as their chief consequence an increase in the number of children who survive to a short and wretched adulthood. Population increase may merely retard economic progress and under some circumstances may promote economic welfare, by increasing the number of those who share it, if it is a by-product of increasing *per capita* incomes operating, through better nutrition, better education, and better sanitary conditions, to enable more children to survive to a healthy and productive adult life. It will be most damaging if the increase in population is mainly the consequence of the application of modern public-health techniques which result in a decrease in infant mortality rates more rapid than the improvement in health conditions at later ages and more rapid than the rate of expansion of opportunities for productive employment.

What is most discouraging is that there are no easy and certain remedies for the overpopulation problem ; that the remedy, birth control, which to most social scientists appears to be the only promising one requires a fairly high level of education and of income to be wisely available and effective, and is moreover bitterly opposed by many on moral and religious grounds ; and that many persons, and many governments, refuse to recognize the existence of a problem here, or, if they do recognize it, to face it frankly and seek for a remedy.

It is a paradox of the population problem that on the grounds of historical experience and of theoretical analysis the attainment of high levels of *per capita* income and of education appear to be almost essential prerequisites of a cure of the problem and that the excessive rate of increase of population is itself the most important barrier to the establishment of these prerequisites. Here once more, the curse of the poor is their poverty, and no easy and certain way to break the vicious circle which is widely acceptable has as yet been discovered.

In this discussion of the obstacles to economic development, I have had occasion to deal with both external and internal obstacles. It is a natural and understandable tendency in underdeveloped countries to stress and to exaggerate the weight of the external obstacles, and to assign major responsibility for the removal of obstacles to economic betterment to governments and peoples other than their own. I do not wish to balance the exaggeration on one side by minimization on the other. The external factors are important, and I would wish to see the world at large, and the richer countries in particular, make their appropriate contribution to a solution of the world's greatest, most serious, economic problem : the problem of much over half the world's population living under conditions of acute poverty. The promotion of general reduction in trade barriers, the freer international movement of capital on reasonable terms, the facilitation of the general diffusion of the world's stock of technical knowledge and skills, these are the major contributions which the more favourably situated countries of the world can make to those less advanced and less prosperous. They are contributions of the greatest importance. But they will not suffice. Without genuine co-operation from the countries to be benefited they will not be effective, except perhaps in increasing still further the amount of hunger, sickness, premature mortality, and poverty in the world.

I do not contend that the underdeveloped countries have their economic futures in their own hands. On the contrary, in the absence of aid from external sources, I would have only pessimistic expectations with respect to the economic future of most of the underdeveloped countries. Given, however, the utmost help from these external factors which there is any reasonable ground to expect, the problem will not even begin to have a practicable solution unless the underdeveloped countries dedicate their own resources, human, physical, and financial, to a sound, large-scale, and persistent attack on those basic internal causes of mass poverty which I have tried to identify and whose nature and method of operation I have tried to explain.

POPULATION GROWTH AND LIVING STANDARDS*

by **Colin Clark**

THE FIRST AND MOST IMPORTANT FACT ON THIS SUBJECT THAT we must take into account is that most religions (using the word religion in its broad sense, to include all the codes of belief and conduct by which men feel themselves bound, so that in this sense of the word all but a minority of mankind has a religion) welcome and encourage the birth of a child. This is as much or more the case with Confucianism, Hinduism or Buddhism as it is with Christianity, Judaism or Islam. It is true that ideas and codes of conduct concerning family life differ somewhat and are subject to qualification between different religions and in different times and places, but the general statement remains true.

The next fact that must be recorded is that many people approach this subject with strong materialistic preconceptions. A basic aversion to religious belief is the essence of their position (glad though they are to receive support, from time to time, from various minority groups within the different religions). Their object of devotion, which takes the place of religion for them, is economic and material welfare. Such welfare is thought of, not only as an object good in itself (a proposition with which all sensible men would agree), but as an objective of such transcendent importance that any belief which conflicts with it has to go by the board. This point of view sometimes shows itself in its most extreme form among some of the younger American writers and propagandists concerned with the development of backward economies. Some religions, they say, such as Hinduism (but meaning others by implication, too) teach that man ought to practise, at any rate in certain circumstances, asceticism, or the renunciation of material goods for the sake of certain religious objectives. As material advancement and the selling of more goods are our basic objectives

* *International Labour Review*, August 1953. Reprinted by permission of the International Labour Office, Geneva, and the author.

(these writers state) it is clear that we must do our best to discredit and destroy such religious beliefs.

Many Malthusians would deny that they had any anti-religious preconceptions. Their point of view, they say, is purely scientific. If that is so there cannot be any other group of scientists so ill informed on the facts with which they are supposed to deal. Many Malthusians have no knowledge of the simplest facts about population ; and those who do know some demography seem to be almost universally uninformed on economics.

In another respect also most Malthusian propagandists give an extraordinary illustration of their unawareness of facts. They believe that if they can have the latest European and American contraceptives sufficiently advertised and cheaply distributed (presumably through some system of subsidization) throughout the oriental countries, the number of children born in the Orient would immediately and permanently fall. Nothing seems more improbable. Children are born in the Orient, as they were among our ancestors, and as most children are born in the Christian world today, because of their parents' wishes and consciences and religious beliefs, not because their parents wish to prevent them from being born but are unable to obtain contraceptives. There have certainly been occasions in the past when men have wished artificially to restrict their families, without any thought or knowledge of modern contraceptives. They have used the method described in the Book of Genesis, which is almost as old as the human race itself. Orientals at the present time would restrict their families if they really desired to do so. Nothing could be more futile—apart from the morality of it—than to attempt to distribute contraceptives among people who do not wish to use them.

It is, however, equally clear—and this is one of the most important of all religious teachings—that we are bound to promote the material welfare of our neighbour. But this objective clearly has qualifications in morals. When Hitler was plundering and enslaving the peoples around him he doubtless reflected with considerable pride on the way he was promoting the material welfare of the German people.

The *International Labour Review* is not, however, the place to discuss disputed points of religion or moral philosophy, though every prudent man should know when his political or economic proposals are likely to involve him in controversy on these subjects.

Subject to these qualifications, we can now discuss the relationship between population increase and economic and material welfare.

It seems to come as a surprise to many people to learn that there are a great many industries—probably the majority of industries in the modern community—which are quite specifically benefited by increasing population. These are the industries that work under the law of increasing returns rather than the law of diminishing returns. This is one of the simplest but at the same time most important propositions in economics. Many modern students of economics have their heads so filled with new but comparatively unimportant formulae that they do not give adequate attention to these important truths. The law of increasing returns prevails in any industry where, as a consequence of an increased scale of output, we can expect to obtain increasing returns per unit of labour or other economic resources employed.

What category of businesses can be more economically run on a large scale ? The list includes most forms of large-scale manufacture, transport, postal communications, banking, insurance and the like. In fact most of the economic operations of a modern community are carried out in such a way that, if there were an increase in the population and the size of the market, organization would become more economical and productivity per head would increase, not decrease. Without the large and densely settled population of North America and Western Europe, most modern industries would be working under great difficulties and at very high costs—it is doubtful, indeed, whether they could have come into existence at all.

Industries working under the law of diminishing returns are agriculture, mining, forestry and fishing, and some others which are dependent upon the use of scarce materials. Certain other industries, such as building, where the limiting economic factor appears to be shortage of men of the right kind of skill and organizing ability, probably work under constant returns, i.e., intermediate between increasing and diminishing returns.

On the other hand, some of the most highly mechanized branches of agriculture—production of sugar-cane is probably the most interesting example—show every sign of working under increasing returns. That is to say, a district organized for producing sugar-cane on a large scale, with its crushing mill and haulage systems laid out accordingly, probably enjoys a higher return per unit of labour than a smaller scale system.

At the time when Malthus wrote—or for that matter Ricardo—the law of diminishing returns was supposed to be universal. Although the businessman must have understood, in his own way, the advantages of production on a large scale, it was not until much later in the nineteenth century, at the time of Marshall and his contemporaries, that the law of increasing returns in industry was more clearly formulated. It is now, of course, fully understood and statistically measurable. (Dr Verdoorn, the Netherlands statistician, has assembled a good deal of evidence to show that something like a definite mathematical law governs the extent to which product per man can rise as the scale of industry is increased.) But at the moment, for various reasons, it seems to receive inadequate attention in economic teaching and practically none in popular writings on economics.

The law of diminishing returns does not in the least mean what most people believe it to mean. It certainly does not mean that the returns from agriculture, or any other economic activity, diminish from year to year. The law has no reference to any supposed diminution in time. What the law of diminishing returns says, or at any rate the form of it which is applicable to our present discussion, is that if you put an increasing number of men to farm a limited area of land, then the returns per man will diminish (though the total returns from the land will increase).

But even stated in this way the law is only valid under certain conditions. A man's experience must be very limited if he does not know of some examples of densely populated farm areas producing more per head than less densely populated areas. The law of diminishing returns can only be said to be, in any sense of the word, a law if two further conditions are fulfilled: first, that the inhabitants of the more densely settled area do not use any different farming methods from those of the less densely settled area, and secondly, that they do not employ any more capital per head.

These two further conditions make the law of very limited application indeed. For the use of improved farming methods and greater quantities of capital per man are precisely the steps taken by progressive countries when they find their population increasing and their area of agricultural land limited. If the law has much validity in practice, the statistician should be able to detect its operation by preparing a diagram in which one co-ordinate measures the number of men engaged in agricultural work per square kilometre of cultivable land and the other co-ordinate measures the real product obtained per man. Anyone who draws a diagram of this sort will soon see that the exceptions are more numerous than the cases in which the rule applies. It is interesting to see, however, that the rule holds moderately well when we are comparing the different provinces or regions within one country—for farming methods and skill and the amount of capital available per head do not differ very much between one region of the country and another.

Agricultural Production and Population

In the following table are summarized the figures for all the countries for which comparable results can be obtained. Density of agricultural population is classified by the number of persons engaged in agriculture per square kilometre of cultivable land (the definition of cultivable land will be given later). The only countries excluded are a few of the highest-income non-European countries. In countries like the United States, Australia and Argentina there is obviously no question of a shortage of land, so there is no need to put such countries in the table.

We have to use some standard of value to compare agricultural production per head in the different countries. As almost every country has its own pricing system for agricultural products, some international system of prices has to be used. For some purposes United States dollar prices can be used. In this case, however, it is more convenient to use Indian rupee prices of the year 1948–49. The relative prices of different agricultural products in India give results more akin to the price relationships prevailing in most of the low-income countries under study than do the United States relative prices.

Classification of 26 countries with respect to the relationship between the intensiveness of cultivation and agricultural output per person engaged in cultivation

Value of agricultural production per person engaged (rupees per year)	Number of persons engaged in agriculture per square kilometre of cultivable land					
	0–5	5–10	10–15	15–20	20–25	25–30
Below 1,000	..	Philippines	..	..	..	India
1,000-1,500	..	..	Turkey Yugoslavia U.S.S.R.	..	..	..
1,500-2,000	..	..	Poland	Rumania	..	Italy
2,000-2,500	Brazil	Greece	Cyprus Bulgaria	Portugal	..	..
2,500-3,000	..	France Austria	Spain	..	Hungary	..
3,000-3,500	Sweden	Ireland	Syria	..	..	..
3,500-4,000	..	..	Germany Czechoslovakia	Belgium	..	..
4,000-4,500	..	..	..	..	..	..
4,500-5,000	..	Britain	..	Netherlands	..	..
Over 5,000	..	..	Denmark	..	..	..

We can see from the table how little relation there is, if any, between density of settlement and average product per head. About the same density of settlement prevails in Denmark as in Soviet Russia, but product per man in one case is five times what it is in the other. Many people are concerned about the density of the agricultural population in India, and it is undoubtedly high. But it is equally high in Italy, where the average cultivator produces about twice as much as does the Indian. There is much talk about the possibility of introducing the Indian to tractors and milking machines and all the most modern agricultural equipment. Let us defer discussing this for the present—its time will come—and meanwhile set ourselves the much easier question, whether the Indian could learn and practise the simple arts of the Italian peasant, and use his simple equipment, for dairying, rice growing, fruit growing and similar activities. For if he could, he would be, within a few years, twice as well off as he is now.

It is difficult to teach the Indians any new agricultural methods. Better to try to obtain the same objective by reducing population density. For the sake of argument, let us consider this latter proposition. To carry it out, you will have to reduce the Indian population to one-quarter of what it is now. (A statistical estimation of the operation of the law of diminishing returns, made by comparing different provinces or regions in the same country, indicates that there is probably an inverse square root relationship between the density of settlement and productivity per man.) The stoutest Malthusian would hesitate at the prospect of having to reduce the population by three-quarters and, in any case, how long would it take him to do it, even if he had his way in every respect, short of murder ?

Any observation of these facts must make us realize what immense improvements are possible in agricultural productivity in most parts of the world. Such improvements cannot, of course, be had for the asking. To get them, an immense dissemination of education and technical knowledge will be needed, new equipment to a steadily increasing degree, and capital to provide equipment, livestock and buildings. Whether there is any hope of obtaining this capital is a question which will be discussed shortly.

The most successful farming, as judged by the ability to obtain the highest product at the highest density of settlement, is to be found in Denmark and the Netherlands, with Belgium and Britain not far behind. In Denmark the high figure is obtained with a density of settlement of 10 men engaged in agricultural work per square kilometre of cultivable land, in the Netherlands with 17. Farm economists in the Netherlands mostly agree, in the interests of efficient operation, that they would not like to see this high density further exceeded. However, the Netherlands farmers have provided very concrete evidence that agricultural land can be worked, and yield a high product, at this high density of settlement. Their country has, however, a soil of unusual fertility, and some may prefer to take Denmark, with ten men per square kilometre, as the reasonable standard. At any rate, it cannot be said that here we are dealing with soil of unusual fertility. Rather the reverse.

Now we must discuss what we mean by cultivable land. In Western Europe we come to think of practically the whole land surface as cultivable (if we include intensive livestock grazing as cultivation) except for a few swamps and extremely mountainous areas. But extending our view we see that limits are imposed by cold (as we approach the Arctic Circle or mountainous regions) or by aridity (as in parts of Spain). In dealing with other parts of the world these climatic limits are of much greater importance.

Cultivable land is measured in climatic terms. It is true that in some countries there are large areas where, although climatic conditions are satisfactory, the soil is believed to be so poor that no cultivation is possible, particularly in tropical areas. But the consensus of opinion among chemists is that these defects can be remedied, though it is costly to do so. Climatic defects, on the other hand, can only be remedied by extremely costly methods (irrigation or glass houses) and we can assume that no really large-scale operations of this nature will be practicable.

Using the Thornthwaite climatic classification,[1] we assume that the poleward limit of cultivable land is where the cold 'taiga' climates begin. At the other end we must exclude all arid deserts and all but a very small fraction of the semi-arid land—of which there is a great deal in India, Africa and Australia—where only sparse grazing is possible. The next category is the subhumid lands, half of which are regarded as cultivable, except that where they have a regular rainy season the proportion may rise to two-thirds or five-sixths. The main body of cultivable land in all continents, however, is the land with wet or humid temperate or subtropical climate. The only

[1] All these workings and classifications were set out in detail in the author's paper to the United Nations Scientific Conference on the Conservation and Utilization of Resources (Lake Success, Aug. 1949).

further exception we must make is that in the areas where high tropical temperatures combine with all-the-year-round rainfall, the land (if fertilized) is capable of growing two crops a year, and is accordingly counted as double in compiling the total estimate of cultivable land.

Denmark has no more than 39,000 square kilometres of cultivable land. Denmark's net exports (i.e., exports less imports) of farm products are as much as 45 per cent of net product (defined as output less seeds and fodder used up in the process of production). Denmark, therefore, in effect, feeds not only her own population of 4·4 million, but another 3·6 million people elsewhere, or 8 million in all; that is, about 200 people are fed per square kilometre of cultivable land.

The question is often asked, how many people can now be fed by one man working on the land? There is, of course, no single answer. Net productivity of a man on the land varies in different places and at different times. We must also remember that the amount of food which people expect to have supplied to them also varies. But, under modern Danish conditions, you have ten men working per square kilometre of land and 200 people supplied thereby, or 20 people supplied by one man. If we take dependants into account, we can say that one farm family supplies about eight families all told—itself and seven others. Or, if you like to put it more prosaically, we can say that if we assume that there is no net import or export of farm products a country with agriculture as productive as in Denmark and with a population whose standards of feeding are as high as those of the Danes will have to keep about 12½ per cent of its labour force occupied in agriculture.

In some of the non-European countries we can of course obtain higher figures of the number of persons fed per agricultural worker, or lower figures of the proportion of the labour force required in agriculture.

At Danish standards, therefore, of productivity on the one hand and of diet on the other, a square kilometre of cultivable land will provide for about 200 people, or a square mile for about 500. On this standard, how much of the world is overpopulated, or how much additional population can it support? On the criterion of having sufficient land to feed one's population at these Danish standards, the only countries in the world which are overcrowded (not counting a few small isolated settlements) are Japan, the Netherlands, Belgium and probably Switzerland (if we take its high proportion of mountainous area into account). The Federal Republic of Germany is just on the borderline. England is overcrowded if considered in isolation, but not if the territory and populations of Scotland and Northern Ireland are considered in conjunction with it. The population of India and Pakistan per square mile of cultivable land is about 400—high, but not above the limit. The corresponding figure for China is lower, probably between 300 and 350. For Indonesia it is much lower, but here the position is complicated by the greater part of the population being concentrated in the one island of Java, while the rest of a very large cultivable area is almost uninhabited.

In countries like Britain, Belgium and Germany it is taken for granted that the population will not try to support itself entirely on its own limited land area and that a substantial proportion of the inhabitants will be engaged in export industries in order to purchase food and raw materials from elsewhere. Until recently this was taken for granted in the case of Japan also. Some people now talk about Japan having difficulty in supporting her increasing population on her limited area. This sort of statement only has meaning if one assumes that Japan is to be excluded from all export trade.

Europe, excluding the U.S.S.R. (pre-war territory), has 1,400,000 square miles of cultivable land. In this area live 450 million people, who obtain (taken altogether) some 95 per cent of their food supplies from European agricultural production. If all of Europe were as closely settled as Denmark, 700 million people would be able to obtain their food supplies from this area. Europe is the most densely settled of the continents. The United States and Canada have 2,275,000 square miles of cultivable land, with only 175 million people on it, only a small fraction of the numbers it could feed, even on European standards of cultivation. Latin America has approximately the same numbers, about 170 million people, but in this case there are 7 million square miles of cultivable land. Africa, with 6 million square miles, has a population of only 210 million and Oceania only 30 million population with a million square miles of cultivable land.

One of the world's most congested regions is the Middle East, where 78 million people live with only 171,000 square miles of cultivable land. Even so, the density is below the limit which we set ourselves ; the land is farmed in the Middle East much less efficiently than in Denmark, and a good deal of now arid land could be brought into cultivation by means of irrigation if sufficient capital were available.

The rest of south-east Asia, apart from Indonesia, is also lightly populated, with only 95 million people on 1,250,000 square miles of cultivable land. There has been so much talk about south-east Asia and its problems that it comes as a shock to realize that a great deal of it is uninhabited. This is the case for almost the whole of Malaya, large areas of Burma and Siam, and a considerable part of the monsoon-climate area of Burma.

Most of the world, therefore, is populated at far below its potential density. The world's total area of cultivable land (allowing for double cropping in the highest-rainfall tropical areas) is 24 million square miles, and at Danish standards of cultivation and consumption could support 12,000 million people, as opposed to the 2,300 million people it supports now.

Now let us leave economics and go back to demography. Some demographers may admit the truth of these economic and geographical facts, but then go on to say that Danish (or any other) standards of high cultivation could never be reached, for the reason that population increases in many of the countries concerned are so unbearably rapid that they are bound to overtake any increase in production. Statements like this, which are often made *a priori* without ascertaining the available facts, soon tend to be generalized until they form a theoretical Malthusian statement that population everywhere and at every time is tending to press upon the means of subsistence. The true facts on this subject are simple, but seem to be known by very few people and conflict with popular belief at almost every point.

The Fertility of the Human Race

If every woman married young, and there were no restriction of births of any kind, what would the average size of the family be ? (We are discussing now not the number of children surviving, but the number born.) The answer is about six. That is to say, this would be the average number of living children born to the average woman who had survived to the age of 45 and had been married all the time. The families of women who died earlier would of course be smaller.

What is the evidence for this ? First, uncertain and imprecise, but covering a very wide range of time and place, comes the evidence of the anthropologists. According to their evidence, this seems to be the average number of children born in primitive communities. In these communities every woman marries young, and, as there is nearly always a surplus of males, a woman left widowed will probably be remarried almost immediately. Practices for the artificial prevention of conception, though known among some primitive peoples, appear to be rare.

The next evidence, much more precise but from far fewer sources, comes from certain countries with a simple agricultural economy where good demographic records are available. (The reader should be aware that outside Western Europe, North America, Australasia and Japan most countries have no proper record of the number of births and deaths, much less the accurate census tables and other material needed for demographic calculation.) Brazil and Ceylon are among the few countries for which proper census records are available from which demographic calculation can be made. China has had no sort of census for more than a century, but one or two carefully conducted sample inquiries by Western observers in limited areas give us some interesting material. The third piece of evidence, from an entirely different source and only recently available, is very concrete. The medical sub-committee of the recent British Royal Commission on Population collected a good deal of information from women which, by an ingenious statistical method, was put together in such a form as to show what the total fertility of the modern English woman would be if she married early and if throughout her married life no restriction were imposed upon conception. The answer here also came to a figure in the neighbourhood of six.

Most people (including many biologists and doctors) have somehow acquired the opinion that the natural fertility of the human race is much higher than this. Popular opinion is even more misinformed. Ask anyone what was the size of the average

Victorian family and he will probably say that it was about 12; in fact the average family in Victorian England (or in most of nineteenth century Europe) was about five.

The next point which must be made clear is that, in the conditions in which mankind has been living throughout the greater part of its history on this earth, and in which the majority of mankind is living today, an average family of six children barely suffices to maintain the population. Primitive populations, generally speaking, do not increase.

At the beginning of the Christian era the estimates of historians put the population of the world at about 250 million. We can accept this estimate with the widest margin of error. It does not matter very much, from our present point of view, whether we put the figure at 150 million or 500 million. The point is that the human race began, so the geologists tell us, 500,000 years ago. (The evidence accepted by geologists and by biologists appears to be of a far lower order of accuracy than that used by economists and demographers, low though that may be; the geologists sometimes behave as if an extra zero in their figure were a comparatively minor matter, while some of the biologists have recently tried to raise the figure from half a million to a million years.) But on this assumption of half a million years we must deduce that the average rate of increase in numbers of the human race, over the greater part of its existence, was not more than ·004 per cent per annum.

Between the beginning of the Christian era and the seventeenth century, for which period we have rather more population information, the average rate of increase of mankind accelerated somewhat, but was still no more than ·04 per cent per annum. A rate of increase of as much as 1 per cent per annum became apparent in Britain and Ireland towards the end of the eighteenth century, and from about the middle of the nineteenth century onwards the average rate of increase of the whole world has been slightly over 1 per cent per annum. In some areas the figure has been as high as 2 per cent per annum and in a few cases as high as 3 per cent (natural increase, apart from immigration), for example in the United States in its early years of development and in modern Ceylon.

It is clear that there is, among primitive people, a mortality such as to require an average family of six just to maintain the population. Though wars and famines do occur among primitive people, it would not be in accordance with the evidence to describe them as chronic. Most of their mortality seems to be due to the general hardships of life and the absence of any form of medical treatment.

But we must also realize how widely these conditions have applied, in the past, among supposedly civilized as well as primitive peoples, and how extensively they still apply today. The evidence of Indian history seems to show that the population was much the same in the fourth century B.C., the seventeenth century A.D., and also in the early nineteenth century. It was quite late in the nineteenth century that any real expansion of the Indian population began. It is obviously wrong to say that India's population over this long period was held in check by some natural limits ; it stood over most of this period at about 150 million, or not much more than a third of the population which India and Pakistan (without any great improvement in agricultural methods) are carrying now. The long history of India shows varying phases of order and good government, followed by war, disorder and anarchy. In the latter phases not only production but also population is reduced.

More or less similar conclusions can be drawn from a study of Chinese history. What very few people realize, however, is that the Chinese population has apparently been in a stationary or declining phase ever since 1850—this is the opinion of two of the world's most careful demographers, Sir Alexander Carr-Saunders and Professor Wilcox. The tragic events of the last two decades have apparently greatly accelerated the decline, and there is evidence now that large areas of cultivable land in China are uninhabited.

Still more striking is the possibility of seeing in our own times an actual change of trend taking place. Indonesia, before 1941, caused some concern among demographers by maintaining a persistent rate of increase, under Netherlands rule, of as high as 2 per cent per annum. The problem was complicated, as has been mentioned before, by the concentration of almost the whole of the population in Java while the other islands were largely uninhabited. But now the (extremely uncertain) estimates of population are only a few per cent above the 1941 level. Sir Alexander Carr-Saunders has evidence to show that in Africa population has been stationary over very long periods. Probably it only began to increase in this century. Still more surprisingly, in Latin America, which was supposedly civilized, there were long periods of stagnation in the seventeenth and eighteenth centuries.

Both the historical and present-day evidence seems to point to the same conclusion, that any appreciable population increase is only possible when two conditions are fulfilled, namely, the establishment of a firm and ordered political system and the dissemination and utilization of some medical knowledge. It is doubtful whether there has ever been, in historical fact, an actual instance of the supposed Malthusian universal, of population overtaking agricultural productivity, multiplying right up to the limits of subsistence, and then being held in check by some new form of 'vice or misery'. Agricultural methods themselves are susceptible of considerable change. In most modern communities improvements in technique lead to a rise in agricultural productivity, without any additional labour force or the cultivation of any additional land, at a rate faster than any probable rate of increase in population. This does not apply in the West alone. In Japan product per man in agriculture has risen steadily since the 1890s at a rate of 2 per cent per annum.

Ireland is sometimes quoted as an example. Population increased fairly rapidly in the eighteenth century, not because of abnormally large families but because of good health and reduced mortality. British legislation forbade this increasing population to find employment in industry, but a new form of agriculture based on potato growing provided adequate food supplies—until the famine of 1845. But the important point is that the Irish population had practically stopped increasing by 1831—emigration was outbalancing almost the whole of the natural increase. The famine was mainly due to a fungal disease of potatoes which could easily be checked under modern conditions, and its worst consequences could have been avoided under more far-sighted and humane administration.

Another example sometimes quoted is that of the irrigation settlements in India. It is said that as soon as additional land is made available for cultivation through irrigation works the population of the district rapidly increases, and density of population per square mile of cultivable land is soon as high as it was before. This is probably true ; but there is no evidence that it is due to either increased births or reduced mortality among the inhabitants ; all the probabilities are against this. What has happened is precisely what one might have expected —the migration of a large number of would-be settlers from other parts of India.

All the above facts and reasoning constitute a very unexpected approach to the problem, though it may be claimed that they are both true and important. Some readers may accept them, but still have misgivings. They may grant that no part of the world has ever yet come within sight of over-population in the Malthusian sense of the term, and that Malthus's ideas of history were as odd as his ideas of agriculture. They may grant that the world still contains enormous areas of cultivable land capable of settlement. But they will also point out the immense acceleration of the pace of medical improvement during the past generation. There is some (not complete) evidence that the rate of decline of mortality in Asia in this century is far more rapid than was the rate of decline of mortality in nineteenth century Europe. With the prospect of continuously decreasing rates of mortality, and with the hope of world peace and good government (for which we are all certainly labouring our hardest), will we not create in the course of the next century a world population problem of quite unmanageable dimensions ? An average of six children per family, which appears to be the natural rate of reproductivity of the human race, just suffices to keep population stationary under primitive conditions and allows for a rate of population increase of 1 or 2 per cent per annum in a settled and civilized agrarian economy, but what might it lead to if the whole world enjoyed rates of mortality as low as those of advanced western communities ? Under such conditions about 90 per cent of the children born survive to child-bearing age, and even if we allow that a certain proportion of them remain unmarried we are still going to get a rate of population increase of about 4 per cent per annum, or population doubling every 20 years. The 3 per cent per annum rates of increase already observed in the early years of the United States and in present-day Ceylon arise from the conjuncture of very large families with low mortality rates.

This all turns on the question of whether the average family is likely to remain as high as six. Instances have been given from the primitive and the modern world. But in India, for which we have a considerable number of sample studies, it appears doubtful whether the average family of Hindus was ever more than five. (Among the Moslem and Christian minorities larger families are found.) This is apparently due to the curious Hindu rule which forbids the remarriage of widows. In Japan we can trace the fall from six at the beginning of the present century to a figure of only four by 1940, and apparently lower again now. Dr Lorimer's study of Soviet Russia traces a similar movement up to 1938. In India sample studies show a considerable fall in the size of family in industrial cities, and some statisticians qualified to judge think that, taking India as a whole, the average family may now be as low as four.

We have not enough information to make a detailed and accurate analysis of what is going on in most of these countries, and it will probably be many years before such information is available. But one point which is brought out in the writings of Dr Ghosh about Indian population is that the marked decline in reproductivity in the partially industrialized areas of the Orient is probably due not to the restriction of births in marriage, but to later marriage. Throughout the Orient very early marriages have been until recently the rule, and a deferment of only a year or two may make a very considerable difference to total fertility. Alike in the medical and statistical evidence of the fertility of the average human family we see clearly that the greater part of the births occur in the comparatively early years of married life.

Even though the statistical interpretations of it may differ somewhat, there can be no doubt about the deceleration of the rate of India's population growth. Prior to 1921 the rate of growth was less than 1 per cent per annum. From 1921 to 1931 India's population grew by 11 per cent, and from 1931 to 1941 by 16 per cent, but between 1941 and 1951 the increase was again only about 11 per cent (taking India and Pakistan together for the latter year). The Bengal famine of 1943 and the massacre of refugees on both sides of the border at the time of the separation of Pakistan from India in 1947 were both dreadful events, but they cannot account for more than a small fraction of the observed deceleration of the population increase. For the decade 1951–61, on the basis of the information available, there is every indication that the net rate of population growth will prove to be less than 1 per cent per annum.

In Ceylon, likewise, there is fairly clear evidence that the average total fertility has fallen from six to five in one generation.

There is neither need nor space to attempt to trace all the causes of these phenomena. In an urban population the desires to accumulate money and achieve social position are a far greater force than in a static peasant community, and the incentives to bring up families are thereby weakened. To what extent religious beliefs become weakened when a peasant community becomes urbanized is also a matter for discussion; sometimes it undoubtedly occurs, but even among those urbanized Hindus, for instance, who retain their religious beliefs in full, there is clearly some tendency to reduce the size of the family.

In India, therefore, which many people thought to possess the world's most intractable population problem, the situation is very different from what is commonly supposed. The work of Indian statisticians shows that the rise in production has since 1870 been far greater than the rise in population, and there is every prospect that, with increasing industrialization, this process will continue.

Neither is this the place to discuss the extraordinary change in the population trend in North America and Western Europe that has occurred during the past decade. Many of these western communities now have a rate of natural increase far higher than that of Asia, and look like maintaining it.

High net rates of population increase are found in Latin America, in Africa, in the Middle East (it is here that the problem is so serious, because resources of land are very limited, and increasing cultivation by irrigation works is bound to be a slow and costly process) and in some, but not all, of the countries of south-east Asia. Most of the countries with the highest rates of population increase are those which have very considerable resources of unused agricultural land. There cannot, therefore, be said to be any serious danger of food shortage, except that which is brought about by their own misgovernment.

Capital Resources

We can now bring this discussion to a conclusion, and also examine one final point—capital accumulation—on which serious misgivings may be felt. For the more advanced countries, which already have a fairly dense population and a good transport system, the obvious line of development is industrialization. Once the earliest difficulties have been overcome—admittedly a slow and hazardous process—the law of increasing returns comes into operation, and every further increase in population makes the industrialization process more remunerative.

Industrialization for the purpose of developing exports is not a possibility open to every country. In some cases even industrialization to supply local needs is hopelessly uneconomic. Generally speaking a sparse population, lack of transport, lack of education and remoteness from world markets are factors which may make industrialization very difficult. The presence or absence of local raw materials is a matter of very secondary importance. Japan and Switzerland are examples of highly successful industrialization, and both are virtually lacking in indigenous raw materials.

Where industrialization is not possible, or involves too great difficulties and hazards, the alternative policy of extended agriculture must be followed. Most of the countries involved have resources of unused land. This is not the case in a few isolated densely populated areas, mostly islands, such as Mauritius, the Cape Verde Islands, and the British West Indies. In such cases, where transport difficulties impede industrialization, emigration is the only satisfactory solution.

But we must mention in this connexion Puerto Rico, which for many years has been sitting heavily upon the American conscience, and has provoked many Americans into believing it to be a case of overpopulation. The American conscience can now be at rest. After a long period of stagnation Puerto Rico has shown since 1939 a rate of development of real income, and economic development generally, without parallel in world history, leaving the Japanese rate of growth far behind. This has depended upon two elements, an intensification and technical improvement of sugar production and a widespread programme of industrialization. Emigration has played a comparatively minor role. Though dependent upon a rather costly shipping service Puerto Rico is near enough to the United States market (and within the same tariff wall) to be able to participate very remuneratively in the United States industrial structure.

But, whether for industrialization or for the extension of agricultural production, considerable capital resources are required. It is very easy to underrate the amounts necessary. Satisfactory agricultural development often requires amounts comparable with those required for industrial development. It is a great mistake to consider solely factories or livestock. Whoever hears now of the Bombay Plan, the project which attracted world-wide attention in 1945, whereby India's real national income was to be doubled in 15 years ? This Plan was prepared by businessmen, and made quite careful estimates of the capital which would be required for the large-scale industrialization of India. These were literally true ; what the Plan forgot was the enormous further investment which would be needed for housing, transport, education and other social needs.

The amount of capital required per head in these countries is generally equal to about four years' income per head. The figures, of course, vary enormously between trades. A carpenter needs no more capital than a bag of tools ; the capital used by a telephone operator is more than she could earn in a lifetime. But generally speaking, averaging all trades together, the four to one rule holds. (Some people may ask, does this mean that each unit of additional capital earns a 25 per cent return ? It does, in the sense that 100 units of capital invested cause national income to rise by 25 units per annum. But of this additional product labour will demand at least 15 units, even in an oriental country—more like 20 units in a western country—leaving something between 5 and 10 units per annum as a remuneration to the investor of the 100 units of capital.)

This means that, to cover an increase in the labour force of 1 per cent, a capital investment equal to 4 per cent of the national income will be necessary. We thus get a very simple rule. Take the expected rate of population increase and multiply it by four. This gives us the percentage of national income which has to be invested in order to provide employment, of the same average kind as now exists, for the increasing population. This investment may come from internal savings or external borrowing. It is only in so far as the rate of investment exceeds the rate of population increase multiplied by four that anything will be left over for industrialization or for raising standards of real income per head.

It is unfortunately impossible to test out this interesting rule because of the almost complete lack of reliable statistics of the rate of saving in the underdeveloped countries. Some figures from India before the war indicate a rate of saving of about 6 per cent of the national income. There are unfortunately some signs that this rate of saving was not resumed in the post-war years, but if anything like this figure prevails now it is well in excess of four times the rate of population growth, and therefore leaves a margin (though less than might be desired) for industrialization, before any inflow of external capital is considered. But India is in a more fortunate position than many of the underdeveloped countries. In many cases, where rates of population increase are higher and rates of saving in all probability lower, there will be a retrogression of economic standards unless a substantial inflow of external capital is possible.

Conclusion

We can bring it all down in the end then to a single conclusion. Any foreseeable rate of population increase, in any part of the world, can be economically provided for at a satisfactory and indeed rising standard of real income, subject to three conditions. The first, which is of comparatively minor importance, is that free emigration should be facilitated from a few isolated overcrowded areas. Here the numbers involved are small. Emigration is not a necessary economic solution for the problems of the larger countries, whatever may be the rights and wrongs of it in general.

The next condition is that for large and densely populated countries, such as India, which have reached the stage where industrialization is obviously their only suitable prospect of economic advancement, the rest of the world, even if it cannot offer direct help for such industrialization, should at least co-operate by leaving markets open for these countries to sell their goods and not place tariff and quota restrictions upon their trade. Japan was treated with gross unfairness by the Western powers in the 1930s, and this played a considerable part in forming her determination to go to war.

Countries which have already reached the size and stage of development of India and Brazil, for instance, will probably be able to proceed with industrialization using their own resources only, though it will be much slower than would be possible if they received external assistance. In the smaller, weaker countries the receipt of external assistance is a necessary condition without which further development will not be possible. How this should be organized, and how the responsibilities should be shared among the different lending countries, cannot now be discussed.

It may well be that many of those who advocate population limitation in the oriental countries do so precisely because they do not like the idea either of emigration or of leaving markets open to oriental goods, or of giving any capital assistance to weaker countries. If there are any such it is time that their uncharitable motives were exposed.

THE PROBLEM OF LIMITED ECONOMIC DEVELOPMENT*

by **Gerald M. Meier**

THESE NOTES CONSIDER A PROBLEM WHICH HAS LONG BEEN central to economic thought—the determinants of differential rates of growth among nations. Although from the time of Adam Smith to the present group of growth theorists there has been a formidable succession of contributions explaining 'the nature and causes of the wealth of nations', the emphasis has usually been on the factors that promote growth—not on the converse problem of limitations to growth ; attention has been given mainly to advanced economies—not underdeveloped countries[1] ; and the analysis has usually concerned a closed economy—not an open economy. It may, therefore, be worth while to consider the more particular problem of why, within the framework of the world economy, development has been retarded in underdeveloped countries. No other period is more illustrative of the process of international development than that of 1870 to 1913. We may, accordingly, consider the problem in this historical context.

It is apparent that during the period 1870 to 1913 some countries proceeded at a rapid rate through the transition from being underdeveloped countries to becoming advanced economies (for example, Argentina, Australia, Canada, New Zealand), while other countries remained underdeveloped (for example, Bolivia, Brazil, Ceylon, China, India, Indonesia, Java, Malaya). Some economies which were economically backward in 1870 are still so ;[2] in some areas there has been a

* *Economia Internazionale*, Vol. VI, No. 4, 1953. Reprinted by permission of the Director of the Istituto di Economia Internazionale, and the author. The author is indebted to Dr Hla Myint and to his colleagues for helpful comments.

[1] We adopt the usual definition of an underdeveloped country as being one which is extremely poor relatively to other economies ; in a ranking of countries of the world by real income per head, the underdeveloped countries would be at the bottom.

[2] Compare the income distribution of countries given in the U.S. Department of State, *Point Four*, Economic Cooperation Series No. 24, January 1950, pp. 113-14.

tendency towards a condition which might be termed 'underdevelopment equilibrium'[1]. What forces may account for this limited development ?

In examining this question we might survey various possible answers and note the extent to which they can explain the situation in underdeveloped countries between 1870 and 1913. It will be seen that the principal explanations of why development was retarded may be found in some basic elements of the classical 'stationary state' and in some implications of the international features of development.

Possible Obstacles to Development

Although a commonplace, it is nevertheless necessary to recognize at the outset that the socio-political environment within a country may or may not be conducive to development. Certain religious and social attitudes are more favourable to development than are others, as has been stressed in the writings of Sombart, Weber, and Professor Tawney, among others. Current literature on development also frequently emphasizes the political and sociological aspects of the problem. The following two quotations are representative :

> 'Economic progress will not occur unless the atmosphere is favourable to it. The people of a country must desire progress, and their social, economic, legal and political institutions must be favourable to it.'[2]

> 'It is the realization that true economic growth is a many-sided individual and social process which is the most important lesson of past attempts to link underdeveloped territories and peoples in a wider world economy. It consists in the re-fashioning of aptitudes, and belief of individuals to give them new freedom in their multitudinous daily tasks—many of them not assessable in accounting or financial terms.'[3]

Assuredly, the socio-political aspects are so important that to a certain extent the problem of why some areas have remained underdeveloped might be answered by merely noting

[1] Ragnar Nurkse, *Some Aspects of Capital Accumulation in Underdeveloped Countries*, Cairo, 1952, p. 4.

[2] United Nations, *Measures for the Economic Development of Underdeveloped Countries*, New York, May 1951, p. 13.

[3] S. H. Frankel, *Some Conceptual Aspects of International Economic Development of Underdeveloped Territories*, Essays in International Finance, No. 14, Princeton, 1952, p. 22.

that they have lacked the socio-political prerequisites for development. The restrictive character of semi-feudal institutions, weak governments, lack of social legislation, absence of incentives, inadequate education, and poor health all bear witness to this. There is, indeed, much truth in maintaining that a country is economically backward because it is politically, socially, and physically backward.

Nevertheless, relevant as the sociological approach is, it is in many respects too easy a way out of the problem, and one may suspect that it does not get to the essence of the problem. Certainly from a purely economic viewpoint, there is more to be said about the process of development *per se*. For the present purposes of analysis, we might leave the socio-political elements on one side and concentrate on the more fundamental problem of whether the economy of an underdeveloped country might not contain within itself certain economic factors and forces which retard the country's rate of advance.

A popular answer to our problem immediately suggests itself—lack of resources and overpopulation. If a country has no natural resources which can be tapped, the possibility of development is, of course, obviated. But regarding how many underdeveloped countries in 1870 could it be said that there were no resources for import-competing commodities, or no resources for increasing exports, or that no increase in food production was possible? The answer must be very few. In fact, in some underdeveloped areas—for example, Africa and Brazil—the amount of resources per head was quite high.

It might, however, be contended that in many countries resources were scarce relatively to existing population or potential population. Although this is now true in several backward areas, it was much less apparent during the 1870–1913 period. The present phenomenon of a low amount of resources per head is the result of either the exhaustion of resources or such a rapid growth in population that overpopulation now puts pressure on the available resources. The beginnings of these trends are noticeable between 1870 and 1913, but, in that period, except for a few areas, population pressure was not the serious problem it now is. In some countries, such as Ceylon, the West Indies, and Malaya, there was even a shortage of labour, and to secure an adequate labour supply immigration was necessary. To explain the lack of development in these countries in terms of population pressure would be anachronistic, so far as their failure to develop in the nineteenth century is concerned.

Where there was population pressure, development was certainly handicapped. Contrary to the stagnation theory, population growth, if it is in a backward country, does not induce capital-widening investment or innovations. Instead, it diminishes the rate of capital accumulation, raises costs in extractive industries, increases the amount of disguised unemployment, and in large part simply diverts capital to maintaining children who die before reaching a productive age. In short, resources go to the formation of population, not capital.[1] As Malthus remarked, 'A man whose only possession is his labour can make no effectual demand if his labour is not wanted. . . . It will be found that those states often make the slowest progress in wealth where the stimulus arising from the population alone is the greatest.'[2]

Yet, overpopulation is not the answer to the problem we have posed. In a real sense, it is the problem ; overpopulation is synonymous with underdevelopment. In Ricardo's words, 'to say there is a great abundance of labour, is to say that there is not an adequate capital to employ it'.[3] The problems of increasing capital per head and raising *per capita* real income are common to all backward economies, whether overpopulated or not. In those countries which had a supra-optimum population the problems were intensified in degree, but not character.

If, then, many underdeveloped countries had resources which could have been utilized, and if overpopulation is simply a manifestation of underdevelopment, what other reasons might be offered to explain why development was retarded in some

[1] For a more complete discussion of problems raised by a supra-optimum population, see J. J. Spengler, 'The Population Obstacle to Economic Betterment', *American Economic Review Papers and Proceedings*, May 1951.

[2] T. R. Malthus, *Principles of Political Economy*, London, 1820, Chapter VII, section ii.

[3] David Ricardo, *Notes on Malthus's Principles of Political Economy*, Sraffa edition, Cambridge, England, 1951, p. 241.

countries ? A review of the literature on development suggests many obstacles to development. Most of these obstacles, however, can be classified under the following three categories : (i) market imperfections, (ii) 'the vicious circle', and (iii) the repercussions of foreign investment. We may now consider each of these in turn.

Market Imperfections

If we may be allowed to conceive of a production frontier (production possibility curve or transformation curve) for the underdeveloped country, it may be said that the actual production frontier has been far within the maximum possible frontier which might have been achieved by an optimum allocation of resources. The production functions which have actually been used have been very much 'inferior' or 'pseudo' production functions.

Many market imperfections might be listed as having prevented an optimum allocation of resources, thereby limiting the extension of the actual production frontier out to the maximum possible frontier. The imperfections most frequently cited are those of imperfect knowledge, imperfect mobility, specificity of factors, and imperfect divisibility of factors. Ignorance of potential resources and ignorance of technique were two manifestations of the imperfect knowledge. Ignorance of domestic, let alone world, market conditions was another. Dominated by custom and status, indigenous labour was immobile both geographically and occupationally. Nor were the prospects of higher economic rewards effective in removing this immobility. Many of the socio-political elements previously mentioned also fall into place here as additional frictions.

Although the imperfections in an underdeveloped economy cannot be denied, their significance would be overemphasized if it were claimed that the problem of development merely consists in a removal of these frictions in order to extend the actual frontier out to the maximum possible frontier, through the achievement of an optimum allocation of resources. For strong doubts may be expressed as to whether the attainment of an optimum allocation of resources, in so far as it depends on the fulfilment of marginal conditions, has much relevance in a backward economy. To gain any substantial increase in output, what is needed is not so much the fulfilment of 'marginal conditions' as 'total conditions'. More important than the 'tightening up' of the economy is a consideration of whether capacity should be created or destroyed—whether the total output might not be increased by introducing or abandoning the production or consumption of a commodity. One can scarcely interpret as a marginal adjustment the production of a new commodity or the introduction of a railway which might alter the entire productive structure of the region. Before marginal refinements become relevant, there must first be many 'once-over' structural changes, plus a great deal of 'hump investment' spread simultaneously over a broad front so that the utilization of the investments will approach full capacity.

Low output in backward countries, therefore, may be more realistically attributed to the absence of these large changes, rather than to the non-fulfilment of marginal conditions. To rely on marginal adjustments for the purpose of pushing the actual inferior production frontier out to the maximum frontier is to seek a will-o'-the-wisp, which, even if its achievement could be gratuitously assumed, would still not yield an increase in output comparable to that which is possible from the large changes involved in the fulfilment of total conditions. So far as an increase in output is concerned, marginal adjustments have been of secondary importance compared to the prime requirement of net capital formation, not only to provide intensive investment, but also to outstrip the growth in population and allow the amount of capital per head to increase.

The foregoing emphasis on total conditions and the minimization of the view that development can be achieved by marginal adjustments should not be interpreted, however, as meaning that market imperfections and frictions have been without significance. On the contrary, they have been important, as we shall see, not so much because they have limited marginal adjustments, but rather because they have been obstacles to the fulfilment of total conditions and have prevented the growth which has occurred in the export sectors of the underdeveloped economy from being diffused throughout the rest of the economy.

The Vicious Circle

According to the second view of underdevelopment, a backward economy remains backward because its total output is low, and reserve stocks are negligible, so that after consumption needs are fulfilled, little remains for capital accumulation. Consequently, there can be no marked increase in output. In the extreme form, such an economy remains a subsistence economy.

As is well known, a host of conditions may combine to limit capital accumulation. Although many underdeveloped areas have possessed potential resources, there was not adequate knowledge of these potentialities. Native peasants, producing for local markets, were unaware of possibilities extending beyond their particular localities. Only with foreign investment and the coming of extra-territorial enterprises was there a reasonable assessment of resources. But this knowledge was possessed by the foreign enterprises, not the native producers. And, due to the low level of home demand and the interest in realizing foreign exchange receipts, the foreign enterprise was attracted by production of exports, not production for the backward country's internal market.[1]

Yet, even if there had been knowledge of resources, the underdeveloped country would still have lacked the co-operant factors necessary for the full utilization of its resources. Without a supply of capital and entrepreneurship, without knowledge of industrial techniques, and without administrative and organizational skills, the economy specialized to a high degree in the production of a few labour-intensive or land-intensive primary products. Much of the production was commonly devoted to food crops, and in some countries only monoculture prevailed. Moreover, the labour supply was inefficient, and although employment per unit of output was

[1] Considering Britain's total foreign investment in the period 1870-1913, more than 40 per cent was used directly in railways, 15 per cent in the development of mines and raw materials, and a large proportion of an additional 30 per cent in governmental loans was directed to these activities. Less than 5 per cent of the value of public issues was for commercial and industrial enterprises serving the borrowing countries' home markets. Cf. Sir George Paish, 'Great Britain's Capital Investments in Individual Colonial and Foreign Countries', *Journal of Royal Statistical Society*, January 1911; A. K. Cairncross, *Home and Foreign Investment*, 1870-1913, Cambridge, 1953.

high, labour supply curves were frequently backward-sloping, and surplus population on the land took the form of disguised unemployment. Feudal systems of land tenure and production for narrow village markets also kept productivity low. A large proportion of labour, accordingly, was required to produce only a small surplus above subsistence needs.

Further, the individual agriculturalist's scale of production was very small because of his limited amount of capital, lack of storage facilities, inadequate cash reserves, and narrow markets. Such concentration on small-scale primary production meant, in turn, that the underdeveloped country's capital stock was not only low absolutely, but also low relatively to investment opportunities, and especially low relatively to the capital stock in an advanced country. For, as measured by the ratio of capital stock to real output, the capital coefficients in the backward economy's main activities of agriculture and mining were generally considerably smaller than are the capital coefficients associated with manufacturing, housing, and public utilities. What negligible manufacturing there was in these countries was characterized by small size of plant and was highly labour-intensive; there was little or no urbanization with attendant developments in housing and metropolitan improvements; and there was not the extensive transportation and communication systems which require large capital coefficients.

All the backward economies were thus primary producing areas in which land and labour were the relatively abundant factors and in which the total capital coefficient was very low. The small capital coefficient and low *per capita* productivity formed the vicious circle. To break the circle, capital accumulation was necessary. But the low level of real income kept the level of home savings low. Moreover, not only was the supply of investible funds small in magnitude, but what there was of it was canalized, because of the strong desire for liquidity, into commercial outlets, real estate, short-term lending, and capital flights, instead of into investment in industry, public utilities, or the processing of primary products.

Nor were the government's fiscal and monetary policies sufficiently refined to allow internal development to proceed via a budgetary surplus. Because of their impracticability or the lack of financial controls, income, profit, and other direct taxes formed but a minor proportion of public revenue. Instead, the revenue structure was dominated by customs receipts. The negligible amount of direct taxes, together with the general inadequacy of taxable resources and the ineffectual budgetary control, meant that a government surplus was infrequent: expenditures generally expanded to or beyond the level of available revenues. Lacking sufficient home savings or a budgetary surplus, the underdeveloped areas, therefore, had to rely on external borrowings for long-term investment funds.

It is interesting to note that, though stated in more modern terminology, much of the foregoing is little more than an elaboration of elements contained in the classical model of development. Smith, Ricardo, Malthus, and J. S. Mill concentrated on how the market might be extended, on the possibilities of increasing productivity by the division of labour, and on the problem of capital accumulation. Instead of restricting their attention to the 'scarcity' concept of the economic problem, to the 'tightening up' of allocative efficiency within a given productive framework, the classical economists actually devoted considerable attention to the problem of 'widening' the economy. Indeed, it has been stated that when

> 'we come to the mainstream of classical economic thought dominated by the Ricardian tradition we find the physical output approach of the labour theory firmly established almost to a complete neglect of the allocative problem. It continued to be so until the "marginal revolution" ... considerations concerning "allocative" efficiency were eclipsed by broader considerations concerning the means of raising the physical productivity of labour and expanding the total volume of economic activity.... The central principle, which successfully unifies the various classical economic doctrines from Adam Smith to J. S. Mill, embodies the following fundamental propositions: viz. the economic welfare of society can be more effectively promoted (i) by increasing the physical productivity of labour, and (ii) by increasing the volume of economic activity, rather than by tamely accepting the given quantity of productive resources and making refined adjustments in allocating them among different industries. From this follow the two major canons of classical economic policy, (i) free trade which extends the scope of division of labour and brings fresh resources into the productive framework, and (ii) capital accumulation which enables society to maintain a greater quantity of labour.'[1]

[1] Hla Myint, *Theories of Welfare Economics*, London, 1948, pp. 6, 12, 13.

It is within this context that we can appreciate Smith's emphasis on capital accumulation as a prerequisite of the division of labour, on the need for a marketable surplus above subsistence, and on increasing real wages. Attention of the classical economists to the wages-fund doctrine, to the principle that 'a demand for commodities is not a demand for labour'[1] and to the relation between population growth and the subsistence level are all close to the core of the problem of limited development. The classical concept of the 'stationary state' is indeed suggestive of some elements which have characterized underdeveloped countries.

Finally, to recognize that such a writer as J. S. Mill clearly realized the problems of the underdeveloped economy, the following, which is really a succinct summary of much recent discussion on the subject, might be quoted:

'In countries where the principle of accumulation is as weak as it is in the various nations of Asia; where people will neither save, nor work to obtain the means of saving, unless under the inducement of enormously high profits, nor even then if it is necessary to wait a considerable time for them; where either productions remain scanty, or drudgery great, because there is neither capital forthcoming nor forethought sufficient for the adoption of the contrivances by which natural agents are made to do the work of human labour; the desideratum for such a country, economically considered, is an increase of industry, and of the effective desire of accumulation. The means are . . . a better government; more complete security of property; . . . a more permanent and more advantageous tenure of land . . . improvement of the public intelligence . . . the decay of usages or superstitions which interfere with the effective employment of industry . . . the introduction of foreign arts, which raise the returns derivable from additional capital to a rate corresponding to the low strength of the desire of accumulation; and the importation of foreign capital, which renders the increase of production no longer exclusively dependent on the thrift or providence of the inhabitants themselves, while it places before them a stimulating example, and by instilling new ideas and breaking the chains of habit, if not by improving the actual condition of the population, tends to create in them new wants, increased ambition, and greater thought for the future.'[2]

[1] We are concerned here with the questions raised by this principle, not the validity of Mill's particular statement.

[2] J. S. Mill, *Principles of Political Economy*, London, 1842, 3rd edition, pp. 230-31.

Somewhat paradoxically, however, for all their attention to the problems of development and foreign trade considered separately, the classical economists did not relate the two problems by considering how international relations might cut both ways so far as development is concerned—in some cases stimulating development, in other cases limiting development. The latter possibility is of immediate relevance and might be investigated further.

Repercussions of Foreign Investment

The need for external borrowings does not mean that the development problem is solely a financial one, solved if only foreign investment is forthcoming. A recollection of nineteenth century experience dispels this view. Many countries which were recipients of large amounts of British capital in the pre-1914 era had made relatively little progress by the end of the period. There was, moreover, no clear positive correlation between the amount of capital inflow and the extent of development. Even though the relative magnitudes of the development problem differed among countries, it is nevertheless significant that by 1914 British foreign investment in Brazil had amounted to four times that in New Zealand, and foreign investment in India surpassed that in Argentina or Australia.

While it has broken the vicious circle, the mere access to foreign capital has not alone been sufficient to guarantee development. The repercussions of the foreign investment are what have been crucial : the direction of the foreign investment, the type of economic organization which accompanied it, and its income effects.

The foreign investor was generally attracted not by opportunities in the underdeveloped country's domestic market, but rather by the expectation of higher profits from its export industries and by the possibilities of realizing foreign exchange receipts. This caused foreign capital to become concentrated in plantations and mines producing for export and in railways connecting export-producing areas with the seaports.

According to the traditional theory of foreign investment, when capital flows from areas where it is relatively abundant and has a low marginal product to areas where it is relatively scarce and has a high marginal product, the flow will contribute to the achievement of an optimum distribution of resources in the world economy and will mean an increase in the combined national incomes. This conclusion, however, depends on the adoption of a cosmopolitan viewpoint, on the implicit assumption that private marginal net product and social marginal net product are equal, and on the qualification of *ceteris paribus* (particularly no change in the terms of trade). If the problem is considered only from the underdeveloped country's standpoint, or a divergence between social and private returns is recognized (especially with respect to external economies), or the *ceteris paribus* clause is relaxed, the traditional conclusion may be contradicted. So far as development is concerned, all we can really say is that for an underdeveloped country some foreign investment is better than no foreign investment, but foreign investment directed according to private profit expectations is not necessarily the best direction.[1]

Nevertheless, an outstanding result of foreign borrowings has been their contribution to a substantial increase in the exports of the recipient countries, an increase which is especially striking over the longer period. Tea production in India and Ceylon, coffee production in Brazil, rice production in Burma —all these show sizeable increases. The same is true for exports of these commodities. In many instances, the export output grew not merely at a steady rate, but at an increasing rate. There may have been a period of gestation before the fruits of the investment appeared, but ultimately there was an increased supply of exportable primary products from most of the borrowing countries.

At bottom, the persistence of underlying differences in comparative costs and a sustained absolute demand for primary products by advanced countries were the principal reasons why the backward country's exports grew. Productivity increased more rapidly in the export sector than in the rest of the underdeveloped economy because a relatively small amount of investment allowed the utilization of a large amount of hitherto untouched natural resources; with the foreign

[1] This applies only to development objectives. It is not meant to apply to the additional question of whether development which is contrary to comparative advantage would diminish, instead of increase, economic welfare.

investment there appeared efficiently-managed and technically-organized plantation and mining units producing for export; and, low as was the total capital coefficient for the whole economy, nevertheless the capital coefficient became highest in the export sector. The latter resulted from the establishment of mills and factories to process some raw materials and food-stuffs for export and the extension of utilities to serve the export industries. Moreover, while productivity rose most rapidly in export production, the pressure of population and lack of bargaining power prevented labour from absorbing through rising money wages the increase in productivity. At the same time, the rate of increase in productivity was greater in industrial nations than in underdeveloped areas, and industrial countries became ever-more industrialized. The upshot was that the underdeveloped country's comparative advantage widened for primary products, and the industrial country's comparative advantage turned against these products.

Now, at this point, it might be thought that instead of disclosing limitations to development, we have done just the opposite and have actually established a favourable case for potential development. After all, we have said that many of the underdeveloped countries have not lacked resources; they have had access to foreign capital; their exports have grown; and with foreign borrowings the capital coefficient has risen in the export sector. It might even be thought that we have assembled the elements for a model similar to Professor Hicks' cycle and growth model.[1] The increasing exports might have had effects analogous to those of increasing autonomous investment,[2] and induced investment might have followed from the increase in exports, so that, based on an upward trend in exports, a multiplier-accelerator process might have caught hold and become the engine of growth.

Yet, it did not. The increased supply of exports was not translated into an increase in demand in the rest of the economy. The proximate reason for this lies in a factor which so far has only been implied in our discussion—the lack of internal

[1] J. R. Hicks, *A Contribution to the Theory of the Trade Cycle*, Oxford, 1950, Chapter 8.

[2] J. S. Duesenberry, 'Some Aspects of the Theory of Economic Development', *Explorations in Entrepreneurial History*, Vol. III, No. 2, 15 December 1950, p. 100.

demand due to a low level of real income. The deficiency of internal demand is but another way of looking at the vicious circle ; the low level of real income is a limitation on the demand side, just as it is on the supply side.[1] As Malthus remarked, 'an inferior mode of living is a cause as well as a consequence of poverty'[2] and 'it is unquestionably true that wealth produces wants, but it is a still more important truth that wants produce wealth. . . . The greatest of all difficulties in converting uncivilized and thinly populated countries into civilized and populous ones, is to inspire them with the wants best calculated to excite their exertions in the production of wealth'.[3] The vicious circle on the demand and supply sides have met at a common point—the low level of real income : 'the capacity to buy depends on the capacity to produce, and the division of labour depends on the extent of the market but the extent of the market depends upon the division of labour.'[4]

Thus, the important question is why the level of real income remained low, even though foreign investment occurred and exports increased. The imperfections and frictions previously mentioned had some influence in preventing the expansion in exports from having an impact on the rest of the economy. So did the fact that external economies were confined to the export sector. It is also generally recognized that certain other factors, acting individually or in combination, may be responsible for smaller incomes to agricultural producers than to non-agricultural producers. These need only be recalled here : low price elasticity of demand for many basic agricultural products, the influence of Engel's Law, periodic overproduction which depresses prices more than the reduction of costs by increasing productivity, immobility of agricultural labour and agricultural capital, and highly competitive conditions of agricultural production.[5] But in so far as these factors have also been present in some primary-producing countries which have none

[1] Nurkse, op. cit., pp. 2-4.

[2] Malthus, op. cit., pp. 427-8.

[3] ibid., p. 428.

[4] Allyn Young, 'Increasing Return and Economic Progress', *The Economic Journal*, Vol. XXXVIII, December 1928, p. 539.

[5] Cf. A. W. Ashby, 'General Causes of Agricultural Poverty', *Farm Economist*, Vol. V, No. 7, 1946 ; E. A. Ojala, *Agriculture and Economic Progress*, Oxford, 1952, pp. 179-80.

the less become advanced countries, we must seek more basic explanations. These might be found in the type of economic organization which secured the increase in exports and in the income leakages abroad which dampened the effects of both the multiplier and accelerator.

The export products which display the most rapid rates of growth—coffee, tea, sugarcane, sisal, and rubber—were produced mainly under the plantation system. Although the superior techniques, knowledge, and capital of the plantation units allowed production and exports to expand, these units were under foreign control. There was, accordingly, a considerable drain of profits and interest out of the underdeveloped economy, even though some profits were reinvested within the country.

Moreover, the plantation system relied on the presence of a large supply of unskilled labour. With the intensive use of labour, labour's marginal product was low, and so were real wages. It may not be too much of an exaggeration to say that in some underdeveloped areas the elasticity of the labour supply has been almost infinite at the subsistence wage level. An internal surplus of food is what has been required, but not achieved, in many countries which have remained backward.

Not all the increase in exports, however, was due to the plantation system. In some areas where population density was too high for the plantation system, peasant production continued to prevail even after the inflow of foreign capital. Foreign enterprises merely advanced credit to peasants and provided transportation and marketing facilities. Other crops such as groundnuts, rice, and jute remained essentially peasant crops. But regarding these instances, some writers allege that it commonly happened that the natives, ignorant of world market conditions and dependent on middlemen operating between them and the foreign company, were in the position of confronting a monopsonistic middleman or foreign company when selling their produce and a monopolist when buying imports, so that the native's real income did not rise as much as it would have if he had sold directly to the foreign market.[1]

[1] Sir Alan Pim, *Colonial Agricultural Production*, London, 1946, pp. 29, 33; W. H. Hancock, *Survey of British Commonwealth Affairs*, London, 1940, Vol. II, pp. 221-2; A. McPhee, *The Economic Revolution in British West Africa*, London, 1926, pp. 98-100.

How much validity there is in this contention is difficult to establish, since the degree of monopoly or monopsony power is at best an ambiguous concept, and evidence of its existence is not easy to obtain or assess.

Considering the 'income effects' of the foreign investment, however, it is clear that although there were basic ingredients for a multiplier-accelerator process, the income-generating forces were dampened considerably by leakages abroad. Because of the remittance of profits, interest, and dividends to the lending country, as well as the high marginal propensity to import and high income elasticity of demand for imports, a given amount of investment in the underdeveloped country generated a much smaller amount of income than would have an equivalent amount of investment in an advanced country.

Although the underdeveloped economy had a high marginal propensity to consume, leakages abroad were high, so the multiplier effect was weak. Similarly, the acceleration effects in the backward country were negligible compared to those in an advanced country. Not only was the total capital coefficient smaller, but whatever induced investment occurred was geared mainly, if not entirely, to changes in foreign demand for exports. This is quite a different situation from that in an advanced country where the total capital coefficient is much higher and where investment is induced not only by changes in foreign demand but also, more significantly, by home demand. It must also be recognized that the additional capital equipment associated with induced investment had to be imported from industrial nations.

Finally, to realize a positive rate of growth the underdeveloped region was dependent on a trend rate of increase in exports. But although exports rose over the long period, so did the propensity to import. As the products of the advanced countries were introduced into the backward region, and as contact was made with superior consumption patterns, the region's propensity to import increased—that is, Professor Duesenberry's 'demonstration effect' might operate internationally as well as domestically.[1] In part, the backward area's marginal

[1] Cf. Ragnar Nurkse, 'Some International Aspects of the Problem of Economic Development', reprinted in the present volume, pp. 256-71. Earlier uses of this concept have been made by Professors Stolper and Kindleberger.

propensity to import tended to be greater, the higher was its level of income, because there was not a once-for-all introduction of the advanced countries' commodities, but rather a more gradual process of preliminary 'want development' for the advanced country's exports,[1] and these commodities, especially consumer goods, were of such a nature that they entered into the backward country's standard of consumption only after the country's income had risen above minimum levels.

It might further be argued that over the long period the distribution of income in the backward country tended to shift in favour of profits and rents, since as the level of activity rose, a multiplicity of intermediary traders emerged and benefited from the secular inflationary pressures, the demand for land increased, and money wages did not rise commensurately because of the abundance of unskilled labour without bargaining power. Traders and landlords may be expected to have a higher marginal propensity to import than do the other classes, so that again for this reason the marginal propensity to import for the community tended to increase as the level of income rose. All these elements, therefore, combined to cause the expansion in exports to be in effect dissipated on imports, and the upward trend in exports had no significant carry-over to output for the domestic market.

Development through Inflation and Protection

Having considered how the obstacles imposed by imperfections, the vicious circle, and the income leakages abroad have been historical limitations to development, we may conclude by briefly enquiring whether development might not have proceeded further if the underdeveloped countries had pursued policies designed to raise the level of home demand and reduce the dependence on foreign trade. Two policy areas are immediately suggested—inflation and protection. Although a thorough study of the effects of these policies would necessitate detailed case studies, we may offer some general observations on a programme of development through inflation and protection.

[1] Elizabeth E. Hoyt, 'Want Development in Underdeveloped Areas', *Journal of Political Economy*, Vol. LIX, No. 3, June 1951.

Deliberate inflation, say through credit creation, may well increase the level of money demand as the supply of money increases, and not all is absorbed in idle cash balances. It is also likely to stimulate investment by raising profit expectations and may be a means of extracting forced savings to match the investment made with bank credit. But the increase in money demand is, of course, not a solution to the problem of the demand side of the vicious circle. What is needed is an increase in real demand. Real income, not money income, must rise before home demand will offer sufficient inducement to home investment.

Concerning the extraction of forced savings and investment through inflation, there is considerable literature indicating the disadvantages of this policy.[1] These need only be recalled here : (*a*) the misdirection of savings into foreign assets, real estate, and inventories instead of to industry and agriculture ; (*b*) the shift in the distribution of real national income in favour of profits ; (*c*) the pressures on the balance of payments and the possibility of continuous currency depreciation ; (*d*) the ever-greater divergencies between private marginal product and social marginal product ; and (*e*) the loss in consumption by some multiple of the amount of investment provided through forced savings.[2]

Although these disadvantages weaken the case for inflation, the advocacy of protection merits more serious attention. Unlike the neo-classical theory of international trade which determines a once-for-all allocation of given resources, the modern arguments for protection disclaim any static interpretation of the division of gains from trade. Instead they proceed from a dynamic theory of comparative costs which associates a different comparative cost structure with each level of income and production. Incorporating an overall view of foreign investment and development, they argue for a distribution of benefits from development more favourable

[1] See, for example, Nurkse, *Some Aspects of Capital Accumulation in Underdeveloped Countries*, op. cit., pp. 53-65 ; United Nations, *Measures for the Economic Development of Underdeveloped Countries*, New York, May 1951, chapter VI ; E. M. Bernstein and I. G. Patel, 'Inflation in Relation to Economic Development', *International Monetary Fund Staff Papers*, Vol. II, No. 3, November 1952.

[2] ibid., pp. 381-2.

to the backward countries in the long period and for a mitigation of cyclical disequilibria in the short period.

Considering the long period problem, those arguments which stem from a naive desire for autarkic industrialization can be readily dismissed; on the other hand, the element of truth in the 'infant industry', 'attracting direct investment', and 'servicing the foreign debt' arguments can be admitted. In a broader context, however, there are other arguments which should be examined further. Specifically, a combination of import duties, export taxes, and subsidies are frequently advocated to (i) avoid a potential deterioration in the terms of trade, or to improve the terms of trade, (ii) to alter the domestic distribution of income, and (iii) to stimulate the movement of resources into secondary production.

It is highly problematical whether protective devices actually can accomplish these objectives and whether they could do so without being at the expense of real income. In general, it might be submitted that the protectionist must prove that gains concentrated at the margin on the terms of trade are not more than offset by diffused average losses from a restriction in the international division of labour: that protective devices which stimulate greater domestic production result in greater total production than could be obtained indirectly by trade; and that alternative domestic and international measures might not yield similar results without the adverse beggar-my-neighbour effects of protection.

More particularly, for the immediate problem, the protectionist must demonstrate that the quantitative efficacy of the devices he advocates is not exaggerated. Such exaggeration is likely to be the case for underdeveloped countries since many of these have relatively little bargaining power and, more significantly, the devices are most effective in the short period, whereas their objectives, in terms of the secular phenomena of development, are of a long run character.

It should also be realized that a decrease in imports is of minor benefit to the underdeveloped country unless the portion of income which was formerly spent on imports is now not spent on home produced consumer goods but is made available for domestic capital formation. If protection is to contribute to development it is necessary to stimulate basic key industries

rather than merely the production of import-competing consumer goods.

Moreover, the several objectives of protection might be mutually inconsistent. As Professor Metzler has shown, if the demand for a country's exports as a whole is sufficiently inelastic, as is probable for many backward primary-producing countries, its terms of trade will improve, and this favourable movement may more than offset the initial effects of the tariff in raising domestic prices of manufactured goods.[1] Without an increase in the domestic prices of imports (including tariffs) relative to the domestic prices of exports, there may be no incentive to shift resources from export to import-competing industries. Then, in contrast to the Stolper-Samuelson conclusion that impediments to imports preserve or increase the 'scarcity' of the scarce factor of production and thereby increase the scarce factor's relative and absolute share of the national income,[2] the result would be that the scarce factor which is relatively most important in the import-competing industries would suffer both a relative decline in its share of the national income and an absolute decline in its real return.

If, then, the foreign elasticity of demand for its products is sufficiently inelastic, a backward country may find it impossible to impose a tariff which will simultaneously improve its terms of trade, attract resources into import-competing industries, and increase the share of labour in the national income (assuming labour is the scarce factor which is used in comparatively large amounts in relation to other factors in the protected industries). As in most problems relevant to welfare economics, the conflict may be between a larger national income and its specific distribution. This is true not only for the tariff, but for most impediments to trade which are essentially reducible to a system of taxes and subsidies affecting the distribution of income as well as the allocation of resources.

Finally, it must be recognized that the objective of development should be not only to raise the level of *per capita* real

[1] L. A. Metzler, 'Tariffs, the Terms of Trade, and the Distribution of National Income', *Journal of Political Economy*, Vol. LVII, No. 1, February 1949, pp. 1-29.

[2] W. F. Stolper and P. A. Samuelson, 'Protection and Real Wages', *Review of Economic Studies*, Vol. IX, November 1941, pp. 58-73.

income but also to reduce the absolute number of individuals and the percentage of total population below a minimum level of real income.[1] Even if protection were successful in raising the level of *per capita* real income, it is conceivable that through the misallocation of resources it might at the same time increase the absolute numbers beneath a minimum level of real income.

[1] Cf. Jacob Viner, 'America's Aims and the Progress of Underdeveloped Areas', in B. F. Hoselitz (editor), *The Progress of Underdeveloped Areas*, Chicago, 1952, p. 187.

ON THE POLITICAL ECONOMY OF BACKWARDNESS*

by **Paul A. Baran**

THE CAPITALIST MODE OF PRODUCTION AND THE SOCIAL AND political order concomitant with it provided, during the latter part of the eighteenth century, and still more during the entire nineteenth century, a framework for a continuous and, in spite of cyclical disturbances and setbacks, momentous expansion of productivity and material welfare. The relevant facts are well known and call for no elaboration. Yet this material (and cultural) progress was not only spotty in time but most unevenly distributed in space. It was confined to the Western world; and did not affect even all of this territorially and demographically relatively small sector of the inhabited globe. Germany and Austria, Britain and France, some smaller countries in Western Europe, and the United States and Canada occupied places in the neighbourhood of the sun. The vast expanses and the multitude of inhabitants of Eastern Europe, Spain and Portugal, Italy and the Balkans, Latin America and Asia, not to speak of Africa, remained in the deep shadow of backwardness and squalor, of stagnation and misery.

Tardy and skimpy as the benefits of capitalism may have been with respect to the lower classes even in most of the leading industrial countries, they were all but negligible in the less privileged parts of the world. There productivity remained low, and rapid increases in population pushed living standards from bad to worse. The dreams of the prophets of capitalist harmony remained on paper. Capital either did not move from countries where its marginal productivity was low to countries where it could be expected to be high, or if it did, it moved there mainly in order to extract profits from backward countries that frequently accounted for a lion's share of the increments in total output caused by the original

* *The Manchester School*, January 1952. Reprinted by permission of *The Manchester School* and the author.

investments. Where an increase in the aggregate national product of an underdeveloped country took place, the existing distribution of income prevented this increment from raising the living standards of the broad masses of the population. Like all general statements, this one is obviously open to criticism based on particular cases. There were, no doubt, colonies and dependencies where the populations profited from inflow of foreign capital. These benefits, however, were few and far between, while exploitation and stagnation were the prevailing rule.

But if Western capitalism failed to improve materially the lot of the peoples inhabiting most backward areas, it accomplished something that profoundly affected the social and political conditions in underdeveloped countries. It introduced there, with amazing rapidity, all the economic and social tensions inherent in the capitalist order. It effectively disrupted whatever was left of the 'feudal' coherence of the backward societies. It substituted market contracts for such paternalistic relationships as still survived from century to century. It reoriented the partly or wholly self-sufficient economies of agricultural countries toward the production of marketable commodities. It linked their economic fate with the vagaries of the world market and connected it with the fever curve of international price movements.

A *complete* substitution of capitalist market rationality for the rigidities of feudal or semi-feudal servitude would have represented, in spite of all the pains of transition, an important step in the direction of progress. Yet all that happened was that the age-old exploitation of the population of underdeveloped countries by their domestic overlords, was freed of the mitigating constraints inherited from the feudal tradition. This superimposition of business *mores* over ancient oppression by landed gentries resulted in compounded exploitation, more outrageous corruption, and more glaring injustice.

Nor is this by any means the end of the story. Such export of capital and capitalism as has taken place had not only far-reaching implications of a social nature. It was accompanied by important physical and technical processes. Modern machines and products of advanced industries reached the poverty stricken backyards of the world. To be sure most, if not all, of these machines worked for their foreign owners—or at least were believed by the population to be working for no one else—and the new refined appurtenances of the good life belonged to foreign businessmen and their domestic counterparts. The bonanza that was capitalism, the fullness of things that was modern industrial civilization, were crowding the display windows—they were protected by barbed wire from the anxious grip of the starving and desperate man in the street.

But they have drastically changed his outlook. Broadening and deepening his economic horizon, they aroused aspirations, envies, and hopes. Young intellectuals filled with zeal and patriotic devotion travelled from the underdeveloped lands to Berlin and London, to Paris and New York, and returned home with the 'message of the possible'.

Fascinated by the advances and accomplishments observed in the centres of modern industry, they developed, and propagandized the image of what could be attained in their home countries under a more rational economic and social order. The dissatisfaction with the stagnation (or at best, barely perceptible growth) that ripened gradually under the still-calm political and social surface was given an articulate expression. This dissatisfaction was not nurtured by a comparison of reality with a vision of a socialist society. It found sufficient fuel in the confrontation of what was actually happening with what could be accomplished under capitalist institutions of the Western type.

The establishment of such institutions was, however, beyond the reach of the tiny middle classes of most backward areas. The inherited backwardness and poverty of their countries never gave them an opportunity to gather the economic strength, the insight, and the self-confidence needed for the assumption of a leading role in society. For centuries under feudal rule they themselves assimilated the political, moral, and cultural values of the dominating class.

While in advanced countries, such as France or Great Britain, the economically ascending middle-classes developed at an early stage a new rational world outlook, which they proudly opposed to the medieval obscurantism of the feudal age, the poor, fledgling bourgeoisie of the underdeveloped countries sought nothing but accommodation to the prevailing order. Living in societies based on privilege, they strove for a share in the existing sinecures. They made political and economic deals with their domestic feudal overlords or with powerful foreign investors, and what industry and commerce developed in backward areas in the course of the last hundred years was rapidly moulded in the straitjacket of monopoly—the plutocratic partner of the aristocratic rulers. What resulted was an economic and political amalgam combining the worst features of both worlds—feudalism and capitalism—and blocking effectively all possibilities of economic growth.

It is quite conceivable that a 'conservative' exit from this impasse might have been found in the course of time. A younger generation of enterprising and enlightened businessmen and intellectuals allied with moderate leaders of workers and peasants—a 'Young Turk' movement of some sort—might have succeeded in breaking the deadlock, in loosening the hide-bound social and political structure of their countries and in creating the institutional arrangements indispensable for a measure of social and economic progress.

Yet in our rapid age history accorded no time for such a gradual transition. Popular pressures for an amelioration of economic and social conditions, or at least for some perceptible movement in that direction, steadily gained in intensity. To be sure, the growing restiveness of the underprivileged was not directed against the ephemeral principles of a hardly yet existing capitalist order. Its objects were parasitic feudal overlords appropriating large slices of the national product and wasting them on extravagent living ; a government machinery protecting and abetting the dominant interests ; wealthy businessmen reaping immense profits and not utilizing them for productive purposes ; last but not least, foreign colonizers extracting or believed to be extracting vast gains from their 'developmental' operations.

This popular movement had thus essentially bourgeois, democratic, anti-feudal, anti-imperialist tenets. It found outlets in agrarian egalitarianism ; it incorporated 'muck-raker' elements denouncing monopoly ; it strove for national independence and freedom from foreign exploitation.

For the native capitalist middle-classes to assume the leadership of these popular forces and to direct them into the channels of bourgeois democracy—as had happened in Western Europe—they had to identify themselves with the common man. They had to break away from the political, economic, and ideological leadership of the feudal crust and the monopolists allied with it ; and they had to demonstrate to the nation as a whole that they had the knowledge, the courage, and the determination to undertake and to carry to victorious conclusion the struggle for economic and social improvement.

In hardly any underdeveloped country were the middle-classes capable of living up to this historical challenge. Some of the reasons for this portentous failure, reasons connected with the internal make-up of the business class itself, were briefly mentioned above. Of equal importance was, however, an 'outside' factor. It was the spectacular growth of the international labour movement in Europe that offered the popular forces in backward areas ideological and political leadership that was denied to them by the native bourgeoisie. It pushed the goals and targets of the popular movements far beyond their original limited objectives.

This liaison of labour radicalism and populist revolt painted on the wall the imminent danger of a social revolution. Whether this danger was real or imaginary matters very little. What was essential is that the awareness of this threat effectively determined political and social action. It destroyed whatever chances there were of the capitalist classes joining and leading the popular anti-feudal, anti-monopolist movement. By instilling a mortal fear of expropriation and extinction in the minds of *all* property-owning groups the rise of socialist radicalism, and in particular the Bolshevik Revolution in Russia, tended to drive all more or less privileged, more or less well-to-do elements in the society into one 'counter-revolutionary' coalition. Whatever differences and antagonisms existed between large and small landowners, between monopolistic and competitive business, between liberal bourgeois and reactionary feudal overlords, between domestic and foreign interests, were largely submerged on all important occasions by the over-riding *common* interest in staving off socialism.

The possibility of solving the economic and political deadlock prevailing in the underdeveloped countries on lines of a progressive capitalism all but disappeared. Entering the alliance with all other segments of the ruling class, the capitalist middle-classes yielded one strategic position after another. Afraid that a quarrel with the landed gentry might be exploited by the radical populist movement, the middle-classes abandoned all progressive attitudes in agrarian matters. Afraid that a conflict with the church and the military might weaken the political authority of the government, the middle-classes moved away from all liberal and pacifist currents. Afraid that hostility toward foreign interests might deprive them of foreign support in a case of a revolutionary emergency, the native capitalists deserted their previous anti-imperialist, nationalist platforms.

The peculiar mechanisms of political interaction characteristic of all underdeveloped (and perhaps not only underdeveloped) countries thus operated at full speed. The aboriginal failure of the middle-classes to provide inspiration and leadership to the popular masses pushed those masses into the camp of socialist radicalism. The growth of radicalism pushed the middle-classes into an alliance with the aristocratic and monopolistic reaction. This alliance, cemented by common interest and common fear, pushed the populist forces still further along the road of radicalism and revolt. The outcome was a polarization of society with very little left between the poles. By permitting this polarization to develop, by abandoning the common man and resigning the task of reorganizing society on new, progressive lines, the capitalist middle-classes threw away their historical chance of assuming effective control over the destinies of their nations, and of directing the gathering popular storm against the fortresses of feudalism and reaction. Its blazing fire turned thus against the entirety of existing economic and social institutions.

The economic and political order maintained by the ruling coalition of owning classes finds itself invariably at odds with all the urgent needs of the underdeveloped countries. Neither the social fabric that it embodies nor the institutions that rest upon it are conducive to progressive economic development. The only way to provide for economic growth and to prevent a continuous deterioration of living standards (apart from mass emigration unacceptable to other countries) is to assure a steady increase of total output—at least large enough to offset the rapid growth of population.

An obvious source of such an increase is the utilization of available unutilized or underutilized resources. A large part of this reservoir of dormant productive potentialities is the vast multitude of entirely unemployed or ineffectively employed manpower. There is no way of employing it usefully in agriculture, where the marginal productivity of labour tends to zero. They could be provided with opportunities for productive work only by transfer to industrial pursuits. For this to be feasible large investments in industrial plant and facilities have to be undertaken. Under prevailing conditions such investments are not forthcoming for a number of important and interrelated reasons.

With a very uneven distribution of a very small aggregate income (and wealth), large individual incomes exceeding what could be regarded as 'reasonable' requirements for current consumption accrue as a rule to a relatively small group of high-income receivers. Many of them are large landowners maintaining a feudal style of life with large outlays on housing, servants, travel, and other luxuries. Their 'requirements for consumption' are so high that there is only little room for savings. Only relatively insignificant amounts are left to be spent on improvements of agricultural estates.

Other members of the 'upper crust' receiving incomes markedly surpassing 'reasonable' levels of consumption are wealthy businessmen. For social reasons briefly mentioned above, their consumption too is very much larger than it would have been were they brought up in the puritan tradition of a bourgeois civilization. Their drive to accumulate and to expand their enterprises is continuously counteracted by the urgent desire to imitate in their living habits the socially dominant 'old families', to prove by their conspicuous outlays on the amenities of rich life that they are socially (and therefore also politically) not inferior to their aristocratic partners in the ruling coalition.

But if this tendency curtails the volume of savings that could have been amassed by the urban high-income receivers, their will to re-invest their funds in productive enterprises is effectively curbed by a strong reluctance to damage their carefully erected monopolistic market positions through creation of additional productive capacity, and by absence of suitable investment opportunities—paradoxical as this may sound with reference to underdeveloped countries.

The deficiency of investment opportunities stems to a large extent from the structure and the limitations of the existing effective demand. With very low living standards the bulk of the aggregate money income of the population is spent on food and relatively primitive items of clothing and household necessities. These are available at low prices, and investment of large funds in plant and facilities that could produce this type of commodities more cheaply rarely promises attractive returns. Nor does it appear profitable to develop major enterprises the output of which would cater to the requirements of the rich. Large as their individual purchases of various luxuries may be, their aggregate spending on each of them is not sufficient to support the development of an elaborate luxury industry—in particular since the 'snob' character of prevailing tastes renders only imported luxury articles true marks of social distinction.

Finally, the limited demand for investment goods precludes the building up of a machinery or equipment industry. Such mass consumption goods as are lacking, and such quantities of luxury goods as are purchased by the well-to-do, as well as the comparatively small quantities of investment goods needed by industry, are thus imported from abroad in exchange for domestic agricultural products and raw materials.

This leaves the expansion of exportable raw materials output as a major outlet for investment activities. There the possibilities are greatly influenced, however, by the technology of the production of most raw materials as well as by the nature of the markets to be served. Many raw materials, in particular oil, metals, certain industrial crops, have to be produced on a large scale if costs are to be kept low and satisfactory returns assured. Large-scale production, however, calls for large investments, so large indeed as to exceed the potentialities of the native capitalists in backward countries. Production of raw materials for a distant market entails, moreover, much larger risks than those encountered in domestic business. The difficulty of foreseeing accurately such things as receptiveness of the world markets, prices obtainable in competition with other countries, volume of output in other parts of the world, etc., sharply reduces the interest of native capitalists in these lines of business. They become to a predominant extent the domain of foreigners who, financially stronger, have at the same time much closer contacts with foreign outlets of their products.

The shortage of investible funds and the lack of investment opportunities represent two aspects of the same problem. A great number of investment projects, unprofitable under prevailing conditions, could be most promising in a general environment of economic expansion.

In backward areas a new industrial venture must frequently, if not always, break virgin ground. It has no functioning economic system to draw upon. It has to organize with its own efforts not only the productive process *within* its own confines, it must provide in addition for all the necessary *outside* arrangements essential to its operations. It does not enjoy the benefits of 'external economies'.

There can be no doubt that the absence of external economies, the inadequacy of the economic milieu in underdeveloped countries, constituted everywhere an important deterrent to investment in industrial projects. There is no way of rapidly bridging the gap. Large-scale investment is predicated upon large-scale investment. Roads, electric power stations, railroads, and houses have to be built *before* businessmen find it profitable to erect factories, to invest their funds in new industrial enterprises.

Yet investing in road building, financing construction of canals and power stations, organizing large housing projects, etc., transcend by far the financial and mental horizon of capitalists in underdeveloped countries. Not only are their financial resources too small for such ambitious projects, but their background and habits militate against entering commitments of this type. Brought up in the tradition of merchandizing and manufacturing consumers' goods—as is characteristic of an early phase of capitalist development—businessmen in underdeveloped countries are accustomed to rapid turnover, large but short-term risks, and correspondingly high rates of profit. Sinking funds in enterprises where profitability could manifest itself only in the course of many years is a largely unknown and unattractive departure.

The difference between social and private rationality that exists in any market and profit-determined economy is thus particularly striking in underdeveloped countries. While building of roads, harnessing of water power, or organization of housing developments may facilitate industrial growth and thus contribute to increased productivity on a national scale, the individual firms engaged in such activities may suffer losses and be unable to recover their investments. The nature of the problem involved can be easily exemplified: starting a new industrial enterprise is predicated among other things upon the availability of appropriately skilled manpower. Engaging men and training them on the job is time-consuming and expensive. They are liable to be unproductive, wasteful, and careless in the treatment of valuable tools and equipment. Accepting the losses involved may be justifiable from the standpoint of the individual firm if such a firm can count with reasonable certainty on retaining the services of those men *after* they go through training and acquire the requisite skills. However, should they leave the firm that provided the training and proceed to work for another enterprise, that new employer would reap the fruits of the first firm's outlays. In a developed industrial society this consideration is relatively unimportant. Losses and gains of individual firms generated by labour turnover may cancel out. In an underdeveloped country the chances of such cancellation are very small, if not nil. Although society as a whole would clearly benefit by the increase of skills of at least some of its members, individual businessmen cannot afford to provide the training that such an increase demands.

But could not the required increase in total output be attained by better utilization of land—another unutilized or inadequately utilized productive factor?

There is usually no land that is both fit for agricultural purposes and at the same time readily accessible. Such terrain as could be cultivated but is actually not being tilled would usually require considerable investment before becoming suitable for settlement. In underdeveloped countries such outlays for agricultural purposes are just as unattractive to private interests as they are for industrial purposes.

On the other hand, more adequate employment of land that is already used in agriculture runs into considerable difficulties. Very few improvements that would be necessary in order to increase productivity can be carried out within the narrow confines of small-peasant holdings. Not only are the peasants in underdeveloped countries utterly unable to pay for such innovations, but the size of their lots offers no justification for their introduction.

Owners of large estates are in a sense in no better position. With limited savings at their disposal they do not have the funds to finance expensive improvements in their enterprises, nor do such projects appear profitable in view of the high prices of imported equipment in relation to prices of agricultural produce and wages of agricultural labour.

Approached thus *via* agriculture, an expansion of total output would also seem to be attainable only through the development of industry. Only through increase of industrial productivity could agricultural machinery, fertilizers, electric power, etc., be brought within the reach of the agricultural producer. Only through an increased demand for labour could agricultural wages be raised and a stimulus provided for a modernization of the agricultural economy. Only through the growth of industrial production could agricultural labour displaced by the machine be absorbed in productive employment.

Monopolistic market structures, shortage of savings, lack of external economies, the divergence of social and private rationalities do not exhaust, however, the list of obstacles blocking the way of privately organized industrial expansion in underdeveloped countries. Those obstacles have to be considered against the background of the general feeling of uncertainty prevailing in all backward areas. The coalition of the owning classes formed under pressure of fear, and held together by the real or imagined danger of social upheavals, provokes continuously more or less threatening rumblings under the outwardly calm political surface. The social and political tensions to which that coalition is a political response are not liquidated by the prevailing system; they are only repressed.

Normal and quiet as the daily routine frequently appears, the more enlightened and understanding members of the ruling groups in underdeveloped countries sense the inherent instability of the political and social order. Occasional outbursts of popular dissatisfaction assuming the form of peasant uprisings, violent strikes or local guerrilla warfare, serve from time to time as grim reminders of the latent crisis.

In such a climate there is no will to invest on the part of monied people ; in such a climate there is no enthusiasm for long-term projects ; in such a climate the motto of all participants in the privileges offered by society is *carpe diem*.

Could not, however, an appropriate policy on the part of the governments involved change the political climate and facilitate economic growth ? In our time, when faith in the manipulative omnipotence of the State has all but displaced analysis of its social structure and understanding of its political and economic functions, the tendency is obviously to answer these questions in the affirmative.

Looking at the matter purely mechanically, it would appear indeed that much could be done, by a well-advised regime in an underdeveloped country, to provide for a relatively rapid increase of total output, accompanied by an improvement of the living standards of the population. There is a number of measures that the government could take in an effort to overcome backwardness. A fiscal policy could be adopted that, by means of capital levies and a highly progressive tax system, would syphon off all surplus purchasing power, and in this way eliminate non-essential consumption. The savings thus enforced could be channelled by the government into productive investment. Power stations, railroads, highways, irrigation systems, and soil improvements could be organized by the State with a view to creating an economic environment conducive to the growth of productivity. Technical schools on various levels could be set up by the public authority to furnish industrial training to young people as well as to adult workers and the unemployed. A system of scholarships could be introduced rendering acquisition of skills accessible to low-income strata.

Wherever private capital refrains from undertaking certain industrial projects, or wherever monopolistic controls block the necessary expansion of plant and facilities in particular industries, the government could step in and make the requisite investments. Where developmental possibilities that are rewarding in the long-run appear unprofitable during the initial period of gestation and learning, and are therefore beyond the horizon of private businessmen, the government could undertake to shoulder the short-run losses.

In addition an entire arsenal of 'preventive' devices is at the disposal of the authorities. Inflationary pressures resulting from developmental activities (private and public) could be reduced or even eliminated, if outlays on investment projects could be offset by a corresponding and simultaneous contraction of spending elsewhere in the economic system. What this would call for is a taxation policy that would effectively remove from the income stream amounts sufficient to neutralize the investment-caused expansion of aggregate money income.

In the interim, and as a supplement, speculation in scarce goods and excessive profiteering in essential commodities could be suppressed by rigorous price controls. An equitable distribution of mass consumption goods in short supply could be assured by rationing. Diversion of resources in high demand to luxury purposes could be prevented by allocation and priority schemes. Strict supervision of transactions involving foreign exchanges could render capital flight, expenditure of limited foreign funds on luxury imports, pleasure trips abroad, and the like, impossible.

What the combination of these measures would accomplish is a radical change in the structure of effective demand in the underdeveloped country, and a reallocation of productive resources to satisfy society's need for economic development. By curtailing consumption of the higher-income groups, the amounts of savings available for investment purposes could be markedly increased. The squandering of limited supplies of foreign exchange on capital flight, or on importation of redundant foreign goods and services, could be prevented, and the foreign funds thus saved could be used for the acquisition of foreign-made machinery needed for economic development. The reluctance of private interests to engage in enterprises that are socially necessary, but may not promise rich returns in the short-run, would be prevented from determining the economic life of the backward country.

The mere listing of the steps that would have to be undertaken, in order to assure an expansion of output and income in an underdeveloped country, reveals the utter implausibility of the view that they could be carried out by the governments existing in most underdeveloped countries. The reason for this inability is only to a negligible extent the non-existence of the competent and honest civil service needed for the administration of the programme. A symptom itself of the political and social marasmus prevailing in underdeveloped countries, this lack cannot be remedied without attacking the underlying causes. Nor does it touch anything near the roots of the matter to lament the lack of satisfactory tax policies in backward countries, or to deplore the absence of tax 'morale' and 'discipline' among the civic virtues of their populations.

The crucial fact rendering the realization of a developmental programme illusory is the political and social structure of the governments in power. The alliance of property-owning classes controlling the destinies of most underdeveloped countries, cannot be expected to design and to execute a set of measures running counter to each and all of their immediate vested interests. If to appease the restive public, blueprints of progressive measures such as agrarian reform, equitable tax legislation, etc., are officially announced, their enforcement is wilfully sabotaged. The government, representing a political compromise between landed and business interests cannot suppress the wasteful management of landed estates and the conspicuous consumption on the part of the aristocracy; cannot suppress monopolistic abuses, profiteering, capital flights, and extravagant living on the part of businessmen. It cannot curtail or abandon its lavish appropriations for a military and police establishment, providing attractive careers to the scions of wealthy families and a profitable outlet for armaments produced by their parents—quite apart from the fact that this establishment serves as the main protection against possible popular revolt. Set up to guard and to abet the existing property rights and privileges, it cannot become the architect of a policy calculated to destroy the privileges standing in the way of economic progress and to place the property and the incomes derived from it at the service of society as a whole.

Nor is there much to be said for the 'intermediate' position which, granting the essential incompatibility of a well-conceived and vigorously executed developmental programme with the political and social institutions prevailing in most underdeveloped countries, insists that at least *some* of the requisite measures could be carried out by the existing political authorities. This school of thought overlooks entirely the weakness, if not the complete absence, of social and political forces that could induce the necessary concessions on the part of the ruling coalition. By background and political upbringing, too myopic and self-interested to permit the slightest encroachments upon their inherited positions and cherished privileges, the upper-classes in underdeveloped countries resist doggedly all pressures in that direction. Every time such pressures grow in strength they succeed in cementing anew the alliance of all conservative elements, by decrying all attempts at reform as assaults on the very foundations of society.

Even if measures like progressive taxation, capital levies, and foreign exchange controls could be enforced by the corrupt officials operating in the demoralized business communities of underdeveloped countries, such enforcement would to a large extent defeat its original purpose. Where businessmen do not invest, unless in expectation of lavish profits, a taxation system succeeding in confiscating large parts of these profits is bound to kill private investment. Where doing business or operating landed estates are attractive mainly because they permit luxurious living, foreign exchange controls preventing the importation of luxury goods are bound to blight enterprise. Where the only stimulus to hard work on the part of intellectuals, technicians, and civil servants is the chance of partaking in the privileges of the ruling class, a policy aiming at the reduction of inequality of social status and income is bound to smother effort.

The injection of planning into a society living in the twilight between feudalism and capitalism cannot but result in additional corruption, larger and more artful evasions of the law, and more brazen abuses of authority.

There would seem to be no exit from the impasse. The ruling

coalition of interests does not abdicate of its own volition, nor does it change its character in response to incantation. Although its individual members occasionally leave the sinking ship physically or financially (or in both ways), the property-owning classes as a whole are as a rule grimly determined to hold fast to their political and economic entrenchments.

If the threat of social upheaval assumes dangerous proportions, they tighten their grip on political life and move rapidly in the direction of unbridled reaction and military dictatorship. Making use of favourable international opportunities, and of ideological and social affinities to ruling groups in other countries, they solicit foreign economic and sometimes military aid, in their efforts to stave off the impending disaster.

Such aid is likely to be given to them by foreign governments regarding them as an evil less to be feared than the social revolution that would sweep them out of power. This attitude of their friends and protectors abroad is no less shortsighted than their own.

The adjustment of the social and political conditions in underdeveloped countries to the urgent needs of economic development can be postponed; it cannot be indefinitely avoided. In the past, it could have been delayed by decades or even centuries. In our age it is a matter of years. Bolstering the political system of power existing in backward countries by providing it with military support may temporarily block the eruption of the volcano; it cannot stop the subterranean gathering of explosive forces.

Economic help in the form of loans and grants given to the governments of backward countries, to enable them to promote a measure of economic progress, is no substitute for the domestic changes that are mandatory if economic development is to be attained.

Such help, in fact, may actually do more harm than good. Possibly permitting the importation of some foreign-made machinery and equipment for government or business sponsored investment projects, but not accompanied by any of the steps that are needed to assure healthy economic growth, foreign assistance thus supplied may set off an inflationary spiral increasing and aggravating the existing social and economic tensions in underdeveloped countries.

If, as is frequently the case, these loans or grants from abroad are tied to the fulfilment of certain conditions on the part of the receiving country regarding their use, the resulting investment may be directed in such channels as to conform more to the interests of the lending than to those of the borrowing country. Where economic advice as a form of 'technical assistance' is supplied to the underdeveloped country, and its acceptance is made a prerequisite to eligibility for financial aid, this advice often pushes the governments of underdeveloped countries toward policies, ideologically or otherwise attractive to the foreign experts dispensing economic counsel, but not necessarily conducive to economic development of the 'benefited' countries. Nationalism and xenophobia are thus strengthened in backward areas—additional fuel for political restiveness.

For backward countries to enter the road of economic growth and social progress, the political framework of their existence has to be drastically revamped. The alliance between feudal landlords, industrial royalists, and the capitalist middle-classes has to be broken. The keepers of the past cannot be the builders of the future. Such progressive and enterprising elements as exist in backward societies have to obtain the possibility of leading their countries in the direction of economic and social growth.

What France, Britain, and America have accomplished through their own revolutions has to be attained in backward countries by a combined effort of popular forces, enlightened government, and unselfish foreign help. This combined effort must sweep away the holdover institutions of a defunct age, must change the political and social climate in the underdeveloped countries, and must imbue their nations with a new spirit of enterprise and freedom.

Should it prove too late in the historical process for the bourgeoisie to rise to its responsibilities in backward areas, should the long experience of servitude and accommodation to the feudal past have reduced the forces of progressive capitalism to impotence, the backward countries of the world will inevitably turn to economic planning and social collectivism. If the capitalist world outlook of economic and social progress, propelled by enlightened self-interest, should prove unable to triumph over the conservatism of inherited positions and traditional privileges, if the capitalist promise of advance and reward to the efficient, the industrious, the able, should not displace the feudal assurance of security and power to the well-bred, the well-connected and the conformist—a new social ethos will become the spirit and guide of a new age. It will be the ethos of the collective effort, the creed of the predominance of the interests of society over the interests of selected few.

The transition may be abrupt and painful. The land not given to the peasants legally may be taken by them forcibly. High incomes not confiscated through taxation may be eliminated by outright expropriation. Corrupt officials not retired in orderly fashion may be removed by violent action.

Which way the historical wheel will turn and in which way the crisis in the backward countries will find its final solution will depend in the main on whether the capitalist middle-classes in the backward areas, and the rulers of the advanced industrial nations of the world, overcome their fear and myopia. Or are they too spell-bound by their narrowly conceived selfish interests, too blinded by their hatred of progress, grown so senile in these latter days of the capitalist age, as to commit suicide out of fear of death ?

AN INTERPRETATION OF ECONOMIC BACKWARDNESS*

by **H. Myint**

In current discussions the terms 'underdeveloped' and 'backward' are generally used as though they were completely interchangeable by applying them to aggregate geographical concepts such as 'countries', 'areas', and 'regions', or by equating them with certain broad indices such as low incomes or capital investment per head. It is more illuminating, in my view, to give these terms different connotations by using the former to mean underdeveloped *resources*, and the latter to refer to the backward *people* of a given area. In this paper I shall argue that this distinction is fundamental to the understanding of the nature of economic backwardness.

I

The difference in approach in terms of 'underdeveloped resources' and in terms of 'backward people'[1] can best be illustrated by examining the current fashion of including not only the natural resources but also the so-called 'human resources' under the generic heading of 'underdeveloped resources', which seems to imply that the two terms we have distinguished really overlap. But is it merely a matter of taste or tact whether we choose to speak of 'backward people' or of 'underdeveloped human resources'? On a close examination it will be seen that each term has its own hinterland of associated ideas and the two cannot be superimposed on each other without creating a number of serious logical difficulties.

* *Oxford Economic Papers*, June 1954. Reprinted by permission of the Clarendon Press, Oxford, and the author.

[1] In order to avoid misunderstanding I had better say at once that in speaking of a 'backward people', in contrast to 'an advanced people', I am referring only to economic life and do not in the least imply general cultural 'backwardness'. The qualifying word 'economic' is dropped merely for the sake of brevity.

In common-sense terms, a 'backward people' may be defined as a group of people who are in some fashion or other unsuccessful in the economic struggle to earn a livelihood. Thus we are starting from a Classical or Marshallian distinction between man, on the one hand, and his environment on the other: only then can we think of a group of people as being successful or otherwise in adapting themselves to their environment. Further, the idea of 'backwardness' inevitably implies a comparison of different degrees of success in this economic struggle: some groups of people are less successful or 'backward' compared with other more successful or 'advanced' groups. Thus the nature of backwardness would lose much of its significance if applied to a homogeneous group of people without international economic relations. It is when a self-sufficient primitive or medieval economy has been opened up to outside economic forces and its people come into contact with other economically more 'advanced' people that the idea of backwardness suggests itself.

This way of approach at once raises a number of issues. Firstly, we shall have to make a more systematic analysis of the continuous process of mutual adaptation between wants, activities, and environment which we have described as 'economic struggle'. Secondly, in order to make a valid comparison of the varying degrees of success in the economic struggle of different groups of people we require the assumption that these different groups are in fact pursuing the same or comparable sets of ends. This is a big assumption which will have to be examined closely. Finally, we shall have to consider whether it is sufficient to measure the degree of 'backwardness' or 'advancement' of different groups of people merely in terms of the relative distribution of final incomes among them; or whether the pattern of distribution of economic activity among the different groups and the different roles they play in economic life might not in the long run offer a more significant clue to the future potential development of each group.

These will be discussed at a later stage (section IV). For the purpose of a preliminary contrast, however, it is sufficient to note that when we adopt the approach in terms of 'backward people' we are by definition making their failure in the economic struggle the centre of the problem and that this involves:

(*a*) a fundamental contrast *between them (the 'backward* people') and the natural resources and the economic environment of their country, and (*b*) a deliberate concentration of attention on their share of incomes or economic activity either within their own country or in relation to the world at large as distinct from the total volume of output or economic activity.

When we turn to the approach in terms of 'underdeveloped resources', however, we are led to quite a different set of ideas. To treat 'human resources' on exactly the same footing as natural resources as part of the common pool of 'underdeveloped resources' is to abandon the older man-against-environment approach in favour of the modern 'allocative efficiency' approach. We are then concerned, not with the success or failure of a given group of people in their struggle against their economic environment (including other groups of people), but with the allocation of given 'resources' among alternative uses as determined by the price system or by the central planner or by a mixture of both. The aim of this allocative process is to maximize total output, and 'underdevelopment' becomes a species of deviation from the productive optimum defined in some sense or other.

We can now see that although, physically speaking, the same people are involved when we speak of 'backward people' and of 'underdeveloped human resources', the standpoint adopted in each case is different. From the first standpoint, these people are regarded as actors (even if unsuccessful ones) in the economic struggle. From the second, they are regarded as impersonal units of 'underdeveloped' resources not distinguishable from units of other types of underdeveloped resources except by the degree of underdevelopment defined in some functional sense. Thus we are not specially concerned with 'human resources' more than with other types of resources except in so far as it could be shown that 'developing' the human resources would in fact increase the total output by a greater extent than by developing other 'material' resources.

The difference between the 'backwardness' and the 'underdevelopment' approach becomes very clear when we exclude human resources from the definition of 'underdeveloped resources' and confine it entirely to natural resources. This is by no means an unusual or deliberately contrived 'strong case' to boost our distinction. As a matter of fact, much of the thinking on the subject is still influenced by the idea of 'underdeveloped countries' as those which (whatever their 'human resources') possess a greater amount of potential natural resources waiting to be developed compared with the 'developed countries' whose natural resources have already been fully brought into use. We may also note how the use of such expressions as 'underdeveloped countries', 'underdeveloped areas', 'underdeveloped regions', etc., tends to foster this belief in the existence of potential natural resources.

Here, once we have excluded the human beings from the 'underdeveloped resources', a number of propositions emerge. Since they will recur again in the course of our argument, they may be summarily stated at this stage. (1) 'Underdevelopment' of natural resources and 'backwardness' of people are two distinct phenomena and they need not even always coexist: thus the inhabitants of the 'overpopulated' countries which admittedly have very little natural resources left for further unaided development are also generally 'backward'. (2) When 'underdeveloped' natural resources and 'backward' people coexist, they mutually aggravate each other in a 'vicious circle'; but this mutual interaction is an essentially dynamic and historical process taking place over a period of time and may be too complicated and qualitative to be easily fitted into the formal quantitative framework of optimum allocation of resources (including capital resources) suggested by the pure 'underdevelopment' approach. (3) Although the 'underdevelopment' of natural resources may cause the 'backwardness' of the people, it does not necessarily follow that any efficient development of natural resources resulting in an increase in total output will always and *pari passu* reduce the backwardness of people. On the contrary, the problem of economic backwardness in many countries has been made more acute, not because the natural resources have remained 'underdeveloped', but because they have been as fully and rapidly developed as market conditions permitted while the inhabitants have been left out, being either unable or unwilling or both to participate fully in the process.

II

Let us now turn to the logical difficulties which arise from attempts to superimpose the 'backwardness' and the 'underdevelopment' approach on each other. These can be best illustrated by examining some of the typical arguments in favour of increasing the flow of investment from the 'advanced' to the 'underdeveloped' countries.

Advocates of plans for the international economic development of the underdeveloped countries generally start by saying that the case for alleviating the poverty and discontent, ill health and ignorance of the peoples of these countries can be made whether we approach the subject from a humanitarian standpoint or purely in self-defence to ease the storm-centres of international relations. At this stage therefore the problem seems to be set out in terms of human misery and discontent, in terms of 'backwardness' rather than in terms of 'underdevelopment' of resources. Indeed, the existence of 'underdeveloped' natural resources at least, far from creating a 'problem' in the relevant sense, may be regarded as part of the means of solving it. When, however, we pass from this initial statement of the problem to the later parts of the economic development plans which contain a more technical treatment of the proposals and 'target figures' for investment, we generally encounter a shift from the 'backwardness' to the 'underdevelopment' approach. The existence of 'underdeveloped' natural resources is no longer regarded as the means of solving the problem ; it has become the problem itself. The argument then proceeds as though the phenomenon of the 'backwardness' of the people can be satisfactorily accounted for purely in terms of the 'underdevelopment' of the resources and deviations from the optimum allocation of world's capital resources.[1]

It is now time to consider the meaning of 'underdeveloped resources' more closely. In the language of optimum theory, it seems to describe two types of deviation : (i) less than optimum amounts of these 'underdeveloped' resources have been used in producing final output, and (ii) less than optimum amounts of capital have been invested to augment the quantity

[1] Cf., for example, United Nations Report, *Measures for the Economic Development of Underdeveloped Countries*, ch. viii.

and improve the quality of these 'underdeveloped' resources. Where the first occurs by itself it would be possible to increase the total output of the underdeveloped countries without outside investment merely by reorganizing their own existing resources by such measures as legal and administrative reforms, the mobilizing of domestic savings, and so on. In current discussion, although this possibility is admitted, it is considered that as a rule the two types of deviation occur simultaneously, the first caused by the second. That is to say, the scope for a more productive reorganization of 'development' of the resources of the underdeveloped countries is limited without first removing the basic cause of 'underdevelopment', viz. an insufficient flow of investment from the 'advanced' countries.

The typical arguments in favour of increasing investment in the underdeveloped countries may now be examined. They may be classified according to the degree of optimism concerning the richness of the 'underdeveloped resources'.

i. The most optimistic type of argument assumes that as a rule underdeveloped countries possess *natural* resources capable of being developed by private investors on a purely commercial basis and this process will automatically help to raise the standard of living of the people of these countries. 'Underdevelopment' is therefore caused by 'artificial' obstacles and restrictions to the free international movement of private capital. Whatever our views about the richness of potential natural resources, this type of argument serves to illustrate a sharp clash between the 'underdevelopment' and the 'backwardness' approach. For, on a closer examination, it turns out that the only type of investment which private investors are willing to undertake in the underdeveloped countries is the exploitation of raw materials, e.g. petroleum, and it is precisely in this field that the governments of the underdeveloped countries are frequently unwilling to admit private foreign capital because they fear that this 'nineteenth-century type of investment' will merely develop the natural resources and not the people and will result in 'foreign economic domination' aggravating the economic 'backwardness' of their peoples. This is a genuine deadlock to which no satisfactory answer can be given in terms of the simple 'underdevelopment' approach. And to dismiss the whole thing merely as irrational economic nationalism seems suspiciously like throwing the baby away with the bath water (see section VI below).

ii. The next type of argument may be regarded as an attempt to retrieve the 'underdevelopment' approach by introducing the Pigovian concept of the 'social' productivity as distinguished from the 'private' productivity of investment. Here it is argued that although the underdeveloped countries may not possess (or are unwilling to make available) resources which can be developed by private enterprise, they can nevertheless very profitably absorb large sums of international investment in the form of public enterprises using a broader criterion of 'social' productivity. These enterprises would include public utilities, transport, hydro-electric and irrigation schemes, &c., which offer economies of large scale and scope for complementary investment and where only a public agency can collect the diffused social returns by means of taxation. A good example of a direct application of this argument may be found in the United Nations Report on *National and International Measures for Full Employment*. Here the authors, after recommending that the International Bank for Reconstruction and Development should be used as the main channel of inter-governmental lending to reduce political risks on both sides, lay down the following conditions:

'The criteria of worthwhileness for the loans should be their effect on national income, taxable capacity and export capacity. The Bank should *not* in general lend, unless it is convinced that in consequence of the loan, the borrowing country's current balance of payments will improve sufficiently to permit interest and amortization payments to be made.'[1]

'Development loans should be made at interest rates uniform for all borrowing countries.' (Op. cit., pp. 93–4.)

These two conditions may be regarded as the logical limits to which the investment policy towards the underdeveloped countries can be liberalized on the basis of the Pigovian concept of 'social' productivity of investment. It may be noted that fairly substantial amounts of capital can still be absorbed

[1] We are not concerned here with the question how far this rule can be reconciled with the authors' practical proposals for stabilizing longer-term lending by fixing target figures. Cf. also A. E. Kahn, 'Investment Criteria for Development Programmes', *Quarterly Journal of Economics*, February 1951.

by some of the underdeveloped countries within these limits. But comparing this view with the general run of discussions on the subject, it soon becomes apparent that many advocates of international development plans would consider the Pigovian conditions as too restrictive to be regarded as a serious basis of investment policy towards the underdeveloped countries. There are two possible ways out of this impasse. The first, which we shall recommend in the later part of this paper, is to make a clean break with the whole 'underdevelopment' approach and to adopt a more direct approach to the problem of economic backwardness of the people. The second and more popular alternative is to try to broaden the 'underdevelopment' approach still further; and this brings us to the third type of the underinvestment argument.

iii. The argument at this stage consists in attempts to stretch the concept of 'social productivity' or 'desirability' by invoking (*a*) the principle of 'needs', and (*b*) the dynamic principle of trying to stimulate further rounds of loan investment by 'productive' grants to 'improve social capital', particularly in the fields of public health, education, and communications. A good example of this may be found in a later United Nations Report on *Measures for the Economic Development of the Underdeveloped Countries*.

Here the authors argue:

(*a*) that 'the amount that can be profitably invested at a 4 per cent rate of interest depends on the amount which is being spent at the same time on improving social capital; and especially on public health, on education and on roads and communications. There is much to be done in this way in the underdeveloped countries before they will be in a position to absorb large amounts of loan capital' (para. 269);

(*b*) that the underdeveloped countries 'cannot borrow' for these purposes, presumably because 'they could not meet the full burden of loan finance' (paras. 270 and 277);

(*c*) that, therefore, grants-in-aid should be made to the underdeveloped countries, but purely for 'productive' purposes (paras. 271 and 276).

The authors do not, however, hesitate to invoke the principle of needs. Thus:

'The principle that the better off should help to pay for the education, the medical services and other public services received by the poorer classes of the community is now well established within every Member nation of the United Nations. The idea that this principle should also be applied as between rich and poor countries is relatively new. It has however been put into practice on several occasions.' (Para. 272.)

How far are these attempts to stretch the idea of 'social' productivity successful?

To begin with, there is an important shift in the basic definition of the 'underdeveloped countries' which is not as clearly stated as it might be. Up to now the main burden of the argument has been on the proposition that 'underdeveloped countries' possess a greater amount of 'underdeveloped' resources than the developed countries and that therefore the 'social' productivity of investment is higher in the former than in the latter. From now on the emphasis has shifted to the fact that the underdeveloped countries have lower *per capita* incomes and therefore suffer from greater needs than the developed countries.

The introduction of the principle of needs does not create any difficulties provided we are prepared to keep it clearly apart from the principle of productivity. Then loans should continue to be made strictly on the productivity principle while grants should be made *separately* on the need principle.

This, however, results in somewhat unpalatable conclusions. (*a*) When we are allocating loans, our main concern is to maximize the total world output and not to equalize international incomes. Thus the social productivity curves of investment must be constructed objectively, and independently of our value judgements concerning needs. This means that capital should not be diverted in the form of low interest loans or grants to the poorer countries simply because they are poor. A more *economic* way of reducing inequalities in the international distribution of income is to allocate the world capital resources in uses where its social productivity is highest even if it happens to be in the richest countries, and to redistribute the resultant output after first ensuring that it is maximized. (*b*) Conversely, when we are allocating grants, our concern is with a more equitable international distribution of incomes and not with their effects on total output. Thus grants should be made in the form of final consumers' goods and services, directed not only towards the poorer countries but also towards the poorer sections within each country. The principle of need in its strict form is an argument for diverting final incomes from the richer to the poorer countries for consumption purposes and not an argument for diverting capital grants for 'productive' purposes.

These conclusions are not without relevance to the practical issues of economic policy in the underdeveloped countries. Thus critics of the unsuccessful developmental ventures of the British Overseas Food Corporation and the Colonial Development Corporation may reasonably maintain that the root cause of the failure lies not as much in the wrong choice of men and inefficient methods of administering the ventures but in the vagueness of the mandate itself which tries to compromise between the principle of obtaining economic returns and the principle of needs. They may say that rather than waste huge sums of money by investing in projects which cannot be justified on the strict productivity principle, it were better to distribute them as free gifts of consumers' goods and services among the poor of Africa. Again, individuals and governments in underdeveloped countries sometimes find themselves with large sums of money which they cannot profitably or safely invest locally ; and then, following the strict productivity principle and the need to protect their capital, they have found it wiser to invest it in the most developed countries such as the U.S.A. or the U.K.

The last example, however, brings out the unsatisfactoriness of trying to apply the static rules of the productive optimum to the problem of the underdeveloped countries. This, however, is rather damaging to the conventional definitions of the 'underdeveloped' countries both in terms of 'underdeveloped' resources and in terms of low *per capita* incomes. For now it begins to transpire : (*a*) that if we take the productivity curves of international investment on the basis of existing economic conditions in the 'developed' and the 'underdeveloped' countries, more often than not capital is likely to be more productive in the former than the latter and the Pigovian distinction between 'social' and 'private' product will not appreciably change the broad picture ; (*b*) that therefore if we were to allocate capital according to the existing productivity curves, even taking a generous view of 'social' productivity, this would still result in relatively greater quantities of capital being invested in the 'developed' than in the 'underdeveloped' countries, accentuating the unequal rate of economic development between the two types of country; and (*c*) that a policy of a more equal redistribution of international incomes based on the pure principle of needs, although it may relieve the burden of cumulative unequal rates of economic development, does not touch the heart of the problem; for fundamentally the problem of the 'underdeveloped' countries is not merely that of low or unequal distribution of final incomes but also that of unequal participation in the processes of economic activity.

Faced with these considerations, those who wish to retain the 'underdevelopment' approach are obliged to 'dynamize' it and to refer to social productivity in the *longer run* as distinct from the *present* social productivity of investment.

We are now in a position to examine the argument of the authors of the United Nations Report on the *Measures for the Economic Development of the Underdeveloped Countries*. It will be seen that the crux of their argument lies in the question how far 'improving social capital' in public health, education, and communications, whether financed by grants or loans, can successfully stimulate further rounds of loan capital. Thus the authors' appeal to the principle of need in para. 272 (also implicit earlier on, e.g. para. 248) turns out to be a side-issue. It is a confusing side-issue at that because the requirements for creating incentives for further investment and those for promoting economic equality do not always conveniently coincide in the same policy as the authors have implied. On the contrary, there are many instances where the incentives for further investment can be created only by pursuing relatively disequalizing policies, such as control of domestic wages, tax exemptions to new (foreign) enterprises, etc.[1]

Turning to their main argument, the extent to which further rounds of loan investment can be effectively stimulated by a policy of 'improving social capital' by grants must depend

[1] Cf., for instance, 'Industrialization of Puerto Rico', *Caribbean Economic Review*, December 1949, by Professor A. Lewis, one of the authors of the Report.

on a wide variety of circumstances which vary from country to country and about which no definite generalizations can be made. We are no longer in the static world where 'under-investment' in a particular line can be deduced in principle by an inspection of the *given* social marginal productivity curves and where there is a definite functional relationship between the quantity of capital invested and the quantity of 'returns' in the form of final output. Thus given favourable circumstances, a small amount of 'investment' in social capital might start a chain-reaction and yield 'returns' in the form of secondary rounds of investment out of all proportion to the initial investment. On the other hand, if circumstances are not favourable, even a larger amount of initial investment might not successfully start these secondary rounds of activities, and there is no real guarantee that increasing the amount of the initial investment still further would induce the desired results. In reply to such objections, the authors can only appeal to the general presumption that if average incomes per head or expenditure per head in the type of social services they have chosen is low, then longer-run social productivity of investment in 'social capital' is likely to be high. This general presumption is not as strong as it appears, and there are two general arguments which may be advanced against it.

The first is clearest in the case of education and technical training although it can be applied also to other types of 'social capital'. It is the fairly common experience of the under-developed countries to find themselves, not merely with an overall shortage of educated people, but also with a relative shortage of those regarded as 'socially productive', such as engineers and doctors, combined with a relative abundance of those regarded as less socially productive, such as lawyers and clerks. The reason for this is, of course, that with the existing social and economic organization of these countries there is a relatively greater market demand for the latter type of person than the former. This would seem to suggest that the problem of creating and organizing demand for trained personnel in the underdeveloped countries may even be more important than the problem of creating the supply by investment in 'social capital'. Given the demand, the supply of trained personnel of most types (including those trained abroad) would seem to respond more automatically and to a greater extent than is usually allowed for. On the other hand, there is less indication that the demand can be effectively stimulated merely by creating the supply without simultaneously introducing far-reaching changes into the economic structure. Thus most underdeveloped countries can provide numerous instances of graduates from technical and agricultural colleges who cannot be absorbed, because the existing economic structure cannot be changed quickly enough to absorb them, although in terms of broad averages the amount of money spent per head of education and technical training is quite modest. The common fate of these people is to suffer a form of intellectual 'disguised unemployment' by taking up appointments as clerks and ordinary school-teachers.[1] Thus there is a genuine tendency for a great deal of investment in 'social capital' to be wasted, although the full extent of this wastage is concealed because expenditure on education and technical training is classed under the head of social services and not subject to the strict profit-and-loss accounting of other types of state enterprises.

This leads us to the second argument, which is rather disconcerting to the economic theorist. The application of fairly sophisticated economic theory involving concepts of social productivity and induced investment tends to create the impression that we have now opened up new possibilities of investment in the underdeveloped countries which were unappreciated and unexplored by the governments and administrators of these countries. This, however, overlooks two circumstances. Firstly, a substantial part of capital inflow into the underdeveloped countries was in the form of government borrowing even in the heyday of private investment. Secondly, the governments of the newly-opened-up countries have always been impelled by a powerful 'self-interest' to try to obtain adequate revenues to meet the expanding costs of administration. Thus, untutored as they may be in economic theory, they have been obliged by practical necessity to borrow and deploy their loans and grants in ways not so different from the

[1] Cf. J. S. Furnivall, *Colonial Policy and Practice*, pp. 380-82.

recommendations of the present-day economic experts.[1] The moral of this argument is not merely that there is less scope for the deployment of 'productive' loans and grants (as distinct from those social service expenditures which are frankly based on the principle of need) than appears at first sight. There is a further consideration which cuts across the whole of the 'underdevelopment' approach. For, as we shall see, ironically enough, where the governments of the underdeveloped countries have been successful in stimulating private (foreign) investment, the result has frequently been too great and rapid an expansion in a few lines of primary production for export which further aggravated the problem of the adjustment of the indigenous peoples of these countries to outside economic forces. Thus again, we are led back from the consideration of the total quantity of investment and the total volume of output and economic activity to a consideration of the type of investment and the distribution of economic activities and economic roles between the backward peoples and the others.

This is a convenient point at which to pause and summarize our argument so far. (i) The problem of the so-called 'underdeveloped countries' consists, not merely in the 'underdevelopment' of their resources in the usual senses, but also in the economic 'backwardness' of their peoples. (ii) Where it exists, the 'underdevelopment' of *natural* resources and the backwardness of people mutually aggravate each other in a 'vicious circle'. (iii) While (ii) is very important, it needs to be handled with care, for it is liable to distract our attention from the real problem of economic backwardness. Thus, impressed by the connexion between the 'backwardness' of the people and the 'underdevelopment' of the resources, many have sought to superimpose these two concepts on each other and to explain the former entirely in terms of the latter. In doing so, however, they are continually obliged to stretch and shift the basis of their argument: from the 'underdeveloped' *natural* resources to the 'underdeveloped' *human* resources; from the 'private'

[1] In some cases, however, there may be an important divergence between the social productivity of investment to the community and the 'private' productivity to the government interpreted narrowly in terms of quick revenue receipts. Sometimes governments may actually discourage new domestic industries to protect their vested interests in customs and excise duties.

to the 'social' productivity of investment; from the principle of 'productivity' to the principle of 'need'; and finally, from the static idea of the optimum allocation of investable resources to the dynamic idea of stimulating further rounds of investment by 'productive' grants. It is fair to say that, in spite of all these contortions, the real issues of backwardness seem to have eluded the grasp of the 'underdevelopment' approach. (iv) Thus in order to push our analysis farther to the heart of the problem, it would seem desirable to make a clean break with the 'underdevelopment' approach and to recognize the problem of 'backwardness' as a major problem in its own right which may occur even where there is no important 'underdevelopment' of resources in any of the acceptable senses. To emphasize this we shall speak from now on of 'backward' and not 'underdeveloped' countries.

III

At this stage it will be seen that there are at least two other 'obvious' explanations of 'backwardness' which must be considered as seriously as 'underdevelopment' in relation to some of the backward countries. But like 'underdevelopment' itself, we shall have to leave them aside in our search for a more general approach to the problem.

The first, of course, is the 'overpopulation' approach which not so long ago used to occupy a central position in discussions now dominated by the idea of 'underdevelopment'. Here again we may agree that backward peoples generally tend to have high birth-rates and that therefore 'overpopulation' and 'backwardness' tend to aggravate each other in another of those 'vicious circles' which are a feature of the whole subject. But this still leaves important gaps in the explanation. While overpopulation may be a major cause of backwardness in some countries, it does not explain why other countries not suffering from manifest population pressure should also be similarly backward. Moreover, some backward countries, e.g. most of those in south-east Asia, initially started from sparse populations in relation to their natural resources. It is only after they have been 'opened up' to international trade that they have tended to become overpopulated, partly because their death-rates have been reduced and partly because their resources have been developed in a few special lines of primary production for export which are subject to diminishing returns. Here, overpopulation cannot be regarded as the cause of backwardness; rather it is a manifestation of the maladjustment of backward peoples to outside economic forces at the physical level. Nor need this maladjustment always take the form of overpopulation. In some cases of extreme backwardness the size of the backward populations has been known to diminish to the point of extinction. Finally, the degree of overpopulation depends, not only on the relation between the physical quantity of natural resources and the size of population, but also on the level of technical and economic development of the people. Thus advanced industrial countries can usually maintain a denser population at a higher standard of living than the backward agricultural and pastoral countries. Further, in the past the advanced countries have absorbed very large increases in population without lowering their standard of living; indeed, many would maintain that these increases were a necessary part of their even greater rates of expansion in output and economic activity.[1] Thus to try to account for economic backwardness purely in terms of population pressure is to leave unanswered the question why the economically backward peoples have been unable to increase their productivity to match the increase in their population while the economically advanced people have managed to increase their standard of living on top of large increases in population.

The second possible line of approach is in terms of the deliberate and legalized political, economic, and racial discriminations imposed on the 'backward' peoples by the 'advanced' peoples. Here again, although this appears to be a major factor in certain countries, notoriously in Africa, it does not explain why the indigenous peoples of other countries who are not subject to such obvious discriminations to the same extent should also be similarly backward. Here, of course, the definition of the nature and extent of discriminations raises very formidable difficulties which we must frankly by-pass if we are to get farther on with our analysis. We shall thus content

[1] Cf. J. R. Hicks, *Value and Capital*, p. 302 n.

ourselves with drawing a somewhat crude working distinction between the deliberate and therefore directly remediable causes of backwardness in the form of open and legalized *discriminations* and the more fortuitous and intractable *disequalizing factors* which may operate even where there is a perfect equality of formal legal rights between different groups of people in their economic relations with each other (cf., however, section V below).

We are now able to sketch the general outlines of our problem. When the backward countries were 'opened up' to economic relations with the outside world, their peoples had to face the problem of adapting themselves to a new environment shaped by outside economic forces. In this, whatever their degree of cultural advance in other spheres, they seem to have been conspicuously unsuccessful or 'backward' compared with the other groups of economically 'advanced' people—whatever their degree of cultural advance in other spheres. Our problem is to explain this gap, to explain why the backward people cannot stand on a 'competitive footing' with the advanced people in this 'economic struggle'. The problem is further complicated by the fact that the gap between the advanced and backward peoples instead of being narrowed has been frequently widened by the passage of time. Thus an inquiry into the causes of economic backwardness essentially consists in searching for those disequalizing factors which instead of being neutralized are cumulatively exaggerated by 'the free play of economic forces'.

In order to isolate these disequalizing factors, we can adopt a 'model' of a backward country which has the following broad negative specifications. (i) Initially the country started with a fairly sparse population in relation to its potential natural resources; so it cannot be said to have been suffering from 'overpopulation' to begin with. (ii) Its natural resources are then 'developed', usually in the direction of a few specialized lines of primary production for export, as fully as the world market conditions permit. This process of 'development' is generally carried out by foreign private enterprise under conditions of *laissez-faire*; but frequently the process may be aided by a government policy of stimulating expansion in investment, export, and general economic activity motivated by a desire to expand taxable capacity. So the country's natural resources cannot be said to be obviously 'underdeveloped'. (iii) Whatever its political status, its native inhabitants at least enjoy a perfect equality of formal legal rights in their economic relations with other people, including the right to own any type of property and to enter into any type of occupation; so they cannot be said to suffer from obvious discriminations in economic matters.

To those who are firmly wedded to the conventional explanations of economic backwardness this may seem like assuming away the entire problem. But when we turn and survey the different types of backward countries, it will be seen that there is a large group, for example those in south-east Asia, British West Africa, Latin America, which approximates more to our model than to any models of obvious 'underdevelopment', 'overpopulation', or 'discrimination' or a combination of all of them, if the first and the second can in fact be combined. Further, even in the other groups of backward countries where these conventional explanations are obviously very important, our model is still useful in turning attention to the residual causes of backwardness which may turn out to be by no means negligible.

IV

Before we consider our 'model' further let us examine the concept of economic backwardness more closely. We may begin by distinguishing between the 'backward country' as an aggregate territorial and economic unit and the 'backward people' who frequently form merely a group within it confined to certain sectors of the economy. Now the disequalizing factors which we are seeking must be considered as operating, not only between the backward and the advanced countries as aggregate units, but also between the backward and advanced groups of peoples within the same backward country itself. Obviously a complete analysis of economic backwardness must take into account both sets of disequalizing factors which are closely interrelated with each other. Even so, we shall come to realize that the familiar 'countries *A* and *B*' approach of the conventional theory of international trade is seriously inadequate for our purpose and that to study the actual impact of outside economic forces on the backward people we shall have to go behind these macro-economic units to those disequalizing factors which operate within the backward country itself.

But much still remains to be done even in terms of the conventional approach, using these versatile letters *A* and *B* to denote the 'advanced' and the 'backward' countries respectively. It is only recently that the general run of economists have turned their attention to the long-run problem of unequal rates of economic growth and productivity among the different countries participating in international trade. But even so, it is fair to say that this has somewhat shaken the belief in the adequacy of the static theory of comparative costs to deal with the essentially dynamic process of growth of the international economy. Thus it is now increasingly admitted that the existing ratios of comparative costs are by no means immutable and rigidly related to the original natural resources of the countries but may be influenced to a great extent by such factors as education, experience, technical skills, and so on, which arise out of the process of international trade itself and may exert a cumulatively disequalizing influence against the countries which have a later start. Following on from this, it would seem that the gains from international trade cannot be adequately measured merely in the form of the conventional 'terms of trade' and the distribution of final incomes among the participating countries; we must also take into account the distribution of economic activities, in the form of induced investment and secondary rounds of employment, growth of technical knowledge and external economies, and all those dynamic stimuli which each participating country receives as a consequence of a given increase in the volume of its trade.[1] Although different views may be held about the practical policies most likely to induce these secondary rounds of investment and economic activity, there is little doubt that the concept of 'induced' investment affords great theoretical insight into the nature of economic backwardness. In a sense, one might say that the difference between the 'advanced'

[1] Cf. H. W. Singer, 'The Distribution of Gains between Investing and Borrowing Countries', *The American Economic Review Papers and Proceedings*, May 1950.

and the 'backward' country lies in the fact that the former, subject to the powerful 'accelerator' effect, can generate its own trade-cycle while the latter merely receives the fluctuations transmitted to it from outside, although of course the size of the impact need not be smaller for that reason.

Having said this, however, it is necessary to add that an approach to backwardness which stops short at this level will be seriously inadequate and that many of the discussions on the subject have been vitiated precisely because they are couched in terms of such geographical aggregates as 'countries', 'areas', 'territories', etc. A natural consequence of this is a preoccupation with such macro-economic quantities as the aggregate and *per capita* national income, total volume of exports, total and average amount of investment, etc. Whence follow those economic development plans which aim to increase either the total or the *per capita* national income by a certain percentage by means of target figures for investment calculated on the basis of average capital requirements per head of population.

This type of macro-economic model of economic development may be suitable for the advanced countries,[1] but there are a number of reasons why it cannot be satisfactorily extended to the backward countries. To begin with, the advanced country, by definition, is in the middle of a self-generating process of economic growth characterized by a steady rate of technical innovation and increase in productivity. Thus is seems reasonable to rule out diminishing returns and assume that a given rate of net investment will, on the whole, result in a corresponding rate of increase in total output or productive capacity. Further, certain basic ratios, such as the propensity to consume, are not obviously unstable and may be used as constants for the process analysis. When we turn to the backward country, however, these assumptions are no longer plausible. The problem here is not to trace the working of the process of economic growth on the basis of certain constant proportions but to try to start that process itself. We cannot stop short at thinking in terms of overall rates of net investment and increase in total output because

[1] Cf., however, T. Wilson, 'Cyclical and Autonomous Inducements to Invest', *Oxford Economic Papers*, March 1953.

the two rates are no longer connected in a determinate manner by a stable average ratio of capital to output.[1] Indeed, even if we could assume constant average productivity of capital, this will not be sufficient for the purpose of many economic development plans because they rely to varying degrees on the assumption of 'external economies' and increasing returns to scale. Further, none of the basic ratios required as constants for the process analysis can be assumed to be stable for the relevant long period. Under the impact of outside economic forces, most of these ratios, such as propensity to consume and import, population growth, etc., have been changed or are in the process of changing. Here again it is the accepted task of economic development policy, not merely to accept these ratios as given, but to try to change them in directions considered to be favourable for development. This is not to say that all economic development plans based on macro-economic analysis will always fail. It is merely to say that it is not sufficient to stop short at this level and assume as a matter of course that, provided the required supply of capital[2] is forthcoming, the process of economic growth will work itself out automatically as it does in the advanced countries. Thus the very nature of our problem, which is to start this process of economic growth, obliges us to go behind the macro-economic units and investigate the actual structure and 'growing-points' of the backward economy. For the same reason, we cannot treat the changes in the basic ratios and propensities as 'exogenous' changes in data but must inquire into their nature and causes.

So far we have been concerned only with the mechanical difficulties of applying the macro-economic models to the backward countries. Even more serious difficulties are encountered when we inquire into the meaningfulness of macro-economic quantities such as the aggregate national income or the *per capita* income to the peoples of the backward countries. These arise in addition to the complication already noted—

[1] 'The law of large numbers' is unconvincing when applied to the industrial sector of backward economies, where instead of *n* number of firms in full working order the State is trying to start a few odd new industrial units.

[2] Including 'productive' grants to stimulate investment. Cf. section II above.

that 'backward peoples' normally form only a sector of the economy of their 'countries'—so that the fortunes of the 'country' and the 'people' cannot be closely identified.

Even in the advanced countries, such concepts as the increase in national income or aggregate output capacity create serious problems of interpretation once we drop the static assumption of given and constant wants and enter the real world of a continual stream of new wants and commodities and improvements in the quality of existing goods. We can, however, put aside these 'index-number' problems in favour of a 'commonsense' interpretation, since we can assume that the 'measuring rod of money' and physical productivity are meaningful to the individuals concerned and broadly approximate to the social goals they are pursuing as groups in a fairly simple and straightforward manner. When we come to the backward countries, however, this assumption has to be carefully re-examined. The peoples of backward countries have had shorter periods of contact with the 'money economy' so that the habits of mind and the symbolism associated with monetary accounting may not be deep rooted in their minds.[1] Further, as groups, they are subject to complex pulls of nationalism and racial status, so that there may not be a simple means-end relationship between the increase in national output and the achievement of their social goals. Thus, in many backward countries, people seem to desire up-to-date factories and other trappings of modern industrialism, not so much for the strictly material returns they are expected to yield as for the fact that they are in themselves symbols of national prestige and economic development. Following Veblen, one might describe this as a case of 'conspicuous production'.

There is then a greater need in the study of backward countries than in that of the advanced countries to go behind the 'veil' of conventional social accounting into the real processes

[1] Cf. S. H. Frankel, *Some Conceptual Aspects of International Economic Development of Underdeveloped Countries* (Princeton, May 1952), now reprinted in *The Economic Impact on Underdeveloped Societies* (Blackwell, Oxford, 1953). My debt to my colleague Professor Frankel cannot, however, be adequately expressed in terms of specific points, for I have had the benefit of discussing with him the fundamental issues of the subject for several years. I cannot, of course, claim his authority for the particular conclusions I have arrived at in this paper.

of adaptation between wants, activities, and environment which we have described earlier on as the 'economic struggle'. When we do this we shall see that the 'problem' of the backward countries as it is commonly discussed really has two distinct aspects: on the subjective side it might be described as the economics of discontent and maladjustment; on the objective side it might be described as the economics of stagnation, low *per capita* productivity and incomes. In principle the latter should be a counterpart to the former and provide us with quantitative indices of it. In practice there is a real danger of the macro-models of economic development 'running on their own steam' without any reference to the fundamental human problems of backwardness on the subjective side.

To illustrate this, let us begin by considering the backward country as a stationary state. In terms of the objective approach this is a standard case of economic backwardness and 'over-population' popularly attributed to the Classical economists.[1] In terms of the subjective approach the situation may not appear so gloomy. Many of the backward countries before they were 'opened up' were primitive or medieval stationary states governed by habits and customs. Their people might live near the 'minimum subsistence level' but that, according to their own lights, did not appear too wretched or inadequate. Thus in spite of low productivity and lack of economic progress, there was no problem of economic discontent and frustration: wants and activities were on the whole adapted to each other and the people were in equilibrium with their environment. This is not to say that everything was idyllic: there may have been frequent tribal wars and insecurity of life and property. But on the whole it is fair to say that there was no 'problem' of backward countries in the modern sense and that the situation perhaps resembled J. S. Mill's picture of the stationary state more than that of his predecessors.[2]

Now consider the second stage particularly in the second half of nineteenth century and the beginning of twentieth century when these stationary backward societies were opened up to the outside economic forces. Here we can see why the term

[1] Cf., however, Ricardo's *Principles*, Sraffa ed., p. 99 and p. 100 n.
[2] Cf. Mill, *Principles*, bk. iv, ch. vi.

'backward' which we have been obliged to use for lack of a better alternative is so loose and liable to different interpretations. For at this stage, and to a certain extent even today, the economic backwardness of a society was simply measured by the lack of response of its members to monetary incentives. This in effect meant measuring the backwardness of a people, not by their inefficiency and inaptness in satisfying their given wants or in pursuing their own social goals, but by their tardiness in adopting new Western standards of wants and activities. Measures for 'economic development' then consisted mainly in attempts to persuade or force the backward people into the new ways of life represented by the money economy—for example, by stimulating their demand for imports and by taxing them so that they were obliged to turn to cash crops or work in the newly opened mines and plantations. Whether it was meaningful or not to the people, the accepted yardstick of economic development of a 'country' was its export and taxable capacity.

'Backwardness' in the sense of economic discontent and maladjustment does not fully emerge until the third stage of the drama when the natural resources of the backward countries have been 'developed' to a large extent, usually by foreign private enterprise, and when the backward peoples have been partly converted to the new ways of life. Here the irony of the situation lies in the fact that the acuteness of the problem of backwardness at this stage is frequently proportional to the success and rapidity of 'economic development' at the second stage. To begin with, it becomes apparent that the backward peoples can be only too successfully converted to new ways of life on the side of wants and aspirations while this cannot be matched by a corresponding increase in their earning capacity. We then have a progressive maladjustment between wants and activities, the former outstripping the latter at each round of 'education' and contact with the outside world. (This may spread from the individual to the national level when at the fourth stage the independent national governments of the backward countries find their resources insufficient to carry out ambitious schemes of economic development and social welfare.) Further, the backward peoples now find that they cannot successfully adapt themselves to the new economic environment shaped by outside forces and that they lag behind in the 'economic struggle' with other economically advanced groups of people who have initiated the 'opening-up' process. Thus they find themselves with a relatively smaller share of the economic activities and the national incomes of their countries although these may be rapidly increasing in the aggregate (at least up to the limits set by the diminishing returns in the new lines of the primary production for export). Here then we have the problem of economic backwardness in its full efflorescence charged with the explosive feeling of discontent and grievance against 'lop-sided economic development', 'foreign economic domination', 'imperialistic exploitation', and so on.

We can now see why it is so unsatisfactory to approach the problem of the backward countries as the source of international tension purely at the macro-economic level of the conventional development plans. Aggregates such as the total national income and volume of exports are very unsatisfactory as indices of economic welfare of a 'plural society' made up of different groups of people such as that which exists in many backward countries. Here the well-known maxim of static welfare economics, that the economic welfare of a country is increased if some people can move to a better position while leaving the others exactly as they were before, must sound somewhat galling to the backward peoples who frequently happen to be those left 'exactly as they were before'.

Nor is *per capita* income very satisfactory as an index of 'poverty'. The sort of maladjustment between wants and earning capacity which we have been describing may occur even if *per capita* incomes are rising. Indeed a greater amount of discontent may be created where incomes rise enough to introduce new commodities into the consumers' budget and then fluctuate and decline (a common experience in export economies) than where incomes per head remain stationary or decline slowly. Further, we should note that the degree of discontent depends, not as much on the absolute level of *per capita* incomes as in their *relative* ranking. Thus motives of 'conspicuous consumption' and the external diseconomies of consumption of higher income groups associated with Veblen and more recently with Professor J. S. Duesenberry should be taken into account.[1]

It is important to point this out since low income per head has now crystallized into the definition of backward countries. Some have even tried to put it on a 'scientific' basis by arguing that since the existing low incomes of the backward peoples are insufficient to provide them with the minimum nutritional requirements, their physical efficiency and productivity is lowered, thus creating a 'vicious circle'. While this may be an important long-run factor, it is a dangerous over-simplification of the complex motivations and aspirations of the backward peoples both at the individual and national levels to assume that Communism can be 'contained' by calories. Even in the backward countries, perhaps particularly there, men do not live by bread alone. Thus as a *Times* correspondent has recently written about the wage claims in the African Copper Belt:

> 'Another factor which drives the African to make demands is his increasing needs. He is beginning to buy smarter clothes; to eat foods he never did before; to drink wine and English beer instead of native liquor. It is, indeed, an almost impossible task today to compile a reasonable family budget because of this transitional stage in African 'consumer' requirements. This, too, however much people may disapprove of the elaborately dressed up African 'spiv' with his cowboy hat, sunglasses, and new bicycle, is a healthy trend; it is obviously essential if the African is to be weaned from a subsistence to a cash economy that he should develop the needs that create incentive.' (*The Times*, 19 January 1953.)

If the backward peoples as individuals desire those commodities one associates with the 'American way of life', at the national level they seem to desire the latest models of social security schemes associated with the 'British Welfare State'. It would thus be a crowning-point of irony if some backward countries were to turn towards Communism through an excessive fondness for the American and British ways of life.

V

In the light of what has been said above, the study of the 'disequalizing factors' at work against the backward peoples within the economies of their countries emerges as an essential

[1] Cf. Ragnar Nurkse, *Some Aspects of Capital Accumulation in Underdeveloped Countries*, Cairo, 1952, Third Lecture.

link between the two aspects of the problem of backwardness: the economics of discontent and maladjustment on the one side and the economics of stagnation or relatively slow rates of growth in total or *per capita* national income and productivity on the other.

When we consider these 'disequalizing factors' we shall see that the exclusion of the 'obvious' explanations in terms of 'underdevelopment', 'overpopulation', and 'discrimination' still leaves us with a great variety of residual causes of backwardness. To analyse them in detail is beyond the scope of this paper. For our purpose of obtaining a general interpretation of the nature of backwardness it is sufficient to point out certain broad patterns of backwardness in which the initial differences in experience, opportunities, capital supply, etc., between the economically backward and advanced groups of people seem to have been 'fossilized' or accentuated by the 'free play of economic forces'. We shall illustrate these patterns with reference to the backward peoples in their typical roles as unskilled workers, peasant producers, and borrowers of capital which between them cover most types of economic contacts between the backward and the advanced peoples.

In order to do this we shall introduce three characteristic features of the 'opening-up' process into our 'model' of the backward economy.

1. The first concerns the nature of 'specialization' for the export market. Now it is commonly realized that 'specialization' does not merely mean moving along the given 'production-possibility' curve of the textbook; and that in practice it involves an irreversible process whereby much of the resources and the productive equipment, e.g. transport and communications, of the backward economy have been moulded and made 'specific' to satisfy the special requirements of the export market. (Hence the well known argument for diversification.) But the habit of thinking in terms of 'countries' or 'areas' leads to the inadequate appreciation of one further fundamental fact: in spite of the striking specialization of the inanimate productive equipment and of the individuals from the economically advanced groups of people who manage and control them, there is really very little specialization, beyond a natural adaptability to the tropical climate, among the backward

peoples in their roles as unskilled labourers or peasant producers. Thus the typical unskilled labour supplied by the backward peoples is an undifferentiated mass of cheap man-power which might be used in any type of plantation or in any type of extractive industry within the tropics and sometimes even beyond it.[1] This can be seen from the range of the primary industries built on the immigrant Indian, Chinese, and African labour. Thus all the specialization required for the export market seems to have been done by the other co-operating factors, the whole production structure being built around the supply of cheap undifferentiated labour.

When we turn to the backward peoples in their role as peasant producers, again the picture is not appreciably changed. Some backward economies 'specialize' on crops which they have traditionally produced, and thus 'specialization' simply means expansion along the traditional lines with no perceptible change in the methods of production (e.g. rice in south-east Asian countries). Even where a new cash crop is introduced, the essence of its success as a *peasant* crop depends on the fact that it does not represent a radical departure from the existing techniques of production[2] (e.g. yams and cocoa in West Africa). Thus as a historian has said about the palm-oil and ground-nuts trade of West Africa : 'They made little demand on the energies or thought of the natives and they effected no revolution in the society of West Africa. That was why they were so readily grafted on to the old economy and why they grew as they did.'[3] Here again one is tempted to say that much of the 'specialization' seems to have been done by nature and the complementary investment in transport and processing. On the side of productive activities, the fact that the crop is sold for the export market instead of for domestic consumption is an accidental detail. It is only on the side of wants that disturbing changes seem to have been introduced, including a decline of skills in the domestic handicraft industries now no longer able to compete against the imported commodities. To prevent

[1] Cf. S. H. Frankel, *Capital Investment in Africa*, pp. 142-6.

[2] If this condition is not fulfilled, the peasant system soon gives way to the plantation system or the peasant is so supervised and controlled that he is reduced to the status of a wage-earner except in name (cf. J. H. Boeke, *The Evolution of Netherland Indies Economy*, p. 11).

[3] A. McPhee, *The Economic Revolution of West Africa*, pp. 39-40.

misunderstanding, it should be added that frequently the peasant methods are found to have lower costs than the 'modern' scientific methods, and that is the reason why peasant production has been able to withstand the competition of the plantation system in some countries. But at the best this merely means the survival of old skills rather than a steady improvement in the methods of production through 'specialization' for the export market.

Thus, paradoxically enough, the process of 'specialization' of a backward economy for the export market seems to be most rapid and successful when it leaves the backward peoples in their unspecialized roles as unskilled labour and peasant producers using traditional methods of production.

ii. The second characteristic feature of the 'opening-up' process is the monopoly power of varying degrees which the foreign business concerns exercise in relation to the backward economy. Here again the actual process of the growth of trade between the advanced and the backward countries differs from the textbook picture of two countries coming into trading relations with each other under conditions of perfect competition. Indeed, if we were to insist on applying the rules of perfect competition to foreign enterprises, very few backward countries would have been 'developed'. The process of opening up a new territory for trade is an extremely risky and costly business, and it is only by offering some sort of monopolistic concessions that foreign business concerns can be induced to accept the risks and the heavy initial costs, which include not only those of setting up transport and communications and other auxiliary services but may also include the ordinary administrative costs of extending law and order to places where it does not exist. Hence the age-old method of economic development by chartered companies. In the case of mining this is reinforced by the technical advantages of large-scale enterprise.

Even where there is no formal concession of monopoly power, as in a peasant economy, conditions are generally very favourable for its growth. To begin with, only fairly big firms with large enough reserves to meet the heavy initial costs and risks may venture into the new territory. Further, although there may be no restriction to free entry, potential competitors may be put off by the 'economies of experience' which give a great differential advantage to the pioneers. Thus there are usually a small number of fairly big export-import firms engaged in a 'cut-throat' competition with each other in their effort to increase their turnover and spread their heavy overhead costs. This need not be limited to 'horizontal' competition among the export-import firms; it may also result in a 'vertical' competition between the export-import firms and the steamship companies which control the trade routes. After some time this trade war generally results in 'pools' and 'combinations' both of the horizontal and vertical types,[1] for 'the small trader must grow to greatness, either in himself, or in combination with others. The alternative is his failure and ultimate disappearance. In fact, economic conditions of England are exhibited on an intenser scale in West Africa, where businesses grow, decay and combine with mushroom rapidity.'[2]

Thus in a typical process of 'development', the backward peoples have to contend with three types of monopolistic forces: in their role as unskilled labour they have to face the big foreign mining and plantation concerns who are monopolistic buyers of their labour; in their role as peasant producers they have to face a small group of exporting and processing firms who are monopolistic buyers of their crop; and in their role as consumers of imported commodities they have to face the same group of firms who are the monopolistic sellers or distributors of these commodities.

iii. The third characteristic feature of the 'opening-up' process is the growth of the middlemen between the big European concerns and the economically backward indigenous populations. They are the necessary adjuncts to any process of rapid economic development and fill in the gaps between the highly specialized Western economic structure and the relatively unspecialized roles of the backward peoples. Although they may operate in the labour market, they are more important in their activities as collectors of produce from the

[1] This 'vertical integration' may also spread downwards towards a greater supervision and control of peasant producers resulting in a 'mixed' system between peasant and plantation systems (cf. Boeke, op. cit., ch. i).

[2] McPhee, op. cit., p. 103; cf. W. K. Hancock, *Survey of British Commonwealth Affairs*, vol. ii, part 2, ch. iii, sec. iii; also J. S. Furnivall, op. cit., pp. 95-7 and pp. 197-8.

peasant farmers, as distributors of imported articles to the indigenous consumers, and, most important of all, as money-lenders. In most backward countries they seem to owe their special position to their longer contact with Western economic life ; frequently they may start as immigrant labour and work their way up as small traders and money-lenders. The racial distribution of the middlemen groups among the backward countries is familiar : thus we have the Indians and Chinese in south-east Asia, Indians in East Africa, Syrians and 'Coast Africans' in West Africa, etc. Thus the economic hierarchy of a typical backward country is generally a pyramid with Europeans on top, then the middle men, and lastly the indigenous people at the bottom.

Each of the characteristic features outlined above tends to reduce the relative share of the national incomes of the backward countries accruing to the indigenous peoples. But, as we have said before, the nature of economic backwardness cannot be fully appreciated until we go beyond the distribution of incomes to the distribution of economic activities : for 'it is to changes in the forms of efforts and activities that we must turn when in search for the keynotes of the history of mankind[1].'

When we consider the backward peoples in their role as unskilled labour, it is important to ask, not merely why their wages have remained low but why they have been frozen into their role of cheap undifferentiated labour with little vertical mobility into more skilled grades. Here, apart from the monopsony power of the employers, various complex factors are at work to stereotype their role ; out of these we may select three as being fairly typical.[2]

The first is the very high rate of turnover of indigenous labour, partly because the backward peoples are unused to the discipline of the mines and plantations, and partly because they have one foot in their traditional tribal and village economies which make them look upon wage labour not as a continuous permanent employment but as a temporary or periodical expedient to earn a certain sum of money. Given

[1] Marshall, *Principles*, p. 85.

[2] Cf. Wilbert E. Moore, *Industrialization and Labor*, ch. v, for a more systematic analysis.

this rapid rate of labour turnover, there is no opportunity to acquire the experience and skill for promotion to skilled grades. If this were the only cause, one might assume that this is a transitional problem which would gradually disappear with the breakdown of the traditional social institutions and the spread of money economy. But unfortunately there are other obstacles.

This brings us back to the difficulties which we by-passed when defining the nature and extent of 'discrimination' against backward peoples. Here, with reference to the lack of vertical mobility of indigenous labour, we must frankly admit that our distinction between 'discrimination' and 'disequalizing factor' wears very thin in many backward countries. Even where there is no official colour bar, unofficial industrial colour bar is fairly widespread (for example, say, the Rhodesian copper-mines). Even where 'discrimination' has not hardened into a 'bar' of any sort, the natural and frequently unconscious tendency of the white employers to mark off 'native' or 'coloured' occupational categories irrespective of individual differences in ability and skill can be very damaging to the backward peoples ; for the educational effect of apprenticeship and promotion to skilled grades in ordinary economic life is more far-reaching than huge sums of money spent on educational institutions.

The third factor which has contributed to the fossilization of the 'cheap labour' convention is the additional supplies of labour which mines and plantation can draw, either from the breakdown of tribal societies (e.g. the Ashanti Wars in West Africa) or from the human reservoirs of India and China. Importation of immigrant labour has been blessed by liberal economic policy as contributing to the international mobility of labour ; and it may be freely admitted that 'economic development' and the rapid growth of output of tropical raw materials could not have been achieved without it. But as a solution to the problem of human backwardness it has been somewhat unhappy. It has not appreciably relieved the population pressure in the donating countries ; and in the receiving countries, apart from the complex social problems it has created, it has robbed the indigenous people of the chance to acquire vertical mobility in the labour market through the automatic operation of the laws of supply and demand and the principle of substitution.

Let us now turn to the backward peoples in their role as peasant producers in relation to the middlemen and the big export-import firms. Here we have the familiar disequalizing factors, such as the peasants' ignorance of market conditions, which are extremely unstable, their lack of economic strength to hold out against middlemen and speculators, and their need to borrow money at high rates of interest, which have reduced the relative share of incomes accruing to the backward peoples. It may also be freely admitted that this has been helped by their well-known 'extravagance' and lack of thrift which are after all the logical consequences of too successful a policy of creating economic incentives for the production of cash crops. The formal framework which offers perfect equality of economic rights offers no protection, and the result of the 'free play of economic forces' under conditions of fluctuating export prices is the well-known story of rural indebtedness, land alienation, and agrarian unrest.[1] Here again we should go beyond the distribution of incomes to the distribution of economic activities. We shall then see that the real damage done by the middlemen lies not in their 'exploitation', considerable as it may be in many cases, but in the fact that they have put themselves between the backward peoples and the outside world and have robbed the latter of the educating and stimulating effect of a direct contact.[2] As a consequence, even after many decades of rapid 'economic development' following the 'opening-up' process, the peoples of many backward countries still remain almost as ignorant and unused to the ways of modern economic life as they were before. On the side of economic activities they remain as backward as ever; it is only on the side of wants that they have been modernized, and this reduces their propensity to save and increases their sense of discontent and inequality.[3]

Finally, we may comment briefly on the backward peoples in their role as borrowers. Here, when we inquire closely why they are obliged to borrow at very high rates of interest from

[1] Cf. Furnivall, op. cit., passim.
[2] Cf. Hancock, op. cit., pp. 225-7.
[3] Cf. Ragnar Nurkse, op. cit., 1952, Third Lecture.

the money-lenders, we frequently find that high risks and the difficulties of finding suitable outlets for liquid funds may be more important than an overall shortage of saving. It is true that the rigid sterling exchange standard of some backward countries (which works like the gold standard) may have a deflationary bias, particularly during periods of rapid extension of the money sector. But, in spite of this, it is difficult to establish that there is an overall shortage of saving for the backward economy as a whole. In the 'advanced' or Western sectors at least, big business concerns can raise loans on the international market on equal terms with the borrowers from the advanced countries and the banks generally tend to have a very high liquidity ratio.

This leads us to the problem which is apt to be obscured by the 'under investment' approach which stresses the overall shortage of capital supply. It is the problem of organizing the *distribution* of credit as distinct from the problem of increasing the total supply of saving. The 'retail distribution' of credit among peasant producers is beyond the capacity of the ordinary commercial bank and, in spite of the rise of the co-operative movement, still remains one of the unsolved problems of the backward countries which may have greater long-run significance than the more spectacular projects for economic development. Further, there is a great need to extend credit facilities not only to the peasant producers but also to the growing class of small traders and businessmen among the backward peoples who would like to enter into the traditional preserves of the middlemen. Here many would-be businessmen from the backward groups frequently complain of the 'discrimination' against them by the commercial banks when the truth of the matter is that they are simply caught up in a vicious circle of lack of business experience resulting in a lack of credit-worthiness. The banks, far from discriminating, are playing strictly according to the 'rules of the game', but these rules tend to put the heaviest handicap on the weakest players.

That the real 'bottleneck' may frequently lie in the difficulties of organizing the distribution of credit and finding suitable outlets for existing savings, rather than in the overall shortage of saving, may also be seen from the fact that domestic saving even where it exists in sizeable amounts is normally used for money-lending on the basis of land and jewellery mortgage since this yields a very much higher rate of return to the savers than any other available form of 'productive' investment.

VI

The idea of economic backwardness put forward in this paper may be better appreciated in terms of the deviations, not from the static concept of the allocative optimum, but from the dynamic presumption concerning the beneficial effects of free trade held by the older generation of liberal economists. For it will be remembered that the Classical case for free competition was based, not as much on the purely static considerations of allocative efficiency as on dynamic considerations of economic expansion. Thus it was believed that the growth of individualism and economic freedom would encourage initiative and enterprise, thrift, industriousness, and other qualities favourable to the dynamic expansion of the economy both horizontally, through the international division of labour and the extension of the market, and vertically, through capital accumulation and technical innovations.[1]

This line of thought is worth pursuing. The Classical economists did not claim that the free play of economic forces would necessarily lead to a more equitable distribution of wealth ; as a matter of fact, they believed that inequalities of incomes (on the basis of equal opportunities) were necessary to provide the incentives for economic expansion : thus a redistribution of incomes from the rich to the poor might discourage saving, and poor relief (whether on a national or an international scale) might aggravate the population problem. As a corollary to this, they denied that the free play of economic forces would set up disequalizing factors which would ultimately inhibit the expansion in the total volume of output and economic activity.

As is well-known, this Classical vision of harmonious economic growth through free enterprise has been shattered by two major factors : the growth of monopoly and imperfect competi-

[1] Cf. L. Robbins, *The Theory of Economic Policy*, p. 16 ; also H. Myint, *Theories of Welfare Economics*, ch. iv.

tion, and the growth of unemployment. These did not, however, immediately lead to a reconsideration of the long-run theory of economic development on the Classical lines, for many economists have been too preoccupied with the purely static effects of imperfect competition, as in much of modern welfare economics, or with purely short-run problems, as in much of modern Keynesian economics. It is only fairly recently that the tide has turned, and the economics of backwardness, apart from its practical interest, may now come to occupy an important position in its own right as an essential element in the new theory of long-run economic development.

One of the most interesting developments in the long-run theory of economic development is Professor Schumpeter's well-known argument that the growth of monopoly, which from a static view would result in a maldistribution of resources, might actually favour technical innovations and economic development.[1] We have already seen a parallel case of this argument when we were led to the conclusion that monopoly was an essential element in the 'opening-up' process of the backward countries to international trade. The question then arises: can the Schumpeter argument be extended to the backward countries or is there a fundamental difference in the operation of monopoly in the backward countries as compared with the advanced countries?

Recently Professor J. K. Galbraith has put forward a theory which seems to provide a part of the answer. He maintains that the growth of monopoly in the advanced countries, particularly in the U.S.A., has been accompanied by a growth of 'countervailing power' on the opposite side of the market, e.g. trade unions, retail chain stores, co-operative societies, farmers' unions, etc. The growth of monopoly increases the gains from building up the countervailing power and induces its growth and this provides a new self-regulatory mechanism to the economy in a world of monopoly.[2] In Professor Galbraith's terminology, then, economic backwardness may be described as a phenomenon which arises because the process of 'economic

[1] J. Schumpeter, *Capitalism, Socialism and Democracy*, chs. vii and viii.

[2] J. K. Galbraith, *American Capitalism*: 'The Concept of Countervailing Power'.

development' has been too rapid and the initial conditions too unfavourable to give rise to an effective 'countervailing power' to check the 'foreign economic domination' of the backward peoples. One remarkable thing about Professor Galbraith's argument is that although he is concerned with the economically most advanced country in the world, the U.S.A., the sectors of the economy which he regards as being particularly in need of the countervailing power—agriculture, consumers' goods market, and the labour market—are exactly paralleled in the backward countries with their export-import monopolies and large scale mining and plantation businesses (cf. Galbraith, op. cit., chs. x and xi).

Now if we were merely concerned with the problem of backwardness in its subjective aspect as the economics of discontent it would be sufficient to show how the working of the disequalizing factors set up by the free play of economic forces in the absence of countervailing power has resulted in the present situation. But we must go on to the other side of the problem and investigate the relation between the disequalizing factors and economic stagnation or the slow rate of growth in total output and economic activity (apart from the unfavourable effects of political and social unrests, both on present production and future investment).

Here, as we have noted above, we must be on guard against the convenient supposition that the requirements of economic equality and economic development always work in the same direction. Bearing this in mind, when we consider the typical process of 'economic development' of most backward countries there seem to be prima facie reasons for thinking that the disequalizing factors have affected not merely the distribution but also the rate of growth in the total volume of output and economic activity.

The fundamental assumption of liberal economics is that the free play of economic forces would lead to the maximum development of *individual* talents and abilities; whereas in practice the free play of economic forces in backward countries has resulted, not in a division of labour according to individual abilities, but in a division of labour according to stratified groups. The accurate selection of the different types and qualities of natural resources by the automatic market mechanism contrasts dramatically with its lack of selectivity concerning human resources which has resulted in the 'fossilization' of the backward peoples in their conventional roles of undifferentiated cheap labour and unspecialized peasant producers. Thus, unless we are prepared to subscribe to the doctrine of inherent racial inferiority of the backward peoples, there seems to be a strong presumption that the potential development of the backward countries has been inhibited by this waste of human resources, leading to a stultification of the possible 'growing-points' of the economy. Nor can the loss of educational opportunities be adequately remedied by 'investment in human capital' as is frequently assumed. Mere increase of expenditure on technical training and education, although it may offer a partial relief, is really too weak and unselective to be an active countervailing force to the deep-seated disequalizing factors. Too great an emphasis on the 'under-investment in human capital' therefore tends to confuse the issues and distract attention from the more potent disequalizing factors.

Further, the disequalizing factors work not only on the supply side but also on the demand side, and unequal distribution of incomes and of activities combine with each other to inhibit economic development. One of the most important reasons why the backward countries have been prevented from enjoying the stimulating effect of manufacturing industry is not the wickedness of foreign capitalists and their exclusive concern with raw material supplies but merely the limitation of the domestic market for manufactured articles.[1]

When we were discussing the concept of 'social productivity' towards the end of section II above, we remarked on the tendency of economic practice to forestall economic theory. So also here, with the concept of 'countervailing power'. Long before the economists were aware of the problem, practical administrators and economic historians of the backward countries were impressed by the fact that the peoples of these countries seem to need some sort of countervailing power to enable them to stand up against the 'free play of economic forces'. Some have sought the countervailing power in the

[1] Cf. Ragnar Nurkse, op. cit., First Lecture.

preservation of the traditional social institutions and, in extreme cases, have even toyed with the idea of a retreat into the self-sufficiency of the traditional stationary state. Others, more forward-looking, have tried to foster countervailing power in the form of co-operative societies and, more recently, by means of trade unions and marketing boards for the peasant produce. Above all this, the disequalizing forces themselves have generated a fierce nationalism among the backward peoples which is the most powerful source of countervailing power in the present times. So we are already in a position to learn a few lessons about the nature and limitations of the countervailing power in the backward countries.

The first lesson is that some sources of countervailing power, like the co-operative societies, themselves need a fairly high degree of business-like behaviour and 'economic advance' and can only be fostered very slowly in the backward countries. The second lesson is that it is easier to redistribute existing incomes than to redistribute and stimulate economic activity by the use of countervailing power. The governments of some backward countries are now able to obtain a larger share of the income from the exploitation of the natural resources, either by striking better bargains with foreign mining concerns or by means of marketing boards in the case of peasant produce; but they are still faced with the problem of reinvesting the money in a directly productive way as distinct from increasing expenditure on general social services. It is difficult enough to find outlets for productive investment in backward countries; it is far more difficult to find those outlets which will increase the direct participation of the backward peoples in the processes of economic activity. It is important to stress this point because the governments of the backward countries, in their desire to have rapid and spectacular economic development, may be tempted to embark on those large-scale projects which, even if they were successful as business concerns, might not appreciably increase the participation of their peoples in the new economic activities.[1] Apart from its failure as a business concern, the fundamental weakness of the famous 'Ground Nut Scheme' of the British Overseas Food

[1] In some countries excessive central planning may give rise to a new class of 'middlemen' in the guise of government agents or officials.

Corporation was that in an attempt to have rapid results on a large scale the Corporation was obliged to minimize the African participation in it.

The final lesson to be learnt is the danger of an excessive use of the countervailing power combined with an extreme economic nationalism. As a counter-measure to the disequalizing forces at the international level, discriminatory and protective measures to change the existing terms of comparative costs and foster the national economies of the backward countries have their place. In certain circumstances, they may even have a favourable effect on the volume of international trade in the long run. But, on the other hand, the dangers of an excessive nationalist policy should not be underrated. The loss to the backward countries in this case is not merely consumers' loss through having to pay a higher price or through having to put up with poorer qualities of commodities substituted for imports; a far heavier loss may lie in the sphere of economic activities when cut off from the stimulating contact with the outside world. This is also true of trade unions. In some backward countries trade unions have the very important function of breaking the industrial colour bar; but in others they may become a crippling burden on the economy and inhibit economic progress.[1]

These considerations should not, however, blind us to the genuineness of the disequalizing factors working against the backward peoples and their real need for countervailing power. From the point of view of these peoples this is where the real rub lies. It is, however, precisely on this point that economists, both of liberal and of central-planning persuasion, have shown the least sympathy and understanding. The liberal economist is apt to believe that the disequalizing factors do not exist and that all attempts to use the countervailing power are the result of 'irrational economic nationalism'. The central planner is apt to seek a solution of the essentially distributive and structural problems of economic backwardness in terms of bigger and better aggregative economic development plans. Thus the study of the disequalizing factors at work against the backward peoples has never really been allowed to emerge from the intellectual underworld of extreme economic nationalism.

[1] Cf. *Report on Cuba*, by the Economic and Technical Mission of the International Bank for Reconstruction and Development, pp. 138-59.

2. THE HISTORICAL CONTEXT

UNDERDEVELOPED COUNTRIES AND THE PRE-INDUSTRIAL PHASE IN THE ADVANCED COUNTRIES

an Attempt at Comparison *

by **Simon Kuznets**

THIS PAPER WAS PREPARED IN RESPONSE TO A REQUEST TO compare 'the present situation in underdeveloped countries with the earlier situation of the more developed countries, with special reference to the factors that seem . . . to be critical in respect of potentialities of development'. The comparison is intended to introduce a series of papers focusing on 'conditions relevant to, and case studies of, the interrelationship between population, economic development, and social change'.

The theme is obviously of wide scope, and touches a field for which testable observations are hard to find. Part of the discussion must be devoted to defining terms, but this in itself should help to clarify the difference between the present state of the underdeveloped countries and the earlier situation of the more developed. It will also indicate the areas in which information for drawing more effective comparisons should be sought ; and permit the presentation of a few relevant and available data.

We begin by distinguishing three definitions of 'underdevelopment'. The first associates it with the failure to utilize fully the potential economic output warranted by existing technological knowledge—this failure being ascribable to obstacles inherent in the 'social' institutions, internal or external to a country. In this sense, all countries are underdeveloped : none utilizes its productive potential to the full. Indeed, a mathematical function in which possible additions to economic product are the dependent variable and the some-

* *Proceedings of the World Population Conference, 1954,* Papers : Volume V. Reprinted by permission of the United Nations Organization and the author.

how measurable 'social' changes are the independent variable may well have a much steeper slope for a 'very advanced' country than for an underdeveloped one.[1] This is obviously *not* the meaning of the term 'underdeveloped' in current discussion. Yet one aspect of this definition is directly relevant : the attribution to social factors of the failure to utilize the technologically feasible potential. If our stock of knowledge permits a much greater economic output than is turned out and if the difficulties lie in the social institutions, underdevelopment must be viewed as a social problem. Our thinking is thus guided into consideration of the social fabric and possible changes in it rather than into channels that it would follow if the shortages of economic performance were attributed, for example, to the inexorable forces of nature or to the irrevocable dictates of divine providence.

The second definition of 'underdevelopment' is backwardness in level and character of economic performance compared with other countries (or units of different type). In this sense, underdevelopment is a matter of degree and most countries, except the necessarily few considered the most advanced, are underdeveloped.

This again is not quite the meaning of the term in current discussion ; but once more, some elements are relevant to the understanding of the current problem. The advanced countries, against whose *realized* performance economic backwardness can be gauged, are an incontrovertible demonstration that higher economic levels are attainable and not just dimly viewed potentials permitted by the stock of knowledge. The tension in underdeveloped countries is generated by the recognition of achievements elsewhere. In addition to this 'demonstration' effect, there is another long recognized aspect. Under certain conditions, economic attainment bestows power

[1] For example, the large productive potential of the United States is one of the major obstacles to an adequate flow of private investment funds into economic development outside of the country—for uses not directly connected with the raw material or other needs of its economy. It need scarcely be added that in an empirical construction of the model suggested in the text, social change, the independent variable, would be most difficult to measure. Note that since the definition includes external social factors, attainment of political independence by a colony would be classified as a social change.

that can be used for aggression, overt or covert. The countries that lag behind others in economic attainment may, for that reason, be unable to defend themselves against aggression, real or fancied, by the more advanced countries. This condition adds to the pressure to match the economic attainments of other members of the world community.

The third meaning of 'underdevelopment', basic in most current discussion, is the failure to provide acceptable levels of living to a large proportion of a country's population, with resulting misery and material deprivation. Where an adequate standard of living has been attained despite failure to realize the technological potential—as in the developed countries—no serious problem arises. Where the lag behind the advanced countries is moderate, as is true of nations just below the top of the economic pyramid (or of some regions within the advanced countries), the problem is also of tolerable dimensions and neither acute nor urgent. However, in the many underdeveloped countries which account for more than half of mankind, economic backwardness means material misery for most of the population and insecurity for the countries themselves. And it is this fact that creates the tension and sharpens the acuteness and urgency of the problem.

The comments just made are directly relevant to finding that 'earlier situation of the more developed countries' with which the present state of the underdeveloped countries should be compared. How do we specify this comparable earlier situation chronologically ?

The question can be discussed more meaningfully if we identify the more developed countries of today. If we judge by the level of *per capita* income either in the post World War II period or during the period between the two world wars, the leading countries are the United States, Canada, Australia, New Zealand, the United Kingdom, Switzerland, the Scandinavian countries (Sweden, Norway, Denmark), Germany, the Netherlands, and at some remove, France and Belgium.[1] The identity of the underdeveloped countries is well known : in

[1] The following publications can be consulted : (1) *National and Per Capita Income, Seventy Countries—1949*, United Nations, Statistical Paper Series E, No. 1, October 1950 ; (2) *Point Four*, U.S. Department

addition to the vast agricultural empires of China and India, most of Asia, with the exception of Asiatic U.S.S.R., Japan, and Israel; most of Africa with the exception of the Union of South Africa; most of Latin America, with the possible exception of Argentina, Uruguay, and more doubtfully Chile. The exceptions noted and the whole complex of Southern and Eastern Europe are in a middle zone between the two extremes.

We may then ask whether an earlier comparable situation of the more developed countries, i.e. essentially of Western and Northern Europe and of their offshoots in North America and Oceania, means a period when they were underdeveloped, i.e. lagged behind the then leading economies; when their backwardness relative to the leaders was as marked as that of the underdeveloped countries of today; when their *per capita* incomes were as low and material deprivation and misery were as widespread as in the latter. If so and if such an earlier situation were found, could we discern the strategic factors that produced the economic leadership of today?

Posed in this fashion, the question has little meaning for the young, relatively 'empty' countries peopled by the Western Europeans and their descendants. In the very early history of the United States, Canada, Australia, and New Zealand, the groups involved were small bands of pioneers, voluntary and involuntary; and many of the early settlers may have suffered material deprivation comparable with that in the underdeveloped countries today. But these troubles were the penalty of pioneering, not of economic backwardness; and the comparison is irrelevant. At no time after these early pioneering days had passed and the settled groups had begun to be significantly large did these countries lag much behind the economic leaders. Thus, in the 1840s, when the United States had about 17 million people and the United Kingdom had 25 million, the *per capita* income of the former was only about a quarter smaller than that of the latter, the economic leader of the time

of State Publication 3719, January 1950, pp. 113-14 (income data for 1939); (3) Colin Clark, *Conditions of Economic Progress*, 2nd edition, London, 1951. These sources yield roughly similar results if allowance is made for the transitory impact of World War II on some countries, e.g. Germany and Japan.

(and twice that of Italy, and over three times that of Russia).[1] There is *no* comparable earlier situation in the history of the economically developed countries of the New World when their *per capita* incomes were so far behind the economic leaders or at such low levels as are those of most underdeveloped countries today.

But even for the older developed countries, the search for an earlier comparable situation so defined would take us back centuries. Western and Northern Europe was well behind the Italian cities in economic development from the 9th to the 15th centuries and the economic attainment of the latter, in the aggregate and through much of the time, lagged behind most of the economies of the Near and Far East. As late as the early 18th century, people in Western Europe were not sure whether any growth in population and economic levels had been attained since the days of the Roman Empire ; and they thought, perhaps correctly, that their political and economic organization was inferior to that of China during the prosperous phases of its long dynastic cycles. But it would take us far afield, both in scope and in time, to look back to the period when the presently developed countries among the older units in Europe were so backward (measured, say by income *per capita*) in comparison with others as to be at all comparable with the underdeveloped countries of today. We would have to step back at least three centuries ; and possibly even further back, in some cases (like France) perhaps to the early Middle Ages. On these periods neither my competence nor, perhaps, the available data can shed much light. More important, the whole complex of conditions, while similar in degree of backwardness, would be so different in many other important ways that its relevance to current problems would be doubtful. Rather than commit myself to what would be, at best, a superficial review of a vast canvas of distant history, I abandoned this particular criterion of comparability.

[1] The figures used here are from Michael G. Mulhall, *Industries and Wealth of Nations* (London, 1896). Mulhall was the Colin Clark of the late 19th century. His estimates are naturally crude ; but they are based on consistent methods for the several countries and on fairly full utilization of the then available data, and are acceptable indicators of the general order of magnitude.

But one important inference should be drawn from this glance into the longer past. We know that the long term acceleration of population growth occurred within the last two to two and a half centuries; that the economic and technological revolutions, the acceleration in the rate of growth of *per capita* national product in most countries, including those at the top, is even more recent, dating back not more than a century and a half. If the 'earlier situations' in the presently developed countries that could be viewed as examples of underdevelopment existed three centuries ago or possibly even earlier, it follows that these older units of the European community must have had a long period of development and rise before the coming of the economic and technological revolutions. It also follows that when the recent rapid pulse of economic growth began, the countries now in the forefront probably were also among the advanced units of that time.

This inference is corroborated by a general view of the earlier history of those parts of Western Europe which, together with their offshoots in the New World, are among the economic leaders today. It can be argued that, in general, the leadership of Western Europe in modern economic development is an outcome of a long process of learning from its more advanced neighbours in the Near and Far East; that the intellectual, political, and geographical revolutions which occurred between the 13th and 16th centuries were important and indispensable antecedents to the economic expansion that followed; and that the countries that led in these major complexes of advance in knowledge and social organization, and their offshoots in the New World, occupy today the top positions on the scale of economic development. It is hardly an accident that among the few leading countries the older European units are England, the Netherlands, the Scandinavian countries, France, and more belatedly Germany—most of which participated in the intellectual and religious revolutions and were situated to take advantage of the geographical revolution; and that England, which led in all three revolutions, was also the pioneer in the fields of economic and material technology. We should finally note that the political independence and initiative of these European units were preserved for centuries while the learning that preceded these revolutions, and of expansion that followed them, was carried on. Conversely, it is hardly an accident that almost all the underdeveloped countries of today were outside the orbit of these revolutions and of the growth that preceded the economic and technological changes which began in the late 18th and continued through the following centuries.

This suggests an important contrast between the currently underdeveloped countries and the situation of the developed countries as it was just before the introduction of the major technological changes that ushered in the modern industrial system—the system whose adoption constitutes much of the content of modern economic development. At that time, mid or late 18th century, many of the developed countries of today were already advanced economically—by contemporary standards; had already experienced fairly sustained growth over the earlier centuries, and enjoyed political independence in doing so; and were the direct participants in and beneficiaries of the extension of knowledge and changes in attitudes that constituted the three revolutions mentioned. In contrast, most underdeveloped countries of today are inheritors of much older civilizations which, however economically superior in the distant past, include strongly entrenched elements that constitute serious obstacles to the adoption of the modern industrial system. They face the problems of development after decades, if not centuries, of political subjection which, granted some beneficial effects, left a heritage against which the newly established independent regimes must struggle. Thus, they must approach the task of utilizing the available potential of economic knowledge not from the position of near leadership and at the end of a cumulative process of preceding growth and learning carried on under conditions of political independence; but from the position of laggards by a long distance and after a period in which internal organization was distorted either by political subjection or by co-existence with the aggressive leaders of the economic civilization of the West.

We may add significant detail to the contrast just suggested by reformulating our criterion of comparability to permit the use of available quantitative evidence. As indicated, the substance of modern economic development lies in the adoption of the industrial system—a term denoting widespread

application of empirical science to the problems of economic production. One corollary that follows is the shift in the distribution of the labour force away from agriculture, first toward manufacturing and public utilities, and subsequently toward trade and service pursuits. This commonly observed shift is due, at bottom, to the structure of human wants, their easy long term satiability by products of agriculture—so that increasing productivity of labour in the latter releases an increasing proportion of labour to other pursuits. The technological revolution was *not* confined to non-agricultural industries: if it were, the share of the labour force in agriculture might not have declined. Rather, the application of science to social and material technology produced both an agricultural and an industrial revolution; and the former, given the structure of human wants, permitted a much lower ratio of workers in agriculture to either total population or total labour force. This in turn led to a whole host of related changes ordinarily discussed under urbanization, growth in the average scale of the economic plant, changes in character of business firms, and the like.

This brief indication of a complex process may possibly permit misleading connotations. But it suffices for our purposes to note that, according to available evidence, the proportion of the labour force in agriculture in the underdeveloped countries today is about six-tenths or more, whereas in the developed countries it is ordinarily one-fifth or less.[1] We can now reformulate the question about the comparable 'earlier situation': what was the situation in that pre-industrial phase of the developed countries when the share of their labour force engaged in agriculture was about six-tenths or more?

In dealing with this question, we can command some evidence although it is far from adequate. In the United States, agriculture accounted for over 60 per cent of the labour force through 1850, and dropped below 50 per cent only by 1880. For Canada the share of the labour force engaged in agriculture was 50

[1] These and additional data cited below are from Colin Clark, op. cit., supplemented by special studies for a few countries. The evidence is summarized in a statistical appendix to a recent paper, 'Toward a Theory of Economic Growth', presented at Columbia University Bicentennial Conference III, May 1954.

per cent in 1871, the earliest figure available to me; and if one may judge by United States experience, the share may have been over six-tenths as late as 1850. In England and Wales, one would have to go back to the end of the 17th century: Gregory King's figures for 1688 suggest that the proportion of the labour force in agriculture was close to six-tenths (it was down to 23 per cent by 1841). For Sweden, the proportion was as high as 64 per cent in 1870; but in Norway and Denmark the proportions were already 49 per cent in 1875 and 52 per cent in 1870 respectively. In France the earliest available figure (for 1866) is 43 per cent of the labour force in agriculture; in Germany 34 per cent for 1880. One would be inclined to set 'the comparable phase' for the older countries of Western Europe in the first quarter of the 19th century, but much earlier for England and perhaps the Netherlands; about the middle of the century for the Scandinavian countries and North America; and perhaps about the same for Australia and New Zealand (the early percentages are 38 in 1870 for the former, and 31 in 1874 for the latter). With the exception of England and perhaps the Netherlands, the comparable pre-industrial phase in the distribution of the labour force of the developed countries is, therefore, between a century and a century and a half ago.

Having placed the phase chronologically, we can use the limited but illuminating evidence provided by the estimates of national income in constant prices, total and *per capita*. For eight countries—the United States, United Kingdom (ex. Southern Ireland), Canada, France, Germany (pre-World War II), Sweden, Denmark, and Italy—all except Italy among those with the highest *per capita* income today—we have records of national income that extend over three-quarters of a century—the periods terminating after World War II for those countries whose economies were not deeply affected by the war, or up to the end of the 1930s for the others.[1] Using the per decade rates of growth in *per capita* national income in *constant prices* we extrapolate back from the present levels and derive rough approximations to their *per capita* income a century earlier. These derived figures, which are in *current*

[1] These data also are summarized in the statistical appendix to the Columbia paper referred to in the note on page 142.

prices of a recent year, can be compared with the *per capita* incomes in current prices of the underdeveloped countries of today.

This extrapolation was made from the 1949 levels given in the United Nations publication cited in the note on page 137; and from the 1939 levels given in the U. S. Department of State publication mentioned in the same note, with the derived estimates shifted to 1949 prices for comparison with more recent *per capita* income levels. The results are as follows. For all the countries listed above, except Italy and Sweden, the derived *per capita* income for the decade between 1840 and 1850, ranges from roughly $150 to about $300. For Sweden it is about $110, and for Italy it is about $90. These are *under-estimates* since rates of growth over the recent three-quarters of a century, which are more heavily weighted by the high rates associated with the industrialization process, are carried back a century into a period well before industrialization and rapid growth began in some countries (e.g. Sweden).

Compared with these figures the current incomes, in the same prices, in many of the underdeveloped countries of today look distressingly low. The United Nations publication referred to above shows *per capita* income under $30 for China and Indonesia ; between $30 and $40 for Southern Korea, Thailand, Burma, Yemen, Saudi Arabia, Ecuador, and Haiti ; between $41 and $60—Philippines, Afghanistan, Pakistan, India, and Bolivia. In fact, over three-tenths of the 2 billion people covered in the 1949 income estimates, had *per capita* incomes of $50 or less. As they stand, the figures suggest that *per capita* incomes in the underdeveloped countries today are from about one-sixth to one-third of the *per capita* incomes of the developed countries a century ago.

Granted that because of the estimating procedure used, the incomes of underdeveloped countries may be understated ; but the same bias affects time comparisons of national income in developed countries, since income in the earlier and less developed decades tends to be understated. Granted also that some of the developed countries among the eight listed, e.g. the United Kingdom and France, had already passed the pre-industrial phase of development by the mid-19th century ; yet what scattered evidence we have concerning even earlier incomes still suggests *per capita* levels much higher than those in the underdeveloped countries today. Despite all these qualifications, one must conclude that the pre-industrial level in the developed countries was several times that of most underdeveloped countries today.

The implications of this finding, coupled with other evidence, can now be briefly summarized.

First, the national income records indicate continuity and consistency over the last century in the relative position of countries judged by *per capita* income. We have rough but usable data for eight major countries covering a half century from the 1840s to the mid-1890s; and data for 24 countries whose relative standing in the mid-1890s and in 1949 can be compared (with just a few adjustments for changes in territory). While the earlier data come from Mulhall and the later from the United Nations studies, the general orders of magnitude are fairly acceptable. However, this sample is largely limited to the European countries and the European settlements in the New World and excludes practically all the underdeveloped countries of today. Although the data reveal some changes in standing—the United States forges ahead to surpass the *per capita* income of the United Kingdom, the slower growth of France causes a recession in its position—by and large, countries at the head of the procession in the beginning are at the head at the end. This conclusion would emerge much more strongly if the underdeveloped countries of today were included in the comparison.[1]

Second, not only have the relative differences among the developed, less developed, and underdeveloped countries, judged by *per capita* income, persisted over the last century, but the disparity has increased. The long term national income records, available largely for the more developed countries, suggest increases in *per capita* income (in constant prices) over a century to between two-and-a-half and over six times the initial value. No such rates of growth in the *per capita* incomes

[1] In other words, the contrast between the high level of *per capita* incomes of Western Europe and the low levels in Asia and Latin America has certainly persisted through the century. Even for the 24 countries for which we have data for both the mid-1890s and 1949, the coefficient of rank correlation in *per capita* income is $+0 \cdot 79$.

can be assumed for the older of the presently underdeveloped countries, or even for those in the New World. Since the present low *per capita* income in most underdeveloped countries is close to the margin of subsistence, a level of even three-quarters of the present magnitude—let alone a half, a third, or a sixth—can hardly be imagined: the population could not possibly survive it. Hence, during the last century the spread must have widened between the underdeveloped countries at one end of the range and the few economically advanced countries at the other. But interestingly enough, this widening in the relative disparity of *per capita* incomes is found even among the sample of largely European countries. For the eight major countries that Mulhall covers (all European except for the United States) the ratio of the unweighted average deviation to the unweighted arithmetic mean is 0·32 in the 1840s and 0·42 in the mid-1890s (if the United States is excluded, the ratios are 0·31 and 0·38). For the 24 countries for which we have data both in the mid-1890s and 1949, the ratio of the average deviation to the arithmetic mean is 0·39 at the earlier date and 0·52 at the later; if we limit the comparison to European countries alone, excluding the five non-European countries, the ratios become 0·32 and 0·53 respectively. Other measures of dispersion, e.g. the relative range, show the widening in international disparities in *per capita* income even more conspicuously.

Third, for most of the older underdeveloped countries (China, India, the countries of the Middle East) but with important exceptions, the rate of growth of total population over the last century to century and a half was appreciably lower than that in the more developed countries of today (again with some exceptions such as France). Since the rate of growth in *per capita* income in the former was also materially lower than in the latter, it follows that the rate of growth in total income, the income mass as it were, was also very much lower. This is of some importance because the rapidity with which the total economy grows is an indication of the ability of a society to adjust itself to continuous expansion of the absolute scale of operation. A slow growth in total volume of economic activity is likely to be accompanied by social institutions geared to such a low rate, institutions that would require substantial modification if the pace of growth in the total were to be accelerated. This suggests problems—which have an interesting counterpart in the more advanced countries, when the pace of growth slackens and when institutions and patterns effective under conditions of rapid growth have to be modified.

The higher economic level and the different historical heritage in the pre-industrial phases of the developed countries must have been associated with patterns of population movement different from those characterizing the underdeveloped countries of today. With this subject, however, I shall deal even more briefly since all firmly established findings should be quite familiar to the readers of this paper; and on any more tentative data I do not feel competent to pass judgment. The few comments listed are presented as questions or hypotheses subject to critical examination by experts.

1. The developed countries of today, in their pre-industrial phases, represented small population groups. At the end of the 17th century the population of the United Kingdom was about 7 million, and even in 1770, on the eve of the Industrial Revolution, that of England and Wales was not much greater. In the 1840s the United States had less than 20 million. Indeed, none of the countries in this group had appreciably more than 30 million before the process of industrialization had begun. Yet among the underdeveloped countries today there are two with enormous population totals, and others whose population is 50 million or more (Brazil, Pakistan, Indonesia). It is often overlooked, although not by demographers, that the large populations of the developed countries of today are a consequence, not an antecedent of their rapid economic growth; and that at the crucial earlier stages the population groups were small. The implication for the magnitude of the problems involved in rapid economic growth is obvious; and this difference in sheer population size between the developed countries in their pre-industrial phase and at least some of the larger underdeveloped countries today (including some half-developed, like Japan and the U.S.S.R.) should be added to the others already noted.

2. For all the developed countries of today the rates of growth in total population during a period preceding the

initiation of industrialization can be measured. While the exact dating is in itself a substantial research problem, it is sufficient to use here the rough chronology suggested on pp. 142-3. We can then calculate rates of population growth in England and Wales and France for five or seven decades prior to 1770, or prior to 1800; also the rate of population growth during the first half of the 19th century in the Scandinavian countries, Germany, Switzerland, the Netherlands, Belgium; and, of course, in the Western European settlements in the New World. These rates of growth, in percentage terms, are naturally very high for the younger, 'emptier' countries like the United States, Canada, Australia, New Zealand. This is to be expected, and it is hardly relevant to the growth of presently underdeveloped countries. Few or none of the latter are that 'empty' and few have a potential of growth similar to that of North America or Oceania in the mid-19th century.

Far more relevant are the rates of growth for the older European countries. These were much lower than for the United States, for example, where they ranged about 35 per cent per decade in the first half of the 19th century. By and large, they were 10 per cent per decade or lower—the only significant exception is for England and Wales where the rate was close to 15 per cent during the first half of the 19th century. Furthermore, in many cases the rates accelerated somewhat *after* the process of industrialization and quickened economic growth began. Thus the rates for England and Wales were higher during the first half of the 19th than during the last quarter of the 18th century; and higher during the second half than during the first half of the 19th century for Germany, Belgium, Holland, and Denmark.

Similar data for the underdeveloped countries during the first half of the 20th century are not as abundant; and one does need records for a substantial period in order to eliminate the distorting effects of transient changes. The scanty data available suggest that in some of the older and densely settled and underdeveloped countries (e.g. India, and presumably China, although that is *terra incognita*) the overall rates of growth are not high—certainly not significantly higher than those quoted above for the older European countries (with some obvious exceptions, e.g. as compared with the low rate for France). However, in a number of underdeveloped countries the rates of growth during the 20th century are significantly higher than in the older European countries in their pre-industrial phase (and even more so compared with later periods). For example, the *Demographic Yearbook of the United Nations* (1952) shows that in the following underdeveloped countries (only those were selected for which population exceeded 1 million in recent years and the period of coverage is over 25 years—for most it is close to 50 years) the decade rate of growth of population during the first half of the 20th century was above 20 per cent : Formosa, Korea, Philippines, Thailand, Federation of Malaya, Cuba, Dominican Republic, Honduras, Bolivia, Brazil, Colombia, and Venezuela. In addition, in the following underdeveloped countries it averaged between 15 and 20 per cent per decade : Ceylon, Egypt, Tunisia, Nicaragua. Granted the need for caution in view of the quality of the data for many of these countries. Nevertheless, the impression—and it is important and should be checked—is that the population of many underdeveloped countries has been growing, in recent decades, at much higher rates than the population of the older developed countries in their pre-industrial phase.

3. A view of the crude birth and death rates—and these measures are subject to even wider margins of error—proves revealing. In general, the crude birth rates in the older of the developed countries ranged, during the first half of the 19th century, between 30 and 35 per thousand (and the level was similar for England and Wales in the 18th century). The only exceptions are some of the German states (Prussia, Bavaria, Saxony) where the crude birth rates reached 38 and even went above 40. The rather spotty data of limited quality for many underdeveloped countries suggest much higher levels. Thus the *Demographic Yearbook of the United Nations* (1952) suggests rates of 40 or more (for 1941-50) for Egypt, Costa Rica, El Salvador, Guatemala, Mexico, Bolivia, and Malaya ; and of about 38 for Honduras, Venezuela, and Ceylon. Thus one possible factor in the higher rate of population growth in many underdeveloped countries today, than in the older developed countries in their pre-industrial phase, may well be a significantly higher crude birth rate.

4. A second factor in the difference may be the crude death rates. By and large, these rates in the older European countries, even those economically advanced, were more than 20 per 1,000 until the last quarter of the 19th century, i.e. during the pre-industrial phase (and naturally were particularly high in those German states where the crude birth rate was high relative to other advanced European countries). This combination of a birth rate of slightly more than 30 and of a death rate of more than 20 yielded rates of natural increase of 10 or less per 1,000. In many underdeveloped countries today, at least during recent decades, reported crude death rates were well below 20. *United Nations Demographic Yearbook* (1952) reports crude death rates for 1940-50 of about 15 or less for the following underdeveloped countries: Costa Rica, the Dominican Republic, Nicaragua, Jamaica, Puerto Rico, Peru, Venezuela, and Thailand. Indeed, of some 20 underdeveloped countries for which the death rate can be calculated for the recent decade, in only two—Egypt and Guatemala—is it over 20 per 1,000.

5. There is, finally, the international migration variable. The older European countries, which entered the phase of rapid population growth and industrialization in the 19th century, could take advantage of the escape valve provided by migration either across the Atlantic (predominantly to the United States) or to the British dominions elsewhere, or, not infrequently, to some other European country. The intercontinental migrations were particularly important. The succession of immigrants to the United States—from the British to the Germans, to the Scandinavians, to the Italians, and to the Eastern Europeans—traces the path through Europe of the introduction of industrialization and of the initiation of the painful period of adjustment to the industrial system. That emigration helped to smooth the way to the economic development of many of these countries can hardly be gainsaid. Nor can it be doubted that the loss by migration reduced the overall rate of population growth in some of them. No such opportunity, at least not in that relative dimension, was available through most of the 20th century to the underdeveloped countries of today. This is a third factor that may account for part of the difference between the rates of

population growth of many underdeveloped countries since 1900 and those in the pre-industrial phase of the older developed European units.

6. In concluding, we should note that their higher birth rates may be said to reflect the lower economic level of many of the currently underdeveloped countries as over against that of older European units in their pre-industrial phase. On the other hand, their lower death rates may be said to reflect the more recent date for which we observe them in the underdeveloped countries of today—mortality thus mirroring the advantages of the technological advance made since the pre-industrial phase of the now developed countries. Finally, with respect to international migration, the underdeveloped countries today are paying the penalty of being late on the scene, since expansion into the 'empty' territories of the New World is no longer politically feasible. Thus, differences in economic level and in historical timing between the developed countries in their pre-industrial phase and the presently underdeveloped countries are reflected in differences in their demographic patterns when we relate the present situation to the earlier 'comparable' one.

It is hardly necessary to summarize here what is already too summary a discussion. And implications for further study in the field are perhaps too obvious to merit explicit formulation. Yet it may be advisable to list the implications bearing upon the possible use of past records of developed countries to shed light on the problems of underdeveloped countries.

1. Both the absolute and relative economic position, as well as the general cast of the immediately antecedent history, of the now developed countries in their pre-industrial phase were cardinally different from the economic position and the immediate historical heritage of the underdeveloped countries of today. It is, therefore, far from safe to extrapolate economic or demographic aspects from the earlier records for the developed countries to current and prospective levels for the underdeveloped.

2. There is today a vast gulf between economic levels, social framework, and, I assume, demographic patterns of the

developed countries at the top and most underdeveloped countries. This widespread is in itself an important factor determining policy and prospects of economic growth in underdeveloped countries. But it should inhibit easy extrapolation in cross-section analysis.

3. The experience of countries that have enjoyed satisfactory growth and have gone through the period of industrialization has varied considerably with their size, their antecedents, and particularly in their sequence, the duration of their lag behind the pioneer countries and their immediate successors. To understand the problems of growth of the currently underdeveloped countries, the analysis of successive experience of the developed countries—with particular emphasis on those whose effective entrance into the process of rapid economic growth and industrialization came late—seems to me of utmost importance. Examination of similarities and differences should be particularly instructive since it would suggest the different roles of various factors as the conditions, set by the changing world scene and the historical heritage of each country, modify the process of adjustment to the industrial system.

4. For many of the late joiners in the circle of the industrialized nations (e.g. Japan and the U.S.S.R.), the process is far from complete and the levels of *per capita* income attained are still very much lower than for the older developed countries at the top. This experience of the late joiners should be particularly valuable in analysing the problems of population, economic development, and social change in underdeveloped countries. There are case-studies of interest to specific groups among underdeveloped countries: e.g. the experience of late comers in Latin America and the Near East might be particularly illuminating to underdeveloped countries in those areas.

5. The very width of the gap between developed and underdeveloped countries today may also be indicative of the wealth and the variety of the economic potential that must exist in the underdeveloped areas. The realization of even a minor share of this potential might mean striking relative increases in their economic performance. It might also mean rapid sustained growth for at least some—once the obstacles have

been removed—and at rates even surpassing those in many of the now developed countries in their past. This makes it all the more important to study the record of the recently industrialized countries—including those that may still be considered partly undeveloped or even still largely underdeveloped—provided that significant steps forward have already been taken.

6. If the emphasis is to be on similarities and differences in the basic characteristics of the process of adoption of the industrial system—for countries distinguished by their size, historical heritage, and the timing of their industrialization process—we obviously need a variety of national studies. In these, the interplay among economic growth, population patterns, and social change must naturally be the main focus of interest. Furthermore, the periods covered should be long enough for rates of secular change to be established without confusion with more transient changes. It is from such long period studies, with emphasis on the interconnexion of secular trends in population, in economic level and structure, in internal political and social institutions, and in the world scene, that we can hope to derive testable conclusions that may be useful in understanding and dealing with the problems of the economic growth of underdeveloped countries. The alternative shortcuts prevalent to date—of cross-country comparisons and of studies of population, economic, and social change, each in isolation—have been helpful as suggesting leads but are far from an adequate guide either to testable analytical conclusions or to formulation of long-term policy.

THE TAKE-OFF INTO SELF-SUSTAINED GROWTH*

by **W. W. Rostow**

THE PURPOSE OF THIS ARTICLE IS TO EXPLORE THE FOLLOWING hypothesis : that the process of economic growth can usefully be regarded as centering on a relatively brief time interval of two or three decades when the economy and the society of which it is a part transform themselves in such ways that economic growth is, subsequently, more or less automatic. This decisive transformation is here called the take-off.[1]

The take-off is defined as the interval during which the rate of investment increases in such a way that real output *per capita* rises and this initial increase carries with it radical changes in production techniques and the disposition of income flows which perpetuate the new scale of investment and perpetuate thereby the rising trend in *per capita* output. Initial changes in method require that some group in the society have the will and the authority to install and diffuse new production techniques ;[2] and a perpetuation of the growth process requires that such a leading group expand in authority and that the society

* *The Economic Journal*, March 1956. Reprinted by permission of the Royal Economic Society and the author. The author wishes to acknowledge with thanks the helpful criticisms of an earlier draft by G. Baldwin, F. Bator, K. Berrill, A. Enthoven, E. E. Hagen, C. P. Kindleberger, L. Lefeber, W. Malenbaum, E. S. Mason and M. F. Millikan.

[1] This argument is a development from the line of thought presented in *The Process of Economic Growth* (New York, 1952), Chapter 4, especially pp. 102-05. The concept of three stages in the growth process centring on the take-off is defined and used for prescriptive purposes in *An American Policy in Asia* (New York, 1955), Chapter 7.

[2] We shall set aside in this article the question of how new production techniques are generated from pure science and invention, a procedure which is legitimate, since we are examining the growth process in national (or regional) economies over relatively short periods. We shall largely set aside also the question of population pressure and the size and quality of the working force, again because of the short period under examination ; although, evidently, even over short periods, the rate of population increase will help determine the level of investment required to yield rising output *per capita* (see below, p. 158, note 2). By and

as a whole respond to the impulses set up by the initial changes, including the potentialities for external economies. Initial changes in the scale and direction of finance flows are likely to imply a command over income flows by new groups or institutions; and a perpetuation of growth requires that a high proportion of the increment to real income during the take-off period be returned to productive investment. The take-off requires, therefore, a society prepared to respond actively to new possibilities for productive enterprise; and it is likely to require political, social and institutional changes which will both perpetuate an initial increase in the scale of investment and result in the regular acceptance and absorption of innovations.

In short, this article is an effort to clarify the economics of industrial revolution when an industrial revolution is conceived of narrowly with respect to time and broadly with respect to changes in production functions.

THREE STAGES IN THE GROWTH PROCESS

The historian examining the story of a particular national economy is inevitably impressed by the long-period continuity of events. Like other forms of history, economic history is a seamless web. The cotton-textile developments in Britain of the 1780s and 1790s have a history stretching back for a half century at least; the United States of the 1840s and 1850s had been preparing itself for industrialization since the 1790s, at the latest; Russia's remarkable development during the two pre-1914 decades goes back to 1861 for its foundations, if not to the Napoleonic Wars or to Peter the Great; the remarkable economic spurt of Meiji Japan is incomprehensible outside the context of economic developments in the latter half of the Tokugawa era; and so on. It is wholly legitimate that the historian's influence should be to extend the story of the British industrial revolution back into the seventeenth century and forward far into the nineteenth century; and that

large, this article is concerned with capital formation at a particular stage of economic growth; and of the array of propensities defined in *The Process of Economic Growth* it deals only with the propensity to accept innovations and the propensity to seek material advance, the latter in relation to the supply of finance only.

Heckscher should embrace Sweden's transition in a chapter entitled, 'The Great Transformation (1815–1914)'.[1] From the perspective of the economic historian the isolation of a take-off period is, then, a distinctly arbitrary process. It is to be judged, like such other arbitrary exercises as the isolation of business cycles and secular trends, on whether it illuminates more of the economic process than it conceals; and it should be used, if accepted, as a way of giving a rough framework of order to the inordinately complicated biological problem of growth rather than as an exact model of reality.

There is difficulty in this set of conceptions for the statistical analyst of economic development as well as for the historian. At first sight the data mobilized, for example, by Clark, Kuznets, Buchanan and Ellis exhibit a continuum of degrees of development both within countries over time and as among countries at a given period of time, with no *prima facie* case for a clearly marked watershed in the growth process.[2] In part this statistical result arises from the fact that historical data on national product and its components are only rarely available for an economy until after it has passed into a stage of more or less regular growth; that is, after the take-off. In part it arises from the fact that, by and large, these authors are more concerned with different levels of *per capita* output (or welfare)—and the structural characteristics that accompany them—than with the growth process itself. The data they mobilize do not come to grips with the inner determinants of growth. The question raised here is not how or why levels of output *per capita* have differed but rather how it has come about that particular economies have moved from stagnation—to slow, piecemeal advance—to a situation where growth was the normal economic condition. Our criterion here is

[1] E. F. Heckscher, *An Economic History of Sweden*, (Tr.) G. Ohlin, (Cambridge, Massachusetts, 1954), Chapter 6.

[2] Colin Clark, *The Conditions of Economic Progress* (London, 1951, second edition); Simon Kuznets, 'International Differences in Capital Formation and Financing' in *Capital Formation and Economic Growth*—A Report of the National Bureau of Economic Research, New York, Princeton University Press, 1955, pp. 19-106; Norman Buchanan and Howard Ellis, *Approaches to Economic Development* (Twentieth Century Fund, New York, 1955). See also the United Nations data presented as a frontispiece to H. F. Williamson and John A. Buttrick, *Economic Development* (New York, 1954).

not the absolute level of output *per capita* but its rate of change.

In this argument the sequence of economic development is taken to consist of three periods : a long period (up to a century or, conceivably, more) when the preconditions for take-off are established ; the take-off itself, defined within two or three decades ; and a long period when growth becomes normal and relatively automatic. These three divisions would, of course, not exclude the possibility of growth giving way to secular stagnation or decline in the long term. It would exclude from the concept of a growing economy, however, one which experiences a brief spurt of expansion which is not subsequently sustained ; for example, the United States industrial boom of the War of 1812 or the ill-fated spurts of certain Latin American economies in the early stages of their modern history.

Take-offs have occurred in two quite different types of societies ; and, therefore, the process of establishing preconditions for take-off has varied. In the first and most general case the achievement of preconditions for take-off required major change in political and social structure and, even, in effective cultural values. In the vocabulary of *The Process of Economic Growth*, important changes in the propensities preceded the take-off. In the second case take-off was delayed not by political, social and cultural obstacles but by the high (and even expanding) levels of welfare that could be achieved by exploiting land and natural resources. In this second case take-off was initiated by a more narrowly economic process, as, for example, in the northern United States, Australia and, perhaps, Sweden. In the vocabulary of *The Process of Economic Growth*, the take-off was initiated primarily by a change in the yields ; although subsequent growth brought with it changes in the propensities as well. As one would expect in the essentially biological field of economic growth, history offers mixed as well as pure cases.

In the first case the process of establishing preconditions for take-off might be generalized in impressionistic terms as follows :

We start with a reasonably stable and traditional society containing an economy mainly agricultural, using more or less unchanging production methods, saving and investing productively little more than is required to meet depreciation. Usually from outside the society, but sometimes out of its own dynamics, comes the idea that economic progress is possible; and this idea spreads within the established *élite* or, more usually, in some disadvantaged group whose lack of status does not prevent the exercise of some economic initiative. More often than not the economic motives for seeking economic progress converge with some non-economic motive, such as the desire for increased social power and prestige, national pride, political ambition and so on. Education, for some at least, broadens and changes to suit the needs of modern economic activity. New enterprising men come forward willing to mobilize savings and to take risks in pursuit of profit, notably in commerce. The commercial markets for agricultural products, domestic handicrafts and consumption-goods imports widen. Institutions for mobilizing capital appear; or they expand from primitive levels in the scale, surety and time horizon for loans. Basic capital is expanded, notably in transport and communications, often to bring to market raw materials in which other nations have an economic interest, often financed by foreign capital. And, here and there, modern manufacturing enterprise appears, usually in substitution for imports.

Since public-health measures are enormously productive in their early stages of application and, as innovations go, meet relatively low resistance in most cultures, the death rate may fall and the population begin to rise, putting pressure on the food supply and the institutional structure of agriculture, creating thereby an economic depressant or stimulus (or both in turn), depending on the society's response.[1]

The rate of productive investment may rise up to 5 per cent of national income;[2] but this is unlikely to do much more than

[1] Historically, disruptive population pressure has been generated in pretake-off societies not only by the easy spread of highly productive measures of public health but also by the easy acceptance of high-yield new crops, permitting a fragmentation of land-holdings, earlier marriage and a rise in the birth rate; e.g., Ireland and China.

[2] The relation of the investment rate to growth depends, of course, on the rate of population rise. With stagnant population or slow rise a 5 per cent investment rate could yield substantial growth in real output *per capita*, as indeed it did in pre-1914 France. On the other hand, as noted below (pp. 170-71) investment rates much higher than 5 per cent can persist in primitive economies which lack the preconditions for growth,

keep ahead of the population increase. And, in general, all this activity proceeds on a limited basis, within an economy and a society still mainly characterized by traditional low-productivity techniques and by old values and institutions which developed in conjunction with them. The rural proportion of the population is likely to stand at 75 per cent or over.

In the second case, of naturally wealthy nations, with a highly favourable balance between population and natural resources and with a population deriving by emigration from reasonably acquisitive cultures, the story of establishing the preconditions differs mainly in that there is no major problem of overcoming traditional values inappropriate to economic growth and the inert or resistant institutions which incorporate them ; there is less difficulty in developing an *élite* effective in the investment process ; and there is no population problem.[1] Technically, much the same slow-moving process of change occurs at high (and, perhaps, even expanding) levels of *per capita* output, and with an extensive growth of population and output still based on rich land and other natural resources. Take-off fails to occur mainly because the comparative advantage of exploiting productive land and other natural resources delays the time when self-reinforcing industrial growth can profitably get under way.[2]

based on capital imports, without initiating sustained growth. For some useful arithmetic on the scale and composition of capital requirements in a growing economy with a 1 per cent population increase see A. K. Cairncross, *Home and Foreign Investment* (Cambridge, 1953), Chapter 1.

[1] Even in these cases there have often been significant political and social restraints which had to be reduced or eliminated before take-off could occur; for example, in Canada, the Argentine and the American South.

[2] Theoretically, such fortunate societies could continue to grow in *per capita* output until diminishing returns damped down their progress. Theoretically, they might even go on as growing non-industrial societies, absorbing agricultural innovations which successfully countered diminishing returns. Something like this process might describe, for example, the rich agricultural regions of the United States. But, in general, it seems to be the case that the conditions required to sustain a progressive increase in agricultural productivity will also lead on to self-reinforcing industrial growth. This result emerges not merely from the fact that many agricultural improvements are labour-saving, and that industrial employment can be stimulated by the availability of surplus labour and is required to draw it off ; it also derives from the fact that the production and use of materials and devices which raise agricultural productivity in themselves stimulate the growth of a self-sustaining industrial sector.

The beginning of take-off can usually be traced to a particular sharp stimulus. The stimulus may take the form of a political revolution which affects directly the balance of social power and effective values, the character of economic institutions, the distribution of income, the pattern of investment outlays and the proportion of potential innovations actually applied; that is, it operates through the propensities. It may come about through a technological (including transport) innovation, which sets in motion a chain of secondary expansion in modern sectors and has powerful potential external economy effects which the society exploits. It may take the form of a newly favourable international environment, such as the opening of British and French markets to Swedish timber in the 1860s or a sharp relative rise in export prices and/or large new capital imports, as in the case of the United States from the late 1840s, Canada and Russia from the mid-1890s; but it may also come as a challenge posed by an unfavourable shift in the international environment, such as a sharp fall in terms of trade (or a war-time blockade of foreign trade) requiring the rapid development of manufactured import substitutes, as in the case of the Argentine and Australia in the 1930s and during the Second World War.[1] All these latter cases raise sharply the profitability of certain lines of enterprise and can be regarded as changes in the yields.

What is essential here, however, is not the form of stimulus but the fact that the prior development of the society and its economy result in a positive, sustained, and self-reinforcing, response to it: the result is not a once-over change in production functions or in the volume of investment, but a higher proportion of potential innovations accepted in a more or less regular flow, and a higher rate of investment.

In short, the forces which have yielded marginal bursts of activity now expand and become quantitatively significant as rapid-moving trends. New industries expand at high rates, yielding profits which are substantially reinvested in new

[1] Historically, the imposition of tariffs has played an important role in take-offs, e.g., the American Tariffs of 1828 (cotton textiles) and 1841-2 (rail iron); the Russian tariffs of the 1890s, etc. Although these actions undoubtedly served to assist take-off in leading sectors, they usually reflected an energy and purpose among key entrepreneurial groups which would, in any case, probably have done the trick.

capacity; and their expansion induces a more general expansion of the modern sectors of the economy where a high rate of plough-back prevails. The institutions for mobilizing savings (including the fiscal and sometimes the capital-levy activities of government) increase in scope and efficiency. New techniques spread in agriculture as well as in industry, as increasing numbers of persons are prepared to accept them and the deep changes they bring to ways of life. A new class of businessmen (usually private, sometimes public servants) emerges and acquires control over the key decisions determining the use of savings. New possibilities for export develop and are exploited; new import requirements emerge. The economy exploits hitherto unused backlogs in technique and natural resources. Although there are a few notable exceptions, all this momentum historically attracted substantial foreign capital.

The use of aggregative national-income terms evidently reveals little of the process which is occurring. It is nevertheless useful to regard as a necessary but not sufficient condition for the take-off the fact that the proportion of net investment to national income (or net national product) rises from (say) 5 per cent to over 10 per cent, definitely outstripping the likely population pressure (since under the assumed take-off circumstances the capital-output ratio is low),[1] and yielding a

[1] The author is aware of the substantial ambiguities which overhang the concept of the capital-output ratio and, especially, of the dangers of applying an overall aggregate measure. But since the arithmetic of economic growth requires some such concept, implicitly or explicitly, we had better refine the tool rather than abandon it. In the early stages of economic development two contrary forces operate on the capital-output ratio. On the one hand there is a vast requirement of basic overhead capital in transport, power, education, etc. Here, due mainly to the long period over which such investment yields its return, the apparent (short-run) capital-output ratio is high. On the other hand, there are generally large unexploited backlogs of known techniques and available natural resources to be put to work; and these backlogs make for a low capital-output ratio. We can assume formally a low capital-output ratio for the take-off period because we are assuming that the preconditions have been created, including a good deal of social overhead capital. In fact, the aggregate marginal capital-output ratio is likely to be kept up during the take-off by the requirement of continuing large outlays for overhead items which yield their return only over long periods. Nevertheless, a ratio of 3–1 or 3·5–1 on average seems realistic as a rough bench-mark until we have learned more about capital-output ratios on a sectoral basis.

distinct rise in real output *per capita*. Whether real consumption *per capita* rises depends on the pattern of income distribution and population pressure, as well as on the magnitude, character and productivity of investment itself.

As indicated in the accompanying table, I believe it possible to identify at least tentatively such take-off periods for a number of countries which have passed into the stage of growth.

Some Tentative, Approximate Take-off Dates

Country	Take-off	Country	Take-off
Great Britain ..	1783–1802	Russia	1890–1914
France	1830–1860	Canada	1896–1914
Belgium	1833–1860	Argentine[3] ..	1935–
United States[1] ..	1843–1860	Turkey[4]	1937–
Germany	1850–1873	India[5]	1952–
Sweden	1868–1890	China[5]	1952–
Japan[2]	1878–1900		

[1] The American take-off is here viewed as the upshot of two different periods of expansion: the first, that of the 1840s, marked by railway and manufacturing development, mainly confined to the East—this occurred while the West and South digested the extensive agricultural expansion of the previous decade; the second the great railway push into the Middle West during the 1850s marked by a heavy inflow of foreign capital. By the opening of the Civil War the American economy of North and West, with real momentum in its heavy-industry sector, is judged to have taken off.

[2] Lacking adequate data, there is some question about the timing of the Japanese take-off. Some part of the post-1868 period was certainly, by the present set of definitions, devoted to firming up the preconditions for take-off. By 1914 the Japanese economy had certainly taken off. The question is whether the period from about 1878 to the Sino-Japanese War in the mid-1890s is to be regarded as the completion of the preconditions or as take-off. On present evidence, I incline to the latter view.

[3] In one sense the Argentine economy began its take-off during the First World War. But by and large, down to the pit of the post-1929 depression, the growth of its modern sector, stimulated during the war, tended to slacken; and, like a good part of the Western World, the Argentine sought during the 1920s to return to a pre-1914 normalcy. It was not until the mid-1930s that a sustained take-off was inaugurated, which by and large can now be judged to have been successful despite the structural vicissitudes of that economy.

[4] Against the background of industrialization measures inaugurated in the mid-1930s the Turkish economy has exhibited remarkable

The third stage is, of course, the long, fluctuating story of sustained economic progress. Overall capital per head increases as the economy matures. The structure of the economy changes increasingly. The initial key industries, which sparked the take-off, decelerate as diminishing returns operate on the original set of industrial tricks and the original band of pioneering entrepreneurs give way to less single-minded industrial leaders in those sectors; but the average rate of growth is maintained by a succession of new, rapidly growing sectors, with a new set of pioneering leaders. The proportion of the population in rural pursuits declines. The economy finds its (changing) place in the international economy. The society makes such terms as it will with the requirements for maximizing modern and efficient production, balancing off, as it will, the new values against those retarding values which persist with deeper roots, or adapting the latter in such ways as to support rather than retard the growth process. This sociological calculus interweaves with basic resource endowments to determine the pace of deceleration.

It is with the problems and vicissitudes of such growing economies of the third stage (and especially with cyclical fluctuations and the threat of chronic unemployment) that the bulk of modern theoretical economics is concerned, including much recent work on the formal properties of growth models. The student of history and of contemporary underdeveloped areas[1] is more likely to be concerned with the

momentum in the past five years founded in the increase in agricultural income and productivity. It still remains to be seen whether these two surges, conducted under quite different national policies, will constitute a transition to self-sustaining growth, and whether Turkey can overcome its current structural problems.

[5] As noted in the text it is still too soon (for quite different reasons) to judge either the Indian or Chinese Communist take-off efforts successful.

[1] A number of so-called underdeveloped areas may have, in fact, either passed through the take-off process or are in the midst of it, e.g., Mexico, Brazil, Turkey, the Argentine and India. I would commend for consideration—certainly no more until the concept of take-off is disproved or verified—the dropping of the concept of 'underdeveloped areas' and the substitution for it of a quadripartite distinction among economies: traditional; pretake-off; take-off and growing. Against the background of this set of distinctions we might then consider systematically two separable questions now often confused. First, the stage of growth, as among growing economies. It is legitimate to regard Mexico and the

economics of the first two stages; that is the economics of the preconditions and the take-off. If we are to have a serious theory of economic growth or (more likely) some useful theories about economic growth, they must obviously seek to embrace these two early stages—and notably the economics of the take-off. The balance of this article is designed to mobilize tentatively and in a preliminary way what an economic historian can contribute to the economics of take-off.

The Take-off Defined and Isolated

There are several problems of choice involved in defining the take-off with precision. We might begin with one arbitrary definition and consider briefly the two major alternatives.

For the present purposes the take-off is defined as requiring all three of the following related conditions:

(*a*) a rise in the rate of productive investment from (say) 5 per cent or less to over 10 per cent of national income (or net national product);

(*b*) the development of one or more substantial manufacturing[1] sectors, with a high rate of growth;

(*c*) the existence or quick emergence of a political, social and institutional framework which exploits the impulses to expansion in the modern sector and the potential external economy effects of the take-off and gives to growth an on-going character.

United States, Great Britain and Australia, France and Japan, as growing economies, although they stand at very different points along their national growth curves, where the degree of progress might be measured by some kind of index of output (or capital) per head. Second, the foreseeable long-run potential of growing economies. Over the long pull, even after they are 'fully developed', the *per capita* output levels that different economies are likely to achieve will undoubtedly vary greatly, depending notably on resource endowments in relation to population. The arraying of levels of output *per capita* for different economies, now conventional, fails to distinguish these three elements; that is, the current rate of growth; the stage of growth; and the foreseeable horizon for growth.

[1] In this context 'manufacturing' is taken to include the processing of agricultural products or raw materials by modern methods; e.g., timber in Sweden; meat in Australia; dairy products in Denmark. The dual requirement of a 'manufacturing' sector is that its processes set in motion a chain of further modern sector requirements and that its expansion provides the potentiality of external economy effects.

The third condition implies a considerable capability to mobilize capital from domestic sources. Some take-offs have occurred with virtually no capital imports ; e.g., Britain and Japan. Some take-offs have had a high component of foreign capital ; e.g., the United States, Russia and Canada. But some countries have imported large quantities of foreign capital for long periods, which undoubtedly contributed to creating the preconditions for take-off, without actually initiating take-off ; e.g., the Argentine before 1914, Venezuela down to recent years, the Belgian Congo currently. In short, whatever the role of capital imports, the preconditions for take-off include an initial ability to mobilize domestic savings productively, as well as a structure which subsequently permits a high marginal rate of savings.

This definition is designed to isolate the early stage when industrialization takes hold rather than the later stage when industrialization becomes a more massive and statistically more impressive phenomenon. In Britain, for example, there is no doubt that it was between 1815 and 1850 that industrialization fully took hold. If the criterion chosen for take-off was the period of most rapid overall industrial growth, or the period when large-scale industry matured, all our take-off dates would have to be set forward ; Britain, for example, to 1819–48 ; the United States to 1868–93 ; Sweden to 1890–1920 ; Japan to 1900–20 ; Russia to 1928–40. The earlier dating is chosen here because it is believed, on present (often inadequate) evidence, that the decisive transformations (including a decisive shift in the investment rate) occur in the first industrial phases ; and later industrial maturity can be directly traced back to foundations laid in these first phases.

This definition is also designed to rule out from the take-off the quite substantial economic progress which can occur in an economy before a truly self-reinforcing growth process gets under way. British economic expansion between (say) 1750 and 1783, Russian economic expansion between (say) 1861 and 1890, Canadian economic expansion between 1867 and the mid-1890s—such periods—for which there is an equivalent in the economic history of almost every growing economy—were marked by extremely important, even decisive, developments. The transport network expanded, and with it both internal and external commerce ; new institutions for mobilizing savings were developed ; a class of commercial and even industrial entrepreneurs began to emerge ; industrial enterprise on a limited scale (or in limited sectors) grew. And yet, however essential these pretake-off periods were for later development, their scale and momentum were insufficient to transform the economy radically or, in some cases, to outstrip population growth and to yield an increase in *per capita* output.

With a sense of the considerable violence done to economic history, I am here seeking to isolate a period when the scale of productive economic activity reaches a critical level and produces changes which lead to a massive and progressive structural transformation in economies and the societies of which they are a part, better viewed as changes in kind than merely in degree.

Evidence on Investment Rates in the Take-off

The case for the concept of take-off hinges, in part, on quantitative evidence on the scale and productivity of investment in relation to population growth. Here, as noted earlier, we face a difficult problem ; investment data are not now available historically for early stages in economic history. Following is such case as there is for regarding the shift from a productive investment rate of about 5 per cent of Net National Product (NNP) to 10 per cent or more as central to the process.[1]

[1] In his important article, 'Economic Development with Unlimited Supplies of Labour,' reprinted in the present volume, pp. 400-49, W. Arthur Lewis indicates a similar spread as defining the transition to economic growth :

'The central problem in the theory of economic development is to understand the process by which a community which was previously saving and investing 4 or 5 per cent of its national income or less converts itself into an economy where voluntary saving is running at about 12–15 per cent of national income or more. This is the central problem because the central fact of economic development is rapid capital accumulation (including knowledge and skills with capital). We cannot explain any 'industrial' revolution (as the economic historians pretend to do) until we can explain why saving increased relatively to national income.'

Presumably Mr Lewis based this range on empirical observation of contemporary 'underdeveloped' areas on which some data are presented below. As in note 2, pp. 158-9 above, it should be emphasized that the choice of investment proportions to symbolize the transition to growth hinges on the assumptions made about the rate of population increase.

A Prima Facie *Case*

If we take the aggregate marginal capital-output ratio for an economy in its early stage of economic development at 3·5–1 and if we assume, as is not abnormal, a population rise of 1–1·5 per cent per annum it is clear that something between 3·5 and 5·25 per cent of NNP must be regularly invested if NNP *per capita* is to be sustained. An increase of 2 per cent per annum in NNP *per capita* requires, under these assumptions, that something between 10·5 and 12·5 per cent of NNP be regularly invested. By definition and assumption, then, a transition from relatively stagnant to substantial, regular rise in NNP *per capita*, under typical population conditions, requires that the proportion of national product productively invested move from somewhere in the vicinity of 5 per cent to something in the vicinity of 10 per cent.

The Swedish Case

In the appendix to his paper on international differences in capital formation, cited above, Kuznets gives gross and net capital formation figures in relation to gross and net national product for a substantial group of countries where reasonably good statistical data exist. Excepting Sweden, these data do not go back clearly to pretake-off stages.[1] The

[1] The Danish data are on the margin. They begin with the decade 1870-79, probably the first decade of take-off itself. They show net and gross domestic capital formation rates well over 10 per cent. In view of the sketch of the Danish economy presented in Kjeld Bjerke's 'Preliminary Estimates of the Danish National Product from 1870-1950' (Preliminary paper mimeographed for 1953 Conference of the International Association for Research on Income and Wealth), pp. 32-4, it seems likely that further research would identify the years 1830-70 as a period when the preconditions were actively established, 1870-1900 as a period of take-off. This view is supported by scattered and highly approximate estimates of Danish National Wealth which exhibit a remarkable surge in capital formation between 1864 and 1884.

Estimates of National Wealth in Denmark

	1,000 millions of kroner	Source
1864	3·5	Falbe-Hansen, *Danmarks statistik*, 1885.
1884	6·5	ibid.
1899	7·2	Tax-commission of 1903.
1909	10·0	Jens Warming, *Danmarks statistik*, 1913.
1927	24·0	Jens Warming, *Danmarks erhvervsor samfundsliv*, 1930.

Swedish data begin in the decade 1861–70; and the Swedish take-off is to be dated from the latter years of the decade.

Kuznets' table of calculations for Sweden follows:

Decade	DGCF[1] as percentage of GNP[2]	DNCF[3] as percentage of NNP	Depreciation to DGCF (percentage)
1861–70	5·8	3·5	(42)
1871–80	8·8	5·3	(42)
1881–90	10·8	6·6	(42)
1891–1900	13·7	8·1	43·9
1901–10	18·0	11·6	40·0
1911–20	20·2	13·5	38·3
1921–30	19·0	11·4	45·2

Note (Kuznets): Based on estimates in Eric Lindahl, Einan Dahlgren and Karin Kock, *National Income of Sweden*, 1861–1930 (London: P. J. Kingston, 1937), Parts One and Two, particularly the details in Part Two.

These underlying totals of capital formation exclude changes in inventories.

While gross totals are directly from the volumes referred to above, depreciation for the first three decades was not given. We assumed that it formed 42 per cent of gross domestic capital formation.

The Canadian Case

The data developed by O. J. Firestone[4] for Canada indicates a similar transition for net capital formation in its take-off

Estimates of National Wealth in Denmark—contd.

	1,000 millions of kroner	Source
1939	28·8	Economic expert committee of 1943, *ϕkonomiske efterkrigsproblemer*, 1945.
1950	54·5	N. Banke, N. P. Jacobsen og Vedel-Petersen, *Danske erhvervsliv*, 1951.

(Furnished in correspondence by Einar Cohn and Kjeld Bjerke.) It should again be emphasized, however, that we are dealing with a hypothesis whose empirical foundations are still fragmentary.

[1] DGCF: domestic gross capital formation. (Ed.)

[2] GNP: gross national product. (Ed.)

[3] DNCF: domestic net capital formation. (Ed.)

[4] O. J. Firestone, *Canada's Economic Development, 1867-1952, with Special Reference to Changes in the Country's National Product and National Wealth*, paper prepared for the International Association for

(say, 1896–1914) ; but the gross investment proportion in the period from Confederation to the mid-nineties was higher than appears to have marked other periods when the preconditions were established, possibly due to investment in the railway net, abnormally large for a nation of Canada's population, and to relatively heavy foreign investment, even before the great capital import boom of the pre-1914 decade :

Canada : Gross and Net Investment in Durable Physical Assets as Percentage of Gross and Net National Expenditure (for Selected Years)

	GCF/GNP	NCF/NNP	Capital consumption as percentage of gross investment
1870 ..	15·0	7·1	56·2
1900 ..	13·1	4·0	72·5
1920 ..	16·6	10·6	41·3
1929 ..	23·0	12·1	53·3
1952 ..	16·8	9·3	49·7

The Pattern of Contemporary Evidence in General[1]

In the years after 1945 the number of countries for which reasonably respectable national income (or product) data exist has grown ; and with such data there have developed some tolerable savings and investment estimates for countries at different stages of the growth process. Within the category of nations usually grouped as 'underdeveloped' one can distinguish four types :[2]

Research in Income and Wealth, 1953, to which Mr Firestone has kindly funished me certain revisions. By 1900 Canada already had about 18,000 miles of railway line ; but the territory served had been developed to a limited degree only. By 1900 Canada already had a net balance of foreign indebtedness over $1 billion. Although this figure was almost quadrupled in the next two decades, capital imports represented an important increment to domestic capital sources from the period of Confederation down to the pre-1914 Canadian boom, which begins in the mid-1890s.

[1] I am indebted to Mr Everett Hagen for mobilizing the statistical data in this section, except where otherwise indicated.

[2] The percentages given are of net capital formation to net domestic product. The latter is the product net of depreciation of the geographic area. It includes the value of output produced in the area, regardless of whether the income flows abroad. Since indirect business taxes are not deducted, it tends to be larger than national income ; hence the percentages are lower than if national income was used as the denominator in computing them.

(*a*) *Pretake-off economies*, where the apparent savings and investment rates, including limited net capital imports, probably come to under 5 per cent of net national product. In general, data for such countries are not satisfactory, and one's judgement that capital formation is low must rest on fragmentary data and partially subjective judgement. Examples are Ethiopia, Kenya, Thailand, Cambodia, Afghanistan and perhaps Indonesia.[1]

(*b*) *Economies attempting take-off*, where the apparent savings and investment rates, including limited net capital imports, have risen over 5 per cent of net national product.[2] For example, Mexico (1950) NCF/NDP[3] 7·2 per cent; Chile (1950) NCF/NDP 9·5 per cent; Panama (1950) NCF/NDP 7·5 per cent; Philippines (1952) NCF/NDP 6·4 per cent; Puerto Rico (1952) NCF(Private)/NDP 7·6 per cent; India (1953) NCF/NDP, perhaps about 7 per cent. Whether the take-off period will, in fact, be successful remains in most of these cases still to be seen.

(*c*) *Growing economies*, where the apparent savings and investment rates, including limited net capital imports, have reached 10 per cent or over; for example, Colombia (1950) NCF/NDP, 16·3 per cent.

(*d*) *Enclave economies*. (1) cases where the apparent savings and investment rates, including substantial net capital imports, have reached 10 per cent or over, but the domestic precondi-

[1] The Office of Intelligence Research of the Department of State, Washington, D.C., gives the following estimated ratios of investment (presumably gross) to GNP in its Report No. 6672 of 25 August 1954, p. 3, based on latest data available to that point, for countries which would probably fall in the pretake-off category:

Afghanistan ..	.. 5 per cent	Pakistan ..	.. 6 per cent
Ceylon ..	.. 5 per cent	Indonesia ..	.. 5 per cent

[2] The Department of State estimates (ibid.) for economies which are either attempting take-off or which have, perhaps, passed into a stage of regular growth include:

Argentine ..	13 per cent	Colombia ..	14 per cent
Brazil	14 per cent	Philippines ..	8 per cent
Chile	11 per cent	Venezuela ..	23 per cent

Venezuela has been for some time an 'enclave economy', with a high investment rate concentrated in a modern export sector whose growth did not generate general economic momentum in the Venezuelan economy; but in the past few years Venezuela may have moved over into the category of economies experiencing an authentic take-off.

[3] NCF: net capital formation; NDP: net domestic product. (Ed.).

tions for sustained growth have not been achieved. These economies, associated with major export industries, lack the third condition for take-off suggested above (p. 164). They include the Belgian Congo (1951) NCF/NDP 21·7 per cent; Southern Rhodesia (1950) GCF/GDP[1] 45·5 per cent, (1952) GCF/GDP 45·4 per cent. (2) Cases where net capital exports are large. For example, Burma (1938) NCF/NDP, 7·1 per cent; net capital exports/NDP, 11·5 per cent; Nigeria (1950–51) NCF/NDP, 5·1 per cent; net capital exports/NDP, 5·6 per cent.

The Cases of India and Communist China

The two outstanding contemporary cases of economies attempting purposefully to take-off are India and Communist China, both operating under national plans. The Indian First Five Year Plan projects the growth process envisaged under assumptions similar to those in paragraph 1, p. 167, above. The Indian Planning Commission estimated investment as 5 per cent of NNP in the initial year of the plan, 1950–51.[2] Using a 3/1 marginal capital-output ratio, they envisaged a marginal savings rate of 20 per cent for the First Five Year Plan, a 50 per cent rate thereafter, down to 1968–9, when the average proportion of income invested would level off at 20 per cent of NNP. As one would expect, the sectoral composition of this process is not fully worked out in the initial plan; but the Indian effort may well be remembered in economic history as the first take-off defined *ex ante* in national product terms.

We know less of the Chinese Communist First Five Year Plan than we do of the concurrent Indian effort, despite the recent publication of production goals for some of the major sectors of the Chinese economy.[3] Roundly, it would appear that, from a (probably) negative investment rate in 1949, the Chinese Communist regime had succeeded by 1952 in achieving a gross rate of about 12 per cent; a net rate of about 7 per cent.

[1] GCF: gross capital formation; GDP: gross domestic product. (Ed.)

[2] Government of India, Planning Commission, *The First Five Year Plan*, 1952, Vol. I, Chapter 1.

[3] These comments are based on the work of Alexander Eckstein and the author in *The Prospects for Communist China* (New York and London, 1954), Part 5, pp. 222-4. The statistical calculations are the work of Mr Eckstein.

On arbitrary assumptions, which have a distinct upward bias, these figures can be projected forward for a decade yielding rates of about 20 per cent gross, 17 per cent net by 1962.

So far as the aggregates are concerned, what we can say is that the Indian planned figures fall well within the range of *prima facie* hypothesis and historical experience, if India in fact fulfils the full requirements for take-off, notably the achievement of industrial momentum. The Chinese Communist figures reflect accurately an attempt to force the pace of history, evident throughout Peking's domestic policy, whose viability is still to be demonstrated. In particular, Peking's agricultural policy may fail to produce the minimum structural balance required for a successful take-off, requiring radical revision of investment allocations and policy objectives at a later stage.

We have, evidently, much still to learn about the quantitative aspects of this problem ; and, especially, much further quantitative research and imaginative manipulation of historical evidence will be required before the hypothesis tentatively advanced here can be regarded as proved or disproved. What we can say is that *prima facie* thought and a scattering of historical and contemporary evidence suggests that it is not unreasonable to consider the take-off as including as a necessary but not sufficient condition a quantitative transition in the proportion of income productively invested of the kind indicated here.

The Inner Structure of the Take-off

Whatever the importance and virtue of viewing the take-off in aggregative terms—embracing national output, the proportion of output invested, and an aggregate marginal capital-output ratio—that approach tells us relatively little of what actually happens and of the causal processes at work in a take-off ; nor is the investment-rate criterion conclusive.

Following the definition of take-off (pp. 164-6, above), we must consider not merely how a rise in the investment rate is brought about, from both supply and demand perspectives, but how rapidly growing manufacturing sectors emerged and imparted their primary and secondary growth impulses to the economy.

Perhaps the most important thing to be said about the behaviour of these variables in historical cases of take-off is that they have assumed many different forms. There is no single pattern. The rate and productivity of investment can rise, and the consequences of this rise can be diffused into a self-reinforcing general growth process by many different technical and economic routes, under the aegis of many different political, social and cultural settings, driven along by a wide variety of human motivations.

The purpose of the following paragraphs is to suggest briefly, and by way of illustration only, certain elements of both uniformity and variety in the variables whose movement has determined the inner structure of the take-off.

The Supply of Loanable Funds

By and large, the loanable funds required to finance the take-off have come from two types of sources: from shifts in the control over income flows, including income-distribution changes and capital imports;[1] and from the plough-back of profits in rapidly expanding particular sectors.

The notion of economic development occurring as the result of income shifts from those who will spend (hoard[2] or lend) less productively to those who will spend (or lend) more productively is one of the oldest and most fundamental notions in economics. It is basic to the *Wealth of Nations*,[3] and it is applied by W. Arthur Lewis in his recent elaboration of the classical model.[4] Lewis builds his model in part on an expansion

[1] Mr Everett Hagen has pointed out that the increase in savings may well arise from a shift in the propensity to save, as new and exciting horizons open up, rather than merely from a shift of income to groups with a higher (but static) propensity to save. He may well be right. This is, evidently, a matter for further investigation.

[2] Hoarding can, of course, be helpful to the growth process by depressing consumption and freeing resources for investment if, in fact, non-hoarding persons or institutions acquire the resources and possess the will to expand productive investment. A direct transfer of income is, evidently, not required.

[3] See, especially, Smith's observations on the 'perversion' of wealth by 'prodigality'—that is, unproductive consumption expenditures—and on the virtues of 'parsimony' which transfers income to those who will increase 'the fund which is destined for the maintenance of productive hands'. Routledge edition, London, 1890, pp. 259-60.

[4] Op. cit.

of the capitalist sector, with the bulk of additional savings arising from an enlarging pool of capitalist profits.

Historically, income shifts conducive to economic development have assumed many forms. In Meiji Japan and also in Czarist Russia the substitution of government bonds for the great landholders' claim on the flow of rent payments lead to a highly Smithian redistribution of income into the hands of those with higher propensities to seek material advance and to accept innovations. In both cases the real value of the government bonds exchanged for land depreciated ; and, in general, the feudal landlords emerged with a less attractive arrangement than had first appeared to be offered. Aside from the confiscation effect, two positive impulses arose from land reform : the state itself used the flow of payments from peasants, now diverted from landlords' hands, for activity which encouraged economic development ; and a certain number of the more enterprising former landlords directly invested in commerce and industry. In contemporary India and China we can observe quite different degrees of income transfer by this route. India is relying to only a very limited extent on the elimination of large incomes unproductively spent by large landlords ; although this element figures in a small way in its programme. Communist China has systematically transferred all non-governmental pools of capital into the hands of the State, in a series of undisguised or barely disguised capital levies ; and it is drawing heavily for capital resources on the mass of middle and poor peasants who remain.[1]

In addition to confiscatory and taxation devices, which can operate effectively when the State is spending more productively than the taxed individuals, inflation has been important to several take-offs. In Britain of the late 1790s, the United States of the 1850s, Japan of the 1870s there is no doubt that capital formation was aided by price inflation, which shifted resources away from consumption to profits.

The shift of income flows into more productive hands has, of course, been aided historically not only by government fiscal measures but also by banks and capital markets. Virtually without exception, the take-off periods have been marked by

[1] *Prospects for Communist China*, Part 4.

the extension of banking institutions which expanded the supply of working capital; and in most cases also by an expansion in the range of long-range financing done by a central, formally organized, capital market.

Although these familiar capital-supply functions of the State and private institutions have been important to the take-off, it is likely to prove the case, on close examination, that a necessary condition for take-off was the existence of one or more rapidly growing sectors whose entrepreneurs (private or public) ploughed back into new capacity a very high proportion of profits. Put another way, the demand side of the investment process, rather than the supply of loanable funds, may be the decisive element in the take-off, as opposed to the period of creating the preconditions, or of sustaining growth once it is under way. The distinction is, historically, sometimes difficult to make, notably when the State simultaneously acts both to mobilize supplies of finance and to undertake major entrepreneurial acts. There are, nevertheless, periods in economic history when quite substantial improvements in the machinery of capital supply do not, in themselves, initiate a take-off, but fall within the period when the preconditions are created: e.g., British banking developments in the century before 1783; Russian banking developments before 1890, etc.

One extremely important version of the plough-back process has taken place through foreign trade. Developing economies have created from their natural resources major export industries; and the rapid expansion in exports has been used to finance the import of capital equipment and to service the foreign debt during the take-off. United States, Russian and Canadian grain fulfilled this function, Swedish timber and pulp, Japanese silk, etc. Currently Chinese exports to the Communist Bloc, wrung at great administrative and human cost from the agricultural sector, play this decisive role. It should be noted that the development of such export sectors has not in itself guaranteed accelerated capital formation. Enlarged foreign-exchange proceeds have been used in many familiar cases to finance hoards (as in the famous case of Indian bullion imports) or unproductive consumption outlays.

It should be noted that one possible mechanism for inducing a high rate of plough-back into productive investment is a rapid expansion in the effective demand for domestically manufactured consumers' goods, which would direct into the hands of vigorous entrepreneurs an increasing proportion of income flows under circumstances which would lead them to expand their own capacity and to increase their requirements for industrial raw materials, semi-manufactured products and manufactured components.

A final element in the supply of loanable funds, is, of course, capital imports. Foreign capital has played a major role in the take-off stage of many economies: e.g., the United States, Russia, Sweden, Canada. The cases of Britain and Japan indicate, however, that it cannot be regarded as an essential condition. Foreign capital was notably useful when the construction of railways or other large overhead capital items with a long period of gestation, played an important role in the take-off. After all, whatever its strategic role, the proportion of investment required for growth which goes into industry is relatively small compared to that required for utilities, transport and the housing of enlarged urban populations. And foreign capital can be mightily useful in helping carry the burden of these overhead items either directly or indirectly.

What can we say, in general, then, about the supply of finance during the take-off period? First, as a precondition, it appears necessary that the community's surplus above the mass-consumption level does not flow into the hands of those who will sterilize it by hoarding, luxury consumption or low-productivity investment outlays. Second, as a precondition, it appears necessary that institutions be developed which provide cheap and adequate working capital. Third, as a necessary condition, it appears that one or more sectors of the economy must grow rapidly, inducing a more general industrialization process; and that the entrepreneurs in such sectors plough back a substantial proportion of their profits in further productive investment, one possible and recurrent version of the plough-back process being the investment of proceeds from a rapidly growing export sector.

The devices, confiscatory and fiscal, for ensuring the first and second preconditions have been historically various. And, as indicated below, the types of leading manufacturing sectors which have served to initiate the take-off have varied greatly. Finally, foreign capital flows have, in significant cases, proved extremely important to the take-off, notably when lumpy overhead capital construction of long gestation period was required ; but take-offs have also occurred based almost wholly on domestic sources of finance.

The Sources of Entrepreneurship

It is evident that the take-off requires the existence and the successful activity of some group in the society which accepts borrowers' risk, when such risk is so defined as to include the propensity to accept innovations. As noted above, the problem of entrepreneurship in the take-off has not been profound in a limited group of wealthy agricultural nations whose populations derived by emigration mainly from north-western Europe. There the problem of take-off was primarily economic ; and when economic incentives for industrialization emerged commercial and banking groups moved over easily into industrial entrepreneurship. In many other countries, however, the development of adequate entrepreneurship was a more searching social process.

Under some human motivation or other, a group must come to perceive it to be both possible and good to undertake acts of capital investment ; and, for their efforts to be tolerably successful, they must act with approximate rationality in selecting the directions toward which their enterprise is directed. They must not only produce growth but tolerably balanced growth. We cannot quite say that it is necessary for them to act as if they were trying to maximize profit ; for the criteria for private profit maximization do not necessarily converge with the criteria for an optimum rate and pattern of growth in various sectors.[1] But in a growing economy,

[1] For a brief discussion of this point see the author's 'Trends in the Allocation of Resources in Secular Growth', Chapter 15, *Economic Progress*, ed. Leon H. Dupriez, with the assistance of Douglas C. Hague (Louvain, 1955), pp. 378-9. For a more complete discussion see W. Fellner, 'Individual Investment Projects in Growing Economies' (mimeographed), paper presented to the Center for International Studies Social Science Research Council Conference on Economic Growth, October 1954, Cambridge, Massachusetts.

over periods longer than the business cycle, economic history is reasonably tolerant of deviations from rationality, in the sense that excess capacity is finally put to productive use. Leaving aside the question of ultimate human motivation, and assuming that the major overhead items are generated, if necessary, by some form of state initiative (including subsidy), we can say as a first approximation that some group must successfully emerge which behaves as if it were moved by the profit motive, in a dynamic economy with changing production functions ; although risk being the slippery variable, it is under such assumptions Keynes' dictum should be borne in mind : 'If human nature felt no temptation to take a chance, no satisfaction (profit apart) in constructing a factory, a railway, a mine or a farm, there might not be much investment merely as a result of cold calculation.'[1]

In this connexion it is increasingly conventional for economists to pay their respects to the Protestant ethic.[2] The historian should not be ungrateful for this light on the grey horizon of formal growth models. But the known cases of economic growth which theory must seek to explain take us beyond the orbit of Protestantism. In a world where Samurai, Parsees, Jews, North Italians, Turkish, Russian, and Chinese Civil Servants (as well as Huguenots, Scotsmen and British North-countrymen) have played the role of a leading *élite* in economic growth John Calvin should not be made to bear quite this weight. More fundamentally, allusion to a positive scale of religious or other values conducive to profit-maximizing activities is an insufficient sociological basis for this important phenomenon. What appears to be required for the emergence of such *élites* is not merely an appropriate value system but two further conditions : first, the new *élite* must feel itself denied the conventional routes to prestige and power by the traditional less acquisitive society of which it is a part ; second, the traditional society must be sufficiently flexible (or weak) to permit its members to seek material advance (or political power) as a route upwards alternative to conformity.

[1] *General Theory*, p. 150.

[2] See, for example, N. Kaldor, 'Economic Growth and Cyclical Fluctuations', *The Economic Journal*, March 1954, p. 67.

Although an *élite* entrepreneurial class appears to be required for take-off, with significant power over aggregate income flows and industrial investment decisions, most take-offs have been preceded or accompanied by radical change in agricultural techniques and market organization. By and large the agricultural entrepreneur has been the individual land-owning farmer. A requirement for take-off is, therefore, a class of farmers willing and able to respond to the possibilities opened up for them by new techniques, land-holding arrangements, transport facilities, and forms of market and credit organization. A small purposeful *élite* can go a long way in initiating economic growth; but, especially in agriculture (and to some extent in the industrial working force), a wider-based revolution in outlook must come about.[1]

Whatever further empirical research may reveal about the motives which have led men to undertake the constructive entrepreneurial acts of the take-off period, this much appears sure: these motives have varied greatly, from one society to another; and they have rarely, if ever, been motives of an unmixed material character.

Leading Sectors in the Take-off

The author has presented elsewhere the notion that the overall rate of growth of an economy must be regarded in the first instance as the consequence of differing growth rates in particular sectors of the economy, such sectoral growth rates being in part derived from certain overall demand parameters

[1] Like the population question, agriculture is mainly excluded from this analysis, which considers the take-off rather than the whole development process. Nevertheless, it should be noted that, as a matter of history, agricultural revolutions have generally preceded or accompanied the take-off. In theory we can envisage a take-off which did not require a radical improvement in agricultural productivity: if, for example, the growth and productivity of the industrial sector permitted a withering away of traditional agriculture and a substitution for it of imports. In fact, agricultural revolutions have been required to permit rapidly growing (and urbanizing) populations to be fed without exhausting foreign exchange resources in food imports or creating excessive hunger in the rural sector; and as noted at several points in this argument, agricultural revolutions have in fact played an essential and positive role, not merely by both releasing workers to the cities, and feeding them, but also by earning foreign exchange for general capital-formation purposes.

(e.g., population, consumers' income, tastes, etc.), in part from the primary and secondary effects of changing supply factors, when these are effectively exploited.[1]

On this view the sectors of an economy may be grouped in three categories:

(*a*) *Primary growth sectors*, where possibilities for innovation or for the exploitation of newly profitable or hitherto unexplored resources yield a high growth rate and set in motion expansionary forces elsewhere in the economy.

(*b*) *Supplementary growth sectors*, where rapid advance occurs in direct response to—or as a requirement of—advance in the primary growth sectors; e.g., coal, iron and engineering in relation to railroads. These sectors may have to be tracked many stages back into the economy, as the Leontief input-output models would suggest.

(*c*) *Derived growth sectors*, where advance occurs in some fairly steady relation to the growth of total real income, population, industrial production or some other overall, modestly increasing parameter. Food output in relation to population, housing in relation to family formation are classic derived relations of this order.

Very roughly speaking, primary and supplementary growth sectors derive their high momentum essentially from the introduction and diffusion of changes in the cost-supply environment (in turn, of course, partially influenced by demand changes); while the derived-growth sectors are linked essentially to changes in demand (while subject also to continuing changes in production functions of a less dramatic character).

At any period of time it appears to be true even in a mature and growing economy that forward momentum is maintained as the result of rapid expansion in a limited number of primary sectors, whose expansion has significant external economy and other secondary effects. From this perspective the behaviour of sectors during the take-off is merely a special version of the growth process in general; or, put another way, growth proceeds by repeating endlessly, in different patterns, with different leading sectors, the experience of the take-off.

[1] *Process of Economic Growth*, Chapter 4, especially pp. 97-102; and, in greater detail, 'Trends in the Allocation of Resources in Secular Growth', see above, p. 177, n. 1.

Like the take-off, long-term growth requires that the society not only generate vast quantities of capital for depreciation and maintenance, for housing and for a balanced complement of utilities and other overheads, but also a sequence of highly productive primary sectors, growing rapidly, based on new production functions. Only thus has the aggregate marginal capital-output ratio been kept low.

Once again history is full of variety: a considerable array of sectors appears to have played this key role in the take-off process.

The development of a cotton-textile industry sufficient to meet domestic requirements has not generally imparted a sufficient impulse in itself to launch a self-sustaining growth process. The development of modern cotton-textile industries in substitution for imports has, more typically, marked the pretake-off period, as for example in India, China and Mexico. There is, however, the famous exception of Britain's industrial revolution. Baines' table on raw-cotton imports and his comment on it are worth quoting, covering as they do the original leading sector in the first take-off :[1]

Rate of Increase in the Import of Cotton-wool, in Periods of Ten Years from 1741 to 1831

	per cent		per cent
1741–1751 ..	81	1791–1801 ..	67½
1751–1761	21½	1801–1811 ..	39½
1761–1771	25½	1811–1821 ..	93
1771–1781	75¾	1821–1831 ..	85
1781–1791	319½		

From 1697 to 1741, the increase was trifling : between 1741 and 1751 the manufacture, though still insignificant in extent, made a considerable spring : during the next twenty years, the increase was moderate : from 1771 to 1781, owing to the invention of the jenny and the water-frame, a rapid increase took place : in the ten years from 1781 to 1791, being those which immediately followed the invention of the mule and the expiration of Arkwrights's patent, the rate of advancement was prodigiously accelerated, being nearly 320 per cent : and from that time to the present, and especially since

[1] E. Baines, *History of the Cotton Manufacture* (London, 1835), p. 348.

the close of the war, the increase, though considerably moderated, has been rapid and steady far beyond all precedent in any other manufacture.

Why did the development of a modern factory system in cotton textiles lead on in Britain to a self-sustaining growth process, whereas it failed to do so in other cases? Part of the answer lies in the fact that, by the late eighteenth century, the preconditions for take-off in Britain were very fully developed. Progress in textiles, coal, iron and even steam power had been considerable through the eighteenth century; and the social and institutional environment was propitious. But two further technical elements helped determine the upshot. First, the British cotton-textile industry was large in relation to the total size of the economy. From its modern beginnings, but notably from the 1780s forward, a very high proportion of total cotton-textile output was directed abroad, reaching 60 per cent by the 1820s.[1] The evolution of this industry was a more massive fact, with wider secondary repercussions, than if it were simply supplying the domestic market. Industrial enterprise on this scale had secondary reactions on the development of urban areas, the demand for coal, iron and machinery, the demand for working capital and ultimately the demand for cheap transport, which powerfully stimulated industrial development in other directions.[2]

Second, a source of effective demand for rapid expansion in British cotton textiles was supplied, in the first instance, by the sharp reduction in real costs and prices which accompanied the technological developments in manufacture and the cheapening real cost of raw cotton induced by the cotton gin. In this Britain had an advantage not enjoyed by those who came later; for they merely substituted domestic for foreign-manufactured cotton textiles. The substitution

[1] The volume (official value) of British cotton goods exports rose from £355,060 in 1780 to £7,624,505 in 1802 (Baines, op. cit., p. 350). See also the calculation of R. C. O. Matthews, *A Study in Trade Cycle History* (Cambridge, 1954), pp. 127-9.

[2] If we are prepared to treat New England of the first half of the nineteenth century as a separable economy, its take-off into sustained growth can be allocated to the period, roughly, 1820-50 and, again, a disproportionately large cotton-textile industry based substantially on exports (that is, from New England to the rest of the United States) is the regional foundation for sustained growth.

undoubtedly had important secondary effects by introducing a modern industrial sector and releasing in net a pool of foreign exchange for other purposes; but there was no sharp fall in the real cost of acquiring cotton textiles and no equivalent lift in real income.

The introduction of the railroad has been historically the most powerful single initiator of take-offs.[1] It was decisive in the United States, Germany and Russia; it has played an extremely important part in the Swedish, Japanese and other cases. The railroad has had three major kinds of impact on economic growth during the take-off period. First, it has lowered internal transport costs, brought new areas and products into commercial markets and, in general, performed the Smithian function of widening the market. Second, it has been a prerequisite in many cases to the development of a major new and rapidly enlarging export sector which, in turn, has served to generate capital for internal development; as, for example, the American railroads of the 1850s, the Russian and Canadian railways before 1914. Third, and perhaps most important for the take-off itself, the development of railways has led on to the development of modern coal, iron and engineering industries. In many countries the growth of modern basic industrial sectors can be traced in the most direct way to the requirements for building and, especially, for maintaining substantial railway systems. When a society has developed deeper institutional, social and political prerequisites for take-off, the rapid growth of a railway system with these powerful triple effects has often served to lift it into self-sustaining growth. Where the prerequisities have not existed, however, very substantial railway building has failed to initiate a take-off, as, for example, in India, China, pre-1895 Canada, pre-1914 Argentine, etc.

It is clear that an enlargement and modernization of Armed Forces could play the role of a leading sector in take-off. It was a factor in the Russian, Japanese and German take-offs; and it figures heavily in current Chinese Communist plans.

[1] For a detailed analysis of the routes of impact of the railroad on economic development see Paul H. Cootner, *Transport Innovation and Economic Development: The Case of the U.S. Railroads*, 1953, unpublished doctoral thesis, Massachusetts Institute of Technology.

But historically the role of modern armaments has been ancillary rather than central to the take-off.

Quite aside from their role in supplying foreign exchange for general capital-formation purposes, raw materials and foodstuffs can play the role of leading sectors in the take-off if they involve the application of modern processing techniques. The timber industry, built on the steam saw, fulfilled this function in the first phase of Sweden's take-off, to be followed shortly by the pulp industry. Similarly, the shift of Denmark to meat and dairy products, after 1873, appears to have re-inforced the development of a manufacturing sector in the economy, as well as providing a major source of foreign exchange. And as Lockwood notes, even the export of Japanese silk thread had important secondary effects which developed modern production techniques.[1]

'To satisfy the demands of American weaving and hosiery mills for uniform, high-grade yarn, however, it was necessary to improve the quality of the product, from the silkworm egg on through to the bale of silk. In sericulture this meant the introduction of scientific methods of breeding and disease control ; in reeling it stimulated the shift to large filatures equipped with machinery ; in marketing it led to large-scale organization in the collection and sale of cocoons and raw silk . . . it exerted steady pressure in favour of the application of science, machinery, and modern business enterprise.'

The role of leading sector has been assumed, finally, by the accelerated development of domestic manufacture of consumption goods over a wide range in substitution for imports, as, for example, in Australia, the Argentine and perhaps in contemporary Turkey.

What can we say, then, in general about these leading sectors ? Historically, they have ranged from cotton textiles, through heavy-industry complexes based on railroads and military-end products, to timber, pulp, dairy products and finally a wide variety of consumers' goods. There is, clearly, no one sectoral sequence for take-off, no single sector which constitutes the magic key. There is no need for a growing society to recapitulate the structural sequence and pattern of Britain, the United States or Russia. Four basic factors must be present :

[1] W. W. Lockwood, *The Economic Development of Japan* (Princeton, 1954), pp. 338-9.

1. There must be enlarged effective demand for the product or products of sectors which yield a foundation for a rapid rate of growth in output. Historically this has been brought about initially by the transfer of income from consumption or hoarding to productive investment ; by capital imports ; by a sharp increase in the productivity of current investment inputs, yielding an increase in consumers' real income expended on domestic manufactures ; or by a combination of these routes.

2. There must be an introduction into these sectors of new production functions as well as an expansion of capacity.

3. The society must be capable of generating capital initially required to detonate the take-off in these key sectors ; and especially, there must be a high rate of plough-back by the (private or state) entrepreneurs controlling capacity and technique in these sectors and in the supplementary growth sectors they stimulated to expand.

4. Finally, the leading sector or sectors must be such that their expansion and technical transformation induce a chain of Leontief input-output requirements for increased capacity and the potentiality for new production functions in other sectors, to which the society, in fact, progressively responds.

Conclusion

This hypothesis is, then, a return to a rather old-fashioned way of looking at economic development. The take-off is defined as an industrial revolution, tied directly to radical changes in methods of production, having their decisive consequence over a relatively short period of time.

This view would not deny the role of longer, slower changes in the whole process of economic growth. On the contrary, take-off requires a massive set of preconditions going to the heart of a society's economic organization and its effective scale of values. Moreover, for the take-off to be successful, it must lead on progressively to sustained growth ; and this implies further deep and often slow-moving changes in the economy and the society as a whole.

What this argument does assert is that the rapid growth of one or more new manufacturing sectors is a powerful and essential engine of economic transformation. Its power derives from the multiplicity of its forms of impact, when a society is prepared to respond positively to this impact. Growth in such sectors, with new production functions of high productivity, in itself tends to raise output per head ; it places incomes in the hands of men who will not merely save a high proportion of an expanding income but who will plough it into highly productive investment ; it sets up a chain of effective demand for other manufactured products ; it sets up a requirement for enlarged urban areas, whose capital costs may be high, but whose population and market organization help to make industrialization an on-going process ; and, finally, it opens up a range of external economy effects which, in the end, help to produce new leading sectors when the initial impulse of the take-off's leading sectors begins to wane.

We can observe in history and in the contemporary world important changes in production functions in non-manufacturing sectors which have powerful effects on whole societies. If natural resources are rich enough or the new agricultural tricks are productive enough such changes can even outstrip population growth and yield a rise in real output per head. Moreover, they may be a necessary prior condition for take-off or a necessary concomitant for take-off. Nothing in this analysis should be read as deprecating the importance of productivity changes in agriculture to the whole process of economic growth. But in the end take-off requires that a society find a way to apply effectively to its own peculiar resources what D. H. Robertson once called the tricks of manufacture ; and continued growth requires that it so organize itself as to continue to apply them in an unending flow, of changing composition. Only thus, as we have all been correctly taught, can that old demon, diminishing returns, be held at bay.

3. THE THEORETICAL CONTEXT

SOME NOTES TOWARDS A THEORY OF DERIVED DEVELOPMENT*

by **Henry C. Wallich**

THE SUBJECT OF THE PRESENT PAPER IS LARGELY THEORETICAL. As Dr Prebisch has said in the introduction to *Theoretical and Practical Problems of Economic Growth*, a proper theoretical basis is essential if effective policies are to be established. There is available, of course, a large amount of theoretical work based on the experience of the more developed countries. But for the less developed countries, this material has the disadvantage that it is written from a very different point of view. In fact, one is compelled to admit that it is distinctly lacking in sympathy for the problems of these countries. Granted that theory must be objective, I nevertheless believe that it will be difficult to do really fruitful thinking about the problems of these countries unless the thinker identifies himself with their point of view. The economic theorist who limits himself to thinking in terms of comparative advantage, of textbook notions of monetary stability and free trade, is likely to discover all kinds of obstacles and reasons why underdeveloped countries cannot develop, and in particular cannot or should not industrialize. This negative kind of theorizing is interesting, but not particularly helpful. The purpose of a positive theory must be, not to find difficulties, but to solve them.

Two representative approaches have been followed in the work done by economists in the more developed countries. One has been to bring to bear upon the various aspects of development, the body of doctrine that has been generated on these subjects. Thus, upon population questions there is brought to bear a theory of population, upon capital formation, a theory of saving and investment, and so forth. This approach is essential if we want to take full advantage of the tools of

* A paper presented at the Third Meeting of Central Bank Technicians of the American Continent, Havana, 1952. Published with the author's permission.

analysis that already exist. It is not a very satisfying one, however, because it lacks organic unity.

The alternative is to bring to bear upon these problems a single unifying theory of development. Schumpeter's sweeping view of the economic process is probably the most outstanding intellectual performance of this kind. The quality that makes this theory so widely admired is, I believe, its internal unity. From a few basic premises it proceeds to conclusions that embrace a large part of the economic scene. Numerous difficult problems suddenly come into focus and find an explanation when illuminated from the vantage point of Schumpeter's theory. The great current interest in questions of economic growth has brought renewed and widespread interest in the Schumpeterian doctrine.

But in applying this doctrine to the less developed countries of our day, we find that it does not fit. In Schumpeter's model, the generating force is provided by the entrepreneur, the process is innovation, the goal is the establishment of a position of wealth and power for the entrepreneur. If we were to attach a general label to these concepts, one might say that they all belong to the sphere of production and supply. Popular living standards are not the goal, although they are likely to be the result. Factors of consumption and demand thus play a secondary role.

That Schumpeter's theory does not satisfy the case of the less developed countries is fairly obvious. The entrepreneur is not the main driving force, innovation is not the most characteristic process, and private enrichment is not the dominant goal. But the three cornerstones of Schumpeter's edifice—motive force, process, and goal—are such as may serve as basis to any other theory of development. It seems possible to feel one's way in the direction of such a theory by contrasting, step by step, the known facts with the postulates of Schumpeter's theory.

A Sketch of the Theory

The Motive Force

To suggest that the entrepreneur is not the main propelling force in the development of less advanced countries is not to deny, of course, that he plays a role. But it is a secondary role. One of the reasons why some countries remained static while others advanced was, very probably, a difference in the national endowment with entrepreneurial qualities. For many years, opportunity has been open to entrepreneurs in these countries, but it has not been seized. It may be taken for granted, of course, that other circumstances have contributed to this stagnation. There is no reason to think, however, that these obstacles have been greater than those overcome elsewhere by vigorous initiative.

The human traits that have kept capitalists in the less developed countries from becoming entrepreneurs are well known. Real estate mindedness, mistrust of industrial ventures, remnants of a feudal past, have all contributed. Every 'survey report' of missions sent out by international agencies and others comments on this point. No doubt the role of the entrepreneur in less developed countries will expand as the countries progress. If it should anywhere become a dominant role, it will make the development process of that country much more like that envisaged by Schumpeter. However, once a development process has begun without the entrepreneur in the vanguard, his chances of achieving leadership seem slim. Socially, politically, and economically the cards seem to be stacked against him almost everywhere. No longer is he the hero of the piece, admired by economists, and, more important, by his compatriots. The law does not aid and abet him and his property interests on all sides, as it did during the heyday of capitalism. He seems to be regarded as a by-product of economic development, to be tolerated because of his usefulness but to be watched and curbed because of his selfish propensities. If in most of the less developed countries his wealth escapes heavy taxation, it is mainly due to administrative inadequacies.

Who, then, are the protagonists in the process of development? In most of the less developed countries, the development process today seems to be predominantly a social, national, and also a nationalistic one. To a greater or lesser degree, the government is its most conspicuous and active agent. But in many cases, the government is in turn the spokesman for intensely felt popular demands. A widespread desire for higher living standards lies behind these demands.

For the first time, such desires, which must always have existed, are made into a real force by the dawning realization that progress is possible. Government action and mass impulses today seem to be the most characteristic motive forces of economic development.

The Process

What brings these government policies and mass impulses into being, and how do they function ? If they are the main motive forces, an analysis of their origin and functioning should lead us to an understanding of the characteristic processes of development. It goes without saying that there are wide differences among countries and that the analysis will be applicable in different degrees to each one of them. What we are looking for is a theory that brings out the most characteristic features from a broad variety of phenomena.

It is probably advisable to distinguish two aspects of the development process. The first has to do with how the process is started. The question to be asked is : what are the stimuli that cause an economy to break out of a mould of stagnation, or to accelerate from a very slow rate of growth ? The second aspect relates to the character of the continuing development process—how does it keep going ? For Latin American countries the first aspect is of no great importance, but it is for Asia and Africa.

Most of the factors likely to produce development can be classified under the headings of pressure or opportunity. Neither pressure nor opportunity evidently are enough, however, since both have been present for most countries during many years without producing visible results. The pressure of extreme need has caused starvation rather than advancement. The challenge of opportunity has not been picked up.

The 'break out' or acceleration seems to have been accomplished mainly through what one may describe as a widening of horizons aided by the pressure of need. What apparently happens is that the objective fact of opportunity is translated into a subjective realization of its presence. The 'demonstration effect' investigated by Duesenberry and Nurkse, brought into action by better communication and transportation, seems to have something to do with this widening of horizons. So no doubt does the exhilaration flowing from the end of colonial rule in some countries. These factors seem to have been of particular importance in Asia and Africa.

Latin American countries have faced a somewhat different set of problems. Here it was less a question of initiating a rise in *per capita* income than of accelerating it. The demonstration effect, however, seems to have had its share in stimulating popular demand for economic development. Governments, too, seem to have been exposed to an effect of this kind. Many of them have been awakened, by the power of example, to wide possibilities of positive action towards development. In addition, Latin American governments have been moved to action by the pressure of events and expectations. The fear of deteriorating terms of trade has been a strong motive of industrial development. The danger of being cut off from foreign supplies, through depression and consequent loss of export markets, or through war, has worked in the same direction.

In general, therefore, it seems to have been a combination of pressure and widening of horizons that has started off or accelerated the development drive. Perhaps one is not saying a great deal when one tries to separate the multiplicity of forces into two such categories. Obviously, there is a different set of specific causal factors behind the development of each country. The important thing is not to classify them, but to understand them. But if the classification is sensible, one may perhaps hope that it will contribute to understanding.

So far, the mechanism described is not very far removed from the Schumpeterian model. The 'widening of horizons' leads, after all, to something resembling 'innovation'. But the continuation of the process, once started, is another matter. One can hardly say that in less developed countries 'innovation' is its most characteristic feature. The process is better described perhaps as one of assimilation. No one would deny, of course, that to organize a new industry in a less developed country is an art of entrepreneurial initiative. But it is evidently very different from the original process of innovation.

Incidentally, one may suspect that the process of assimilation, being easier and quicker, engages less of the vital forces of the people and provides less of an outlet for creative energy. This would in turn be reflected in the lesser position awarded in society to the entrepreneur.

In other respects, too, present day development differs from that envisaged by Schumpeter. He, as well as Robertson and many continental economists, view innovations as an important or even as the main cause of business fluctuations. This is much less true of the process of assimilation. In the first place, there is less danger of temporary lulls in the flow of investment opportunities, as long as foreign technology remains to be caught up with. In the second place, the cycle of most of the less developed economies is generated mainly in their international sectors, through changes in exports. It is much less a function of domestic investment. We shall encounter the implications of this and other differences between development through assimilation, and development through innovation, in the later parts of this paper.

Goals

If the entrepreneur does not play the first fiddle in derived development, neither can his profit rank first among the goals of this process. Even in a Schumpeterian economy, entrepreneurial profit is not of course the national objective, as formulated by the government or the people. But in Schumpeter's framework, neither the government nor the people are prime movers. In the less developed countries, higher living standards seem to be the characteristic goal—except in some totalitarian countries to which we shall revert later. That is the natural consequence of the fact that the locus of leadership lies, not in the entrepreneurial but, in the governmental and popular sphere. Governments—even when they have no ambition of power politics—might perhaps prefer to hold back consumption and postpone the rise in living standards in the interests of higher investment. But under present day conditions, their strength often depends on their ability to assume and carry out commitments to the electorate for rapid social improvement. It is not easy for them to go slow deliberately. The force of the development drive is almost inevitably directed toward higher consumption.

Consumption-oriented Development

We started out by saying that one of the characteristics of Schumpeterian development is its orientation towards production. It draws its motive power from the sphere of supply. Of the other development process, one can say that it is predominantly oriented towards consumption. Its most characteristic elements belong to the sphere of demand. These characteristics are the result—not an inevitable one—of the fact that the process is based, not on innovation but on the assimilation of existing innovations. It is this feature that suggests the general concept of derived development—derived from innovations made elsewhere.[1]

The implications of the consumption- and demand-oriented character of derived development are far reaching. Like the imprint which is given to the Schumpeterian development process by its orientation towards the sphere of production and supply, the influence of orientation towards consumption is traceable in many phases of development. We shall find it reflected in the paucity of savings, in the secular tendency towards inflation, in the failure of the market process to be fully effective in distributing resources, and in the greater consequent importance of the political process. We shall also observe its impact upon the direction that development takes, and upon the speed with which development progresses. The orientation towards consumption and demand is, I believe, the most important and distinctive feature of the development of the less developed countries.

It goes without saying that the distinction here drawn rests upon emphasis and not upon some absolute. Consumption has its place in the Schumpeterian model and production has its in the theory of derived development. Moreover, the Schumpeterian model does not seek to describe the totality of an advanced 19th century economy. It deals only with the most characteristic features. Thus, the development of the British economy had many aspects in which consumption and demand

[1] The term 'derived development' is not meant to suggest of course a colonial process of development resulting passively from the growth of other countries. This is the type of development that Dr Prebisch has called the 'development of the past'. Cf., *Theoretical and Practical Problems of Economic Growth*, p. 5 (United Nations Economic Commission for Latin America, 1950).

played an important role. The growth of the United States and of Germany had, at first, some of the marks of derived development. The governments of these countries in particular have been development-conscious almost from the very beginning. But the characteristic spirit of the *laissez-faire* days is well portrayed by the Schumpeterian thesis. The emphasis upon production in Adam Smith's economics corroborates our view of the basic orientation that prevailed.

Likewise, the de-emphasis of the role of the entrepreneur in the theory of derived development does not imply that the entrepreneur does not fulfil a vital function. His role may well grow as countries progress. Production-consciousness exists and is increasing. These are all aspects of reality which it would be absurd to deny. What cannot be argued, however, is that they are dominant or characteristic aspects.

Neither is the distinction between a supply-oriented and a demand-oriented economy a statistical proposition. Supply and demand always balance *ex post*—the amount sold is the same as the amount bought. Nevertheless, a persistent inflationary or deflationary bias is significant. Nor can much be proved by measuring the propensity to save, although a comparison of savings ratios at given *per capita* income levels would be instructive.

The distinction made depends basically upon the spirit that animates the economy. It is social values that count—the approval bestowed respectively upon thrift, profit, and business success, or upon welfare, social security, and equality of income. It is obvious that even in the more advanced countries, which started out as production-oriented economies, these values have been shifting enormously. In many of the less developed countries, however, a consumption-oriented scale of values prevails from the very beginning.

No value judgement is implied in labelling some economies as oriented towards production, others towards consumption. The Schumpeterian economy has a certain romantic appeal, but its *laissez-faire* implications would be hard to swallow for most people today. The social values of a consumption economy are in many respects much more attractive. This appraisal by our contemporary civilization is implied in the current trend towards the welfare state, in which demand and consumption play a leading role. If one looks for some 'ideal' economy, it would probably be one that combined the individual virtues of the Schumpeterian with the social values of a consumption economy.

No judgement likewise is implied regarding the relative efficiency of either type of economy in achieving the goal of rapid development. The possible 'loaded' character of the terms 'production' and 'consumption' is unintended and must not be allowed to mislead in this connexion. In its ability to draw on innovations and savings generated abroad, derived development obviously has an advantage of a very high order. There can be no doubt in fact that derived development is capable of making much faster strides than innovating development ever did. In analysing the process in detail we shall find other facets of strength as well as of weakness that distinguish it from innovating development. It is not the purpose of the distinction to point to virtues on one side and vices on the other. The purpose is to isolate some of the factors that are most characteristic for advancement of less developed countries. In this way, a few steps can perhaps be taken towards an integrated theory of their development.

The Implications of Derived Development

A theory is useful in so far as it explains things or predicts them. We shall now try to work out the implications of the concept of Derived Development and shall apply them to the phenomena of the development process. To the extent that this attempt is successful, it should provide both a better understanding of the process and a confirmation of the theory. In that event, some policy conclusions should also become possible.[1]

The Direction of Development

What does the theory sketched in the preceding pages suggest as to the probable direction of the development of an economy oriented toward the sphere of consumption and

[1] The author is compelled to offer his apologies for the inadequate treatment of many of the topics that will suggest themselves to the reader under the present heading. In part he may attribute it to the pressure of time under which the paper had to be prepared.

demand? Perhaps the chief alternatives can be summarized under the headings of specialization, respectively, in primary production and industry. It seems clear that a process of derived development of the kind here analysed predisposes an economy toward industrialization. One reason is that the demonstration effect is heavily biased in the direction of urban forms of living and that it intensifies particularly the demand for manufactured goods. This is likely to lead to an identification of progress with urbanization and industrial production.

A second reason is that the assimilation of foreign methods of production tends to be particularly dynamic in the fields of manufacturing. It is the spectacle of large industrial installations more than the contemplation of improved agricultural methods that is likely to capture the imagination. The reader will have no difficulty to find examples in his own experience. The fact that governments are becoming increasingly skilled in applying the protective devices and stimuli needed to overcome the initial high cost of new manufacturing ventures works in the same direction.

This 'pedagogical' aspect of industrial activity is perhaps the strongest argument in favour of a policy of deliberate industrialization. I believe that we are all agreed that an increase in industrial activity is one of the most important components of development. We need as solid an intellectual base as possible for a policy of this kind, and a contribution can perhaps be made within the framework of the theory here presented.

This contribution may be derived from a variant of the demonstration effect, applied to production instead of consumption. It has often been observed that industrial work seems to be more effective in communicating new skills and in thus making labour more productive, than is agricultural work. This tendency seems to be particularly strong in countries where agricultural labour is tied to ancient traditions that are hard to break, or where such work leads into deadening routines, such as Dr Ramiro Guerra has pointed out in the case of cane sugar production.[1] This view of the proliferating pedagogical advantages of industry gives us a basis for

[1] Ramiro Guerra y Sanchez, *Azúcar y Población en las Antillas*.

industrialization that justifies new manufacturing ventures even where productivity initially is no higher or, even somewhat lower, than in primary production. The justification lies in the reasonable expectation that industrial work will raise the quality of the labour force and will thus eventually lead to a level of productivity higher than would prevail in primary production. This approach seems to be broader and more defensible than the familiar 'young industries' argument. The latter refers to the productivity of a particular industry, while the approach here presented rests upon the improvement in the labour force in general, which would provide a source of external economies to all industries.

To sum up on the direction of derived development : The theory suggests that the natural course of this type of development is toward industrialization. It gives us a basis for a policy of deliberate industrialization that stresses productivity and is not shaken by temporary fluctuations in the terms of trade. Finally it warns us against the bias, inherent in development by assimilation, toward overambitious industrial projects, and reminds us of the danger of going too fast and too far in that direction.

Supply of Productive Factors

We may next ask ourselves what the effect of derived development is likely to be upon the supply of productive factors, chiefly savings and labour. Here it seems to be necessary to distinguish two stages. One stage is that of the primitive economy, with a largely non-monetary character, where simple wants are filled with a minimum of capital and in some cases also of a minimum of labour effort. Here the introduction of new possibilities of consumption is likely to stimulate productive effort. The idea of 'incentive goods' is a familiar one. The result is likely to be an increase in the supply of labour, and perhaps also some stimulation of savings, if originally these were close to zero.

The second stage is more interesting from our point of view, and here the effects are likely to be different. The demand for advanced types of consumer goods almost certainly tends to reduce the supply of savings. The demonstration effect is hostile to saving—it was from this point of view that the concept was originally evolved. The inflationary environment which is likely to accompany a process of derived development in turn discourages the growth of thrift. Efforts to reduce the inequality of income, in so far as they are successful, probably work in the same direction.

The supply of labour may conceivably benefit from the greater desire for the blessings of civilization even in a fairly advanced economy. But this effect may be more than offset by another circumstance. There may be a tendency for the popular drive for higher living standards to become associated with demands for shorter working hours, limitations upon productivity, early retirement, and the like. Examples will readily come to mind. In one sense this is no more than would have to be expected under any circumstances, for when income rises, so does the demand for leisure. But there is probably more than just this to the tendency to limit the supply of effort, particularly since attempts in that direction often seem to be made when there has been no significant increase in living standards. Underemployment no doubt shares in the responsibility. But one may suspect that attempts to limit labour effort also reflect a prevailing social psychology, which leads an individual to view himself more as a beneficiary of a social process of development, to which his personal effort can contribute little, than as one who benefits primarily from his own productive work.

The net conclusion seems to be that derived development, in its advanced stages, is less favourable to the supply of productive factors, and particularly to saving, than originating development. Among the important goals of economic policy must be, therefore, measures to stimulate saving and to create an environment favourable to greater productivity-consciousness.

The Role of the Government

It is evident that in a process of derived development, the role of the government is very different from that assigned to it in originating development. The essence of the latter is that development is carried forward by the entrepreneur. The government's role is secondary or passive. This at any rate is the implication of the Schumpeterian theory. As a matter of historical record, we know that while the British government seems to have hampered rather than aided development during its early stages, the governments of the United States and Germany, for example, as well as of other countries, often took active steps to promote development. This, as said before, suggests that the development of these countries had in it something non-Schumpeterian, partaking of the nature of derived development.

In the less developed countries, where private enterprise is weak, development is not likely to go forward rapidly if the government likewise remains passive. Thus, derived development calls for some measure of government intervention. A second reason why one must expect more government action in a derived development process is that much of the popular demand for higher living standards, which is one of the characteristics of the process, takes the form of political pressure. In so far as the government is sensitive to such pressure, it must act to give expression to them. A third reason for more government action is that in a development process carried forward by broad popular demand, a considerable part of total investment is likely to be in 'social overhead'. These are investments that only a government can undertake. A fourth reason lies in the prospect that savings will be low owing to the orientation of the process toward consumption. This suggests that the government will have to use the tax power in order to increase investment.

Finally, and perhaps most importantly, one may argue that intervention in the process of derived development is perhaps more suited to the abilities of government than intervention in originating development. Originating development is a process of experimentation, requiring imagination and the willingness to take chances, and a capacity for correcting mistakes. These are not the things at which governments excel. The strength of government is organization, and it may be suggested that derived development is a process predominantly of organization. Innovation is not required, for the techniques are well known through examples abroad. The primary task is to organize their application.

This does not mean that the government should undertake all new economic activity. But the government is in a good position to orient the development of the economy through the familiar means, direct and indirect, of economic planning. The unfortunate counterpart to this is the threat to political liberties implicit in increased government activity.

Again, perhaps, there is nothing new in saying that in the process of derived development the government must have a substantial role. Certainly it is nothing new to economists in the less developed countries. But for economists in the more advanced countries, some of whom would like to see development to proceed with a minimum of government interference, it may be useful to be reminded of the very deep-seated nature of the causes that force the government into action.

The Inflationary Bias of Derived Development

The inflationary bias evident in present-day development has often been commented upon. Inflationary impulses as an accompaniment of development are nothing new. In Schumpeter's system, they form an integral part of the process. The entrepreneur, according to Schumpeter, resorts to bank credit to finance his innovation. Rising prices and forced saving follow, until a peak in the movement is reached and deflation sets in ; eventually the cycle repeats itself.

The essential feature of this Schumpeterian process, is that it involves no secular inflation. The long term price level remains approximately stable. Both premises—cyclical inflation and long term stability—are confirmed by the history of the major countries during the 19th century. Their experience confirms what one would expect *a priori* of an economy oriented toward production and supply and aiming at the accumulation of private property. Secular inflation would not be consonant with the recurrent tendency toward oversupply, nor with the savings and property instincts of the ruling groups.

The essential part of the mechanism is that bank credit is limited and that the bulk of investment must therefore be financed out of voluntary saving. There exists thus a nexus between saving and investment : those interested in investment must themselves save or be able to borrow the savings of others. Thus the lure of profits stimulates the accumulation of savings, and the availability of the latter limits—although not completely—the amount of investment.

This nexus between the inducement to save and to invest is weakened when development is propelled by popular desire for higher living standards. What was briefly mentioned in connexion with the supply of savings seems worth developing here.

In a consumption economy, saving is not as important a means for improving one's lot, as it is in a production-oriented economy. It is more rational to expect one's lot to be improved by outside events—by the government, by the labour union, or by the growth of the economy in general. To this growth, the savings of the beneficiary can contribute very little. The government can build just as many roads or health centres, entrepreneurs as many movies or restaurants, whether any one person saves or not. The would-be beneficiary of development is in the position of an atomistic competitor, whose actions do not affect those of others in a manner to produce repercussions upon himself.

Of course it is still true that a person can save and invest and benefit thereby. But this is no longer the typical way of looking at the benefits from economic progress. In a production-oriented society, the logical way of looking at this is to visualize the benefits coming from one's productive effort. In a consumption-oriented society, the tendency is to look at personal progress as something in which one shares as a result of overall progress. Thus, the typical case is that of a man who expects to benefit from investment and saving, not as the owner, but as the user and consumer of what that investment produces. In that capacity, a man's interest is still in an increase in the total volume of saving and investment, but he has no direct interest in himself adding to it.

The weakening of the nexus between saving and investment is likely to have adverse effects upon the prospects for a stable price level. Savings tend to be less, while there is growing pressure to increase investment, in order to satisfy desires for higher living standards. But the disequilibrium goes beyond an imbalance between saving and investment. When the implications of a demand-oriented economy are viewed in their broadest sense, the inflationary forces appear even more powerful. Social demand, working through political and labour union channels, seeks to extract from the economy more than what, through domestic production and international trade, it can be made to yield. It is not only development and the associated investment that are responsible for inflationary tendencies, but the entire social climate of a demand-oriented economy. We must be aware of the deep roots of these forces when we talk about whether and how to control inflation.

INVESTMENT, INCOME AND THE MULTIPLIER IN AN UNDERDEVELOPED ECONOMY*

by **V. K. R. V. Rao**

IT IS CONVENIENT TO BEGIN BY SUMMARIZING THE MAIN CONTENT of the Keynesian theory on the subject, which, incidentally, makes no attempt to give a separate treatment to underdeveloped economies. The volume of employment and of income is determined by the level at which aggregate demand price is equal to aggregate supply price. The propensity to consume is such that when Y_w increases, C_w increases but not to the same extent. The gap has to be made up by I_w or investment. The nature of the propensity to consume is such that marginal propensity to consume declines with increasing income and unless investment increases sufficiently, aggregate demand price will fall short of aggregate supply price, so that income and employment will decline till equality is attained between the two. Savings and investment are always equal, but this equality is brought about because of appropriate changes in the volume of income and employment. Saving is a residual, while it is investment which is the crucial factor. Increase in investment results in increase in income and the increase in income leads to an increase in saving. The marginal propensity to consume determines the relation between an increment of investment and the appropriate increment of income such as will induce the increment of saving necessary to maintain the equality of saving and investment. This relationship between increment of investment and that of income is determined by k or what is called the multiplier, the formula being $\Delta Y_w = k\ \Delta I_w$, where $1 - \frac{1}{k}$ is equal to the marginal propensity to consume. As the marginal propensity to consume declines with increasing income, increasingly larger increments of investment become necessary for securing

* *The Indian Economic Review*, February 1952. Reprinted by permission of *The Indian Economic Review* and the author.

given increments of income at increasing levels of income. As the marginal propensity to consume is likely to be not far short of unity in the case of poor communities, the multiplier has a high value in their case with the result that comparatively small increments of investment are likely to bring about full employment. At the same time, as their average propensity to consume is also high, investment accounts for a smaller portion of the value of their aggregate output which is the same thing as the volume of their income; fluctuations in investment, therefore, account for smaller fluctuations in total employment than they do in the case of richer communities whose average propensity to consume is less and in whose case, therefore, investment accounts for a larger share of the value of the aggregate output. The paradoxical situation, therefore, arises that the poorer the community the greater the ease of obtaining for it a condition of full employment and the smaller the fluctuations in its employment caused by changes in its net investment; while the richer the community the more difficult it is to secure full employment, while the greater are the fluctuations in its total employment due to fluctuations in its net investment. Add to this the fact that fluctuations in net investment are more likely in a richer community, the conclusion seems to follow that instability in employment is a characteristic of increasing national income, and with it there is an increasing tendency towards the growth of involuntary unemployment unless offset by an increased investment that is possible only with the abandonment of both *laissez faire* and balanced budgeting. Keynes is mainly concerned with the problem of involuntary unemployment in the richer communities, and his whole thesis relates to the question of how to secure full employment in the case of these countries. The remedies he puts forward, viz. cheap money, deficit financing, redistributive taxation, and public investment have all become current coin in national economic policies, with full employment as the major objective. Unfortunately Keynes did not formulate the economic problem of underdeveloped countries, nor did he discuss the relevance to these countries of either the objective or the policy that he proposed for the more developed, i.e. the industrialized countries. The result has been a rather unintelligent application—not on Keynes's part—of what may be called Keynesian economics to the problems of the underdeveloped countries. Thus it is common ground with most writers on the economics of underdeveloped countries that what was required for their economic development was an increase in the purchasing power of the people. Deficit financing and created money have figured in practically all the plans, both official and unofficial, that have been put forward, e.g. for the economic development of India: while cheap money seems to have become as much an article of financial faith in the underdeveloped countries as in the industrialized economies. It is, therefore, of some importance to examine the problem of investment, income and the multiplier in the special context of underdeveloped economies with a view to finding out how far Keynesian ideas on economic policy are relevant and applicable to the problems of economic development. I shall deal with this question with special reference to my own country, viz. India.

Take first the question of full employment. Everyone is agreed that full employment is a major desired goal of economic policy. According to Keynes, in a poor country where the marginal propensity to consume is high and the multiplier, therefore, also high, comparatively small increments of investment are sufficient to secure full employment. It must be pointed out that according to Keynes an increase in employment is identical with an increase in real income whether measured in terms of wage units or of output. Full employment, therefore, involves the maximization of output that is possible with the elimination of involuntary unemployment and the full utilization of existing capacity and technical knowledge. Once this stage is reached, any attempt to increase investment sets up a tendency in money prices to rise without limit or leads to the emergence of a state of true inflation, where rising prices will no longer be associated with an increasing aggregate real income. Progress beyond this stage is not discussed in Keynes, the implicit assumption being that there is a unique level of full employment and when that is reached the desired objective has been attained. Even when subsequent writers have discussed the next step by linking up the multiplier principle with that of acceleration, what is visualized is a change in the nature of employment, with a larger proportion now going into investment industries, rather than an increase in total employment. Let me now examine these concepts in the context of an underdeveloped economy like India.

To begin with, we have here a predominantly agricultural country, where capital equipment is low and the standard of technical knowledge applied to production vastly inferior to that in the west. Moreover, the number of employees or workers employed on a wage is comparatively small, the vast majority of earners falling under the category of self-employees or household enterprises. Added to this is the fact that a significant proportion of the national output is not produced for the market but is intended for self-consumption. Under these circumstances, the multiplier principle does not work in the simple fashion visualized by Keynes primarily for the industrialized economies. An increase in investment leads to an increase in income and in employment. The next increase ought to come from a secondary increase in income, employment and output in the consumption-goods industries, to be followed by a tertiary increase and so on, till income, output and employment have increased by k times the initial increase in investment, and saving has increased by an amount equal to the additional investment. I am aware that the investment multiplier and the employment multiplier are not identical, and that increase in output cannot be proportional either to the increase in money income, or to that in employment, but for purposes of argument, it is convenient to ignore these differences at this stage. Now in the case of a country like India the secondary, tertiary and other increases in income output and employment visualized by the multiplier principle do not follow, even though the marginal propensity to consume is very high and the multiplier should, therefore, function in a vigorous fashion. This is because the consumption-goods industries to which the increased demand is directed are not in a position to expand output and offer effective additional employment. The most important reason for this is the technical nature of the chief consumption industry to which the additional demand would presumably be directed, viz. food. This means in most underdeveloped countries primarily the agricultural industry. Now, agriculture all over the world is notoriously an industry where the supply curve is steeply inelastic in the short period. Further, variations in agricultural output in a country like India, where irrigation accounts for less than 20 per cent of the cultivated area, are largely dominated by the vagaries of nature, and response to price increases is less effective in terms of aggregate output than in those of individual crops. Moreover, the belief is widely held, and not without justification, that the supply curve of agricultural industry as a whole is not only inelastic but also tends to be backward-rising, so that an increase in the value of output need not necessarily lead to a subsequent increase in the volume of output. The primary increase in income following on a given increment of investment does get spent to a large extent on the output of agriculture, and leads, therefore, to an appropriate increase in the income of the agricultural producers. But it is not followed up by these producers increasing their own output and thus adding to both employment and real income.

Apart from the reasons mentioned above, the agricultural producer is rather reluctant to act in the way postulated for entrepreneurs by classical economists or even by Keynes himself in response to increase in profits. The presence of price control and governmental procurement both act as psychological disincentives, while uncertainty regarding the duration of high prices and their future also has the effect of dampening immediate response to price stimuli. Moreover, even to the extent to which agricultural producers want to increase output, they do not get the facilities necessary either by way of technique or of supplies to carry out their intentions. One may call all this either bottlenecks or shortages or inelasticity in the supply curves of the factors of production ; the net result is the same, viz. that it is not possible significantly to increase output in the short period in spite of willingness to expend money on doing so. This means that while income increases, output does not increase in anything like the same measure in the agricultural sector. In other words, the income multiplier is much higher in money terms than in real terms, and to that extent prices rise much faster than an increase in aggregate real income.

The same conclusion also applies when we consider the behaviour of agriculturists as consumers in response to the increase in their money income resulting from the initial investment. Marginal propensity to consume being high, the larger proportion of the increased income will be sought to be spent on consumption goods. As the agriculturists are themselves producers of food, the increase that follows in their consumption of foodgrains—the increase in consumption may take the form of either increasing the quantity consumed or substitution of better quality grains for coarse grains—leads to a reduction in the marketable surplus of foodgrains. This means in turn that the non-agricultural sector of the economy now has to pay still higher prices for its foodgrains without an appropriate response on the part of production in the agricultural sector. The tendency, therefore, for prices to rise without a rise in aggregate real income is further strengthened by the working of the marginal propensity to consume on the part of the receivers of additional agricultural incomes. One may perhaps expect that the position would be different in respect of the increased consumption of non-agricultural goods on the part of the agriculturist consumers. But, even here, the position is not far different in the case of a country like India. This is due to many reasons such as the absence of effective excess capacity in industries, difficulty of obtaining raw materials and other ingredients for additional production, inelastic supply of skilled workers, and various bottlenecks arising out of controls and the general environment of a shortage-dominated economy. To the extent, therefore, that agriculturist consumers do spend a part of their additional income on non-agricultural goods, the tertiary increase in money income does take place, but not a corresponding or even a noticeable increase in either output or employment. To the extent that agriculturists find that they are unable to effect an increase in their real income in terms of non-agricultural goods in spite of expending a larger money income, the effect is to decrease the marginal utility of the additional income with the result that in terms of Keynes' second proposition presented in Chapter II of his *General Theory*, identity between utility of the wage—in this case the cultivator's income—and the marginal disutility of that amount of employment—in this case the cultivator's own labour—is reached at the existing level of the volume of labour in the agricultural industry, in spite of an increase in the money value of the output of that labour, and may even be reached at lower levels of the volume of labour expended in the agricultural industry. Thus the primary increase in investment and, therefore, increase in income and employment leads to a secondary and a tertiary increase in income, but not to any noticeable increase in either output or employment in either the agricultural or the non-agricultural sector. The multiplier principle, therefore, works with reference to money income but not with reference either to real income or employment. To the extent that the increases in money income do not get absorbed by a rise in prices and leave a margin of additional real income in certain sections of the community such as agricultural producers and industrial producers, they are dissipated either by an increase in food consumption on the part of the former or by an increase in imports or in cash balances on the part of the latter ; in neither case do they lead to an increase either in real income or in employment for the community as a whole.

The position may be summed up as under. In the Keynesian scheme of things the supply curve of output as a whole is comparatively elastic in the short period under conditions of involuntary unemployment. Therefore there is a relation, if not of identity, of at least comparative identity in value between the multipliers relating increment of money investment to increment of money income, of increment of money investment in terms of wage units to increment of money income in terms of wage units, of increment in investment output to increment in total output and of increment of employment in investment industries to increment in total employment. It is only on these assumptions that an increment of investment, operating on the basis of the multiplier principle, helps to increase output, real income, and employment, and leads to what may be called an automatic self-financing of the increased investment.[1]

[1] 'An increment of investment in terms of wage-units cannot occur unless the public are prepared to increase their savings in terms of wage-units. Ordinarily speaking, the public will not do this unless their aggregate income in terms of wage-units is increasing. Thus their effort to consume a part of their increased incomes will stimulate output until the new level (and distribution) of incomes provides a margin of saving sufficient to correspond to the increased investment. The

Undoubtedly the multipliers k and k' would be smaller than the multiplier linking up increment in money investment to increment in money income, for the supply curve of output is not perfectly elastic but is, on the other hand, inelastic, though the inelasticity becomes marked and increasing only as one approaches full employment. But there is no doubt that all the multipliers mentioned above must be positive and moving in the same direction if the Keynesian thesis is to apply in practice. This implies in turn that for the multiplier principle to work, there must exist the following:

(*a*) Involuntary unemployment.

(*b*) An industrialized economy where the supply curve of output slopes upwards towards the right but does not become vertical till after a substantial interval.

(*c*) Excess capacity in the consumption-goods industries.

(*d*) Comparatively elastic supply of the working capital required for increased output.

These assumptions do not hold in the case of an underdeveloped economy. Involuntary unemployment of the Keynesian type is necessarily associated with a free-enterprise wage economy where the majority of earners work for wages and where production is much more for exchange than for self-consumption. But this type of economy is of comparatively recent origin, which also explains the fact that over the whole range of human history unemployment in the modern sense is, comparatively speaking, a rare and local phenomenon. Mrs Robinson has pointed out that in a society in which there is no regular system of unemployment benefit, and in which poor relief is either non-existent or 'less eligible' than almost any alternative short of suicide, a man who is thrown out of work

multiplier tells us by how much their employment has to be increased to yield an increase in real income sufficient to induce them to do the necessary extra saving, and is a function of their psychological propensities. If saving is the pill and consumption is the jam, the extra jam has to be proportioned to the size of the additional pill. Unless the psychological propensities of the public are different from what we are supposing, we have here established the law that increased employment for investment must necessarily stimulate the industries producing for consumption and thus lead to a total increase of employment which is a multiple of the primary employment required by the investment itself.' Keynes, *The General Theory of Employment, Interest, and Money*, pp. 117-18.

must scratch up a living somehow or other by means of his own efforts: Mrs Robinson goes on to point out that such persons do not figure in the list of unemployed but take up some other work, subject however to the proviso that their productivity is less than in the occupations they have left. She continues: 'Thus a decline in demand for product of the general run of industries leads to a diversion of labour from occupations in which productivity is higher to others where it is lower. The cause of this diversion, a decline in effective demand, is exactly the same as the cause of unemployment in the ordinary sense, and it is natural to describe the adoption of inferior occupations by dismissed workers *disguised unemployment*.'[1] Mrs Robinson has pointed out further that the existence of disguised unemployment introduces a complication into the formal scheme of the General Theory of Employment, the function relating total investment ceasing to be unique, since a given rate of investment will be accompanied by a greater rate of consumption the more unemployment is disguised. Underdeveloped economies are conspicuous for the extent to which they contain disguised unemployment. Only the kind of disguised unemployment they have is not of the type visualized by Mrs Robinson, where it results from a decline in effective demand and can exist in an industrialized economy only provided there is no unemployment dole or other not disagreeable social means for enabling the unemployed to exist. In an underdeveloped and agrarian economy with little capital equipment and a somewhat low state of technical knowledge like India, on the other hand, disguised unemployment is a normal feature of the economy. The term is not applied, as Mrs Robinson applies it, to wage labour taking to less productive work on account of unemployment. It is applied in the case of India to persons who are employed in the sense that they are engaged in household enterprise but who are really in a state of disguised unemployment in the sense that no difference will be made to output by their withdrawal from the occupations concerned. As is pointed out in the recent report of the U.N. Committee of Experts on *Measures for the Economic Development of Underdeveloped Countries*, 'the disguised unemployed are those

[1] Joan Robinson, *Essays in the Theory of Employment*, p. 84.

persons who work on their own account and who are so numerous, relatively to the resources with which they work, that if a number of them were withdrawn for work in other sectors of the economy the total output of the sector from which they were withdrawn would not be diminished even though no significant reorganization occurred in this sector, and no significant substitution of capital'[1]. This kind of disguised unemployment makes a significant difference to the working of the theory of the multiplier. If unemployment in underdeveloped economies takes the form of disguised unemployment rather than that of involuntary unemployment, then the secondary, tertiary and other effects of the initial primary employment created by the initial increment of investment do not follow, apart from other reasons, for this reason that there is no labour force willing to accept employment at the current wage, and involuntarily unemployed because of lack of employment opportunities. By definition, involuntary unemployment implies an elastic supply of labour at the current wage level. Those who are suffering from disguised unemployment do not fall under this category. They are, first of all, not aware that they are unemployed and are not, therefore, on the look-out for employment. Secondly, they are already in receipt of a real income which presumably gives them at least the same satisfaction as they would get by taking up employment at the current wage level. In actual fact, a wage considerably higher than the income they are receiving in their existing occupations would be necessary in order to induce them to offer themselves for employment. In other words, they are not really involuntarily unemployed in the Keynesian sense; and yet they are unemployed in clearly economic sense in which we have defined disguised unemployment. The particular form which unemployment takes in the underdeveloped countries, viz. that of disguised unemployment, makes the economy for Keynesian purposes practically analogous with one of full employment; and to that extent prevents the multiplier from working in the direction of an increase in either output or employment. The presence of disguised unemployment thus prevents the working of the Keynesian law that

[1] p. 7 of the Report.

'increased employment for investment must necessarily stimulate the industries producing for consumption and thus lead to a total increase of employment which is a multiple of the primary employment required by the investment itself'.

Apart from the difficulties caused by the presence of disguised unemployment, the agrarian nature of the economy makes for a supply curve that, at best, is much more inelastic than that of an industrialized economy such as Keynes primarily had in mind when formulating his theory of employment. This, in turn, tends to widen the difference between the multiplier linking up increments of money investment with increments of money income from that linking up increments of investment output with increments of total output, with the result that money incomes and prices rise much faster than real incomes and output. Savings, therefore, fail to rise to equality with investment; and with deficit financing, the inflationary process sets in earlier and proceeds faster in an agrarian or underdeveloped economy as compared with an industrialized or developed economy. The case for investment supported by deficit-financing for the purpose of inducing a given increase in output is, therefore, much weaker in an underdeveloped economy as compared with that in a developed economy.

This conclusion gets further reinforcement when we look at the organizational nature of an underdeveloped economy. In an industrialized economy the community consists of a small number of employers and a large number of employees, production for market is the rule, and consumers purchase the goods and services they require, with the result that when there is an increase in income, the marginal propensity to consume leads to an increase in the market demand for consumption goods and thereby to an increase in output and employment in the consumption-goods industries. In the case of an underdeveloped economy, however, household enterprises predominate, and production is much more for self-consumption than for the market with the result that when there is an increase in income the marginal propensity to consume leads to an increase in the demand for self-consumption rather than for purchases in the market. While this increased demand may partly be met by increased output on the part of the consumers themselves, at least a portion, if not actually the bulk, of the increased demand will be met by a diversion of output from the market to their self-consumption. Thus a reduction in the marketable surplus rather than an increase in output makes available the extra quantity of consumption goods required by this class following an increase in their income, and to this extent the extra employment induced by their increased consumption is less than what it would have been if their increased consumption had been purchased in the market. In Keynesian terms, the effect of this is to reduce the value of the multiplier below the level calculable from the marginal propensity to consume. Such a conclusion would appear to undermine the theory of the multiplier, the whole basis of which is the marginal propensity to consume, and yet that seems inevitable in an underdeveloped economy dominated by household enterprises and production for self-consumption. It is, of course, possible to preserve the formal structure of the multiplier theory by regarding an increment of self-consumption as a leakage analogous to the leakage that takes place when the increased consumption resulting from increased income takes the form of increased imports. It may perhaps be added that the former type of leakage is more likely in underdeveloped economies while the latter is more likely in industrialized economies.

Another factor preventing the appropriate increase in the output of consumption-goods industries and the employment therein following an increase in income, arises from the absence of excess capacity in consumption-goods industries, coupled with a comparatively inelastic supply of the working capital needed for increasing production, which is characteristic of an underdeveloped economy. In effect, this is but analogous to the conditions that obtain in an industrialized economy as it approaches conditions of full employment ; but there is this difference, viz. that it begins to operate much earlier and is quite consistent with the existence of disguised unemployment in the underdeveloped economy.

My conclusion, therefore, is that the multiplier principle as enunciated by Keynes does not operate in regard to the problem of diminishing unemployment and increasing output in an underdeveloped economy, an increment of investment based on deficit financing tending to lead more to an inflationary rise in prices than to an increase in output and employment. It would, however, be possible to give formal validity to the Keynesian law even in the case of underdeveloped economies by treating them as economies in a state of full employment or near-full employment. Full employment, however, is identified in the public mind with an optimum economic condition and carries with it the implication that it is accompanied by the maximum utilization of labour, capital and natural resources in the economy. That is why it is regarded as the major objective of present-day national and international economic policy and figures so prominently in the aims and objects of the U.N.O. and its specialized agencies. To describe underdeveloped economies as being in a state of full or near-full employment, therefore, is to do violence to the accepted connotation of that phrase even though it may satisfy the formal requirement of the Keynesian concept of full employment. Under the circumstances, I would prefer to say that the economic policy of deficit financing and disregard for thrift advocated by Keynes for securing full employment does not apply in the case of an underdeveloped economy. The policy that holds good for an underdeveloped economy is more on the lines formulated by the classical economists ; and if the Keynesians would say that this is because of the existence of full employment in the underdeveloped economies, there can be no *formal* objection to their statement. In any case it would follow that the economic policy that would be advocated for underdeveloped economies for increasing incomes, output, and employment would be radically different from that so universally associated with Keynes and formulated by him primarily for application to the developed or industrialized economies. In that sense, the multiplier principle with its accepted relationship between increments of investment and increments of incomes, output, and employment does not hold for an underdeveloped economy like India.

The further conclusion also seems to follow that the existence of disguised unemployment, household enterprise, production for self-consumption, dominance of agriculture, and deficiency of capital equipment and of technical knowledge—all characteristic of an underdeveloped economy—create conditions analogous to those of the full employment visualized by Keynes, when in actual fact there is no full employment in the economic, or even the popularly accepted, sense of the term. The formal effect of this on the General Theory of Employment still remains to be undertaken ; but I have the feeling that the answer lies in giving up the assumption that there is one unique level of full employment. Apart from the level of full employment visualized by Keynes, there are as many levels of full employment as there are different stages of economic development. Indeed it is the transition from the level of full employment appropriate to a lower stage to another appropriate to a higher stage which constitutes the process of economic development. The economic process consists of two distinct categories, one where given the level of economic development, you move from low employment to full employment, and the other where you move from full employment at a given level of economic development to full employment at the next level of economic development. The Keynesian thesis applies only to one of these categories, viz. where, given the level of economic development, you move from low employment to full employment ; it is the classical thesis which is operative for the other category where you move from one level of economic development to a higher level of economic development. The mixing up of these two categories and a consequent blind application of the Keynesian formulæ to the problems of economic development has inflicted considerable injury on the economies of underdeveloped countries and added to the forces of inflation that are currently afflicting the whole world. The old-fashioned prescription of 'work harder and save more' still seems to hold good as the medicine for economic progress, at any rate as far as the underdeveloped countries are concerned.

GROWTH MODELS AND UNDERDEVELOPED ECONOMIES*

by **Henry J. Bruton**

THE POST-WAR LITERATURE ON GROWTH ECONOMICS HAS TENDED to distinguish the growth process in a relatively highly developed country from that in a so-called 'underdeveloped' area. In the former case the analyses have been characterized by severe rigour, with consequent imposition of restrictive assumptions setting definite and specific boundaries to the problems. To a large extent, work in this area is an extension of the savings-investment analysis of Keynes into more dynamic formulations. In discussions of the developmental process of underdeveloped countries, however, there is the exactly opposite approach ; the problem is usually very generally defined, rigour is frequently completely absent, and the variables considered inevitably spill over into areas which economists have long treated as beyond the scope of the discipline (for example, population, and technological change). In the absence of a general framework—a model—within which to examine the problems of the underdeveloped country, much of the discussion has taken place in a virtual theoretical vacuum and consequently is often unsatisfactory both logically and practically.

The purpose of this paper is to examine a modified version of the growth theory developed by Domar, Harrod, Fellner,[1] and others in the light of the more commonly known

* *The Journal of Political Economy*, August 1955. Reprinted with the permission of the University of Chicago Press, the publishers of this journal, and of the author.

[1] See R. F. Harrod's *Towards a Dynamic Economics* (London : Macmillan & Co., Ltd, 1952) ; Evsey D. Domar, 'Capital Expansion, Rate of Growth, and Employment', *Econometrica*, Vol. XIV (April 1946) ; William Fellner, 'The Capital-Output Ratio in Dynamic Economics', in *Money, Trade, and Economic Growth* (New York : Macmillan Co., 1951). There are many other articles, of course ; Professor Fellner's paper has a short bibliography on the subject.

characteristics of the underdeveloped country and to attempt to make a more systematic and rigorous statement than has hitherto been made of the developmental process and problems in these countries. The procedure is as follows: I shall examine the assumptions made in existing growth models and the conditions necessary to make these assumptions (or alternative ones) valid. Then, on the basis of readily available data for the United States and the United Kingdom, I suggest hypotheses about the conditions that have actually obtained in the economic growth of these countries. These hypotheses are then transplanted to the underdeveloped country, and their implications are examined for an economic system with the general features of the modern underdeveloped country.

It seems necessary to digress a moment in order to state explicitly what the 'general features of the modern underdeveloped country' are and to indicate the form of the growth theory that I shall use. Of course, no two underdeveloped countries are exactly alike; but the descriptive literature[1] on such countries suggests enough similarity that we may confidently describe a 'representative underdeveloped country', which, although not an exact replica of any one country, is a reasonably accurate description of all. Of course, low *per capita* income and consequently low savings are the chief criteria of underdevelopment, but there are other characteristics equally significant. There is a significant amount of disguised unemployment; some workers, though nominally employed, contribute nothing to total output. Further, the country has a narrow range of output, chiefly raw materials and agricultural products. The level of technology is low relative to that known elsewhere, and a corollary of this is a relative shortage of entrepreneurial and management capacity. Finally, although this is less clear-cut than the other characteristics, an underdeveloped country trades chiefly with the more highly developed countries and very little with its fellow under-

[1] Such literature is turned out chiefly by the United Nations (see especially the Economic Commission for Asia and the Far East's annual issues of *Economic Survey of Asia and the Far East* and the Economic Commission for Latin America's annual issues of *Economic Survey of Latin America*).

developed countries. Other peculiarities might be mentioned,[1] but this list will suffice for the purposes of this paper. For the sake of brevity, I shall call the representative underdeveloped country 'Country U'.

For the 'representative highly developed country' I shall refer simply to the United States and the United Kingdom; it is unnecessary to describe these countries. I shall speak of the representative developed country as 'Country D'. The discussion will be in terms of only two countries, U and D, but this is mere convenience of exposition and not analytically significant.

The central proposition of the Harrod-Domar theory arises from introducing the rather obvious assumption that investment is capacity-creating as well as income-generating. Thus, if the new capacity is to be utilized, the equivalent new demand must be generated. Given a constant ratio between saving and income—call it s—and a constant capital-output ratio—call it k—it is evident that capacity will increase by $s/k\ Y$ (where Y is income). Then the increase in income must equal the increase in capacity: $\Delta Y = \frac{s}{k} Y$, and, dividing through by Y, we get $\frac{\Delta Y}{Y} = \frac{s}{k}$; that is, income demand must grow at a constant percentage rate, s/k, in order to assure no idle capacity of capital equipment.[2] Now s/k may be looked at from two points of view: on the one hand, it may be thought of as the rate of growth of income *required* to use the newly created capacity. On the other hand, it may be thought of as the maximum *allowable* rate of growth possible without inflation. The two are the same, of course; but this terminology is useful in suggesting the deflationary bias of the mature economies and the inflationary bias inherent in almost all the underdeveloped—immature—economies.

[1] Population problems vary markedly among countries. Some discussion of the rate of population growth in economic development occurs in the text.

[2] The equation in an *ex post* form is, of course, a tautology; to make it an equilibrium condition, the rate of growth must be that which is consistent with the propensity to save and the capital-output ratio which keeps the stock at the intended level in relation to output (see Harrod, op. cit.; and Fellner, op. cit.)

The rate of growth derived here applies to capital capacity. We may also approach the growth problem from the point of view of labour.[1] Thus if the labour force grows at a constant percentage rate, l, and productivity increases by a constant percentage rate, p, then, in order for labour to be fully employed, income must grow at a rate equal to $l + p + lp$. Once more we may speak of the 'required' rate and the 'allowable' rate; the growing labour force must be matched by increasing income, but the labour force also imposes a limit above which demand may not go without causing inflation.

The deflationary-biased economies could experience unemployment as a consequence of the inability of the system to invest the savings that would be forthcoming at the required rate of growth. For the capital-shortage countries, unemployment could result from the insufficiency of the supply of capital to employ the growing labour force. These difficulties are a consequence of the assumption of constant coefficients of production.

Under the assumptions usually made,[2] we have two independent rates of growth, which must be equal to each other and to the percentage rate of growth of income, or the system will stumble. I proceed now to look more closely at the implications of this set of ideas for the underdeveloped countries in the light of their characteristics and the historical experience of the United States and the United Kingdom.

One further point may be made here. The growth models, virtually without exception, are in real terms, and the effects of price changes are not analysed. The literature on underdeveloped areas, virtually without exception, is dominated by reference to changing terms of trade. Since my analysis is carried out within the framework of the growth models, I assume no price changes and hence constant terms of trade. In this respect, if in no other, this paper is virtually unique in the literature on underdeveloped countries.

[1] See D. Hamberg, 'Full Capacity vs. Full Employment Growth', *Quarterly Journal of Economics*, Vol. LXVI (August 1952).

[2] Harold Pilvin has worked out an analysis in which the assumption of constant input coefficients has been dropped and the two independent rates become tied to each other (see his 'Full Capacity vs. Full Employment Growth', *Quarterly Journal of Economics*, Vol. LXVII (November 1953).)

As indicated earlier, the assumption of a constant k is strategic to the model. When the theory was first formulated, little attention was paid to the empirical validity of this assumption ; however, data are now available which suggest that for both the United States and the United Kingdom there have been virtually no significant changes in the capital-output ratio which cannot be accounted for by cyclical changes in output or by wartime activity.[1]

If we accept a constant k as empirically valid, it becomes necessary to explain the factors responsible for this stability. In principle, four such factors must be considered : (1) the behaviour through time of the interest rate ; (2) the nature of the production function with respect to returns to scale ; (3) the nature of technological innovations ; and (4) the nature of changes in the composition of output.

Harrod[2] has recently deprecated the role of changes in the interest rate in changes in capital intensity. For short-run analyses this seems reasonable, but in the determination of the input-mix over long periods the relative prices of the inputs surely are important. If this were not the case, it would be exceedingly difficult to account for much of international trade and for the fact that in different countries different input-mixes are used to produce the same product.[3]

[1] Data supporting this position are readily available and need not be reproduced here. See Simon Kuznets, *National Product since 1869* (New York : National Bureau of Economic Research, 1946) ; B. Weber and S. J. Handfield Jones, 'Variations in the Rate of Economic Growth in the United States of America, 1869-1939', *Oxford Economic Papers*, Vol. VI, N.S. (June 1954) ; E. H. Phelps Brown and S. J. Handfield Jones, 'The Climacteric of the 1890's', *Oxford Economic Papers*, Vol. IV, N.S. (October 1952) ; E. H. Phelps Brown and B. Weber, 'Accumulation, Productivity, and Distribution in the British Economy, 1870-1938', *The Economic Journal*, Vol. LXIII (June 1953) ; and R. W. Goldsmith, 'The Growth of Reproducible Wealth of the United States of America from 1805 to 1950', in *Income and Wealth Series*, Vol. II (1952) of the International Association for Research in Income and Wealth.

[2] See his comments appended to the Pilvin paper (op. cit.). In his book, however, he attaches considerable importance to the rate of interest.

[3] A bit of empirical evidence is provided by the study of Daniel Creamer, *Capital and Output Trends in Manufacturing Industries, 1880-1948* (Occasional Papers, No. 41 [New York : National Bureau of Economic Research, 1954]). His data show the major rise in the ratio of fixed capital to output in manufacturing industries as occurring from 1880 to 1910 ; for most of this period interest rates were falling and/or very low.

It is no simple matter to measure changes in the interest rate; but in both the United States and the United Kingdom the available evidence suggests that all interest rates have fallen absolutely (and in relation to real wage rates) over the last seventy or eighty years.[1] Accepting this evidence, we would expect the behaviour of the interest rate to contribute to a secular upward tendency in the capital-output ratio.

As for returns to scale, there are no data to contradict the classical assumption of diminishing returns. This is especially true for that part of the economy which makes significant use of natural resources. As the availability of such natural resources as coal and iron ore is reduced (a reduction in their availability has, of course, occurred in the United States and the United Kingdom), the effectiveness of labour and capital applied to them is lowered and K/O should tend to increase. Similar reasoning is applicable, although less strikingly so, to agriculture. Surely, there should be no quarrel with the assumption of the general appropriateness of diminishing returns, more or less a major factor, depending on the extent to which the economy is raw-material- and agriculture-oriented.[2]

If we accept the conclusions about the declining rate of interest and diminishing returns, then we are left to explain the constancy of the capital-output ratio in terms of innovations and/or shifts in the composition of output.

[1] Here, too, I shall simply refer to readily available data. See Phelps Brown and Weber, op. cit., appendix; E. H. Phelps Brown and S. V. Hopkins, 'The Course of Real Wages in Five Countries', *Oxford Economic Papers*, Vol. II, N.S. (June 1950); Weber and Handfield Jones, op. cit.; *Historical Statistics of the United States, 1789-1945* (Washington: U.S. Department of Commerce, 1949), secs. D and N.

[2] Diminishing returns are represented in a production function of the type $O = AK^{a_1} L^{a_2}$ by $a_1 + a_2 < 1$. But if *all* factors were included in the equation rather than merely capital and labour (K and L), then surely the sum of exponents would be at least unity; that is, diminishing returns could not obtain. Diminishing returns to scale then means diminishing returns to capital and labour combined, with something else—for example, natural resources—held constant. Similarly, when it is said that innovations counteract diminishing returns, this must mean that 'innovations' have been omitted from the production function and the productivity of capital and labour then appear to increase (or not to decrease); more accurately, perhaps, we should say that innovations are substituted for capital and labour, in which case there would be no diminishing returns for the complete production function—one including innovations.

Although the concept of innovations is almost always used to refer to any kind of alteration in the productive technique, there is a persistent tendency to imply such major changes as the assembly line and the Bessemer process. Consequently, there is also the presumption that innovations are capital-using; that is, they tend to increase the capital-output ratio.[1] Much of cycle history is frequently explained in terms of such innovations, all requiring large investment outlays; all requiring a prolonged increase in demand, to be profitable; and all producing major structural changes in the system. But there seems little reason to assume that this is the only kind of innovation or even the most common kind. In particular, it appears that two kinds of technological change increase the efficiency with which capital is utilized.

First, there are those changes which reduce the capital tied up in goods in the pipeline.[2] Major improvements in transportation and distribution have reduced significantly the time needed to move finished goods from producer to user. Second, the alterations and changes generally classified as organizational changes have resulted in a more efficient use of capital and hence have worked to reduce K/O.

However, the most important factor working to increase the productiveness of capital appears to be the growth of general, social overhead facilities. Any given investment outlay now produces a larger increase in capacity than it would have, had these facilities not been in existence. Especially important in this respect is the extent of education and the consequent availability of a skilled labour force. But also important are transportation and power facilities, which create external economies for new enterprises as compared to ones undertaken earlier.[3] Not only do such general facilities contribute to the

[1] A neutral innovation is one that leaves the capital-output ratio unchanged, and capital-using and capital-saving innovations are defined correspondingly; this is Harrod's definition in *Towards a Dynamic Economics* (p. 22).

[2] Joan Robinson, *The Rate of Interest* (London: Macmillan & Co., Ltd, 1952), pp. 42-3.

[3] Compare John H. Adler, 'The Fiscal and Monetary Implementation of Development Programs', *American Economic Association Papers and Proceedings*, Vol. XLII (May 1952); Tibor Scitovsky, 'Two Concepts of External Economies', reprinted in the present volume, pp. 295-308; J. E. Meade, 'External Economies and Diseconomies in

increasing productiveness of specific investments, but there is also evidence that such projects as utilities and transportation systems build ahead of the market. This means that, as increased use is made of their facilities, their capital-output ratio declines.

It is argued here that the following sequence is generally characteristic of technological progress: first, major changes are made in productive technique, which require capital deepening. Such major innovations occur sporadically and are made only in anticipation of long-range increases in demand. Once these methods are in general use, however, numerous routine changes occur, representing more effective use of existing capital equipment. In many cases the simple replacement of worn-out equipment results in more effective use of a given stock of capital.[1] These organizational, routine innovations require little initial outlay and consequently can be made with virtually no significant commitment. I suggest that it is this kind of technological innovation that produces the year-in, year-out increases in the effectiveness with which the United States and the United Kingdom exploit their available resources.[2]

My hypothesis, then, is that day-to-day routine innovations are of the capital-saving variety and that these, together with particular external economies, provide the necessary counteracting force to a declining rate of interest and diminishing

a Competitive Situation', *The Economic Journal*, Vol. LXII (March 1952); and P. N. Rosenstein-Rodan, 'Problems of Industrialization of Eastern and South-eastern Europe', reprinted in the present volume, pp. 245-55.

[1] Phelps Brown and Handfield Jones, op. cit.; Phelps Brown and Weber, op. cit.

[2] This is a difficult position to support with quantitative evidence. In addition to the argument in the text, perhaps the best support that can be given it now is to observe that it is consistent with most theoretical discussions of the innovational process, discussions which, in general, are not concerned with the problem raised here. See especially Schumpeter's *Business Cycles* (New York: McGraw-Hill Book Co., 1939), chaps. i-v; B. S. Keirstead, *The Theory of Economic Change* (Toronto: Macmillan Co., 1948), chap. viii; W. W. Rostow, *The Process of Economic Growth* (New York: W. W. Norton & Co., 1952), chap. iv; Moses Abramovitz, 'Economics of Growth', in Bernard F. Haley (ed.), *A Survey of Contemporary Economics*, Vol. II (Homewood, Ill.: Richard D. Irwin, Inc., 1952); and A. P. Usher, *History of Mechanical Inventions* (New York: McGraw-Hill Book Co., 1929), *passim*.

returns, thus producing a constant capital-output ratio. I further hypothesize that such innovations—and evidently such external economies—occur only after the major capital-using innovations have already become effective and generally acceptable throughout the system.

As for the effects of shifts in the composition of output on the capital-output ratio, there appears to be no *a priori* reason to expect them to be other than neutral. Changes in the composition of output presumably reflect changes in final demand, and there is nothing to suggest that demand changes in such a way that the overall capital-output ratio is consistently pushed in one direction. The only readily available data on this are contained in Creamer's study cited earlier. He finds that only about one-sixth of the change in the capital-output ratio between 1880 and 1919 can be explained by a change in the composition of manufacturing output; after 1919 the capital-output ratio (in total manufacturing) declined, in spite of the altered composition of output. This evidence, though slight, added to the absence of any theoretical reason to expect otherwise, justifies the assumption that changes in the composition of output act randomly on the overall capital-output ratio.[1]

Now what is the relevance of all this for the underdeveloped countries? Since their output is very low relative to that of the more highly developed countries, their chief objective is to increase the capacity output of their economies as rapidly as possible. To do this, it is evidently desirable to have capital as productive as possible—that is, K/O as low as possible. To the extent that the rate of interest reflects the shortage of capital relative to labour, the low K/O will obtain. But this means low productivity per worker and hence low real *per*

[1] This may be the appropriate point at which to note that Creamer's findings show a clear-cut increase in the capital-output ratio for manufacturing industries from 1880 to 1920 and a sharp decline thereafter. William Fellner (*Monetary Policies and Full Employment* [Berkeley: University of California Press, 1947], p. 80) shows about the same thing for capital and output as a whole. Creamer's data are convincing, but the evidence that K/O for output as a whole behaved in the same way is not yet clear. Further disaggregating may show that it has behaved similarly. Even if this is the case, the burden of the argument in the text will not be affected, and my hypothesis about the sequence of innovations will still be valid.

capita income. Therefore, to increase *per capita* income, we must increase the proportion of capital in the input-mix ; we must move around the equal-product curve, using more capital and less labour to achieve the same output. This process is, by definition, capital-deepening and can be accomplished only by increasing the supply of capital relative to that of labour. This would release labour, and, assuming that the released labour will be employed—more on this in a moment—total output and *per capita* output would increase.

However, there is also evidence that the isoquant map itself is not the same for Country U as it is for Country D. This evidence suggests that, even with the same relative quantities of labour and capital, output is likely to be less in the former country than in the latter. This means simply that the level of technology in U is lower than that in D. Two requirements are then evident for the underdeveloped country. On the one hand, it must seek to increase its available supply of capital relative to that of labour ; this will result in increased labour productivity and, under certain assumptions (to be discussed), increased *per capita* income. But in order to achieve a rate of productivity and a rate of productivity increase comparable to that in the developed countries, there must also be a substantial raising of the technological level in the underdeveloped country.[1] I have argued earlier that the major innovations in the United States and the United Kingdom—those resulting in the most pronounced increase in output—were capital-using ; that is, they resulted in an increase in the capital-output ratio. These major, capital-using innovations were necessary before the minor, routine, capital-saving innovations could be made. To the extent that Country U imports its improved technology, it would appear necessary for it to go through the same sequence.

If this is true, then it means that the initial innovations[2] in U must run counter to the dictates of the relative factor-supply situation ; where the capital-labour ratio calls for labour-

[1] Conceivably, of course, technology could do the job alone ; what is meant here is that technological level achieved by the more highly developed countries.

[2] For Country U, 'innovation' refers to the *importation* of new techniques not now used in U, from Country D.

using, capital-saving innovations, modern technology calls for a series of innovations which are the exact opposite *before* the capital-saving innovations are possible. Also, it is a much simpler matter to import major new processes than it is to import changes which are associated with organization and which seem to be chiefly a function of the experience, initiative, and enthusiasm of management. Thus in the earlier stages of the reorganization of the economy of an underdeveloped country, such a country will have a high K/O at the time it can very least afford it. As the new methods become more firmly and widely understood and as the external economies become effective, K/O will begin to decrease. This creates a rather severe problem : because of the abruptness with which low-income countries are attempting to reorganize their general economic system, they are forced—by modern technology—to introduce methods of production that their factor-supply situation will not justify.[1]

And this leads to another problem. There is, in general, not enough capital for a complete reorganization of the economy of the underdeveloped country.[2] A (relatively) small amount of capital, if introduced so as to achieve maximum productivity, will be insufficient to employ all labour in the most effective way. Indeed, increased unemployment may result, for the introduction of technological changes that substitute capital for labour releases some of the latter resource. Unless more capital is available to employ the released workers, unemployment is the consequence. A somewhat paradoxical situation develops in which output and unemployment are both increasing.

The unemployment is caused by a shortage of investment, but the shortage of investment is caused not by a deficiency of aggregate demand but simply by a shortage of capital.[3]

[1] This argument is discussed in the Economic Commission for Latin America's *Theoretical and Practical Problems of Economic Growth* (1950).

[2] Someone has estimated that it would require one trillion dollars of investment to provide China and India with enough capital to achieve the capital-worker ratio that obtains in the United States. One cannot be sure exactly how much a trillion dollars really is, but one can be sure that it is much more than is available.

[3] This kind of unemployment is usually referred to as 'Marxian'; Ricardo was also worried about it (see Hamberg, op. cit.).

Not only must capital be available for the existing labour force, but evidently in many underdeveloped countries $l + p + lp > s/k$, and the situation is growing secularly more severe.

In the case of the developed countries, the threat of unemployment loomed imposing because of the inability of demand to grow with the capacity generated by investment. For Country U, unemployment looms imposing because of the insufficiency of savings ; there is too little capital to employ all labour at the maximum productivity allowed by modern technology.

I turn now to the savings function. Here, too, the assumption usually made is that the average propensity to save (and hence the marginal propensity) is constant. It seems impossible, however, to state the necessary and sufficient conditions for constancy and work through them as we just did for the capital-output ratio. Present data are insufficient to test in any reasonably satisfactory way all the many hypotheses that could be used to explain the relationship between S and Y over long periods.[1] Until we know more about the behaviour of the saving-income relation through time in the highly developed countries, it seems futile to speculate on its behaviour in an underdeveloped country. Perhaps a safe generalization—and one that will enable me to pass on to matters that I am able to talk about—would be that there is no convincing historical evidence that S/Y adjusts itself so as to alleviate (or even to tend to alleviate) inflationary or deflationary situations or so as to affect the level of employment. Such hypotheses can be made, of course, but there is little reason to accept any one over any other.

There are, however, two frequently encountered arguments about the savings-income ratio to which a brief reference should be made. Professor Ragnar Nurkse[2] has suggested that 'when people come into contact with superior goods or superior

[1] The findings of Raymond W. Goldsmith, *A Study of Saving in the United States* (Princeton, N.J. : Princeton University Press, 1955), may shed light on this question. Volumes I and II of this work appeared after this paper was prepared.

[2] *Problems of Capital Formation in Underdeveloped Countries* (New York : Oxford University Press, 1953).

patterns of consumption, with new articles or new ways of meeting old wants they are apt to feel after a while a certain restlessness and dissatisfaction. Their knowledge is extended, their imagination stimulated; new desires are aroused, the propensity to consume is shifted upwards.'[1] If such a 'demonstration effect' were operative, it would mean that S/Y was maintained at a lower value in U than in D as long as the former country had relatively low incomes, that is, as long as it was underdeveloped. This, of course, would add to the difficulties for the underdeveloped country outlined in the previous section (and to those to be discussed in the next section). However, one might equally well assume that the inequality of income among nations resulted in the lower-income countries having a larger S/Y because they were aware that this was the best way to catch up with high-income countries. *A priori*, each behaviouristic assumption is equally plausible, and we must await more empirical data before attempting to settle on specific assumptions.

The second argument has to do with the effect of inequality in the distribution of income on the propensity to save out of a given level of income. Available data show that income is less equally distributed in a representative underdeveloped country than in a highly developed economy, and this fact should tend to make S/Y higher for Country U than for Country D. However, there is one difficulty with this potential advantage. The highest individual incomes in underdeveloped countries are largely received from land and house rents. Inequality in such countries arising out of relatively high rental incomes does not favour the accumulation of productive capital equipment but rather has led to such things as speculative housing projects—frequently of a luxury type—or conspicuous consumption. Thus inequality alone is not sufficient to assure productive capital accumulation; the inequality must favour those who know how to and are willing to invest their surplus income productively. Landowners in underdeveloped countries are certainly not in this category. Therefore, it is possible that a more equal distribution of income in Country U would result in a more rapid rate of capital accumulation if this greater

[1] ibid., pp. 58-9.

equality was achieved at the expense of rents and in favour of larger returns to owners of productive capital equipment.[1]

International trade has been introduced into the growth models only in a perfunctory way;[2] but when these models are applied to an underdeveloped country, considerably more attention to it is required. Formally, foreign trade may be introduced into the growth equation easily enough, simply as the foreign account counterpart of savings. We write M for all debit items on current account and X for all credit items, then take the ratio of $M - X$ to income, call this b, and write the growth equation as

$$\frac{\Delta Y}{Y} = \frac{s + b}{k}$$

It is evident that if b is negative, that is, if $X/Y > M/Y$, the percentage rate of growth of income required to utilize all the increasing domestic capacity is less than it would be in the absence of trade. Similarly, if b is positive, then the allowable rate of growth of income is higher than it could be in the absence of trade. The problem then is to attempt to establish the time path of the relationship between imports and exports.

The traditional approach is to set up a sequence somewhat as follows[3] and argue that all countries pass from one stage to the next:

Borrowing debtor	Increasing import surplus
Debtor	Constant import surplus
Paying debtor	Decreasing import surplus
Lending creditor	Increasing export surplus
Creditor	Constant export surplus

[1] On this point, see the interesting article by W. A. Lewis, 'Economic Development with Unlimited Supplies of Labour', reprinted in the present volume, pp. 400-49.

[2] See Harry G. Johnson, 'Equilibrium Growth in an International Economy', *Canadian Journal of Economics and Political Science*, Vol. XIX (November 1953). He provides the most complete analysis of the role of international trade. R. F. Harrod also has something to say on the subject in his *Towards a Dynamic Economics*, pp. 101-15.

[3] Professor Charles P. Kindleberger makes use of this approach in some detail (see his *International Economics* [Homewood, Ill.: Richard D. Irwin, Inc., 1953], chaps. xix-xx). It can also be found as far back as J. E. Cairnes, *Some Leading Principles of Political Economy* (New York, 1900), pp. 360-62.

Receiving creditor	Decreasing export surplus
Mature creditor	Import surplus

Progression through this sequence is also the progression from low income to higher income and from inflationary-biased economies to deflationary-biased ones. Therefore, if all countries followed this sequence, the foreign-trade sector would tend to make the attainment of a higher allowable rate of growth possible when this is the desired situation, and then to make the required rate lower when that is desirable, namely, when deflation threatens. In the early phases of development a positive b is made possible by capital imports from those mature economies that need an export surplus to counter savings that cannot be matched by domestic investment. Hence the allowable rate of growth of the underdeveloped country is increased, and the required rate of growth of the mature economies is decreased.

But this simplified reasoning rests on certain assumptions which require examination before they can be realistically incorporated into the analysis. The sequence rests on the argument that the rate of return on capital invested domestically falls through time relative to the rate obtainable abroad. As a country provides more and more savings, its investors seek to send those savings to areas where there is less capital in relation to other resources and hence the return per unit of capital is higher. The sequence then appears to rest on the generally acceptable notion of variable proportions and so to have a rather firm base. However, some problems may be indicated which complicate matters.

We are interested in the ratios M/Y and X/Y and their behaviour through time. The sequence of developments described in the first paragraphs of this section follows a well-defined path; defining this path requires further assumptions about the changes that occur in the structure of the system with respect to international trade. These structural adjustments create the complicating problems previously referred to.

Consider, first, the question of imports. The simplest assumption to make is, of course, that the average propensity to import—and hence the marginal propensity—is constant. We may ask the same question about M/Y that we asked about K/O; namely, what are the necessary conditions for constancy (assuming S/Y constant)?

It is fairly legitimate procedure to consider the equations determining K/O as essentially, if not purely, technological in nature.[1] In like manner the savings function may be considered a behaviouristic equation. The import function, however, requires consideration of both a technological and a behaviouristic kind.

From the standpoint of Country D, on the technological side, imports of raw materials are an essential input of the productive process and so are to be treated like any other input. It is necessary, then, to consider the time path of the ratio between imports of raw materials, M_r, and output of manufactured products, O_m. Decreasing values of this ratio could be accounted for in one of two ways: first, by innovations whose consequences were that imported raw materials would be used in a more and more efficient manner and, second, by changes in the composition of manufactured output that would produce changes in M_r/O_m. Such changes could result from changes in tastes or from governmental policy, which, by artificially restricting imports, forced manufacturing output into areas that required smaller amounts of imports. Increasing values of the M_r/O_m ratio could be accounted for by the same phenomena acting in the opposite direction. The assumption of a constant M_r/O_m then either requires that there be no technological change—a completely impossible assumption in any kind of growth analysis—and no change, or only random changes, in the composition of manufactured output, or it requires that if such changes occur, they cancel out.

Available data are consistent with the hypothesis that for the United States and the United Kingdom M_r/O_m has a downward trend over time.[2] There seems to be no reason to

[1] An opposing point of view can be found in Trygve Haavelmo, *Contribution to the Theory of Economic Evolution* (Oslo: Universitetets Social-økonomiske Institutt, 1951), pp. 43-4.

[2] See A. K. Cairncross and J. Faaland, 'Long-Term Trends in Europe's Trade', *The Economic Journal*, Vol. LXII (March 1952); Economic Commission for Latin America, *Economic Survey of Latin America, 1949* (New York, 1951); and the same group's *A Study of Trade between Latin America and Europe* (Geneva, 1953); John H. Adler, Eugene R. Schlesinger, and Evelyn van Westerborg, *The Pattern of United States Import Trade since 1923* (New York: Federal Reserve Bank of New York, 1952); and Hans Neisser and Franco Modigliani, *National Income and International Trade: A Quantitative Analysis* (Urbana: University of Illinois Press, 1953), chap. xii.

assume that changes in the composition of output due to changes in tastes in either of these countries were other than random in their effect on import content. To the extent that tariff and exchange policy had an effect, they undoubtedly worked to reduce imports. However, such policies were largely aimed not at raw-material imports[1] but at imports of finished goods and agricultural commodities. Therefore, I conclude that the falling M_r/O_m is the result of import-saving technological changes.[2] There is much evidence to support this conclusion: the development of synthetics, the increasingly effective use of by-products, and the general overall increasing efficiency with which all inputs are used, which is commonly accepted as a feature of the economic history of the United States and the United Kingdom.

On the behaviouristic side, the problem is to find hypotheses to explain the pattern of consumption through time as income increases. There seems little reason to assume that consumers prefer imported products to domestic ones merely because they are imported. There may be some increase in imports of consumer goods because of conspicuous or ostentatious consumption behaviour. Probably a portion of the purchases of such imported goods as perfumes and wines would fall in this category, as would some foreign tourism, but in an aggregative model of the United States or the United Kingdom this is insignificant enough to be ignored.

Similarly, there is no evidence to justify the assumption that, as *per capita* income increases and as a country exploits its resources in more and more effective ways, an increasing proportion of consumer products—as opposed to services—are domestically produced. This is probably the case in the United States, but here it is to be explained in terms of our competitive strength in consumer durables, which attract an increasing portion of incremental expenditures of consumers. Therefore, the imports of consumer products of a country whose competitive strength lay elsewhere than in consumer

[1] The emphasis on national defence nowadays requires that this statement be qualified to some extent.

[2] The effect of import-saving innovations in highly developed countries has been discussed in the Economic Commission for Latin America publication cited in note 1 on p. 229.

durables would tend to increase as *per capita* income increased. These remarks suggest that no hypothesis about the importation of consumer products would be generally applicable; the nature of resource endowments must be specified.

More important is the hypothesis that, as consumption rises, an increasing percentage of the increment will be in the form of consumption of services as opposed to products. If this is true—and the data suggest that it is[1]—then the behaviour of the ratio of total imported consumer goods, M_c, to total consumption, O_c, depends chiefly on the division of expenditures on services between domestic services and foreign. It seems probable that much the greater part of the increment in the consumption of services will be of domestic services. Increased expenditures on health, education, entertainment, domestic travel, and financial and legal services are clearly a positive function of real *per capita* income and require virtually no expenditure in foreign currencies.

The hypothesis then suggests itself that the ratio of expenditures on imported consumer products to total consumption, M_{cp}/O_c, behaves randomly over time so far as all countries are concerned—it would not for one country—while the ratio of expenditures on imported consumer services to total consumption expenditure, M_{cs}/O_c, decreases. And if we further accept the proposition that expenditures on consumer services become an increasing proportion of total consumer spending—certainly after a given level of *per capita* income has been reached—then the ratio of total spending on consumer imports of goods and services to total consumption, M_c/O_c, must fall through time.

Now if we combine the technological side and the behaviouristic side of the import equation, we can see the necessary conditions for stability of M/Y through time. Both the M_r/O_m ratio and the M_c/O_c ratio must remain constant, or the two ratios must move in such a way as to cancel each other out. For the country whose nonconsumption imports are chiefly raw materials, the presumption is strong that M_r/O_m will decrease through time. On the consumption side, the reasoning and evidence are less conclusive; though we can be confident

[1] Kuznets, op. cit., Part III.

about the falling import content of services, imported consumer products may rise relative to consumer spending (and income), and this could counter the technological effect. But such cancellation appears unlikely, and the most reasonable hypothesis seems to be that M/Y will fall. For both the United States and the United Kingdom, M/Y has been falling,[1] and probably both technological and behaviouristic factors have been working in the same direction. Also it has been falling faster and more consistently in the United States than in the United Kingdom, and this is what we expect, since technological change has occurred more steadily and *per capita* income has increased more in the United States than in the United Kingdom over the last seventy or eighty years.

Assuming the availability of foreign exchange, the underdeveloped country in the early stages of its development is, as noted, in the borrowing-debtor stage. This requires M/Y to be increasing relative to X/Y. That imports would increase if possible is readily acceptable, for both the technological and the behaviouristic aspects of the import function would work in this direction. Technologically, Country U needs capital equipment to increase the productivity of its labour force. Whereas for the developed countries the technological aspect of the import equation was discussed in terms of the raw-material input of these countries' production, for the underdeveloped country the situation is somewhat reversed. As development gets under way, imports of capital equipment will increase because of the relationship between capital input and the output of Country U. Thus, where the developed countries must import raw materials to go with their capital, the underdeveloped countries must import capital to go with their raw materials and labour.

I have argued earlier that innovations have historically been of an import-saving kind, which for the developed countries meant essentially raw-material saving. These same innovations would appear to be import-using from the standpoint of Country U. But I have also argued that organizational and management innovations play a significant role in the process of innovation; these changes require little or no increase in

[1] See the sources cited in note 2 on p. 234.

imports and are surely a requisite for increasing output in the underdeveloped country. On the basis of this reasoning—there are no data, of course—we may conclude only that it is very unlikely that, for technological reasons, M/Y will decrease as income increases through time but that such increases should work to raise this ratio or leave it approximately constant.

On the behaviouristic side, imports should increase also. At the levels of income characteristic of most modern underdeveloped countries, expenditures on services seems to constitute a relatively small part of the increment of consumption expenditures. This may be explained by the fact that many underdeveloped countries have considerable resources—chiefly labour—in service activities.[1] And it is not until *per capita* income has increased substantially that existing service facilities will become inadequate. As income increases, therefore, expenditures will be directed largely toward purchases of consumer products, as opposed to services. The range of output in U is limited to a few primary products; increments of consumer spending will therefore be, to a very large extent, directed toward products that are not domestically produced, with prevailing rates of productivity.

If these are the factors determining M/Y, there appears to be no reason to assume that this ratio will decrease as the country develops. Indeed, the analysis of the preceding two paragraphs suggests that, if M/Y changes at all, it will increase. If this is true—if imports grow at least at the same percentage rate as income—then the availability of foreign exchange imposes a definite ceiling on the rate of growth of income.[2] There is no reason under my assumptions for the rate of growth of income allowed by the import function to be equal to the rate of growth of income required to maintain the labour force fully employed in such a way that its productivity is maximized or even that its marginal productivity is positive.

Earlier, in the analysis of s and k, I argued that, because of the shortage of capital and the specified behaviour of k,

[1] Richard Holton, 'Marketing Structure and Economic Development', *Quarterly Journal of Economics*, Vol. LXVII (August 1953).

[2] Here, perhaps, the two-country assumption is misleading, since shortage of specific exchange may cause trouble. Elaboration of this problem cannot be undertaken here.

unemployment threatened as $s/k < l + p + lp$. Here it is argued that the percentage rate of growth of imports also imposes an upper limit on the percentage rate of growth of income. The rate of growth of import-earning power is simply the rate of growth of exports and capital inflow, $x + c$. Thus, if $x + c < l + p + lp$, there will be unemployment—indeed, increasing unemployment—due to the inability of import-earning power to reach the rate of growth, which, if attained by income, would result in all labour being employed productively.

In examining the time path of M/Y for the developed countries, I also implied something about the time path of the exports of Country U. If exports are the sole source of exchange-earning power for U, the percentage rate of growth of income for this country must be less than that for the developed countries. I have argued that $\Delta M_u/M_u = \Delta Y_u/Y_u$ and $\Delta M_d/M_d < \Delta Y_d/Y_d$, and, since $\Delta M_d/M_d = \Delta X_u/X_u$, then $\Delta X_u/X_u < \Delta Y_d/Y_d$. (The subscripts u and d refer to underdeveloped and developed countries, respectively.) Since the rate of growth of income in U has a ceiling set by the rate of growth of foreign exchange and since this rate of growth is less than the rate of growth of income of the developed countries, U's income must necessarily grow at a lower rate than that of the developed countries.[1] Without capital imports, therefore, the underdeveloped country not only will be unable to achieve the rate of growth of income of the developed countries but may suffer unemployment as well. A rapid growth of income in the developed country is necessary to keep the percentage rate of growth of U's exports from declining ; but this means that the absolute difference between the incomes of D and U will increase and the underdeveloped country will fall further and further behind.

Evidently, capital imports would alleviate the situation, but—and this is the key point—they would be *permanently* necessary. A constant rate of capital inflow into U would raise the allowable rate of growth (possibly as high as for the developed countries) ; but, given the technological and behaviouristic

[1] It should be remembered that I have assumed constant prices all around ; changes in the terms of trade would introduce a new variable here, which might alter the conclusion in the text.

patterns described here, such capital imports would have to continue indefinitely. Once they stopped or slowed down, U would fall back again. It is to be emphasized that a rising income in U resulting in more savings is not a sufficient condition to overcome this problem. Even if the underdeveloped country reaches the point at which it has excess domestic savings and can lend abroad, the nature of the demand for its exports prevents this from occurring. The developed countries are able to earn all their imports ; Country U will still be limited by its capacity to import. In order to follow the development sequence described earlier, not only must the modern underdeveloped country experience an increase in *per capita* income, but there must also be an alteration in the technological and behaviouristic conditions I have outlined ; otherwise the underdeveloped country will remain dependent upon capital inflow. A constant percentage rate of net capital inflow is not conceptually impossible,[1] but it surely is unlikely, and it certainly is not an assumption upon which a realistic development programme can be built.

I can now summarize briefly. In the literature on economic development and in public statements by leaders of underdeveloped countries, emphasis is always placed on the need for more and more capital. This is surely correct and was never a secret. It would appear, however, that, though more capital is a necessary condition for speeding up the rate of development, it is not a sufficient condition. In particular, the preceding analysis has revealed the fundamental role of the nature and pattern of technological change. Liquid capital is perfectly adaptable and can be directed in whatever way is appropriate ; the same is not true of modern technology. Modern technology was developed and is being advanced in a few countries with particular and highly local characteristics, and the technological developments reflect these characteristics. There is no reason at all to assume that the technology thus developed can be bodily transferred to other countries with other characteristics

[1] Evsey D. Domar has shown that permanent outflow of capital, that is, a permanent export surplus, is not impossible (see his 'The Effect of Foreign Investments on the Balance of Payments', *The American Economic Review*, Vol. XL [December 1950]).

and there perform in the way it has performed in the area to which it is indigenous. Indeed, as we have seen, it may perform in a way that is actually harmful to development.

In the international sector similar reasoning is applicable. The argument for the industrialization of the underdeveloped countries usually involves the hypothesis that the terms of trade show a secular tendency to improve for the industrialized countries at the expense of the unindustrialized.[1] This hypothesis, even if it is correct, has surely been asked to support a heavier argument than it can bear.[2] But it does appear that there must be some major change in the technological and behaviouristic parameters of the import equation if the rate of growth of the underdeveloped countries is to approach that of the more highly developed countries. This means essentially that the ceiling imposed on the rate of growth of income by the availability of foreign exchange must be raised above that imposed by the limited rate of savings. Technologically the requirement appears once more to be the development of an improving technology consistent with the resource endowment of the given country. 'Behaviouristically' the way is not very clear. Controls that reduce consumer imports may be necessary to change the pattern of consumption or to gain time until domestic output can be increased and its composition changed so that an increased proportion of consumption can be met by domestic production. But this may involve a non-optimum allocation of resources and will itself serve to limit the rate of growth of output.

As for removing the difficulties through international capital movements, I have shown that unless there are the technological and behaviouristic changes, the import of capital does not solve the problem but merely relieves its immediacy. Further, the countries where capital is scarce, for reasons indicated, may not always offer capital its most productive employment. But foreign capital, even if available, cannot solve the technological problem ; this must be a purely domestic achievement of the underdeveloped country.

[1] See almost any publication of the Economic Commission for Latin America.

[2] Jacob Viner, *International Trade and Economic Development* (Free Press, Glencoe, Ill., U.S.A., 1952).

4. EXTERNAL ECONOMIES AND BALANCED GROWTH

PROBLEMS OF INDUSTRIALIZATION OF EASTERN AND SOUTH-EASTERN EUROPE*

by **P. N. Rosenstein-Rodan**

'I SHOULD LIKE TO BUY AN EGG, PLEASE,' SHE SAID TIMIDLY. 'How do you sell them ?' 'Fivepence farthing for one—twopence for two,' the Sheep replied. 'Then two are cheaper than one ?' Alice said in a surprised tone, taking out her purse. 'Only you *must* eat them both, if you buy two,' said the Sheep. 'Then I'll have *one*, please,' said Alice as she put the money down on the counter. For she thought to herself, 'They mightn't be at all nice, you know.' (Lewis Carroll, *Through the Looking-Glass*.)

It is generally agreed that industrialization[1] of 'international depressed areas' like Eastern and South-Eastern Europe (or the Far East) is in the general interest not only of those countries, but of the world as a whole. It is *the* way of achieving a more equal distribution of income between different areas of the world by raising incomes in depressed areas at a higher rate than in the rich areas. The assumptions in the case under discussion are : that there exists an 'agrarian excess population' in Eastern and South-Eastern Europe amounting to 20–25 million people out of the total population of 100–110 million, i.e., that about 25 per cent of the population is either totally or partially ('disguised unemployment') unemployed. The waste of labour is by no means confined to rich industrial countries. It is considerably greater in poor agrarian countries. If the principles of international division of labour are to be applied, labour must either be transported towards capital (emigration), or capital must be transported towards labour (industrialization). From the point of view of maximizing the

* *The Economic Journal*, June-September 1943. Reprinted by permission of the Royal Economic Society and the author. This article is included in the report of the Economic Group of the Committee on Reconstruction, Royal Institute of International Affairs.

[1] One might consider the industrialization of these countries as one chapter of agrarian reconstruction, or one might treat the improvement of agrarian production as one chapter of industrialization. What matters is to remember that the two tasks are interconnected parts of one problem.

world income, the difference between these two ways is one of transport costs only, and may be assumed to be negligible. Emigration and resettlement would, however, present so many difficulties in immigration areas (and in emigration areas) that it cannot be considered feasible on a large scale. A very considerable part of the task will have to be solved by industrialization.

In order to reach an 'optimum size' of the industrial enterprises, the area of industrialization must be sufficiently large. This fact, as well as the possibility of lowering the marginal risk of investment, make it imperative to aim at an economic unit comprising the whole area between Germany, Russia and Italy. Though large in terms of square miles or population, it is not large in terms of output. The total national income of this economic unit amounts to £2,000 million—i.e., 40 per cent of the income of Great Britain.

There are two fundamentally different ways of industrialization of that area :

(i) That Eastern and South-Eastern Europe should industrialize on its own, on the 'Russian model' (by which we do *not* mean communism), aiming at self-sufficiency, without international investment. That would imply the construction of all stages of industry, heavy industry, machine industry, as well as light industry, with the final result of a national economy built like a vertical industrial concern. This way presents several grave disadvantages : (*a*) It can only proceed slowly, because capital must be supplied internally at the expense of a standard of life and consumption which are already at a very low level. It implies, therefore, a heavy and, in our opinion, unnecessary sacrifice. (*b*) It will lead finally, since there are appropriate natural resources in the area, to an independent unit in the world economy implying a reduction in the international division of labour ; i.e., the output of the world as a whole would be less than it might be, the world would be poorer in material goods. (*c*) The difference in world economic structure is most clearly seen in the case of heavy industries. Building up heavy industries in Eastern and South-Eastern Europe at a great sacrifice would only add to the world excess capacity of heavy industry, and would constitute from the world's point of view largely a waste of resources.

(ii) The alternative way of industrialization would fit Eastern and South-Eastern Europe into the world economy, which would preserve the advantages of an international division of labour, and would therefore in the end produce more wealth for everybody. It would be based on substantial international investment or capital lending. This way presents several advantages: (*a*) It could proceed more quickly and at a small sacrifice of consumption of this area. From the point of view of international political stability there may be all the difference in the world if 50 per cent of the agrarian excess population in Eastern and South-Eastern Europe were profitably employed within ten years after the war instead of, say, 20 per cent. (*b*) The sound principles of international division of labour postulate labour-intensive—i.e., light industries in overpopulated areas. (*c*) Even for the purposes of an expanding world economy, the existing heavy industries in the U.S.A., Great Britain, Germany, France and Switzerland could certainly supply all the needs of the international depressed areas.

Clearly this way of industrialization is preferable to the autarkic one. It is a tremendous task, almost without historical precedent. There is no analogy to the process of industrialization in the early nineteenth century for a number of reasons which may be mentioned briefly before being examined in more detail. (*a*) International investment in the nineteenth century was largely self-liquidating, based on exchange of agrarian and industrial products. Nowadays liquidation can no longer be assumed to be 'automatic', although the problem can be solved if it is properly planned. (*b*) Existing institutions of international investment (floating of shares and loans) are inappropriate to the task of industrialization of a whole area. They deal with too small units and do not take advantage of external economies. Capital mostly goes to individual enterprises. There has never been a scheme of planned industrialization comprising a simultaneous planning of several complementary industries, which is part of our plan for Eastern and South-Eastern Europe (pages 249-51). (*c*) Technical progress was the main driving-force in the nineteenth century. Industrialization in international depressed areas, on the other hand, implies the application of *given* technical knowledge. (*d*) The increase in overhead costs and fixed capital since the nineteenth century has raised the risk of loss of capital and lowered the mobility of resources and the flexibility of the economic system. It has vastly increased the average size of the firm. (*e*) Political risks of international investment are very much greater today than in the nineteenth century, when it was assumed that certain things were 'not done'. State supervision and guarantees can, therefore, substantially lower risks, and for that reason constitute the *conditio sine qua non* of international investment on a large enough scale. Active participation of the State in economic life is a new factor which must be taken into account as a new datum. (*f*) People (even Eastern Europeans!) are not as tough today as they used to be. Social conscience would not stand for as much misery in peace-time as was taken for granted in the Darwinist nineteenth century. Milder methods must be used.

An institutional framework different from the present one is clearly necessary for the successful carrying out of industrialization in international depressed areas. In what follows arguments are submitted tending to show why the whole of the industry to be created is to be treated and planned like one huge firm or trust.

The first task of industrialization is to provide for training and 'skilling' of labour which is to transform Eastern European peasants into full-time or part-time industrial workers. The automatism of *laissez-faire* never worked properly in that field. It broke down because it is not profitable for a private entrepreneur to invest in training labour. There are no mortgages on workers—an entrepreneur who invests in training workers may lose capital if these workers contract with another firm. Although not a good investment for a private firm, it is the best investment for the State. It is also a good investment for the bulk of industries to be created when taken as a whole, although it may represent irrecoverable costs for a smaller unit. It constitutes an important instance of the Pigovian divergence between 'private and social marginal net product' where the latter is greater than the former. Training facilities (including transport and housing) of one million workers per annum would involve costs of certainly more than £100 million per annum —a sum which may be too great to be borne by the State (or the Eastern European national economy) if taken *apart* from the costs of the 50 per cent participation in its own 'Eastern European Industrial Trust'[1] that we shall propose. It should be counted as capital investment in the Eastern European Industrial Trust (E.E.I.T.).

That is not, however, the most important reason in favour of such a large investment unit.

Complementarity of different industries provides the most important set of arguments in favour of a large-scale planned industrialization. In order to illustrate the issues involved, let us adopt the somewhat roundabout method of analysing two examples. Let us assume that 20,000 unemployed workers in Eastern and South-Eastern Europe are taken from the land and put into a large shoe factory. They receive wages substantially higher than their previous meagre income *in natura*. It would be impossible to put them into industry at their previous income standard, because they need more foodstuffs than they had in their agrarian semi-unemployed existence, because these foodstuffs have to be transported to towns, and because the workers have to pay for housing accommodation. If these workers spent all their wages on shoes, a market for the products of their enterprise would arise representing an expansion which does not disturb the pre-existing market, and 90 per cent of the problem (assuming 10 per cent profit) would be solved. The trouble is that the workers will not spend all their wages on shoes. If, instead, one million unemployed workers were taken from the land and put, not into one industry, but into a whole series of industries which produce the bulk of the goods on which the workers would spend their wages, what was not true in the case of one shoe factory would become true in the case of a whole system of industries : it would create its own additional market, thus realizing an expansion of world output with the minimum disturbance of the world markets. The industries producing the bulk of the wage goods can therefore be said to be complementary. The planned creation of such a complementary system reduces the risk of not being able to sell, and, since risk can be considered as cost,

[1] The name is provisional for want of a better one. It will have to be changed because of the unpleasant associations connected with the term 'trust'. Eastern European Industrial Corporation, Board—or Holding Company might be considered.

it reduces costs. It is in this sense a special case of 'external economies'.

It may be added that, while in the highly developed and rich countries with their more variegated needs it is difficult to assess the prospective demand of the population, it is not as difficult to foresee on what the formerly unemployed workers would spend their wages in regions where a low standard of living obtains.

Two other types of 'external economies' will arise when a system of different industries is created. First, the strictly Marshallian economies external to a firm within a growing industry. The same applies, however (secondly), to economies external to one industry due to the growth of other industries. It is usually tacitly assumed that the divergence between the 'private and social marginal net product' is not very considerable. This assumption may be too optimistic even in the case of a crystallized mature competitive economy. It is certainly not true in the case of fundamental structural changes in the international depressed areas. External economies may there be of the same order of magnitude as profits which appear on the profit and loss account of the enterprise.

The existing institutions of international and national investment do not take advantage of external economies. There is no incentive within their framework for many investments which are profitable in terms of 'social marginal net product', but do not appear profitable in terms of 'private marginal net product'. The main driving-force of investment is the profit expectation of an individual entrepreneur which is based on experience of the past. Experience of the past is partly irrelevant, however, where the whole economic structure of a region is to be changed. An individual entrepreneur's knowledge of the market is bound to be insufficient in this case because he cannot have all the data that would be available to the planning board of an E.E.I.T. His subjective risk estimate is bound to be considerably higher than the objective risk. If the industrialization of international depressed areas were to rely entirely on the normal incentive of private entrepreneurs, the process would not only be very much slower, the rate of investment smaller and (consequently) the national income lower, but the whole economic structure of the region would be different. Investment would be distributed in different proportions between different industries, the final equilibrium would be below the optimum which a large E.E.I.T. could achieve. In the international capital market the existing institutions are mostly used to invest in, or to grant credit to, single enterprises. It might easily happen that any one enterprise would not be profitable enough to guarantee payment of sufficient interest or dividend out of its own profits. But the creation of such an enterprise, e.g., production of electric power, may create new investment opportunities and profits elswhere, e.g., in an electrical equipment industry. If we create a sufficiently large investment unit by including all the new industries of the region, external economies will become internal profits out of which dividends may be paid easily.

Professor Allyn Young's celebrated example elucidates our problem. He assumed that a Tube line was to be built in a district and that an accurate estimate was made of costs and receipts. It was found that the rate of profit would be below the usual rate of yield on investments obtainable elsewhere. The project was found not profitable and was abandoned. Another enterprising company bought up the land and houses along the proposed Tube line and was then able to build the line. Although the receipts from the passenger traffic would not pay a sufficient rate of profit, the capital appreciation on the houses and land more than made up the deficiency. Thus the project was realized, the Tube line was built. The problem is : Is it desirable—i.e., does it lend to an optimum allocation of resources and maximization of national income—that this form of capital gain (external economy) be included as an item in the calculus of profitability, or is it not ? Allyn Young hints that it is not desirable because the capital appreciation of houses and land along the Tube line due to an influx of people from other districts has an uncompensated counterpart in a capital depreciation of houses and land in districts out of which people moved into the Tube-line district. Agricultural land in Eastern and South-Eastern Europe will, however, not depreciate when the agrarian excess of population moves out. In this case external economies should be included in the calculus of profitability.

External economies are often invoked as an argument in favour of a different programme of industrialization. National and international investment should concentrate at the start on building of 'basic industries' and public utilities which give rise to new investment opportunities. 'Let us build railways, roads, canals, hydro-electric power-stations, the rest will follow automatically.' Where the lack of transport facilities is a flagrant obstacle to economic progress, as, for instance, in China and parts of Latin America, that may indeed be the best start of development investment. The situation is different, however, in Eastern and South-Eastern Europe. There is no comparable deficiency in railroads there. Rail mileage per £ million of national income is very much higher than in the Far East. A general vision of the future economic structure is necessary in order to know where to build communications, how much of them, and what for. The quality of 'basic' industries is not confined, moreover, to some public utilities. We have seen how complementarity makes to some extent all industries 'basic'.

If sufficient capital (national and international) is available for investment in 'basic industries' the normal multiplier effect will 'naturally' lead to further industrialization according to the advocates of this programme. The argument assumes, however, a smooth working of the equilibrium mechanism of balance of payments and capital movements which is not likely to obtain in the structural disequilibrium situation after the war. Industrialization of international depressed areas, once it is accomplished, may create an equilibrium, from which onwards normal private incentives may operate successfully. But it seems hopeless to rely on them before that point is reached. 'Most of the countries of the world are undertaking national development or will undertake it after the war on the basis of imported capital equipment—locomotives, steel, tractors, steam shovels, cement mixers, turbines. In some instances they have foreign assets which can be used to purchase this equipment. In the majority of cases, however, they will be able to acquire it only by cutting down imports of consumer goods and pushing exports, to develop an export surplus, or by borrowing. Private investors . . . after the experience of the last twenty years, will probably not be willing to lend monies in sufficiently large amounts or low rates of interest to enable national development in debtor areas to get off to a good start. The alternative is for governments in creditor countries to guarantee the loans, or to lend the funds themselves. . . . The availability of foreign funds, foreign technical assistance and foreign machinery, however, will transform the process of national development from one which would threaten to disrupt international economic relations and trade into one which can make a key contribution to the expansion of world income and the reorganisation of world trade.'[1]

Governments in creditor countries will not guarantee the loans or shares unless they see how interest or dividend service is assured. If they have sufficient control on the board of E.E.I.T. they will be able to give the guarantee at no cost or risk to themselves, since the real risks of the whole enterprise is very much lower than the risks relating to parts of the whole would be. But while the investment 'pays' in Eastern and South-Eastern Europe, it is not necessarily self-liquidating. Liquidation will have to be planned—i.e., one part of the industries created in Eastern and South-Eastern Europe will have to be export industries. The flow of their exports will have to be sold in creditor countries. These exports will represent the main part of the rich countries' share in the world expansion. The placing of these exports has to be foreseen and planned in such a way as to minimize the burden of necessary adjustment of economic resources in the creditor countries. Eastern and South-Eastern Europe will most probably cease to be an exporter of cereals. It will export processed foods and light industrial articles.

International trade in the nineteenth century functioned more or less smoothly because all countries had a high income elasticity of demand for imports. On the higher standard of living in the rich countries of the twentieth century the income elasticity of demand for imports may be lower. There may be only one good for which the income elasticity of demand is high : leisure which does not require imports of material goods. Accordingly, the rich countries may have to accept a part of their share in economic expansion in the form of more leisure.

[1] *International Development Loans*, Planning Pamphlets, National Planning Association, No. 15, p. 14. (New York, 1942.)

They may have a 40- or 35-hour week, while Eastern Europe maintains a 48-hour week.

Attention is confined here to what ought to be done rather than how it is to be done. The institutional implementation of this programme must be left over to another occasion. Its main outlines are : At least 50 per cent of the capital required must be supplied internally. 'Creditor' and 'debtor' countries acquire each 50 per cent shares of a trust formed of all the industries to be created in the region. They will plan and proceed as business partners with Government representatives on the board. The creditors acquire shares in the trust which are redeemable after twenty years at 10 per cent above parity if an average dividend service of 4½ per cent at least has been maintained in the past. An *average* dividend service of 3 per cent is guaranteed by Governments on the shares subscribed in their countries. Private investments in Eastern and South-Eastern Europe requiring foreign credits are licensed. Shares may be acquired by contributions *in natura* : for instance, the establishment of branch factories. Guarantees of non-discrimination in the internal taxation policy will be obtained from Eastern European authorities.

The aim of industrialization in international depressed areas is to produce a structural equilibrium in the world economy by creating productive employment for the agrarian excess population. It may be assumed that creditor countries will not be willing to enter into commitments for more than ten years. How much can be achieved in that period, and what is the rough order of magnitude of the capital required ?

Industrial employment has to be found for (*a*) 20 million of the agrarian excess population + (*b*) 7–8 million = 40–50 per cent of the increase in population during the next decade (assuming that 50–60 per cent will be absorbed by agriculture) = 28 million people = 9 million active men and 3 million active women = 12 million workers. Up to 2 million workers can be employed in idle capacity. Capital has to be found for 10 million workers. Since the available capital is scarce, labour-intensive —i.e., light industries—will prevail. According to such statistics as are available, the following classification of industries is proposed : (1) light industries—capital equipment per head

£100–£400 ; (2) medium industries—capital equipment per head £400–£800 ; (3) heavy industries—capital equipment per head £800–£1,500. Since some heavy industries cannot be avoided, let us assume that £300–£350 per head will be required, including housing, communications and public utilities. That amounts to £3,000 million, to which has to be added £1,800 million on maintenance of old and new capital in ten years, giving a total of £4,800 million. Eastern Europe would have to supply at least 50 per cent—i.e., £2,400 million. Another £1,200 million of capital will be necessary for the improvement of agriculture, of which we assume that the bulk would have to be provided internally,[1] so that Eastern and South-Eastern Europe would have to supply £3,600 million capital internally between, say, 1946 and 1956.[2] Since its total income is £2,000 million per annum, that would represent a rate of investment of 18 per cent (equal to that of Russia). Even if we take account of the gradually rising national income, rates of savings beginning with 8 per cent and leading at the end of a ten-year period to 15 per cent would seem to represent the maximum one can plan for. Assuming a national income rising annually by 4 per cent, and an average rate of investment of 12 per cent, the internal capital supply would only amount to £3,000 million. It appears, therefore, that even a bold and rather optimistic programme of industrialization cannot abolish the whole of the surplus population in the next decade. At best 70–80 per cent of the unemployed workers could be employed. It follows that emigration will still have to supplement industrialization. Besides that, however, German reparations in the form of capital equipment might provide one part of the capital of the E.E.I.T. Reparations in money to the rich Western countries created a problem of the last war. There is no difficulty with reparations *in natura* to poor countries. Germany can increase her consumption above the war-time standard, and transfer reparations *in natura* representing 25–50 per cent of what she used to spend on armaments.

[1] A small part of it may be borrowed from abroad, but in this case in the form of bond credit.

[2] The immediate transition period of the first two years after the war is not included in these calculations, so that *de facto* it is a twelve-years plan, not a ten-years plan.

SOME INTERNATIONAL ASPECTS OF THE PROBLEM OF ECONOMIC DEVELOPMENT*

by **Ragnar Nurkse**

'A COUNTRY IS POOR BECAUSE IT IS POOR.' THIS SEEMS A TRITE proposition but it does express the circular relationships that afflict both the demand and the supply side of the problem of capital formation in economically backward areas. This paper will discuss some international aspects of the difficulties on both sides. It will take up only a few points and cannot even attempt to give anything like a balanced picture.

The inducement to invest is limited by the size of the market. That is essentially what Allyn Young[1] brought out in his reinterpretation of Adam Smith's famous thesis. What determines the size of the market ? Not simply money demand, nor mere numbers of people, nor physical area. Transport facilities, which Adam Smith singled out for special emphasis, are important ; reductions in transport costs (artificial as well as natural) do enlarge the market in the economic as well as the geographical sense. But reductions in any cost of production tend to have that effect. So the size of the market is determined by the general level of productivity. Capacity to buy means capacity to produce. In its turn, the level of productivity depends—not entirely by any means, but largely—on the use of capital in production. But the use of capital is inhibited, to start with, by the small size of the market.

Where is the way out of this circle ? How can the market be enlarged ? Although in backward areas Say's Law may be valid in the sense that there is generally no deflationary gap, it never is valid in the sense that the output of any single

* *The American Economic Review,* May 1952. Reprinted by permission of the American Economic Association and the author's widow.

[1] 'Increasing Returns and Economic Progress', *The Economic Journal,* December 1928.

industry, newly set up with capital equipment, can create its own demand. Human wants being various, the people engaged in the new industry will not wish to spend all their income on their own products.[1] Suppose it is a shoe industry. If in the rest of the economy nothing happens to increase productivity and hence buying power, the market for the new shoe output is likely to prove deficient. People in the rest of the economy will not give up other things in order to buy, say, a pair of shoes every year, if they do not have enough food, clothing, and shelter. They cannot let go the little they have of these elementary necessities. If they were willing to give up some of their present consumption in exchange for an annual pair of new shoes, these things would be available for the shoe workers to make up the balance in their own consumption needs. As it is, the new industry is likely to be a failure.

The difficulty is not due fundamentally to discontinuities in the technical forms of capital equipment, though these may accentuate it. It is due above all to the inevitable inelasticity of demands at low real-income levels. It is in this way that lack of buying power cramps the inducement to invest in any individual industry.

The difficulty is not present, however, in the case of a more or less synchronized application of capital to a wide range of different industries. Here the result is an overall enlargement of the market and hence an escape from the deadlock. People working with more and better tools in a number of complementary projects become each other's customers. Most industries catering for mass consumption are complementary in the sense that they provide a market for, and thus support, each other. This basic complementarity stems, of course, from the diversity of human wants. The case for 'balanced growth' rests ultimately on the need for a 'balanced diet'.

The notion of balance is inherent in Say's Law. Take Mill's formulation of it : 'Every increase of production, if distributed without miscalculation among all kinds of produce in the proportion which private interest would dictate, creates, or rather

[1] See Paul N. Rosenstein-Rodan, 'Problems of Industrialization of Eastern and South-Eastern Europe', reprinted in the present volume, pp. 249-50.

constitutes, its own demand.'[1] Here, in a nutshell, is the case for balanced growth. An increase in the production of shoes alone does not create its own demand. An increase in production over a wide range of consumables, so balanced as to correspond with the pattern of consumers' preferences, does create its own demand.

How do we get balanced growth ? Ordinary price incentives may bring it about by small degrees, though here the technical discontinuities can be a serious hindrance ; besides, slow growth is just not good enough where population pressure exists. In the evolution of Western industrial capitalism, rapid growth was achieved, in Schumpeter's view, through the action of creative entrepreneurs producing spurts of industrial progress. Even though innovations originated each time in a particular industry, the monetary effects and other circumstances were such as to promote each time a wave of new applications of capital over a whole range of industries. It is easy to see how a frontal attack of this sort can succeed while yet any sizable investment in any particular industry may be discouraged by the limits of the existing market.

Other types of society may feel a need for some degree of central direction to produce the desired effect—at any rate initially. But whether balanced growth is enforced by government planning or achieved spontaneously by private enterprise is, in a sense, a question of method. Whichever method is adopted, the nature of the solution aimed at may be the same, though the 'miscalculation' Mill warned against seems hard to avoid in either case.

On the international plane, these general considerations apply first of all to the problem of international investment. Why is it that private business investment abroad has tended in the past—in the last few years as well as in the nineteenth century—to shy away from industries working for the domestic market in underdeveloped areas and to concentrate instead on primary production for export to the advanced industrial centres ? The facts do not support the view that the so-called 'colonial' type of investment—in mines and plantations

[1] J. S. Mill, *Essays in Some Unsettled Questions of Political Economy* (London School of Economics reprint, 1948), p. 73.

producing for export to the industrial creditor countries—was typical of nineteenth century foreign investment as a whole. They do suggest, however, that it was, and still is, fairly typical of private business investment in backward areas. American direct investments abroad definitely conform to this pattern. In underdeveloped countries, they work mostly in extractive industries—oil-fields, mines, and plantations—producing for export markets ; only in advanced areas (Canada and Western Europe) do they, significantly, show any great interest in manufacturing for local consumption.[1]

The reluctance of private business capital to go to work for domestic markets in underdeveloped countries, in contrast with its eagerness in the past to work there for export to the industrial nations, reflects no sinister conspiracy or deliberate policy. There is the obvious economic explanation : on the one hand, the poverty of the local consumers in the backward countries ; on the other, the large and, in the nineteenth century, vigorously expanding markets for primary products in the world's industrial centres. In these circumstances it was natural for foreign business investment to form mere outposts of the industrial creditor countries, to whose needs these outposts catered.

Incidentally, the weakness of the market incentive for private investment in the domestic economy of a low-income area can affect domestic as well as foreign capital. It may help in some degree to account for the common observation that such domestic saving as does take place in underdeveloped countries tends to be used unproductively : hoarded, exported, or put into real estate.

Private investment generally is governed by the pull of market demand, and private international investment is no exception to this. A particular instance of the relation between investment incentives and market demand appears in our old friend the acceleration principle. The relation holds, albeit in a different way, in space as well as in the time dimension. The conventional theory of factor proportions and capital movements is that in countries where there is little capital in relation to land and labour, the marginal productivity and

[1] See H. J. Dernburg, 'Prospects for Long-Term Foreign Investment', *Harvard Business Review*, July 1950, p. 42.

hence the yield of capital will be high, and that, if it were not for extraneous impediments, capital would move to these countries from the areas where it is relatively abundant. This view is subject to the qualification that the high potential yield of capital in capital-poor areas may be capable of realization only through investment undertaken simultaneously in a number of complementary industries (or in public overhead facilities that serve to raise productivity in a number of different lines). A balanced increase in production generates external economies by enlarging the size of the market for each firm or industry. There is on this account as well as for other possible reasons, a discrepancy between the private and the social marginal productivity of capital. Even if we abstract from political and other risk factors, there is no guarantee that the motives that animate individual businessmen will automatically induce a flow of funds from the rich to the poor countries. The marginal productivity of capital in the latter compared with the former may be high indeed, but not necessarily in private business terms.

While the doctrine of balanced growth leaves plenty of room for international investment, it does reveal limits to the role of direct business investment. An individual foreign investor may not have the power, even if he had the will, to break the deadlock caused by low productivity, lack of real buying power, and deficient investment incentives in the domestic economy of a backward area. Even in the heyday of private foreign investment, however, capital outlays carried on by public authorities by means of private foreign loans were an important form of international investment. Loans to governments accounted for 30 per cent of Britain's total overseas investments outstanding in 1914, with another 40 per cent in railway securities and 5 per cent in public utilities.[1] Clearly this does not leave any major proportion for the strictly colonial type of investments—in mines and plantations producing for the creditor countries.

Investment by public authorities financed from private—or public—foreign funds is a form of 'autonomous' investment, since it does not depend closely, if at all, on the current state

[1] H. Feis, *Europe, the World's Banker, 1870-1914* (Yale University Press, 1930), p. 27.

of market demand. By contrast, direct business investment must be classed as a form of 'induced' investment since it generally has to be induced by tangible market demand, already existing or visibly coming into existence. Thus the general distinction between autonomous and induced investment is applicable in a certain sense to international investment as well.

International investment on private business account is attracted by markets, and for the poorer countries the big markets in the past were the markets for export to the great industrial centres. Investment was induced by the investing countries' own demand. Foreign investment in extractive industries working for export is not to be despised, since it usually carries with it various direct and indirect benefits to the country where it is made. Why is even this type of investment now flowing out in only a small trickle? Aside, again, from the obvious political impediments, perhaps the answer is that the export markets for primary commodities have not been enjoying anything like the same rate of secular expansion as that which came about in the nineteenth century from the extraordinary growth of population as well as productivity in the Western industrial countries, and also from Britain's willingness to sacrifice her own agriculture to the requirements of international specialization. In recent decades, synthetic substitutes have affected unfavourably the demand for a number of staple products. The present raw-material boom is widely regarded as being due to special circumstances which may not last. In any case, it may take more than a boom—it may take something like a secular expansion of demand—to induce private foreign investment in underdeveloped areas for the production of primary commodities for export.

Reliance on direct business investment for the capital needed for economic development is therefore liable to a double disappointment. Not only is there little or no incentive for private business capital to go to work for the expansion of the domestic economies of low-income countries; even for the expansion of raw-material supplies for export, private business funds may not want to move out in any steady or sizable flow. But this, I repeat, applies to induced investment. It does not, or need not, affect international investment of the autonomous sort.

The case which the underdeveloped countries advance in favour of their 'balanced growth' and 'diversification' is not always well received. Does it not mean turning away from the principle of comparative advantage ? Why do these countries not push their exports of primary products according to the rules of international specialization, and import the goods they need for a balanced diet ? The answer is : because the notion of balance applies on the global scale as well. For fairly obvious reasons, expansion of primary production for export is apt to encounter adverse price conditions on the world market, unless the industrial countries' demand is steadily expanding, as it was in the nineteenth century. To push exports in the face of an inelastic and more or less stationary demand would not be a promising line of development. If it is reasonable to assume a generally less than unitary price elasticity of demand for crude foodstuffs and materials, it seems reasonable also to contend that, under the conditions indicated before, economic growth in underdeveloped countries must largely take the form of an increase in production for the domestic market.

These are some of the considerations that explain the desire for balanced growth and provide some economic justification for it. They do not constitute a case for autarky. As productivity increases and the domestic market expands, while the composition of imports and exports is bound to change, the volume of external trade is more likely to rise than to fall. But even if it remains the same there is not necessarily any harm in balanced growth on the domestic front. Take a country like Venezuela : petroleum accounts for about 90 per cent of its exports but employs only about 2 per cent of its labour force ; the majority of the people work in the interior for a precarious subsistence in agriculture. If through the application of capital and increased productivity the domestic economy were to grow so that people working formerly on the land alone would now supply each other with clothing, footwear, houses and house furnishings as well as food products, while all the time petroleum exports remained the same and imports likewise constant in total volume, nothing but gain would result to the inhabitants without any loss to the outside world. No doubt there would be a fall in the proportion of foreign trade to national income. But could it not be that this proportion, in the many peripheral countries of this type, has been kept unduly high in the past simply by the poverty of the domestic economy? World income is a more basic criterion of world prosperity than the volume of international trade.

The characteristically important role which international trade played in the world economy of the nineteenth century was partly due to the fact that there was a periphery—and a vacuum beyond. The trade pattern of the nineteenth century was not merely a device for the optimum allocation of a given volume of resources ; it was, as D. H. Robertson put it, 'above all an engine of growth',[1] but of growth originating in and radiating from the early industrial centres. Even in this country we have been so accustomed to regard the early nineteenth century pattern as normal that we seldom stop to notice that the economic development of the United States itself has been a spectacular departure from it.

With the spread of industrialization, we have, however, noticed that the major currents of international trade pass by the economically backward areas and flow rather among the advanced industrial countries. Balanced growth is a good foundation for international trade, as well as a way of filling the vacuum at the periphery.

Let us turn now to the supply side of the problem of capital formation for economic development. Here the circular relationship runs from the low-income level to the small capacity to save, hence to a lack of capital, and so to low productivity. It seems to be a common view that the capacity for domestic saving in underdeveloped countries depends on an initial increase in productivity and real income, because the existing level is too low to permit any significant margin of saving, and that some form of outside help—say, foreign investment—is required to bring about this initial improvement and so break the vicious circle.

This theory begins to look a bit shaky as soon as we realize that it is not only the absolute but also the relative level of real income that determines the capacity to save. Although the absolute level of even the poorest countries has risen, it

[1] 'The Future of International Trade', *The Economic Journal*, March 1938, p. 5.

is doubtful whether saving has become any easier ; on the contrary, it may have become more difficult for them, because there has occurred at the same time a decline in their relative income levels in comparison with those of the economically advanced countries. The hypothesis seems to me plausible and, at any rate, worth considering. The great and growing gaps between the income levels of different countries, combined with increasing awareness of these gaps, may tend to push up the general propensity to consume of the poorer nations, reduce their capacity to save, and incidentally strain their balance of payments.

As we have seen from J. S. Duesenberry's recent book, *Income, Saving and the Theory of Consumer Behavior,* the hypothesis that individuals' consumption functions are interrelated rather than independent helps to account for certain facts that have seemed puzzling. The interdependence of consumers' preferences can affect, in particular, the choice between consumption and saving. The reason, for instance, why 75 per cent of families in the United States save virtually nothing (see page 39) is not necessarily that they are too poor to save or do not want to save ; the main reason is that they live in an environment that makes them want new consumption goods even more. The reason is largely what Duesenberry calls the 'demonstration effect' (page 27) of the consumption standards kept up by the top 25 per cent of the people. When individuals come into contact with superior goods or spending patterns, they are apt to feel a certain tension and restlessness : their propensity to consume is increased.

These forces, it seems to me, affect human behaviour to a certain extent in international relations as well. The consumption functions of different countries are in some degree interrelated in a similar way. On the international plane, also, knowledge of or contact with superior consumption patterns extends the imagination and creates new wants.

The leading instance of this effect is at present the widespread imitation of American consumption patterns. The American standard of living enjoys considerable prestige in the world. And it is always easier to adopt superior consumption habits than improved production methods. True, American production methods are also widely imitated ; sometimes, indeed, too closely. But generally this requires investible funds. The temptation to copy American consumption patterns tends to limit the supply of investible funds.

The intensity of the attraction exercised by the consumption standards of the economically advanced countries depends on two factors. One is the size of the gaps in real income and consumption levels. The other is the extent of people's awareness of them. Even though the poorer countries have probably all increased their *per capita* income over the last hundred years, the gaps have tended to widen. The position we have now reached is that two-thirds of the world's income goes to less than a fifth of the world's population in the most advanced countries, while at the bottom of the scale two-thirds of the world's population receives less than a sixth of the world's income ; and that the average *per capita* income of the former group is about seventeen times as high as that of the latter.[1] The estimates on which these calculations are based are in many cases extremely crude, but probably not grossly misleading. They do not, of course, take account of voluntary leisure, which is one way in which the advanced nations have taken out their gains.

The gaps are great, but equally important is the fact that contact and communication are closer than ever before, so that knowledge of these gaps has increased. Think of such recent inventions as the radio, aviation, and the American movies. Communication in the modern world—in the free world at any rate—is close, and so the attraction of advanced consumption standards can exert itself fairly widely, although unevenly, in the poorer parts of the world.

This attraction is a handicap for the late-comers in economic development. It affects not only voluntary personal saving but also makes it politically more difficult to use taxation as a means of compulsory saving and to resist demands for government spending on current account. Some of the backward countries have large masses of disguised unemployment on the land, which could be mobilized for real capital formation, but not without strict curbs on any immediate rise in consumption. Others may hope to introduce improvements in agricultural

[1] *National and Per Capita Incomes in 70 Countries, 1949* (Statistical Office of the United Nations, 1950).

techniques so as to release labour from primitive subsistence farming and make it available for capital works, but again not without restraints to prevent the increment from being immediately consumed. The use of potential domestic sources of capital can be seriously hampered by the dissatisfaction and impatience which the demonstration effect tends to produce.

The traditional view of international economic relations generally implies that a high level of productivity and real income in one country cannot hurt other countries and that, on the contrary, prosperity tends to spread. Of course there are many ways in which a country's prosperity will help its neighbours. But the particular effect now discussed is unfavourable. It puts an extra pressure on countries with a relatively low income to spend a high proportion of it. (This is quite apart from and in addition to the fact that some nations suffer from a cultural aversion to saving, due to the presence of traditional forms of conspicuous consumption. However, the 'demonstration effect' imposes no additional strain on saving capacity when it leads merely to a switch from native to imported forms of consumption.)

A very poor society might find it extremely hard to do any saving even if it knew nothing about higher living standards in the outside world. The vicious circle that tends to keep down the volume of saving in low-income countries is bad enough by itself. The point is that it is made even worse by the stresses that arise from relative as distinct from absolute poverty.

The poorer nations, in contact with the richer, feel continually impelled to keep their money incomes and outlays above what is warranted by their own capacity to produce. The result is an inflationary bias at home and a persistent tendency towards disequilibrium in the balance of payments. The doctrine of comparative advantage is, in my opinion, an effective answer to the simpler forms of the productivity theory of the dollar shortage. Yet here we seem to have reached, by the back door as it were, a theory of balance-of-payments disequilibrium based similarly upon differences in general levels of productivity. However, the comparative cost principle is fully respected. Disequilibrium results, not because productivity determines a country's export costs and competitive strength in the world market, not because the most productive country necessarily undersells all the others in all lines ; disequilibrium results because a country's productivity determines its real income and consumption level and because differences in levels of living, when they are very large and widely known, exert an upwards pressure on the consumption propensity of the poorer countries. In the classical view, a lack of balance in international trade can persist only because some countries try to 'live beyond their means'. We have now a simple explanation of why some countries do, in fact, persist in trying to live beyond their means.

The inflationary pressures and balance-of-payments difficulties are not, as such, the basic trouble. They could conceivably come from increased capital outlays and not from consumer spending. The trouble is that the demonstration effect leads directly to increased consumption, or attempts at increasing consumption, rather than investment. At least it makes an increase in saving peculiarly difficult as and when incomes and investment increase. It is for this reason that international income disparities may have to be treated not merely as a source of strain in the balance of payments but actually as an impediment to capital formation in the poorer countries.

The almost universal countermove of the underdeveloped countries both to suppress the disequilibrium in their balance of payments and, what is more important, to offset the attraction of superior consumption patterns is the restriction of imports and especially of imports of a so-called 'luxury' or 'semi-luxury' character. There is a widespread notion that a country, by cutting down imports of consumption goods through direct controls or prohibitive duties, can make more real capital available for its economic development in the form of imports of capital goods. Governments seem convinced that they are promoting the formation of capital whenever, in their commercial policy, they banish consumable imports in favour of imports of machinery and equipment.

This simple idea that more capital can be got merely by pinching and twisting the foreign trade sector of the economy seems to me to be an instance of the fallacy of misplaced concreteness. The foreign trade sector of the economy enters into the circular flow of income. Every piece of capital equipment imported represents an act of investment which, in the absence of external financing, presupposes and necessitates a corresponding act of saving at home. If this act of saving is not forthcoming, the capital equipment imported may be offset by reduced investment or by disinvestment in the domestic economy, if the expenditure of money previously spent on consumable imports now draws away domestic factors from capital construction or maintenance. Only if this money is left unspent is the requisite saving generated quasi-automatically; this is possible but quite improbable. It is more likely that any net investment that may result from the increased imports of capital goods will be financed by the forced saving of inflation, as long as inflation has not yet passed the point where it ceases to be effective as an instrument of forced saving. It is possible, therefore, although not certain, that 'luxury import restrictions' will lead to some increase in the rate of capital formation in an underdeveloped country.

Besides the quantity of investment, however, there is also a question of quality. Import restrictions unaccompanied by corresponding domestic restrictions will set up a special inducement to invest in domestic industries producing the goods—or substitutes for the goods—that can no longer be imported. If the domestic market is considered at all sufficient to warrant the establishment of such industries, the inducement may prove effective. But since it applies to the luxury and semi-luxury type of goods, whose imports are restricted, the result will be that the country's capital supplies, scarce as they are, and painfully brought into existence, will be sucked into relatively unessential uses.

The luxury import restrictions of the underdeveloped countries in the world today seem to represent, in the last analysis, a desperate effort to offset the handicap which the demonstration effect imposes on the poorer nations—an effort to isolate the local consumption pattern from that of the advanced countries and so to make possible more domestic saving and capital formation. This effort deserves our sympathy. But it attacks only the surface of the problem. It attacks only that part of the propensity to consume which directly involves expenditure on imported goods. The demonstration effect tends, however, to operate through an upward shift in the general consumption function and not in the import consumption function alone. Luxury import restrictionism does not stop this pervasive indirect influence of international discrepancies in consumption levels. A more basic attack would be compulsory saving through public finance, although this is precisely one of the things that is made politically more difficult in the poorer countries by the great discrepancies in living standards.

Far more radical forms of isolation than luxury import restrictions have played a part in the development of two important countries. It is well known that Japan, in the early course of her industrialization, imitated the Western World in everything except consumption patterns. She had kept herself in a state of isolation for centuries, and it was comparatively easy for her to maintain this isolation in regard to consumption patterns. There is no doubt that this was part of the secret of her success in domestic capital formation.

The other instance of radical isolation is Soviet Russia's iron curtain (which of course is not merely a result of the present tension but was well established before World War II). While it certainly has other reasons for its existence, I am inclined to attach significance also to its economic function; that is, to the possible 'materialist interpretation' of the iron curtain. Anyway, it illustrates the possibility that isolation may help to solve the economic problem of capital formation, in a world of great discrepancies in national living standards, by severing contact and communication among nations. Without communication, the discrepancies, however great, may become of little or no consequence and the 'demonstration effect' may lose at least some of its potency.

That this might be a possible and perhaps a necessary solution is a disquieting thought, and one naturally turns in search of an alternative.

Could it be that the alternative lies in unilateral income transfers or, in plain English, gifts from rich to poor countries? The foreign aid programmes of the United States have certainly departed from traditional practices, and it may be that we have seen the beginnings of a system of international income transfers, comparable to the transfers that take place within a country as an automatic result of taxation proportional to income or, still more, of progressive taxation. A system of international grants-in-aid does not stem from any economic mechanism of the market-place; nor does the principle of progressive taxation. Both are based on political value judgements, and both arise from pressures having to do with the coexistence and increasingly close association of people at widely different levels of material welfare.

Suppose we have a model, then, where on the one hand international income disparities open up gaps in the balance of payments and on the other unilateral income transfers come in to fill these gaps. Is this a sufficient and satisfactory solution to the problem of capital formation in the poorer countries? Clearly it is not. If nature is left to take its course, the income transfers coming in will be used in these countries for the satisfaction of the higher propensity to consume that is brought about by the disparity in real-income levels. No permanent basis will be created within the country for higher living standards in the future. It is nearly always possible to some extent to substitute foreign aid for domestic saving so that consumption is increased and no net contribution is made to the rate of total capital formation. It can happen even if the foreign resources are tied to specific productive projects. The point is not, of course, that this is bad, but that it fails to contribute to the foundations of economic development. The attraction of advanced living standards can thus interfere, not only with the harnessing of domestic saving potentials, but also with the effective use of external resources for economic development. It makes it more than ever necessary for an underdeveloped country to keep a tight rein on the national propensity to consume.

This applies obviously to autonomous international investment and, perhaps less obviously, also to improvements in the terms of trade. An improvement in the terms of trade puts at the country's disposal additional outside resources that can be used to promote economic development. By itself, however, it means simply an increment in the country's current income, derived from foreign trade. Without the corresponding domestic saving, this increment cannot lead to any net increase in the rate of investment. Here again the real task is not to extract more capital goods from foreign trade but to extract more saving from the national income.

The upshot is that external resources, even if they become available in the most desirable forms, are not enough. They do not automatically provide a solution to the problem of capital accumulation in underdeveloped areas. No solution is possible without strenuous domestic efforts, particularly in the field of public finance.

EXTERNAL ECONOMIES AND THE DOCTRINE OF BALANCED GROWTH*

by **J. Marcus Fleming**

THE OBJECT OF THIS PAPER IS TO EXAMINE AN ARGUMENT advanced by some of the most distinguished writers on the theory of economic development, to consider to what extent and under what conditions it is valid, and to point to some of its implications.

The argument in question runs roughly as follows. In underdeveloped countries there is little incentive to invest capital in the introduction of modern efficient methods of large-scale production in individual industries producing goods for domestic consumption because the markets for the respective industries are too small. Since, however, the adoption of such methods in any one such industry would increase the demand for the products of the other industries, the incentive would be much greater if investments in a wide range of consumer-goods industries were undertaken, or at least considered, in conjunction. The adoption of investment projects which, though unprofitable individually, would be profitable collectively would, it is implied, be a good thing. This argument is frequently referred to as the 'doctrine of balanced growth'.

Certain elements in the doctrine are adumbrated in Allyn Young's celebrated article on 'Increasing Returns and Economic Progress'.[1] The doctrine itself is set forth briefly in Professor Rosenstein-Rodan's 'Problems of Industrialization of Eastern and South-Eastern Europe'[2] and more fully in Chapter I of Professor R. Nurkse's *Problems of Capital Formation in Underdeveloped Countries*. The argument as presented in the present paper, however, does not purport to reproduce exactly the views of any of these writers. In the first place they differ

* *The Economic Journal*, June 1955. Reprinted by permission of the Royal Economic Society and the author.

[1] *The Economic Journal*, December 1928.

[2] ibid., June-September 1943 (reprinted here, pp. 245-55).

to some extent among themselves, and secondly, my presentation is either, as outlined above, too rough and ready, or else, as expounded below, too pedantically precise, to mirror faithfully the explicit thought of any one of them. What I have tried to do is to reconstruct the logical presuppositions of a doctrine which, with certain variations noted below, is common to Rosenstein-Rodan and to Nurkse.

We must now attempt to analyse the argument under discussion into its explicit and implicit elements. These are as follows:

(*a*) The installation in any one of a wide range of home market industries in an underdeveloped country or region of a new plant capable of operating at a unit cost lower than that of existing production in the industry might be financially unprofitable because of the smallness and inelasticity of the market for the industry within the country or region in question;[1]

(*b*) if demand for the product of such an industry were increased the installation of the new plant would become more profitable or less unprofitable;

(*c*) any increase in output, involving a reduction in unit cost of production, in a typical consumer-goods industry will tend to increase real income and hence real demand for the products of most other consumer-goods industries and thus to increase the profitability of installing more efficient plants in the latter provided, however, that interest rates do not rise too much;[2 3 4]

[1] '. . . the small size of a country's market can discourage or even prohibit the profitable application of modern capital equipment by any individual entrepreneur in any particular industry' (Nurkse, op. cit., p. 7).

[2] 'Although the initial displacement may be considerable and the repercussions upon particular industries unfavourable, the enlarging of the market for any one commodity produced under conditions of increasing returns generally has the net effect . . . of enlarging the market for other commodities' (Allyn Young, op. cit., p. 537). 'The industries producing wage goods can thus be said to be complementary' (Rosenstein-Rodan, present volume, p. 249).

[3] 'Where any single enterprise might appear quite inauspicious and impracticable a wide range of projects in different industries may succeed because they will all support each other in the sense that the people engaged in each project now working with more real capital per head and with greater efficiency in terms of output per man hour

(*d*) it follows that the installation of more efficient plants of the type described in each of a wide range of consumer-goods industries, though unprofitable if undertaken separately, might be profitable if undertaken jointly.

Moreover:

(*e*) The joint installation of such plants, if profitable, would be desirable (i.e., would tend to increase real national income); and

(*f*) because of its effects on the incentive to install efficient new plants in other industries the installation of a single plant, though unprofitable, might tend to raise real national income.

The rather odd-sounding proviso about interest rates at the end of step (*c*) in the argument has to be introduced into my scheme to take account of the fact that Rosenstein-Rodan and Nurkse usually describe the inter-industry relationships dealt with under (*c*) and (*d*) above as affecting not the profitability—net of interest—of installing efficient new plants but the 'inducement to invest' or 'marginal efficiency of investment', i.e., the return on the capital invested in such new plants, including interest as well as profits. Now anything which enhances the rate of return on a new plant will enhance its profitability also, provided that the relevant interest rate does not rise 'too much', i.e., provided that the supply of capital is not 'too inelastic'.

Let us now consider various steps in the argument in greater detail. Step (*a*) is clearly valid. In a country of low *per capita* income and/or scattered population and/or poor communications the demand in a given region for the output of even a generally consumed manufactured product may be so small that the output (at minimum unit cost) of a single modern plant whose installation is under consideration would exceed the total previous output of the product in that region. The particular demand curve for the output of the projected new plant, though elastic over the range of output for which it is displacing previous production, might be highly inelastic and

will provide an enlarged market for the products of the new enterprise in the other industries' (Nurkse, op. cit., p. 13).

[4] Our authors would not confine the scope of this interaction to consumer-goods industries. They do, however, emphasize its applicability as between such industries, and it is on this, as we shall see, particularly vulnerable application that I wish to focus my criticism.

steeply downward sloping for higher outputs. The unit cost curve of the new plant, even though it lies, for larger outputs, below the unit cost of pre-existing production, may lie, for smaller outputs, above that unit cost, and for all outputs may lie above the demand curve for the plant. Under these conditions it would not be profitable to install the new plant.

Step (*b*) in the argument is likewise a valid one. If the particular demand curve for such a plant as has been described should be raised, *while cost conditions remain unchanged,* the effect would obviously be to reduce the loss associated with its operation, possibly to turn the loss into a profit.

The qualification is, however, all-important. If the raising of the demand curve were to be accompanied by a raising of the unit-cost curve the outcome might well be different. For a rise in the cost curve, taken by itself, would tend to reduce the profits, or increase the losses, of operating the plant, would reduce the scale of the plant's output if it were in operation and might make it unprofitable to install the plant at all.

We come now to the central question, with which step (*c*) in the argument is concerned, as to the circumstances in which the installation of a low unit-cost plant in one industry will increase the profitability of a similar installation in another industry.

In a closed economy any increase in the supply of any consumer goods A, the supply of other such goods remaining unchanged, will tend to increase the prices of each of the latter products relative to that of A, though in the case of close substitutes the increase will be small. The increase in real income associated with the expansion in output of A will normally lead to some increases in the demand for non-A commodities as well as for A, and, in order that the increase in demand should be confined to A, the price of non-A commodities must rise relative to that of A, i.e., there will be an increase in the real price of the average non-A commodity.[1]

This increase in the real price of non-A commodities, provided that it is associated with no change in real factor prices, will tend to cause the output of non-A commodities, taken as a group, to expand even under existing methods of production,

[1] i.e., an increase in the average price of non-A commodities relative to the average price of all commodities including A.

and may make it profitable to install new large-scale plants. The extent to which this will occur will be greater: (*a*) the lower the income elasticity of demand for A, (*b*) the less the elasticity of substitution between A and non-A, and (*c*) the greater the elasticity of supply in non-A. But there will always be *some* positive reaction so long as the income elasticity of demand for A is less than unity, and the elasticity of substitution between A and B less than infinite, and so long as there is a positive elasticity of supply for non-A.

Step (*d*) in the argument follows directly from the previous steps.

Steps (*e*) and (*f*) are of a different character from the others in that they entail welfare-economic considerations. It is convenient to consider them in terms of a conceptual scheme which distinguishes in the case of any change in the output of a plant, between: (1) the increment in profits (IP), net of return on capital, (2) the increment in direct (social) net product (IDNP), and (3) the increment in real national income (IRNI). The IP corresponds to the Pigovian marginal (or additional) private net product and the IRNI to the Pigovian marginal social net product. The IDNP consists of the sum of the IP and the net benefits in the form of real income transferred from the firm operating the plant to its consumers, workers, suppliers, etc., as a result of the price changes resulting from the change in production. The IDNP is measured by the value of the additional output less the value of additional factor input, output and input being valued at the average prices prevailing over the relevant intervals of the corresponding product-demand and factor-supply curves. That the IDNP should be positive is the well-known Dupuit test of desirability of a finite change in production. The IRNI exceeds the IDNP to the extent that the change in production gives rise to economies outside the plant in question. An analysis of such external economies, given in the Appendix, shows them to include such items as changes in net product in other plants, changes in factor supply and changes in the national terms of trade.

Returning to point (*e*) in the argument, the introduction of large-scale plants in a variety of increasing return industries will tend to reduce product prices (without reducing factor prices) in those industries, and will therefore confer transfer benefits on the rest of the community. If the net profit of the new plants is positive, therefore, the increment in direct net product resulting from their introduction will be still more positive. Unless, as is improbable, the new plants reduce aggregate factor supplies, bring about a deterioration in terms of trade or otherwise give rise to diseconomies outside the industries in question, their introduction is bound to enhance national real income.

As regards point (*f*), for reasons analogous to those just discussed, not only any introduction of new plants but also any increased output in existing plants which is profitable under imperfect competition is likely to have a positive direct net product and make a positive contribution to national income. Consequently if expansion in industry A renders profitable the expansion of imperfectly competitive industry B the total contribution to national income of the former expansion will include, not only the transfer benefits which it itself confers, but also the economies to which it gives rise in industry B. Even if the expansion at A is unprofitable, its total contribution may be positive, thanks to these transfer benefits and external economies.

A further point, which our authors might have made, but did not, is that the expansion of demand for an industry will increase not only the profit but also the direct net product involved in introducing a new plant there. Consequently, if conditions are such that the joint introduction of plants in a variety of industries may be profitable though the plants are individually unprofitable they will also be such that the plants would jointly yield a positive net product, even though individually none of them would do so.

As we have seen, the validity of step (*c*) depends on the assumption that real factor prices will not be affected when the supply of A is increased and that of non-A goods remains unchanged. This, however, could happen only in a limiting case. Normally real factor prices will be raised or lowered, or some raised and others lowered. There is, therefore, a possibility that the real prices of the factors entering into the operation of modern plants in non-A industries may rise to such an extent as to outweigh the rise in the real prices of non-A products, and thus to induce a contraction rather than an expansion in output and investment in non-A industries.

In what follows, we shall assume, in conformity with what appears to be the intention of the balanced-growth doctrine, that the influence exercised by an increase in the supply of A on the real demand for other products is randomly distributed among non-A industries with respect to the possibilities for obtaining economies from increased output and investment in such industries. In other words those industries which are of a critical size in this respect are not, on the average, either specially complementary to or specially competitive with, industry A.

Suppose, now, there is only one stage of production and only one homogeneous factor of production, 'labour', which is available in fixed supply. Under these conditions the installation of the new plant[1] at A will increase the incentive to install efficient new plants in non-A industries provided that the wage-rate does not rise so far as to prevent an expansion of output in the average non-A industry. And output in the average non-A industry will expand only if labour-input in non-A industries as a whole expands. Since the supply of labour is fixed, this can happen only if the input of labour at A contracts, i.e., if the employment of labour at the new plant is less than the amount of labour released from the other production units in the industry.

Clearly the employment of labour at A cannot contract if A is a completely new industry at which there has been no previous production. Even, however, if there has been some previous production, it is probable in an underdeveloped country that this will be carried on in small units under conditions of constant (long-term) real unit cost. In this case if the new plant is unprofitable it is impossible that the employment of labour in the industry should decline.

For since the pre-existing production units operate at constant labour cost, the price of the product in terms of wage units will remain constant so long as any of the pre-existing units continue to operate. Aggregate demand for the product will also remain constant, so that the output of the new plant

[1] A 'plant', in this model, may be conceived as a group of workers co-operating in some process that requires a minimum number of workers to achieve any output at all.

will at first merely replace output of pre-existing units. If, at the point at which the new plant is itself producing practically the entire previous output of the industry, it is still not profitable, though the product price in terms of wage units is almost at the level which made pre-existing production units profitable, the aggregate labour-cost—and employment—of the new plant must be higher than that of the entire industry prior to its installation. If the output of the new plant is further increased, though its *average* labour cost may fall, its *aggregate* employment of labour must be still further increased.

It would appear therefore that where there is a single factor of production in fixed supply the installation of an unprofitable new plant in industry A, even though its unit cost, at the least unprofitable output, is below that of pre-existing production, is likely[1] to induce contraction rather than expansion in other consumer-goods industries, to yield external *dis*economies rather than external economies. The installation, over a wide range of such industries, of a set of unprofitable large-scale plants would render them not less but more unprofitable than if they had been installed singly. It would, moreover, tend to reduce the real national product. At first sight, this might appear to be contrary to common sense, since the new plants were described as being more efficient and working at lower unit cost than pre-existing production in their respective industries. But this is only true of plants which are installed singly. If all the plants are installed together the rise in wages will force the typical new plant to operate at a level which keeps the labour requirement of its industry approximately what it was under pre-existing methods of production, and at this level, as we have seen, the unit costs of the new plants will be greater than those of pre-existing production.

The situation might be roughly expressed by saying that, whereas the balanced-growth doctrine assumes that the relationship between industries is for the most part complementary, the limitation of factor supply ensures that that relationship is for the most part competitive.

[1] This conclusion would be certain but for the possibility that this output from pre-existing production units might operate under conditions of diminishing returns. This, however, is more likely to occur where several factors of production exist, and is considered below.

Taking account of the multiplicity of factors of production introduces certain complications and qualifications into the argument without greatly altering its conclusions. Each industry and method of production is likely to have factors which are more or less specific to it. Thus when the new plant is introduced at A there is likely to be some fall in the price of factors specific to the old-fashioned methods of production in the industry. As output in the old sector of the industry is curtailed there will be a decline in product price, and a corresponding decline in marginal cost in the form of non-specific factors released to other industries, so that the aggregate receipts of the new plant will fall short of the value of factors released from the older sector of the industry and the plant may be unprofitable even though it employs fewer resources than those released from the older sector. This creates a possibility, though by no means a certainty, that an unprofitable plant, with a positive direct net product, may effect a net release of factors from the industry and thus create external economies.[1]

Another probable consequence of the multiplicity of factors of production is that the weighting or 'mix' of factors used in running the new modern plant at A may resemble more closely the factor-mix employed in running actual or potential modern plants in other industries than the combination of factors employed in production outside A taken as a whole. In this case it is possible that even if the plant installation at A on balance increases the supply of factors to non-A industries it will so raise the prices of those factors which are particularly in demand for the running of modern plants that the net effect on the installation of such plants will be discouraging.

It would appear therefore that, so long as factors of production are in fixed supply, the introduction of large-scale production units in consumer industries is likely to give rise not to

[1] If the direct net product is negative, the new plant cannot possibly create external economies. For the direct net product of the new plant is measured by its price integral *less* its marginal-cost integral. And the net release of resources from the industry is measured by that part of its output which is curtailed, less the marginal cost integral of the new plant. And the price integral of the new plant cannot possibly fall short of the marginal-cost integral on the curtailed output of the older sector of the industry. So that the direct net product of the new plant must always exceed the net release of resources from the industry.

economies but to diseconomies in other industries competing for the consumer market unless the former industries are already big enough for the introduction of the new plant to make possible a net reduction in the resources employed there: that this is unlikely to occur where the new unit is unprofitable, and cannot occur unless it passes the Dupuit test of the desirability of a 'large' investment, i.e., unless it has a positive direct net product.

It is noteworthy that the introduction of more efficient production methods in a large competitive industry such as agriculture is not only certain to be profitable but likely to release factors to other industries so long as the elasticity of demand for the industry as a whole is less than unity. This suggests that if underdeveloped countries were to press ahead with improvements of a financially profitable character in agriculture they might do more to make profitable large-scale efficient production in other industries, such as manufacturing, which are in a phase of increasing returns, than by trying to develop simultaneously a wide range of such manufacturing industries.

Thus far we have assumed a closed economy. The introduction of foreign trade makes little difference to the argument. Indirectly, through the various mechanisms whereby external equilibrium is maintained, the demand for exports varies with the demand for imports. If the scope for economies of scale is equal in export and in home-market industries it makes no difference which gains at the expense of the other. It will still be true that the expansion of industry A will create a balance of economies or diseconomies elsewhere, according as A absorbs less or more factors than before. It is, however, sometimes argued that in underdeveloped countries the export trades sell on more perfect markets than do the domestic trades, so that fewer unexploited opportunities for economies of scale remain in the former. If so the expansion at A will be more likely to generate external economies of scale than the previous argument would imply if, as is often the case, the industry A happens to be one which is more competitive in product markets with imports, and/or more competitive in factor markets with exports, than it is, in the respective markets, with purely domestic industries.

In order really to salvage the doctrine of external economies under examination, however, it is necessary to drop the assumption that the supply of factors of production is fixed in favour of the assumption that the supply varies positively with real factor prices. For then, in order that an expansion in A should increase the profitability of additional output and the installation of new plants in industries producing other consumer goods, thus generating economies, it is no longer necessary that the employment of factors in A should actually decline as output increases, but merely that factor employment there should not rise more than the increased factor supply evoked by the rise in real factor prices. As we have seen, of our authors, only Rosenstein-Rodan explicitly assumes an elastic supply of labour in his illustration of the doctrine, though Nurkse, in arguing in terms of the inducement to invest, is in effect assuming some elasticity in the supply of capital.

It should be noted that the possibility of expanding the supply of labour at a given money wage by increasing the level of money demand would not constitute factor elasticity in the sense relevant here, since the whole argument is concerned with 'real' demand, and full employment is assumed from the start. There are, however, a number of *prima facie* reasons why the supply of factors in an underdeveloped country or region may show a measure of elasticity of a sort relevant to the present argument. Not all of them, however, are very conclusive. For example:

(1) The supply of labour from individual workers may increase when real wages increase, because the workers are better able and more willing to work. But the opposite result is at least as likely to happen because the worker wishes to take out part of his real income in leisure, and 'absenteeism'.

(2) Higher real wages may attract workers on the margin of the labour force into employment, and higher rents may make it profitable to bring poorer qualities of land into cultivation. On the other hand, higher family incomes may lead to a withdrawal of marginal women, children and older workers from the labour force.

(3) Higher real rewards may tempt workers and capitalists to migrate into the country or region in question, thus increasing the supply of factors there. Economies facilitated by this

means in the area of immigration, however, may be balanced by diseconomies in the area of emigration.

(4) Higher real wages in a country at an early stage of demographic development may bring about an expansion of population which will entail an expansion in the labour force a couple of decades later. At a later stage of demographic evolution, however, higher real wages may have a zero or a negative effect on population growth.

For the purpose in hand the main potential sources of elasticity in the supply of factors of production are the three listed below, which will be discussed at greater length.

(5) In so far as factors of production are themselves products of an earlier stage of production—and here we depart from the assumption that there is only one stage of production—an increase in the real prices of those product-factors may bring about an increase in their supply and in the aggregate amount of factors supplied to subsequent stages of production.

(6) A rise in the demand for factory labour may attract workers from employments, such as agriculture, where their productivity is very low, and thus give rise to a virtual increase in the supply of labour or at least an increase in its supply to that sector of industry in which economies of large-scale operation are to be obtained.

(7) Higher interest rates may increase the supply of capital, especially from abroad.

First, let us take account of the 'vertical disintegration' of production—the fact that industries buy the products of other industries, as well as original factors of production, and that some industries are predominantly suppliers of other industries rather than of final consumers. Thus far we have considered industries as acting on each other 'horizontally', through the interrelated markets which they serve or the interrelated factors which they buy. But industries also affect each other in greater or lesser degree in a more direct manner, i.e., 'vertically' as suppliers or customers. We are concerned with the effect of this 'vertical' connexion on the 'horizontal' one, to which the balanced-growth doctrine, as expounded by Rosenstein-Rodan and Nurkse, primarily refers.

The introduction, in industries serving final consumers, of more efficient large-scale methods of production may encourage increased output in factor-producing industries if it tends to raise the prices of produced factors (intermediate products) more, or reduce them less, than the prices of the original factors of production used by the latter group of industries. Now, as a matter of fact, the type of technical changes associated with the substitution of large-scale for smaller-scale production not only tend to raise the demand for capital relative to labour but also to raise the demand for intermediate products as compared with original factors as a whole.

We may assume that, in an underdeveloped country, the industries producing factors of production—especially those producing power, transportation, minerals and capital goods—will, like the consumer-goods industries, frequently operate under conditions of imperfect competition, where efficient production is hampered by the smallness of the market. The stimulus given by the installation of large-scale production in consumer-goods industries to profitability, production and investment in the supplying industries will therefore give rise to an increase in the net product of the latter. This means that the increased use, if any, of original factors in expanding the factor-producing industries will permit a more than equivalent increase in the supply of produced factors, so that the industries producing for final consumption will secure a net increase in the supply of the two sorts of factors taken together. It follows from this that the installation of modern large-scale production in one consumer-goods industry, even though it involves an increased use of factors of production—in both kinds—may nevertheless, in the manner described, leave other consumer-goods industries better supplied with factors than before, thus giving rise to economies there.

It is noteworthy that the chances that the introduction of more efficient large-scale operation in one consumer-goods industry will generate economies in another such industry are here increased only by reason of economies generated at an earlier stage of production. The latter, or 'vertical', type of external economies will, of course, enhance real national income just as surely as the former or 'horizontal' type, and in magnitude are likely to be the more important of the two. Moreover, the 'vertical' generation of economies operates not only from later to earlier stages of production, but also with even greater probability, from earlier to later stages. Thus the expansion of output in a producer-goods industry, provided that it involves an increase in net product, will tend to increase the profitability of other industries in general, and will encourage economies in such of those industries as are operating under increasing returns.

There can be little doubt but that the conditions for a 'vertical' transmission of external economies—whether forward from supplying industry to using industry, or backward from using industry to supplying industry—are much more favourable than for a 'horizontal' transmission between industries at the same stage. There is, therefore, a much stronger case for joint planning of the development of industries at earlier and later stages of the same 'line' of production than of industries at the final stage of different 'lines'. The fact that our authors, other than Allyn Young, seem to lay more emphasis on the 'horizontal' rather than the 'vertical' variant of the balanced-growth doctrine is probably due to the fact that the external economies underlying the former are less frequently discussed in the literature than those underlying the latter. But the 'horizontal' transmission of economies may have been neglected by Marshall and his commentators precisely because, where it exists at all, it is relatively unimportant.

Let us now turn to the possibility, listed at (6) above, that the enhanced real demand for labour arising in various branches of secondary industry as a result of the expansion and modernization of one such industry may be satisfied by drawing labour away from an overcrowded agriculture where its marginal productivity is negligible or relatively low. As already mentioned, Rosenstein-Rodan, in expounding his version of the 'horizontal' variant of the balanced-growth doctrine, explicitly assumes that the labour supply for industrial expansion is drawn from agriculture where it would otherwise be underemployed.

There can be no doubt of the fact, attested by many observers, that underemployment, in the sense specified above, exists in the agriculture of many underdeveloped countries. There can also be little doubt but that an expansion in the real demand for labour in any particular industrial branch would attract some of the underemployed agricultural labour to secondary industry, and to that extent would improve the prospect of reaping economies of scale in the industrial sector as a whole. The crucial question, however, so far as the creation of external economies is concerned, is whether the expansion of industrial branch A would lead to a transference of labour from agriculture to industry sufficient to permit an expansion of branches of industry *other than A*.

It is by no means clear how this question should be answered. Much will depend on the reasons for the prior existence of the agricultural underemployment. It is assumed that this is no mere case of inadequacy of monetary demand combined with rigidity of money wages in secondary industry. There remain two possible lines of explanation. One is that the underemployment is voluntary in the sense that real rewards for unskilled labour in industry are insufficiently in excess of those in agriculture to attract sufficient labour to equalize marginal productivity in the two sectors. Even though the marginal product of labour in agriculture be far below that in industry, labour may stay on the land partly because of a family system under which the individual worker is paid according to the *average* product of peasant labour rather than its *marginal* product, and partly because of inertia, and lack of enterprise.

In this event, however, it seems unlikely that more workers would be attracted from agriculture than are absorbed by the initial expansion in industry A. For expansion in A, output remaining constant elsewhere, is likely to increase the demand-price for food at least as much as for the products of other secondary industries. In so far as this expansion entails an increase in real income, it will no doubt tend to raise demand for manufactures in higher proportion than for food ; but the increased output of A is likely to be more competitive with other manufactures than with food, and the probable transference of income from taxpayers—or whoever bears the losses of the expansion at A—to peasants and workers will tend to raise demand for food rather than manufactures. For these and other reasons[1] the real demand-schedule for labour

[1] Though any influences transmitted 'vertically' to basic industries, or any repercussions on other industries of the economies generated in basic industries, are more likely to favour secondary production than agriculture, on the other hand, the latter is less likely to be affected by scarcity of capital or intermediate products resulting from the initial expansion at A.

in secondary production outside A appears more likely to fall than to rise relative to the schedule of real *per capita* income in agriculture. If the demand for labour A is sufficiently strong to draw labour from agriculture it will be sufficiently strong to draw it from other secondary industries also. The availability of underemployed agricultural labour may enable A's labour force to expand without that of other secondary industries having to contract as much as it otherwise would : it will not permit the latter to expand as well.

A second line of explanation for the initial state of under-employment in agriculture is that workers, while desirous of moving from agriculture to secondary industry, are unable to obtain employment there owing to the artificially high level of industrial wages maintained by labour unions, etc. In this event much depends on how these wages are determined. It is assumed that as the demand for labour expands in industry A industrial money wages will rise at least as fast as prices in general : otherwise the agricultural unemployment would be of a type curable by mere monetary expansion—a hypothesis which we have excluded. If, as might well happen, the unions were to take advantage of the increased demand for labour in industry A to prevent any whittling away of the original disparity between industrial wages and agricultural incomes, this would entail a decline in secondary industries other than A unless the prices of non-A manufactures were to rise faster than those of agricultural products, which, as we have seen, is unlikely. Even if the unions were to confine themselves to preventing a decline in industrial real wages, it is quite possible, for the reasons discussed in the foregoing paragraph, that the rise in agricultural prices would so far outstrip the rise in prices of non-A manufactures as to entail a decline in the real demand-schedule for the latter, and hence a decline rather than an expansion of employment in non-A industries.

In all probability some tendency for industrial wages to be artificially maintained in relation to agricultural incomes is fairly general in underdeveloped countries. It is obvious that real wages are not in practice raised so fast in response to a rise in the real demand for industrial labour as to prevent all movement from country to town. This, however, does not prove that wages do not rise fast enough to nullify the benefits which the several industries would otherwise derive from *each other's* expansion.

Even if secondary industries other than A do not succeed in adding to or retaining their labour force, they may still expand if other factors of production become more plentiful. But the mere fact that agricultural labour is seriously under-employed provides no guarantee that an expansion in A which absorbs more factors than are created by associated economies in basic industries will draw sufficient labour out of agriculture to permit an increase in output, profits and net product in secondary industries other than A.

Let us now turn to the third main possibility of factor elasticity, mentioned at (7) above, namely that the supply of capital is to some extent elastic with respect to the rate of interest. This assumption, as we have seen, has from the start been, in effect, woven into the balanced-growth doctrine by Rosenstein-Rodan and by Nurkse in so far as they express that doctrine in terms of the inducement to invest (see pp. 273-4 above).

An elastic supply of capital would undoubtedly facilitate the creation of external economies of scale. If capital were in infinitely elastic supply, so that additional capital requirements in any industry had no effect on the cost or availability of capital for the use of other industries, and if all requirements could be met from domestic saving, then any expansion in industry A which did not involve an increased use of factors of production *other than capital* would be fairly certain to generate expansion, and the economies associated therewith, in other industries.

A distinction must be drawn, however, between capital obtained from foreign and from domestic sources respectively. When development is financed by foreign capital additional interest or dividends will have to be paid to capitalists resident abroad. In order to transfer the sums the country in which the development occurs will have to generate an export surplus partly by reducing imports and partly by increasing exports. So long as export industries offer the same sort of opportunities for economies of scale as those producing for the domestic market, the increase in exports will have no ill effect. If, on the other hand, no economies of scale are possible in export industries only that part of the addition to the national factor supply which accrues to home-market industries will generate such economies.[1]

How elastic is the supply of capital in fact likely to be in an underdeveloped country or region? This is a question which cannot be satisfactorily answered, or even formulated, in terms of the comparative static analysis used in this paper—at least so far as capital of domestic origin is concerned. Any increase in real income associated with the expansion of capital and output at A would tend to raise the domestic supply of *saving* and gradually and cumulatively the domestic supply of *capital*. In the very long run the expansion at A might evoke an additional supply of domestic capital large enough to meet its own requirements and leave some over for other industries. Within the sort of time period which is of interest for the purposes of economic policy, however, capital-expansion in one industry is likely to be at the expense of capital-expansion in other industries, unless additional capital is available from abroad in highly elastic supply.

The transfer of capital from abroad, unlike the increase in supply from home saving, is responsive to the increase of interest rates or profit opportunities rather than to that of real income in the developing country. Though the two types of responsiveness in capital supply resemble each other in operating only over time, the bulk of any additional supply forthcoming from foreign sources in response to the higher interest rates, etc., is likely to appear much sooner than the bulk of any additional supply accumulated from new domestic savings.

It is impossible to generalize about the elasticity of supply of capital from abroad. In certain cases the supply curve may even be downward-sloping, as when the fact that *some* foreign capital is willing to venture into an underdeveloped country encourages additional supplies at even lower interest rates and lower profit expectations. Or the curve may be highly elastic for moderate amounts and inelastic for large amounts

[1] The net addition, if any, to the factor supply of home-market industries will be the larger the greater the share of import saving in the aggregate improvement in the real trade balance, and the smaller the proportion of that improvement which is required to offset deterioration in the terms of trade.

(if the capital is drawn from somewhat restricted circles of investors abroad). Or it may be elastic for some industries and inelastic for others. (Frequently the industries for which foreign capital supply is inelastic will be precisely the home-market industries where the economies of scale are most to be expected.) Or, in the case of countries having forfeited the confidence of investors, the supply of foreign capital may be highly inelastic all round.

Inelasticity in the supply of capital from abroad tends to render the doctrine of balanced growth not so much invalid as inapplicable. Even where a diversified investment programme would yield a higher return on capital invested than would the projects taken individually, the higher cost of capital might make the large-scale programme as unprofitable as the piecemeal approach. More fundamental is the criticism already noted that even where capital is available in elastic supply the mere fact that it is obtained from abroad reduces the extent to which it can be used to exploit economies of scale in home-market industries and reduces the chances that the combined investment programme will in fact yield a higher return to capital than would the projects taken one by one.

Conclusion

This paper has examined the basic assumptions underlying a modern variant of the balanced-growth doctrine, namely that the introduction of lower (unit) cost methods of production involving expansion in the output of an industry even if itself unprofitable, will enhance the profitability of other industries not specially related to it as customers or suppliers, and, if these industries are operating under imperfect competition, will promote economies of larger-scale production there.

We have concluded that the argument, as usually presented, overemphasises the repercussions on the demand for, and ignores repercussions on the costs of, the other industries, and that, in an economy where factors of production are in fixed supply, the introduction of unprofitable though efficient large-scale production in one industry is more likely to reduce than to increase the profitability of other industries.

We have seen, however, that the chances are much better for a 'vertical' propagation of external economies, from customer industry to supplying industry, and especially from supplying industry to customer industry, and that developments in industries at different stages in the same 'line' of production are more likely to afford each other mutual support than those in different lines of production.

Moreover, the chances that expansion in one industry will generate economies in other industries not 'vertically' related to it will be increased if economies are generated 'vertically' in factor-producing industries. This has the effect of introducing a measure of elasticity into the supply of factors of production which is in general favourable to the creation of external economies.

Conditions of elastic supply of labour or capital likewise tend to favour the applicability of the balanced-growth doctrine. The overall elasticity of the labour supply is, however, likely to be low, and the ease with which labour can be transferred from agriculture to non-agricultural industry, where the opportunities for economies of scale are greater, has frequently been exaggerated.

As to capital, the domestic supply is likely to be practically inelastic within any short period of years. Access to imported capital, on the other hand, varies very much from country to country and from time to time ; and, in any case, foreign capital is less effective than domestic capital in widening the market and promoting economies of scale.

The chances that diversified development in a variety of industries will play a mutually supporting, mutually validating role, as required by the balanced-growth doctrine, are greatest when the necessary additional capital is obtainable on easy terms, when unions can be prevented from pushing up real wages in industry, when reserves of underemployed agricultural labour are eagerly waiting to obtain industrial employment, when there are opportunities for economies of scale in the basic, factor-producing industries, and when, taken singly, the investments in question are only just not profitable. When too many of these conditions are absent the combined installation over a variety of industries of unprofitable though efficient undertakings may have the effect of rendering each of these undertakings still more unprofitable than if it had been set up by itself.

APPENDIX

A Note on External Economies

The term 'external economies', since it was introduced by Marshall, has been employed in a variety of senses, often confusing and misleading. The usage which I consider to be most convenient for the purpose of welfare economics, and which represents a development of that introduced by Professor Kahn in 'Some Notes on Ideal Output'[1], is the following:

Let us adopt the following definitions:

(1) The *increment in direct net product* of a firm is the sum of any net increase in the volume of its sales, *less* any net increase in the volume of its purchases (including purchases of labour and other original factors of production), *plus* any net increase in its real stock of physical assets. This is a sum of physical increments valued at current prices.[2] (The fact that output is netted not only of purchases from other firms but also of purchases from factor-owners makes this a different concept from that of an increase in real 'value added'.)

(2) The *increment in net factor supply* of a factor-owner (worker, capitalist, landowner) is the sum of any increases less any reductions in the supply of his factors to different uses. (A transfer of labour to a better-paid use would constitute such an increase, but not, of course, an increase in remuneration for labour in a given use.)

(3) The *increment in tax quantum* associated with any type of transaction is the increase in the volume of transactions of this type *times* the current tax rate. Subsidies are counted as negative taxes.

(4) The *increment in government services* consists in the money equivalent of any net increase in government services provided without charge, other than those provided to firms.

(5) The *increment in net psychic income* of any individual is the money equivalent of all additional advantages less additional disadvantages accruing to him, other than those arising through

[1] *The Economic Journal*, March 1935.

[2] Where adjustments large enough to alter prices are in question the price of each increment will be the average price over the corresponding interval of variation on the relevant product-demand or factor-supply curve. This average price will be a function of the 'path' of variation and thus of the convention whereby that path is determined.

changes in his money income, or in the nominal purchasing power of that income. This is something of a hold-all residual item, containing, for example, not only all changes in satisfaction associated with a change in occupation as such, but also those associated with changes in the availability of consumer goods at unchanged prices.

Now the sum of all increments of the first three types will together constitute that part of the increment of the real national product which is marketed and is statistically measurable.[1] Inclusion of the increments of types (4) and (5) will add the non-marketed and the intangible elements in the real national product. In a closed economy this sum will also represent the increment in the real national income. In an economy with foreign trade, however, we must add :

(6) The increment, resulting from change in the terms of trade, in the import equivalent of the existing volume of exports.

Now, any increment in one of the above-mentioned categories may be termed, if positive, an 'economy' and, if negative, a 'diseconomy', and any economy or diseconomy which is brought about by the actions of a particular firm, other than a change in its own direct net product, I shall refer to as an 'external' economy or diseconomy, respectively, generated by the operations of that firm.

External economies affecting direct net product, factor supply, tax quantum or psychic income can be cross-classified into two main categories :

A. economies which affect production and enjoyment functions in such a way as to increase the outputs of affected firms for given inputs or to increase the satisfaction derived by persons from given employment and consumption patterns ;

B. economies arising out of production adjustments, employment adjustments or consumption adjustments, undertaken by the affected firms, workers or consumers in response

[1] Summation of the first two types of increments alone would have given us a measure of the increment in real national product in which individual products are weighted according to their factor cost—a faulty weighting from a welfare-economic standpoint. Inclusion of type (3) increments alters the basis of weighting to that of market price.

to changes in the market situation resulting from the initial operation.

Where perfect competition is pervasive only external economies of Category A can occur.[1] Economies of Category B can occur only in connexion with firms, workers or consumers operating under imperfect competition or price-fixing or subject to indirect taxation. Such economies can accompany infinitesimal adjustments only where production (or employment or consumption as the case may be) has previously been uneconomically organized. Thus a small expansion of input and output in a firm resulting from an expansion in product demand can lead to an increase in direct *net* product only when, for reasons of profit-maximization or *force majeure*, product price has previously been in excess of marginal cost. Where *large* individual adjustments are concerned, however, such as installation of new plant, a change in market conditions can make economic an adjustment yielding an increase in direct net product, even though such adjustment was previously uneconomic.

[1] Cf. J. E. Meade, 'External Economies and Diseconomies in a Competitive Situation', *The Economic Journal*, March 1952.

TWO CONCEPTS OF EXTERNAL ECONOMIES*

by **Tibor Scitovsky**

THE CONCEPT OF EXTERNAL ECONOMIES IS ONE OF THE MOST elusive in economic literature. Our understanding of it has been greatly enhanced by the active controversy of the twenties over the nature of the 'empty economic boxes'; but full clarity has never been achieved. Definitions of external economies are few and unsatisfactory. It is agreed that they mean services (and dis-services) rendered free (without compensation) by one producer to another; but there is no agreement on the nature and form of these services or on the reasons for their being free. It is also agreed that external economies are a cause for divergency between private profit and social benefit and thus for the failure of perfect competition to lead to an optimum situation; but for this there are many reasons, and it is nowhere made clear how many and which of these reasons are subsumed under the heading of 'external economies'. Nor do examples help to clarify the concept. The literature contains many examples of external economies; but they are as varied and dissimilar as are discussions of the subject. Some give the impression that external economies are exceptional and unimportant; others suggest that they are important and ubiquitous. Indeed, one might be tempted to explain this strange dichotomy by ideological differences between the different authors; but such an explanation would be both unwarranted and unnecessary. For, with the increasing rigour of economic thinking and separation of the different branches of economic theory, it is becoming increasingly clear that the concept of external economies does duty in two entirely different contexts. One of these is equilibrium theory, the other is the theory of industrialization in underdeveloped countries. It is customary to discuss these two subjects at different levels of abstraction and on the basis of very different sets of assumptions: no

* *The Journal of Political Economy*, April 1954. Reprinted by permission of the University of Chicago Press and the author. Copyright (1954) by the University of Chicago. The author is indebted to Professor Bernard Haley and Mr Ralph Turvey for many helpful suggestions.

wonder that 'external economies' stand for very different things in the two contexts. Indeed, I shall argue that there are two entirely different definitions of external economies, one much wider than the other; and that external economies as defined in the theory of industrialization include, but go far beyond, the external economies of equilibrium theory. The latter have been discussed and rigorously defined in Professor Meade's 'External Economies and Diseconomies in a Competitive Situation';[1] but, since they form part of external economies as defined in the theory of industrialization, we shall deal with them briefly here.

Equilibrium theory, in both its general and its partial form, is a static theory, concerned with the characteristics of the economic system when it is in equilibrium. Most of its conclusions are based on the assumptions of (1) perfect competition on both sides of every market and (2) perfect divisibility of all resources and products. These assumptions underlie the main conclusion of general equilibrium theory, viz., that the market economy leads to a situation of economic optimum (in Pareto's sense), provided that every economic influence of one person's (or firm's) behaviour on another person's well-being (or firm's profit) is transmitted through its impact on market prices. Expressed differently, equilibrium in a perfectly competitive economy is a situation of Paretian optimum, except when there is interdependence among the members of the economy that is direct, in the sense that it does not operate through the market mechanism. In general equilibrium theory, then, direct interdependence is the villain of the piece and the cause for conflict between private profit and social benefit.

One can distinguish four types of direct (i.e., non-market) interdependence (and one of these—the last one in the following enumeration—is known as 'external economies'): (1) The individual person's satisfaction may depend not only on the quantities of products he consumes and services he renders but also on the satisfaction of other persons. In particular, the high income or consumption of others may give a person pain or

[1] *The Economic Journal*, Vol. LXII (1952), pp. 54-67.

pleasure; and so may his knowledge that some others are less well off than he is. This is known as the 'interdependence of consumers' satisfaction'. (2) A person's satisfaction may be influenced by the activities of producers not only through their demand for his services and supply of the products he buys but also in ways that do not operate through the market mechanism. These may be called the producer's 'direct' (i e., non-market) influence on personal satisfaction and are best known by the example of the factory that inconveniences the neighbourhood with the fumes or noise that emanate from it. (3) The producer's output may be influenced by the action of persons more directly and in other ways than through their offer of services used and demand for products produced by the firm. This is a counterpart of the previous case, and its main instance is inventions that facilitate production and become available to producers without charge. (4) The output of the individual producer may depend not only on his input of productive resources but also on the activities of other firms. This is a counterpart of case 1 and may be called 'direct interdependence among producers' but is better known under the name of 'external economies and diseconomies'.[1]

Of these four cases of direct interdependence, the first, interdependence among consumers, is undoubtedly important. It is (together with the case mentioned in the footnote) among the main reasons for the current controversy in welfare economics and the reluctance of economists to make any welfare statements concerning the consumer. Nowadays, welfare statements are usually confined to the field of production, where the main conclusion of general equilibrium theory seems to stand on firmer ground, primarily because the remaining three cases of direct interdependence (all of which involve the producer) seem exceptional and unimportant. The second case seems exceptional, because most instances of it can be and usually are eliminated by zoning ordinances and industrial regulation concerned with public health and safety. The third case is unimportant, because patent laws have eliminated the

[1] A fifth and important case, which, however, does not quite fit into the above classification, is that where society provides social services through communal action and makes them available free of charge to all persons and firms.

main instance of this form of direct interdependence and transformed it into a case of interdependence through the market mechanism.[1] The fourth case seems unimportant, simply because examples of it seem to be few and exceptional.

The last statement appears at first to be contradicted by the many examples of external economies and diseconomies quoted in the literature ; but most of these are *not* examples of direct interdependence among producers, which is the only meaning that can be attributed to the term 'external economies' within the context of equilibrium theory. It will be useful in this connexion to have a rigorous definition of direct interdependence among producers. Meade gave such a definition when he defined external economies ; and I can do no better than to reproduce it. According to him, external economies exist whenever the output (x_1) of a firm depends not only on the factors of production ($l_1, c_1, \ldots$) utilized by this firm but also on the output (x_2) and factor utilization ($l_2, c_2, \ldots$) of another firm or group of firms.[2] In symbols, $x_1 = F\ (l_1, c_1, \ldots\ ; x_2, l_2 \ldots)$, where the existence of external economies is indicated by the presence of the variables to the right of the semicolon. Since $F(*)$ is a production function, external economies as here defined are a peculiarity of the production function. For this reason it is convenient to call them 'technological external economies'.[3] While this will distinguish them from another category of external economies to be introduced presently, we must bear in mind that technological external economies are the only external economies that can arise, because of direct interdependence among producers and within the framework of general equilibrium theory.

The examples of external economies given by Meade are somewhat bucolic in nature, having to do with bees, orchards, and woods. This, however, is no accident : it is not easy to

[1] i.e., patent laws have created a market and a market price for the inventor's services, which in the absence of such laws would often be free goods. The case where the results of government-sponsored research into industrial and agricultural methods are made gratuitously available to industrialists and farmers belongs in the category mentioned in the note on p. 297.

[2] Op. cit.

[3] The term is used in Jacob Viner's 'Cost Curves and Supply Curves', *Zeitschrift für Nationalökonomie*, III (1931), pp. 23-46.

find examples from industry. Going through the many examples of external economies quoted in the literature, I found only two that fit the above definition : the case in which a firm benefits from the labour market created by the establishment of other firms and that in which several firms use a resource which is free but limited in supply.[1] For a more detailed discussion the reader is referred to Meade's article, which will, I think, convince him of the scarcity of technological external economies.

The other field in which the concept of external economies occurs frequently is the theory of industrialization of underdeveloped countries, where the concept is used in connexion with the special problem of allocating savings among alternative investment opportunities. This last is one of the many practical problems to which economists are wont to apply the conclusions of general equilibrium theory. Most of them realize, of course, that general equilibrium theory is limited in its assumptions and applicability ; but the only limitation taken seriously by most economists is that imposed by the assumption of perfect competition ; and this—as is well known—is not always a necessary condition for the conclusions of equilibrium theory to hold good. In particular, many economists regard a uniform degree of monopoly as all that is necessary for market forces to bring about an optimum allocation of investment funds ; and this weaker condition is held to be more nearly fulfilled in our society. Whether for this reason or for some other, the private profitability of investment is usually considered a good index of its social desirability, at least as a general rule.

To this rule, however, the exceptions are too great and obvious to be ignored, especially in underdeveloped countries ; and it is customary to impute most of them to external economies. While the nature of these external economies is often discussed, I have been unable to find a definition of the concept in the literature dealing with underdeveloped countries. It is

[1] Instances of this are the oil well whose output depends on the number and operation of other wells on the same oil field ; the fisherman whose catch depends on the operations of other fishermen in the same waters ; and the firm that uses a public road (or other publicly owned utility) and is partly crowded out of it by other firms using the same road.

possible, however, to infer a definition from the many examples, discussions, and *obiter dicta*. It seems that external economies are invoked whenever the profits of one producer are affected by the actions of other producers. To facilitate comparison with Meade's definition, we can express this in symbols by the function $P_1 = G\ (x_1, l_1, c_1 \ldots ; x_2, l_2, c_2, \ldots)$, which shows that the *profits* of the firm depend not only on its own output and factor inputs but also on the output and factor inputs of other firms ; and we shall say that in the context of underdeveloped countries external economies are said to exist whenever the variables to the right of the semicolon are present.

This definition of external economies obviously includes direct or non-market interdependence among producers, as discussed above and defined by Meade. It is much broader, however, than his definition, because, in addition to direct interdependence among producers, it also includes interdependence among producers through the market mechanism. This latter type of interdependence may be called 'pecuniary external economies' to distinguish it from the technological external economies of direct interdependence.[1]

Interdependence through the market mechanism is all-pervading, and this explains the contrast between the exceptional and often awkward examples of external economies cited in discussions of equilibrium theory and the impression one gains from the literature on underdeveloped countries that the entrepreneur creates external economies and diseconomies with his every move.

What is puzzling, however, is that interdependence through the market mechanism should be held to account for the failure of the market economy to lead to the socially desirable optimum, when equilibrium theory comes to the opposite conclusion and *relies* on market interdependence to bring about an optimum situation. Pecuniary external economies clearly have no place in equilibrium theory. The question is whether the concept is meaningful elsewhere. To answer this question we must first investigate the nature of the pecuniary external economies, to which interdependence through the market mechanism gives rise.

[1] Cf. Viner, op. cit.

Investment in an industry leads to an expansion of its capacity and may thus lower the prices of its products and raise the prices of the factors used by it. The lowering of product prices benefits the users of these products ; the raising of factor prices benefits the suppliers of the factors. When these benefits accrue to firms, in the form of profits, they are pecuniary external economies—Marshall called, or would have called, them (together with the benefits accruing to persons) consumers' and producers' surplus, respectively. According to the theory of industrialization, these benefits, being genuine benefits, should be explicitly taken into account when investment decisions are made ; and it is usually suggested that this should be done by taking as the maximand not profits alone but the sum of the profits yielded and the pecuniary external economies created by the investment.

This prescription seems to be in direct conflict with the results of equilibrium theory. For, according to the latter and subject to its usual assumptions and limitations, market interdependence in the competitive system insures that the maximization of profit by each firm and of satisfaction by each person brings about an optimum situation, which, as is well known, is sometimes described as a situation in which consumers' and producers' surpluses are maximized. In other words, equilibrium theory tells us that in equilibrium the sum of consumers' and producers' surpluses will be maximized, although they do not enter explicitly, as part of the maximand, the economic decisions of any producer.[1] Assuming that these conflicting views are both right, the conflict can be resolved only if we should find that the limitations of general equilibrium theory render it inapplicable to the problems of investment. This, indeed, must often be so ; but in the following we shall single out three special cases, which seem especially important and in which the above conflict is resolved.

(*a*) One reason why the conclusions of general equilibrium theory may be inapplicable to the practical problem of

[1] Cf. J. R. Hicks, 'The Rehabilitation of Consumers' Surplus', *Review of Economic Studies*, Vol. VIII (1941), pp. 108-16. We need not enter here the debate on the usefulness of this terminology. Nor is it necessary to stress that this way of stating the results of perfect competition is characteristic of partial equilibrium analysis.

investment is that the former's assumption of perfect divisibility is not always fulfilled. Perfect competition leads to a position of economic optimum, because under perfect competition the marginal conditions of economic optimum are contained (in the absence of direct interdependence) in the marginal conditions of profit maximization by producers and satisfaction maximization by householders. Indivisibilities, however, may prevent the producer from fulfilling these marginal conditions. For example, he may find himself unable to equate marginal costs to price and, instead, face the choice of producing either less or more than the output that would equate these two quantities. In such a case one of the available alternatives will still yield him a higher profit than all others ; but this need no longer be the one that is also the best from society's point of view. Hence the need, in such cases, to take society's point of view explicitly into consideration.

This fact was recognized as early as 1844 by Dupuit.[1] He was looking for a criterion of the social desirability of investment in such public utilities as canals, roads, bridges, and railways—the typical examples of indivisibilities in economics —and he found this criterion not in the actual profitability of such investments but in what their profitability would be in the hypothetical case in which the operator of the utility practised price discrimination and thus appropriated to himself the consumers' surplus that would normally (i.e., in the absence of price discrimination) accrue to the users of the public utility. In other words, Dupuit's test of social desirability is whether the sum of profit and consumers' surplus is positive.[2] Dupuit's test and his use of the consumers' surplus concept underlying it were vindicated by Professor Hicks ;[3] but neither Hicks nor Dupuit makes clear the role of indivisibilities in rendering the above test necessary. For this last point, as well as for an excellent statement of the entire argument, the reader should

[1] Cf. Jules Dupuit, 'De la mesure de l'utilité des travaux publics', *Annales des ponts et chaussées*, 2nd ser., Vol. VIII (1844) ; reprinted in *International Economic Papers*, No. 2 (1952), pp. 83-110.

[2] This is so whether the consumer's surplus accrues to persons or represents external economies accruing to firms.

[3] Cf. J. R. Hicks, 'L'Économie de bien-être et la théorie des surplus du consommateur', and 'Quelques applications de la théorie des surplus du consommateur', both in *Économie appliquée*, No. 4 (1948), pp. 432-57.

consult chapter xvi of Professor Lerner's *Economics of Control*.[1]

(*b*) The second reason for the inapplicability of general equilibrium theory to the problems of investment is that the former is a static or equilibrium theory, whereas the allocation of investment funds is not a static problem at all. According to equilibrium theory, the producer's profit-maximizing behaviour brings about a socially desirable situation *when the system is in equilibrium*; or, to give this result a more dynamic, if not entirely correct, interpretation, profit-maximizing behaviour brings closer the socially desirable optimum if it also brings closer equilibrium. Investment, however, need not bring the system closer to equilibrium; and, when it does not, the results of equilibrium theory may not apply.

Profits are a sign of disequilibrium; and the magnitude of profits, under free competition, may be regarded as a rough index of the degree of disequilibrium.[2] Profits in a freely competitive industry lead to investment in that industry; and the investment, in turn, tends to eliminate the profits that have called it forth. This far, then, investment tends to bring equilibrium nearer. The same investment, however, may raise or give rise to profits in other industries; and to this extent it leads away from equilibrium. For example, investment in industry A will cheapen its product; and if this is used as a factor in industry B, the latter's profits will rise. This, then, is a case where the price reduction creates, not a consumers' surplus proper, accruing to persons, but pecuniary external economies, benefiting firms. Is this difference sufficient to render the conclusions of general equilibrium theory inapplicable?

To answer this question, we must pursue the argument a little further. The profits of industry B, created by the lower price of factor A, call for investment and expansion in industry B, one result of which will be an increase in industry B's

[1] A. P. Lerner, *Economics of Control* (New York: Macmillan Co., 1944). Lerner's solution is slightly different and, I believe, more correct than Dupuit's, in that he takes account also of producers' surplus. It might be added in passing that the type of indivisibility considered by Dupuit establishes a relation among the users of the public utility that is similar in all essentials to direct interdependence among consumers.

[2] However, the absence of profits is not a sufficient condition of equilibrium.

demand for industry A's product. This in its turn will give rise to profits and call for further investment and expansion in industry A ; and equilibrium is reached only when successive doses of investment and expansion in the two industries have led to the simultaneous elimination of profits in both. It is only at this stage, where equilibrium has been established, that the conclusions of equilibrium theory become applicable and we can say (on the usual assumptions and in the absence of direct interdependence) that the amount of investment profitable in industry A is also the socially desirable amount. This amount is clearly greater than that which is profitable at the first stage, before industry B has made adjustment. We can conclude, therefore, that when an investment gives rise to pecuniary external economies, its private profitability understates its social desirability.

Unfortunately, however, the test of social desirability applicable in the previous case is not applicable here, although it would probably give a better result than a simple calculation of profitability. This can easily be seen by comparing the situation under consideration with that which would obtain if industries A and B were integrated (although in such a way as to preserve the free competition assumed so far). In this case the pecuniary external economies created by investment in industry A would become 'internal' and part of the profits of the investors themselves. Investment in A would be more profitable and pushed further than in the absence of integration ; but, *without investment and expansion also in industry B*, it would not be pushed far enough. For what inhibits investment in A is the limitation on the demand for industry A's product imposed by the limited capacity of industry B, the consumer of this product ; just as investment in industry B is inhibited by the limited capacity of industry A, the supplier of one of industry B's factors of production. These limitations can be fully removed only by a simultaneous expansion of both industries. We conclude, therefore, that only if expansion in the two industries were integrated and planned together would the profitability of investment in each one of them be a reliable index of its social desirability.

It hardly needs adding that the relation between industries A and B discussed above illustrates only one of the many possible instances of pecuniary external economies that belong in this category. Expansion in industry A may also give rise to profits (i) in an industry that produces a factor used in industry A, (ii) in an industry whose product is complementary in use to the product of industry A, (iii) in an industry whose product is a substitute for a factor used in industry A, or (iv) in an industry whose product is consumed by persons whose incomes are raised by the expansion of industry A—and this list does not include the cases in which the expansion causes external *dis*economies. It is apparent from this list that vertical integration alone would not be enough and that complete integration of all industries would be necessary to eliminate all divergence between private profit and public benefit. This was fully realized by Dr Rosenstein-Rodan, who, in dealing with the 'Problems of Industrialization of Eastern and South-Eastern Europe',[1] considered most instances of pecuniary external economies listed above and advocated that 'the whole of the industry to be created is to be treated and planned like one huge firm or trust'.[2] To put this conclusion differently, profits in a market economy are a bad guide to economic optimum as far as investment and industrial expansion are concerned; and they are worse, the more decentralized and differentiated the economy.

This entire argument can be restated in somewhat different terms. In an economy in which economic decisions are decentralized, a system of communications is needed to enable each person who makes economic decisions to learn about the economic decisions of others and co-ordinate his decisions with theirs. In the market economy, prices are the signalling device that informs each person of other people's economic decisions; and the merit of perfect competition is that it would cause prices to transmit information reliably and people to respond to this information properly. Market prices, however, reflect the economic situation as it is and not as it will be. For this reason, they are more useful for co-ordinating current production decisions, which are immediately effective and guided by short-run considerations, than they are for co-ordinating investment decisions, which have a delayed effect and—looking

[1] Reprinted in the present volume, pp. 245-55.
[2] p. 248.

ahead to a long future period—should be governed not by what the present economic situation is but by what the future economic situation is expected to be. The proper co-ordination of investment decisions, therefore, would require a signalling device to transmit information about present plans and future conditions as they are determined by present plans ; and the pricing system fails to provide this.[1] Hence the belief that there is need either for centralized investment planning or for some additional communication system to supplement the pricing system as a signalling device.

It must be added that the argument of this section applies with especial force to underdeveloped countries. The plant capacity most economical to build and operate is not very different in different countries ; but, as a percentage of an industry's total capacity, it is very much greater in underdeveloped than in fully industrialized economies. In underdeveloped countries, therefore, investment is likely to have a greater impact on prices, give rise to greater pecuniary external economies, and thus cause a greater divergence between private profit and social benefit.

(*c*) I propose to consider yet another reason for divergence between the profitability of an investment and its desirability from the community's point of view ; but this is very different from those discussed in the last two sections and has to do with the difference between the national and international points of view. In appraising the social desirability of an economic action from the international point of view, all repercussions of that action must be fully taken into account, whereas, from the national point of view, the welfare of domestic nationals alone is relevant and the losses suffered and benefits gained by foreigners are ignored. The two points of view need not necessarily lead to different appraisals ; but they usually do when the economic action considered is the allocation of investment funds among purely domestic, import-competing, and export industries. From the international point of view, all external economies and diseconomies must be taken into consideration ; from the national point of view, one must count only the

[1] Professor Kenneth Arrow pointed out to me, however, that, in a formal sense, futures markets and futures prices could provide exactly such a signalling device.

external economies and diseconomies that accrue to domestic nationals and leave out of account the pecuniary external economies accruing to foreign buyers from the expansion of export industries and the diseconomies inflicted on foreign competitors by the expansion of import-competing industries. Accordingly, investment in export industries is always less, and that in import-competing industries is always more, desirable from the national, than from the international, point of view.

In discussions on investment policy this difference between the national and international points of view usually appears in the guise of a difference between the criteria of social benefit and private profit. For social benefit, when considered explicitly, is usually identified with national benefit in our society, whereas private profit, although an imperfect index of social desirability, accounts or fails to account for external economies and diseconomies without national bias and therefore probably comes closer to registering the social welfare of the world as a whole than that of a single nation. Hence investment tends to be more profitable in export industries and less profitable in import-competing industries than would be desirable from a narrow nationalistic point of view.

It is worth noting that this argument is in some respects the reverse of the argument found in (*b*) above. There it was the failure of profit calculations to take into account pecuniary external economies that caused the divergence between private profit and social benefit ; here the divergence is caused by the entry into the profit criterion of pecuniary external economies and diseconomies that accrue to foreigners and should therefore be excluded from social accounting concerned with national, rather than world, welfare. The argument is well known as the 'terms-of-trade argument' and has been used to explain the failure of foreign investments in colonial areas to benefit fully the borrowing countries.[1] The divergence between national welfare and private profit depends on the foreigners' import-demand and export-supply elasticities ; and it can be offset by an appropriate set of import and export duties. This has

[1] Cf. H. W. Singer, 'The Distribution of Gains between Investing and Borrowing Countries', *The American Economic Review* (*Proceedings*), Vol. XL (1950), pp. 473-85.

been shown by Mr J. de V. Graaff, in his 'Optimum Tariff Structures'.[1] De Graaff presents his optimum tariff structure as one that will bring about that flow of goods and services which optimizes[2] the nation's welfare; but the same tariff structure will also bring about the allocation of investment funds that is optimal from the national point of view.

[1] *Review of Economic Studies*, Vol. XVII (1949-50), pp. 47-59.
[2] In Pareto's sense.

CAPITAL FORMATION AND ECONOMIC DEVELOPMENT*

by **Celso Furtado**

THE SIX LECTURES DELIVERED IN BRAZIL BY RAGNAR NURKSE on Problems of Capital Formation in Underdeveloped Countries may be regarded as one of the most serious attempts on the part of economists of 'developed' countries to understand the problems with which underdeveloped economies are at present faced. The extremely encouraging results of that study afford ample grounds for optimism concerning the application of modern instruments of analysis to the problem of the development of backward areas today.

The absence of basic information and the resultant ignorance of the real economic facts have given rise, among economists in the underdeveloped countries, to the habit of reasoning by analogy, in the mistaken belief that, up to a certain point, economic phenomena are the same everywhere. Unfortunately, it is not always possible to draw conclusions applicable to concrete situations from theories which, although logically sound, are largely abstract constructions. It is to be hoped, however, that the huge statistical research effort at present being made in many underdeveloped countries may contribute

* *International Economic Papers*, No. 4, 1954. Reprinted by permission of the International Economic Association and the author. Translated by J. Cairncross. 'Formaçao de Capital e Desenvolvimento Econômico', *Revista Brasileira de Economia*, Vol. 6, No. 3, Sept. 1952. This paper is a comment on six lectures delivered by Professor Ragnar Nurkse, of Columbia University, at the Brazilian Institute of Economics in July and August 1951. These were published in Portuguese in *Revista Brasileira de Economia*, Dec. 1951 ; a revised version of them has since been published in Ragnar Nurkse, *Problems of Capital Formation in Underdeveloped Countries*, Oxford, 1953. For the convenience of English-speaking readers, references in this article to the Portuguese version of the lectures have throughout been replaced by references to that book.

A rejoinder by Professor Nurkse was published in *Revista Brasileira de Economia*, March 1953. In substance this is a re-statement of some points stressed in the above-mentioned book ; it corrects certain misleading impressions about Professor Nurkse's views which the reader might gain from this Paper.

to the transformation of economic thought in those countries into as powerful an instrument for the analysis of social reality as it is in other parts of the world.

Many of the points raised by Professor Nurkse in his lectures are extremely topical and deserve fuller treatment. In the present study we will deal with three of these points—the theory of economic development, the relation between the propensity to consume and the rate of development and the effects of investment on the balance of payments.

The Theory of Economic Development

One of the most interesting problems dealt with by Professor Nurkse, right at the outset, is that of the theory of economic development. He draws attention to the fact that, in developed countries, economists have always taken the phenomenon of economic growth for granted, which explains why it has seldom been subjected to systematic analysis.

A scientific theory presupposes the existence of one or more problems which some social group is anxious to solve. It is indispensable, therefore, to recognize the existence of a problem if the search for its solution is to stimulate enquiry. It is practically only in our own days that economic development has become a 'problem' in this sense. The price mechanism was taken to ensure that the most rational possible use was made of the community's productive resources, and, besides, it was common ground that the spirit of enterprise, stimulated by the dynamism of a liberal form of society, offered sound guarantees for economic progress.

Government action in the whole of the economic sphere began to be acceptable when the need for counter-cyclical policy was recognized. And it was as a by-product of cyclical theories that ideas about the process of economic development made their appearance.[1] Since the economic process takes on a cyclical form in a free enterprise economy, it would be unrealistic to reason in terms of an ascending linear movement. Moreover, while it is true that the mere observation of a number

[1] Historians, social philosophers and sociologists in the field of social dynamics had previously devoted a good deal of attention to economic development: cf., for example, the magnificent work of Max Weber, Henri Pirenne, H. See and others, on the origins of capitalism.

of consecutive cycles gave rise to the formulation of secular trend theories, it proved extremely difficult to tackle the problem of growth without first understanding the mechanism of the cycle. As a clearer insight into that mechanism was obtained, counter-cyclical policy grew from elementary measures of a monetary nature into co-ordinated action on the dynamic elements of the economic system. Thus, one part of counter-cyclical policy now consists in deciding what targets are to be achieved in a given time in specific sectors of the economy, which are regarded as having a dynamic part to play. In a given situation of full employment one may, for example, decide that, in order to maintain the level of activity, or, more exactly, the optimum use of the factors of production, it is necessary that the gross social product increase by x per cent over a period of six years. Once that objective has been laid down and the amount of consumer expenditure—which is a function of that objective—is known, it is possible to work out the appropriate total of public and private investment to be carried out by the economy. Counter-cyclical policy will, in that case, consist of a series of measures aimed at the realization of that amount of investment.

In proceeding from a price stabilization policy to the co-ordination and planning of investment, the proponents of counter-cyclical measures were brought up against the need for a theory which would not only analyse the causes of fluctuations in the level of employment but would explain the general process of economic development. This explains the present widespread interest in studies of capital accumulation and of the relation between the amount of investment and national income, and also the fresh efforts to measure national wealth which are particularly marked in the United States. Similarly, it is not surprising that input-output studies are attracting great attention since they allow a much clearer insight into the interdependence of the economic system. The same is true of the recent studies on economic dynamics by Harrod, Domar and other economists.

Professor Nurkse's approach to the theory of economic development is based, broadly speaking, on Schumpeter's analysis. His version of that theory, however, is an extremely personal one. We will therefore consider his contribution separately and only incidentally offer certain observations on Schumpeter's own theory.

The central point of Nurkse's interpretation is the small size of a country's market as a factor limiting economic development. 'In the exchange economy of the real world,' he says, 'it is not difficult to find illustrations of the way in which the small size of a country's market can discourage, or even prohibit, the profitable application of modern capital equipment. . . . Many articles that are in common use in the United States can be sold in a low-income country in quantities so limited that a machine working only a few days or weeks can produce enough for a whole year's consumption.'[1]

The basic problem of underdeveloped countries, on that reasoning, is not a shortage of saving but rather the lack of investment incentives due to the limited size of the market. However interesting this problem may be, Professor Nurkse exaggerates its importance. If underdeveloped countries had the chance of investing with an eye to the external market, there would be no problem. The fundamental question, therefore, is the absence of an expanding external market. We should, then, distinguish between development when foreign trade is expanding and when it is stationary or contracting. That is a fundamental problem and we will address ourselves to it when we come to the connexion between disequilibrium in the balance of payments and the direction investment takes.

There is a further and more serious reason which leads us to dissent from the way Professor Nurkse regards the small size of the market as an obstacle to development. A market is small only in relation to something. And, in the case in question, the market of underdeveloped countries is small in relation to the type of equipment used by developed countries. This is not a fundamental difficulty in the process of economic development, but is merely fortuitous. In the development of countries which are today highly industrialized, technical innovations were adopted when they were economically justified. The factor of production labour was replaced by the factor of production capital, wherever this was justified by a reduction of costs. But the introduction of automatic boot-

[1] Op. cit., p. 7.

making machinery into a primitive community would certainly mean not a reduction, but a considerable increase in costs, just as it would have raised costs in the countries which are today industrialized, if it had been introduced a hundred years ago. Moreover, it is not necessary to introduce the most modern equipment in order to achieve a marked increase in productivity in an underdeveloped country. In many parts of Brazil the mere introduction of the wheel would spell a notable advance. Even the laying of a road can bring about a considerable increase in productivity in an agricultural area.

The aim of economic development must be to increase the physical productivity of labour. In an underdeveloped economy the introduction of automatic boot-making machinery will not mean an improvement in the physical productivity of labour for the community as a whole if the workmen who previously produced boots are left without any work. Moreover, the entrepreneur who introduces this kind of machinery will suffer too, since it will have to stay idle five days in the week. But the entrepreneur who introduces improvements in the tools used for the production of boots by hand, thereby making possible an increase in productivity, will turn out more boots with the same number of man-hours without a disproportionate increase in other costs.

But let us return to Professor Nurkse's argument. 'The enlargement of the market through the rise in productivity that would result from increased capital-intensity of production is inhibited by the initial smallness of the market.' Professor Nurkse then states: 'We perceive a constellation of circumstances tending to preserve any backward economy in a stationary condition. . . . Economic progress is not a spontaneous or automatic affair.'[1] In conclusion, he equates this 'automatic stagnation' with Schumpeter's 'circular flow'.

It is interesting to note that in this way Professor Nurkse gives a historical content to Schumpeter's circular-flow economy which seems to exist in that author's mind as a mere abstraction. The great methodological weakness of Schumpeter's theory consists precisely in that, having created that

[1] Op. cit., p. 10.

abstraction, he then, in contrast to it, worked out a model which is intended to represent concrete situations.

According to Schumpeter the central figure in the process of economic development is the creative entrepreneur, who introduces 'new combinations' and whose action gives rise to 'spontaneous and discontinuous changes in the channels of the circular flow'.

The difficulty about this theory of economic development, as considered at the present time, derives from the fact that Schumpeter formulated it before the first world war, in circumstances which were entirely different from those of our own days. He claimed to explain why economic reality was a constantly changing and not merely a repetitive process. He did not directly concern himself with the possibility of increasing capital intensity or real income, but with the 'dynamics' of the economic process. 'Development in our sense,' he says, 'is a distinct phenomenon, entirely foreign to what may be observed in the circular flow or in the tendency towards equilibrium. It is spontaneous and discontinuous change in the channels of the flow, disturbance of equilibrium, which forever alters and displaces the equilibrium state previously existing. Our theory of development is nothing but a treatment of this phenomenon and the processes incident to it.'[1]

How can we identify the entrepreneur, that dynamic element which disturbs equilibrium? He introduces 'innovations'. Schumpeter lists five types of innovation which may be defined as new goods, new methods of production, new markets, new sources of raw material, and new forms of organization. But in reality the distinctive characteristic of the entrepreneur is the creation of profit. In the circular-flow economy profit does not exist, the entrepreneur is a mere administrator. If those ideas are to be at all valid, we must assume a perfect market, in which profit would only exist as a result of a temporary semi-monopolistic situation, created by any innovation whatsoever.

The essence of Schumpeter's theory of economic development may therefore, be summed up as follows: The economic process in our society is not circular because there is a class

[1] *The Theory of Economic Development* (Harvard, 1951), p. 64.

with a dynamic outlook—the entrepreneurs—which, by means of innovations, constantly tends to disturb the equilibrium. Should we not ask : And what factors make for the existence of such a class in our society ? Why do certain individuals have that social function ? Indeed, the problem of economic development is but one aspect of the general problem of social change in our society, and cannot be fully understood unless we give it a historical content. We should have to consider the whole cultural pattern which grew up in Europe with its rational mode of thinking, its social mobility, its scale of social values reflecting, to a large extent, the scale of personal wealth, in order to explain the dynamics of the capitalist economic process. Schumpeter's simplification makes us lose sight of the real economic problem of development and is, moreover, of little use as a general explanation of the phenomenon.

Nurkse diverges from Schumpeter's theory of development and seeks to explain the passage from a state of equilibrium to one of development by certain concepts (the so-called 'waves of investment') in that author's cyclical theory. 'Where any single enterprise might appear quite inauspicious and impracticable, a wide range of projects in different industries may succeed. . . .'[1] That phenomenon can only be understood within the framework of the cyclical process in developed economies, because, at certain stages of the cycle, when there are many idle factors, it is essential that the movement should begin simultaneously on a broad front so that some sectors create a market for the others. To use this theory as an explanation of the initiation of a process of growth in an underdeveloped economy seems very wide of the mark. For an underdeveloped economy to start a process of development with its own resources and by the spontaneous action of its entrepreneurs is, to use a current expression, like raising oneself by one's own bootstraps. It is true that process of development, once it is launched, can gather momentum from its own forces, as we shall show when dealing with the high propensity to consume of underdeveloped economies today. But that is no justification for claiming that such a development can start off the process.

[1] Op. cit., p. 13.

The concept of innovations is certainly Schumpeter's most interesting theoretical contribution. But his manner of defining them is too vague—for, if, as he maintains, innovations tend to upset the circular flow or the equilibrium of the system, we are practically back where we started, since the circular flow is a mere abstraction. It is possible to conceive of an economy coming within Schumpeter's categories in which the action of a group of entrepreneurs constantly disrupts the equilibrium by the introduction of new products, without necessarily increasing productivity. The new products may simply displace others and the new entrepreneurs' profits may be offset by the losses sustained by others.

The Process of Development

The theory of economic development in its general form does not fall within the categories of economic analysis. This is a point of view fairly widely accepted nowadays, and it should hardly be necessary to refer to the Seminar on Economic Development held at the University of Chicago in 1951, at which sociologists, anthropologists and historians sat side by side with economists. Economic analysis cannot say why any society starts developing and to what social agents this process is due. Nevertheless it can describe the mechanism of economic development and it is this description which we now propose to discuss.

At bottom the process of development consists of a series of changes in the manner and proportions in which the factors of production are combined. We will not dwell on the analysis of the social reasons for these changes, since that would take us too far. Through those changes people try to work out more rational combinations of the factors of production subject to the limitations of current technology, with the aim of increasing the productivity of labour. The aim of the theory of economic development, then, is not to explain why an economy is constantly changing, but why in that economy the productivity of labour goes on increasing.

Developed and Underdeveloped Countries

The process of development involves either new combinations of existing factors at the current technical level, or the introduction of technical innovations. If we may simplify the problem, those regions may be termed fully developed in which, at a given moment, none of the factors are unemployed and it is possible to increase productivity (real *per capita* income) only by introducing new techniques. Further, areas the productivity of which is increasing or could be increased by the simple introduction of techniques which are already known should be considered as suffering from a different degree of underdevelopment. The growth of a developed economy, then, is mainly a problem of accumulation of new scientific knowledge and progress in the application of that knowledge. The growth of underdeveloped economies is above all a process of assimilation of the techniques existing at the time.

In an underdeveloped region there is always underemployment of the factors of production within the limits of known techniques. Such underemployment, however, does not necessarily spring from a faulty combination of existing factors but usually from scarcity of capital. One factor—labour—is squandered because another—capital—is deficient. But capital, as is well known, is nothing else but work carried out in the past, the product of which was not consumed. We are therefore led to conclude that work is badly utilized today because all the product of former work has been consumed. That vicious circle, as we shall subsequently explain, is in the most backward countries almost always broken by the action of external factors.

Productivity and Capital Accumulation

Economic development consists of the introduction of new combinations of factors of production which tend to increase the productivity of labour. Modern technique is the sum of procedures, the application of which makes such an increase in productivity possible. As productivity grows—provided certain factors which will be examined later do not intervene—there is an increase in real national income, that is, in the quantity of goods and services available. Moreover, the increase in remuneration resulting from a rise in real income leads to a change in the structure of consumer demand. By a process of action and reaction, then, the increase in productivity leads to a rise in real income, and the resulting increase in demand leads to a change in the structure of production. In the study of economic development it is essential, therefore, to know how productivity increases and how demand reacts to an increase in the level of real income.

As we noted earlier on, the increase in the physical productivity of labour is, in the main, the fruit of capital accumulation.[1] However, the relations between those two phenomena—increased productivity and capital accumulation—must be studied very closely if we are to understand the difficulties to be overcome in the initial stages of the process of development.

When productivity is very low, the satisfaction of elementary needs absorbs a high proportion of productive capacity. In very backward economies, for example, 80 per cent or more of the active population has to work in order to satisfy the community's needs for food and clothing. When productivity is at such a low level, it is difficult to start a process of capital accumulation within the economy. Let us see why. In all human communities, the demand for non-agricultural products tends to increase with the income available for consumption. In the most advanced communities, this demand absorbs up to 80 per cent of the society's productive capacity. In the most backward communities the inequality in the distribution of wealth results in certain social groups having a relatively high demand for non-agricultural goods and services. Let us consider for example the community referred to above, in which 80 per cent of the labour force works in agriculture, and let us assume that all its members are employed, that they all have the same productivity and that there is no foreign trade. Let us assume further that 5 per cent of the members of that community are in receipt of incomes markedly above the average: let us say that they have 20 per cent of the total income and that they devote 50 per cent of their income to the purchase of farm produce. The low income group (95 per cent of the population) will have to devote 87·5 per cent of its income to the satisfaction of its needs (the purchase of agricultural products) in order that it may make available produc-

[1] A simple technological innovation may increase the physical productivity of labour. It should be remembered, however, that the most important innovations are incorporated in new equipment, thus requiring some net investment.

tive resources which will enable the high income group to spend 50 per cent of its income on the purchase of non-agricultural goods and services. There would thus be no net investment, and, unless the population were stationary, this economy would not even be able to maintain its level of real *per capita* income.

The main obstacles in the path of development, therefore, are encountered at the lowest levels of productivity. Once the process of growth has been launched, the movement's own dynamics ensure that part of the increase in income is set aside for capital investment. A backward community has a very great tendency to remain stagnant without being able, on its own, to set the process of development in motion. The initial impulse to overcome those difficulties has always come from sources outside the community.[1]

The creation of a flow of foreign trade enables an economy with low level of productivity to get development under way without previous capital accumulation. As we observed above, the increase in productivity, which is the essence of economic development, derives in the last analysis from the introduction of more productive combinations of the factors of production. These new combinations normally call for an increase in the supply of the scarce factor (i.e. available capital). But, in certain circumstances, it is possible to introduce more productive combinations without increasing the amount of capital available, provided it is possible to integrate the economy in question into a wider market. The opening up of foreign trade will allow that economy to make a fuller and more rational use of those factors which are available to it in relative abundance, i.e. land and labour. By obtaining larger quantities of goods

[1] This is true not only in the case of those peoples which are underdeveloped at the present time. In Europe, at the end of the Middle Ages, the transition from an economy composed almost entirely of closed and static units, to a progressing economy, was due largely to the trade which the Levantine peoples—particularly the Byzantines after the Arab invasion—brought to the coastal populations of Italy and the South of France. Once under way, the process spread along the great rivers to the whole continent, creating growing opportunities for the division of labour, increases in productivity and capital accumulation. See Henri Pirenne, *La Civilisation Occidentale au Moyen Age*, Vol. VIII of the collection *Histoire Générale*, edited by Glotz, Presse Universitaire, Paris.

than would be possible if production were only for the home market, the economy will have increased its productivity. The increase in real income thus obtained will provide the necessary margin to enable the process of capital accumulation to begin. This simple outline of the problem brings out the great importance for underdeveloped countries of the expansion of world trade. Consider, for example, the great upheavals forced upon the underdeveloped countries' economies by the persistent contraction of world trade which followed the great depression. Many of the countries with the lowest level of development, which, under the stimulus of foreign trade, had started expanding before the depression, have in the last two decades, as a result of population pressure, lost part of the increase in productivity which they had achieved.

Initially, the impulse from outside benefits those sectors directly linked with foreign trade, mainly through the increase in remuneration other than wages. If the impulse is sustained, it will act as an incentive to increase production by means of the investment of the additional profits created by the trade. At this point a series of familiar developments is set in motion by which the accumulation of capital and improved technical methods first set free labour and land and then absorb them, with a resultant increase in the average social productivity. If the impulse from abroad stops when the average level of productivity is still very low, the process of development will probably be nipped in the bud. But once the economy has succeeded in reaching levels of productivity which permit a considerable amount of capital formation, the relative importance of external stimuli on the process of growth will tend to diminish. As productivity increases, real income grows and demand becomes more diverse, so new opportunities of investment are opened up, as we shall see later.

Growth of Income and Diversification of Demand

As average social productivity grows owing to the accumulation of capital, the community's real income increases. However, although there is a very close positive correlation between those two phenomena, we must stress certain factors operating in the opposite direction. We must bear in mind the specific characteristics of a free enterprise economy where the phenomena of growth assume a cyclical form which gives rise to periodical unemployment of the factors of production. Moreover, there are certain phenomena over which we have no control and which interfere with the productivity of labour, e.g. weather conditions in the case of agriculture. Lastly, mention should be made of the market mechanism, which can completely wipe out the effects on income of an increase in the physical productivity of labour. Depending on the elasticity of demand for exports and on the position of the country concerned in the international market, the whole of the benefit of the increase in the physical productivity of labour in the export sector may be transferred abroad by a fall in prices. But, with the exception of special cases such as these, we may assume that real income closely follows the movement of the average physical productivity of labour.

The increase in productivity, then, confers an increase in income on the sector affected. In the early stages of development, as we have seen, that increase is almost entirely absorbed by profits, which make possible the accumulation of capital necessary to raise production. This takes place under the constant stimulus of growing foreign demand. Once the process of growth is consolidated and the demand for labour increases, real wages will tend to rise. In consequence, the increase in real income will tend to be distributed between consumption and investment. The additional consumer demand will affect prices in certain sectors and will ensure that new investment will be channelled towards them, thus absorbing the additional saving created. The new investment will call forth increases in productivity in other sectors and the previous chain reaction will be repeated.

The way demand develops, therefore, is a basic factor governing the direction of the new investment. The development of demand by virtue of the growth of national income is in its turn largely determined by institutional factors. If the increases in income are concentrated in the hands of small closed groups, the process of development started by external pressure will not create reactions within the economy tending to speed up that process. This phenomenon may be observed in certain underdeveloped economies with a large labour surplus where the stimulus from outside is relatively weak. All the benefits from foreign trade accrue to small groups who buy abroad a large part of the goods they consume. Where foreign demand is not intense, the incentive to new investment is small and real wages remain stationary. The benefits from foreign trade merely allow certain social groups to enjoy more sophisticated forms of consumption copied from highly developed countries. We will not stop to indulge in an historical analysis of the way people disposed of institutional factors which impeded the fanning out of the process of development. But, on the basis of economic analysis in the strict sense of the term, we may say that the moment the demand for labour in the export sector allows higher wages to be paid there than in the economy in general, development tends to expand.

Experience shows that demand tends to become more varied as real average wages in an economy rise. Surveys of the most divergent social groups confirm this tendency towards diversification of demand. Thus, the demand for food increases sharply in the early stages of development, but the pace slackens once a certain level of real *per capita* income is reached. The demand for manufactured consumer goods shoots up when the rate of growth of food consumption begins to decline. Durable consumer goods follow a specific pattern of their own.

The evolution of demand and the increase in productivity are independent variables in the process of development. With the increase in productivity, the productive capacity of the economy increases. But, unless demand becomes diversified once the basic needs of the population are satisfied, a growing part of that capacity would tend to remain idle. At a certain level of *per capita* income, the only result of development would be the creation of more leisure for the whole or part of the population.

New investment is carried out largely with an eye on future demand. As that demand becomes more varied, the structure of production tends to be modified with the increase in real income. However open an economy may be, there is always a great quantity of goods and services which cannot be imported. This is why even those economies which have evolved towards more and more complete integration into international trade have constantly branched out into the production of new goods.

The Propensity to Consume and Intensity of Growth

Another very interesting problem discussed by Professor Nurkse is that of modern underdeveloped countries' high propensity to consume. This phenomenon was stressed in a number of studies by the Economic Commission for Latin America and gives food for thought to all concerned with the policy of economic development. Professor Nurkse's contribution in this field is important as his approach is broader than is usually the case and as he fits it into a general theory of consumer behaviour. This theory is based on a thorough analysis of consumer behaviour in the United States and statistical research subsequent to its formulation has not impaired its validity. It is interesting to note that this theory, which claims to explain the great stability of the consumption function in the United States, is now used to explain its instability in backward countries. With the growth of real *per capita* income in the United States, the consumption : national-income ratio has not noticeably changed, for the simple reason that medium and low income groups were increasing their propensity to consume. The theory which was worked out to explain this phenomenon is used by Nurkse to explain the proven fact that a country which today has a real *per capita* income of $200 tends to save a smaller part of it than a country which had the same real income thirty to fifty years ago. Just as the low-income social groups tend to copy the consumption patterns of people at the top of the social scale, poor countries tend to imitate their rich neighbours' way of life. If real *per capita* income increases more rapidly in rich countries than in poor ones, the latters' propensity to consume is thereby increased. With the consequent decline in the poor countries' propensity to save, their rate of growth is also diminished, which tends to accentuate the disparity between the real incomes of the two groups of countries.

This observation is important because it brings out the fact that, in the present state of affairs, the process of development cannot spontaneously reach its optimum rate in underdeveloped countries. The tendency of the propensity to consume to increase arising as it does from inequality of real income between nations, involves a progressive reduction in the spontaneous rate of growth of those countries which lag behind in the process of development. This observation leads to certain further considerations concerning the mechanism of economic development.

The intensity of growth of an economy is a function of two ratios : (*a*) investment to national income, and (*b*) reproducible wealth employed in the productive process to national income.

The second of these ratios refers to the average productivity of capital in a given period of production, that is, to the return obtained per unit of reproducible capital employed in the economy as a whole. This ratio depends to a great extent on the development potentialities of the relevant region's economy. To understand this point, we need only consider the limiting case of a desert area, where the possibilities of development are practically nil. Even if the inhabitants of the desert were to make a great effort of capital investment and were to receive considerable sums from abroad for that purpose, the capital so employed could not possibly have a high productivity. On the other hand, a country with large stretches of fertile but not yet cultivated land will be able, by means of relatively small investments, to achieve large increase in its national income. In the latter country, the average productivity of the capital employed is bound to be high.

These observations deserve attention because real *per capita* income does not necessarily indicate the degree of capital accumulation achieved by an economy, that is, the effort already made to develop the area in question. A particular area can make a great effort to develop its resources and reach a high degree of capital intensity thanks to a spirit of enterprise, without its *per capita* income on that account reaching the level of other areas still at much more rudimentary stages of development. This difference emerges clearly from a comparison between Japan and Argentina. The former country has a much higher average capital intensity than the second, but its *per capita* income is markedly lower. The abundance of fertile land in Argentina is conducive to a very high average productivity of capital employed, while overpopulation in Japan forces it to use even its less fertile land and its most inferior natural resources, thereby heavily reducing the average productivity of capital.

Calculations made for the North American economy[1] show a relatively high average productivity for capital invested there and, at the same time, a high degree of stability in the ratio—making corrections for the cyclical unemployment of the factors of production. Each unit of real investment effected in the United States produces an annual yield varying approximately from 0·35 to 0·70 according to the degree of utilization of factors during the cycle. We may take a ratio of approximately 0·65 as characteristic of the North American economy in conditions of full employment. This is certainly a very high rate of capital productivity and reflects the excellence of North America's natural resources and the relative sparseness of her population. A calculation made by us for Chile's economy gives a ratio of approximately 0·45 and a preliminary calculation for Brazil one of 0·50 for 1949. The higher productivity of capital invested in Brazil, as compared with Chile, is possibly due to the greater difficulties faced by agriculture in Chile, where costly irrigation works are often unavoidable.

The other factor which determines the rate of an economy's growth is the ratio of investment to national income, that is, the proportion of the previous period's national income which is invested. From the available statistics this ratio can be established in the form of a percentage of gross investment to gross national product, or of net investment to net national product. In our analysis we will consider the second ratio.

Let us now see how these two factors combine to give the rate of an economy's growth. If the productivity of capital can be expressed by 0·5, that is, if it is necessary to invest 2 in order to obtain 1 at the end of the first productive process, it follows that, if this economy invests 10 per cent of its net national product, its annual rate of growth will be 5 per cent.

As the coefficient of the productivity of capital is known to be relatively stable in any economy, since it reflects the whole of that economy's potentialities,[2] we may assume that the rate of

[1] Cf. Raymond W. Goldsmith, *The Growth of Reproducible Wealth of the United States of America from 1805 to 1950*. Study submitted for discussion to the 1951 meeting of the International Association for Research in Income and Wealth.

[2] Separate consideration must evidently be given to the possibility of an economy increasing the average productivity of capital by means of a growing foreign trade. If figures comparable with those for the

annual growth is mainly determined by the ratio of investment to national income, which we will term the coefficient of investment.

In the process of development, the behaviour of the coefficient of investment is strongly influenced by institutional and other factors having an effect on the propensity to consume. This problem was to some extent understood by sociologists like Max Weber, who went into the question of the influence of certain forms of the religious spirit, more especially of Puritanism, on the habits of consumers at the early stages of capitalism, and also by Veblen, that great critic of neo-classical economics, who displays certain points of affinity with the thesis of Duesenberry[1] used by Nurkse.

The Keynesian approach attaches great importance to the fact that the psychological motives of the saver are different from those of the investor. But, if we switch our attention from the problem of cyclical fluctuations in the level of employment to the problem of growth of productive capacity, it will be clear that it is quite as important to distinguish between the psychological motives of the investor and the consumer. When a process of development is started in a free enterprise economy, the investor receives a greater incentive than the consumer. The rate of growth is closely connected with this initial disparity between the intensity of the incentives to invest and to consume. A concrete example will help to make the point clear. Let us take the case of an economy where the average productivity of capital is, as in the previous case, 0·5 and in which, for some reason or other,[2] a process of growth

United States were available for England or Japan, it would no doubt be seen that the ratio of reproducible capital to national income does not always have secular stability. It is fairly obvious that England, but for the high degree of international division of labour enjoyed by it, particularly within the British Commonwealth, could not have achieved its high average productivity of capital. But, even in such cases, it would be necessary to observe the phenomenon over a number of years in order to note substantial changes in the coefficient of the productivity of capital.

[1] James S. Duesenberry, *Income, Saving and the Theory of Consumer Behavior* (Harvard University Press, 1949). Cf. in particular Chapter III where he expounds the theory of the 'demonstration effect'.

[2] In primitive economies, as we said before, the process of development is generally started by the action of external factors: inflow of capital and techniques, influence of external demand, substantial

is initiated, that is, net investment increases to a point where productive capacity grows more rapidly than the working population. Sticking to the previous example, let us suppose that investment absorbs 10 per cent of the net national product, i.e. that the coefficient of investment increases to 0·1. When investment rises to that level, the economy in question will start growing at an annual rate of 5 per cent.

There are good grounds for believing that during the first production periods consumption will not be stimulated as strongly as production. It will therefore be possible for the rate of growth of production to increase. This was the process referred to in the previous section, when we asserted that, once launched, development could continue by its own momentum. Let us suppose that, in the first years of development, consumption grows by only 2·5 per cent annually. In that case the growth of the net national product will be speeded up as follows:

	Net National Product (*a*)	Consumption (*b*)	Investment (*c*)	Coefficient of investment (*c*/*a*)
1st Year ..	100·0	90·0	10·0	0·10
2nd Year ..	105·0	92·25	12·75	0·121
3rd Year ..	111·4	94·56	16·48	0·148
4th Year ..	119·6	96·92	22·68	0·190
5th Year ..	130·9	99·34	31·56	0·241

It will be seen that net investment rose from 10 to 32, thereby increasing the coefficient of investment from 0·1 to

improvement in the terms of trade, etc. In countries which have already effected considerable capital accumulation and whose economies are temporarily stagnant, the process of development may be traced back to the action of internal factors: intensification of the growth of population, technological innovations, discovery of richer natural resources, etc.

0·24 in the fifth year. This increase allowed the rate of annual growth of the net national product to rise from 5 per cent to 9·4 per cent. If consumption had grown at the same rate as net product, the latter's rate of growth would have remained at the level reached in the first year, as is shown below:

	Net National Product (*a*)	Consumption (*b*)	Investment (*c*)	Coefficient of investment (*c/a*)
1st Year ..	100·0	90·0	10·0	0·1
2nd Year ..	105·0	94·5	10·5	0·1
3rd Year ..	110·25	99·25	11·0	0·1
4th Year ..	115·76	104·16	11·6	0·1
5th Year ..	121·55	109·35	12·2	0·1

As we pointed out earlier, the historical process of development of the capitalist economy is a vast problem which transcends economic analysis. Nevertheless, it is more or less common ground that the process originated in the cultural contacts resulting from the currents of trade which, coming from without, created in Western Europe an entrepreneur class. That class was profit-minded and formed a dynamic social element which came into collision with the feudal communities. Consumer habits, still under the influence of religious and social traditions, changed more slowly.

Nowadays the process is practically the other way round. Thanks to the enormous power of propaganda media and means of communications, the cart comes before the horse and consumer habits are the first to change. There are grounds, therefore, for believing that the spontaneous development of countries at present undeveloped is proceeding at a much slower rate than their economic potentialities and the level of technical progress would lead one to expect. There is no doubt that one of the most vital problems facing economists in our time is how to overcome those difficulties.

Investment Criteria and the Balance of Payments

Much more could be said on the question discussed in the previous section. We could enquire, for example, what is the effect on the balance of payments of underdeveloped countries of their high propensity to consume. That leads us to consider an assertion by Professor Nurkse in his sixth lecture on the problem of how to use foreign investments: '. . . when additional capital becomes available to a country, the country will want, or should be urged, to invest it in the form that yields the highest possible return, taking into account any external economies created by the project as well as the direct commercial yield. On the other hand, the particular goods through which the interest is transferred abroad are determined by the scale of comparative costs in international trade (though this scale need not be regarded as fixed and may well change as a result of the investment itself). No particular relation is required between the marginal-productivity-of-capital schedule and the comparative-cost schedule. So long as the two conditions stated above are met, there is no inherent difficulty in the servicing problem from the debtor's end.'[1]

This passage raises two questions of considerable interest. The first concerns the basic criterion to be adopted in determining the direction of investment. According to Nurkse, this criterion should be that of marginal social productivity. This is an extremely important affirmation which we notice is made by increasing numbers of economists of repute.[2] The micro-analytical criterion of marginal productivity, in which the productivity of the last unit of investment in each sector is considered from the point of view of the profitability of the firm, is being abandoned in favour of the social criterion, related to national income as a whole, of the productivity of the last unit of investment.

This criterion had already been suggested in the theory of external economies, but has only now been worked out as fully as it deserves. It is of the greatest importance, if we remember that the proportions of the factors of production

[1] Op. cit., pp. 136-7.

[2] Cf. Alfred E. Kahn, 'Investment Criteria in Development Programs', *The Quarterly Journal of Economics*, Feb. 1951.

vary from one country to another. Thus, in an economy like our own, in which labour is not the limiting factor and in which industry pays higher wages than the other sectors employing labour, it may be said that an industry which pays higher wages per unit of net product (i.e. income produced by that industry) has a higher social productivity. But, as labour cannot be regarded as completely elastic, the most generally applicable criterion is the ratio of the volume of investment to the industry's added value (i.e. income produced). To obtain the social productivity, we should also take into account the effects of the investment on the other sectors of the economy. These effects may take the form of substantial reductions of costs, particularly when the investment is in a key sector, such as transport or the production of energy.

The adoption of this criterion leads us to the conclusion that the mechanism of market prices does not of itself make possible the optimum use of resources. Or rather, it might, in special cases, make it possible, but it is not sufficient to ensure such use. Here we come to a fundamental point of the theory of economic development. In a highly developed economy, where the natural resources are more or less all known, marginal productivity is approximately the same in all sectors and hence wages for the same levels of skill and degrees of effort are also approximately equal; in an economy of this type the social productivity of an investment should approximate to its productivity from the point of view of the firm, that is, of the return on the capital. In that case, the price mechanism alone may be regarded as a safe guide to investment. This does not apply to an economy in its early stages of development. There we find a marked disparity in the degree of utilization of the factors of production as between one sector and another. The mere transfer of factors of production or the introduction of new combinations thereof may bring about a substantial increase in social productivity. This increase, however, need not necessarily be reflected in the profitability of the firm. There are, then, strong grounds for believing that the rate of development may be speeded up if the inadequacies of the market as the governing mechanism of economic progress are eliminated and if investments are effected according to a co-ordinated comprehensive plan.

The other problem dealt with by Professor Nurkse in the paragraph in question is the repercussion of foreign investment on the balance of payments. This may be direct, *via* the servicing of dividends, or indirect, *via* the income effects, that is, the increase in imports in consequence of the rise in real income. This is a much wider problem than might be assumed from the passage from Nurkse we have just quoted and should not be restricted to foreign investments since the income effect, which is the heart of the matter and to which we will confine ourselves, operates in the case of the investment of domestic capital as well. This problem was discussed admirably by Kahn[1] and his arguments may be summed up as follows: (1) The increase in real income resulting from the investment in question need not bring about an increase in money income. That is so, for example, in the case of an improvement in food production where the increase is completely absorbed by the producers themselves and does not lead to an increase in the volume of commercial transactions. Indeed, as a second hypothesis, an increase in production might be accompanied by a reduction in the price level. (2) Money income may increase in the same proportion as real income. Once the investment has been made and the new activity started, the income of the factors of production employed—which we shall call F—depends on the sales of the new products (added value) to other recipients of incomes—we shall call them G. In any case, provided G do not buy the new products by inflationary means (by reducing their usual rate of savings, by raising a loan or by mobilizing idle balances), the new money income available to F will be offset by a corresponding absorption of G's purchasing power, who have been forced to reduce their expenditure on other goods by an equivalent amount. It is an open question whether the net effect of F's additional purchases (imported goods or other goods produced in the country) and of the change in the direction of G's purchases (switch to F's production from imported goods or other goods produced in the country) will be an increase or decrease in imports.

We have devoted special attention to this issue in view of the fact that the Economic Commission for Latin America

[1] Op. cit.

in a number of studies has asserted that the process of development of Latin American countries in the last two decades has been accompanied by a chronic tendency to unbalance in foreign payments. As we have contended, this tendency is inherent in the process of spontaneous development in certain conditions of world economic development. It is evident that (as was the case in the last century and in the first three decades of the present one) given a strong flow of capital to countries in the early stages of development, or, even in the absence of such a flow, given a steadily expanding international market capable of absorbing products available in increasing quantities from those countries, the problem of external disequilibrium would not arise or would be a problem of world market conditions only. But the real situation in the last two decades was completely different ; the volume or world trade declined steadily and has continued to drop in even recent years, more specifically from 1947 to 1949.

An analysis of this problem in purely abstract terms might be logically coherent but would be of very little practical use. Thus, Kahn's analysis stands or falls on the soundness of certain premises which are, as we shall see, implicit in it.

The first case referred to by Kahn is one in which real income increases without a corresponding increase in money income. It is of very limited interest. We may conceive of a case in which the discovery of a new process of seed hybridization improves output per hectare in the production of, say, millet, which in certain communities is entirely consumed by the producers. The income accruing to the farmers would be increased and hence real income as well, without money income being affected. But how, in that case, can the increase in real income be attributed to a new 'investment'? And if there is in reality no new investment, how does this case fit into a discussion of criteria for the direction of new investment? This case is in fact of only academic interest.

As to the second hypothesis, in which, owing to a fall in prices, there is an increase in real, but not in money income, there are a number of suppositions implicit in it as regards the elasticity of demand for the products the output of which has increased. Let us suppose, for example, that some astute investment in agriculture leads to an increase in productivity and that the farmers decide to transfer the benefit of this improvement to the consumers by cutting prices and increasing supplies. Let us suppose that they offer three oranges for one cruzeiro instead of two, without any change in profitability. If demand adjusted itself automatically to supply and everybody increased his demand for oranges by 50 per cent there would, by definition, be no pressure on the balance of payments. But, as it is, this ideal of automatic adjustment, which may be postulated in an abstract model, bears little relation to actual fact, particularly in countries in the early stages of development.

The next case, which is of greater interest to us, may help to clear up both the basic concepts and the limitations of Kahn's argument as defended by Professor Nurkse. This is the case where it is assumed that the increase in real income is accompanied by an increase in money income of the same proportion. An inflationary increase in the means of payment is therefore ruled out. Let us suppose that investment is effected in a specific sector of industry—say, textiles—and that this results in an additional production of 100. Consumers will try to acquire those 100 units of textiles and will simultaneously cease buying goods to an equivalent value in various other sectors. Now those goods will be available to people who have had their incomes increased by the sale of the additional 100 units of textiles. The reasoning is similar to the previous argument and will conform to the facts if we assume income elasticity of demand to correspond exactly to the increases in supply resulting from the new investment. But even at this level of abstraction, the reasoning is still open to criticism. In reality, it is implicity assumed that the income created by the production of the 100 units of textiles will be completely transformed into income consumed. The people who stop buying other consumer goods in order to acquire the 100 units of textiles create a supply of consumer goods equal in value to the sales price of the 100 units of textiles. If, in order to simplify matters, we disregard the incidence of taxes, expenditure on raw materials and depreciation, it must still be supposed that, of the new incomes created by the new production, some part will be saved. Therefore, the balance available for expenditure on consumption must be lower than the 100 of the supply of consumer goods created by the introduction into the market of the 100 from the new textile production. The rest of the income created (and saved) will be directed to the capital-goods sector, where there is no corresponding reduction in demand. The real position will be, therefore, that there will be an excess supply in the consumer-goods sector and an excess demand of the same magnitude in the capital-goods sector. Whether this disequilibrium is resolved by an increase in the export of consumer goods and in imports of capital goods, or whether by a fall in the prices in the consumer-goods sector and the reduction of investment, is another problem which we do not propose to discuss. All we are concerned to show is that Kahn's theoretical model appears logically sound only on the surface.

This argument has taken us some distance from the central aspect of the idea we intended to criticize, i.e. the repercussion of investment on the balance of payments. The heart of Kahn's argument is that the group of consumers who buy the 100 new units of textiles cease buying an equal amount of articles produced in the country or imported from abroad; while the group of consumers whose incomes are increased by the production of new textiles, will start buying additional home or foreign goods. The amount of goods imported resulting from the algebraical sum of the two quantities of demand may be greater or smaller and should not be arrived at by *a priori* methods. The marginal propensity to import may be positive or negative, according to whether that propensity is greater in the group buying the 100 new units of textiles or in the group whose incomes were increased with the rise in textile production.

This is a field in which theoretical reasoning does not get us very far and it is essential, therefore, to stick to observable facts. Experience shows that in highly developed economies the marginal propensity to import may just as well be negative as positive. It is well known that the coefficients of income elasticity of demand vary as between different groups of consumer goods. There are certain goods, the demand for which grows more than proportionately to the increase in income, others for which demand grows less than proportionately and others for which demand even diminishes. If the goods imported by a country belong to those for which demand increases only slightly or falls with the increase in national income, it is possible for the amount of imports to remain unchanged or even to decline without any alteration in the price level. In that case we could safely endorse Nurkse's affirmation that 'no particular relation is required between the marginal-productivity-of-capital schedule and the comparative-cost schedule'.

Experience shows, however, that in countries in the early stages of development the course of events is different. The demand for consumer goods imported by these countries has a high income elasticity. This is so in the case of manufactured items in general and of durable consumer goods in particular. It may be observed, for example, that demand for the latter type of goods increases by a coefficient of 2 to 4 as real income rises. Nor is this all. Countries in the early stages of development depend to a great extent on imports for the acquisition of capital goods. As we have already seen, demand for those goods tends to increase more rapidly than national income when the rate of economic development is rapid. Why, faced with those facts, should we allow ourselves to be paralysed by doubts as to whether the marginal propensity to import is negative or positive ? This is an error of perspective typical of economists who try to draw conclusions of universal validity from the kind of economy about which they are accustomed to think.

How can we reconcile a country's tendency to increase imports, which is inherent in its development, with its inability to increase its capacity to import ? For this was in effect the situation familiar to us from 1930 until quite recently. Some economists, who are expert in turning economic problems into questions of semantics, argue that the unbalance in question results from an inflationary situation. Now, when imports exceed the capacity to import, it may be asserted that investment exceeds saving and therefore that an inflationary situation has arisen. As imports will have to be reduced somehow or other in order to put the balance of payments right, that step and the unbalance which led to it may be said to flow from an inflationary situation. But this reasoning disregards the basic aspect of the problem, which is that supply cannot increase and change its composition automatically with the expansion of and in sympathy with the change in the composition of demand. As long as exports (considered as a constant in relation of foreign trade) do not increase *pari passu* with the demand for imports, the process of growth will create disequilibria which take the form of an excessive internal production and of an unfavourable balance of payments. The correction of those disequilibria is a slow and almost always a painful process. And this makes a policy of stabilization difficult and tends to make inflation inseparable from the process of development.

At bottom, therefore, the inflation which accompanies economic development in our country is not a monetary problem. The basic cause of the unbalance is the disparity between the growth in income and the capacity to import. It is therefore indispensable, if this unbalance is to be rectified, to modify the structure of production so as to increase exports or to find substitutes for imports.

A reduction in investments—which is the remedy usually proposed—if applied indiscriminately by means of credit restriction, will not necessarily rectify the unbalance and will certainly not put the other troubles right. In order to avoid the emergence of such maladjustments, certain steps must be taken in advance to direct investments. If it is possible to foresee these disequilibria up to a certain point, it should also be possible to avoid them. Once again, therefore, we are led to conclude that, given the present conditions of the world economy, underdeveloped countries cannot spontaneously achieve a degree of growth consonant with their potentialities and with the technical level at their disposal. Co-ordinated action is indispensable and this is implicitly recognized by Professor Nurkse when he attributes the leading role in economic development today to fiscal policy.

Indeed, Professor Nurkse's most important contribution in his lectures is perhaps the way he relates fiscal policy to saving in underdeveloped countries. Although this is the central problem of economic development today, it is generally misunderstood. What our economy lacks is not incentives to invest but incentives to save. The problem goes much deeper than the mere organization of the capital market. In view of the powerful stimuli to consume exercised by more advanced economies, which Professor Nurkse explains so lucidly, it is extremely difficult for our economy, at its present stage of development, spontaneously to reach a high level of saving. If we wish to achieve a greater and more balanced degree of development, we must give high priority to the problem of saving. A country like Brazil has a large potential margin of savings waiting to be tapped by some form of compulsory saving. It is completely unrealistic to think that we can recreate in Brazil the forms of spontaneous saving typical of the nineteenth century. Professor Nurkse does not fall into that error and it is certainly the best lesson he has to teach us.

5. UNDEREMPLOYMENT AND FACTOR-DISEQUILIBRIUM

UNDEREMPLOYMENT IN UNDERDEVELOPED ECONOMIES*

by **Alfredo Navarrete Jr and Ifigenia M. de Navarrete**

THIS PAPER TREATS OF SOME PROBLEMS OF UNDEREMPLOYMENT which arise mostly in underdeveloped economies, as a consequence of insufficiencies, not in effective demand, but in the supply of means of production.

We shall not analyse cyclical unemployment, which is characteristic of industrialized countries and which is due to lack of effective demand, nor shall we deal with other types of visible unemployment arising from structural changes in taste and technology. We shall also leave aside frictional unemployment, which is relatively small where effective demand is high.[1]

If we take the size of the labour force as given, underemployment may be described as a situation in which the withdrawal of a certain quantity of the factor labour to other uses, will not appreciably diminish the total output of the sector from which it is withdrawn. This is as much as to say that the marginal productivity of these units of the factor labour in their original employment is zero, or very close to

* *International Economic Papers*, No. 3, 1953. Reprinted by permission of the International Economic Association and the authors. Translated by Elizabeth Henderson from 'La Subocupación en las Economias Poco Desarrolladas', *El Trimestre Económico*, Vol. XVIII, No. 4, October/December 1951, Fondo de Cultura Económica, Mexico (a paper presented to the Mexican Scientific Congress, Economic Section, Mexico, D.F., September 1951). This work puts forward the authors' personal points of view, which must in no way be associated with those of the International Monetary Fund and the Organization of American States, respectively.

[1] This does not mean that these types of unemployment do not exist in underdeveloped countries, but simply that, in those countries, the overriding problem is the more effective use of existing human resources and the elimination, as far as possible, of the latter's unproductive application. For the definition of the various types of visible unemployment, cf. W. H. Beveridge, *Full Employment in a Free Society* (London, 1944), pp. 408–10.

zero. It is characteristic of backward economies in process of development that a more or less considerable part of their labour force is always ready to increase its productive activity, at existing nominal wage rates (though at decreasing real wages), if jobs are available.[1]

For the purposes of our discussion we shall distinguish between cyclical (disguised) underemployment, structural (hidden) underemployment, and the underemployment of expansion.

In academic circles, interest in disguised underemployment stems from Joan Robinson's use of the term disguised unemployment, which she defined as follows: 'It is natural to describe the adoption of inferior occupations by dismissed workers as *disguised unemployment*'.[2]

In this case it is assumed that the productive equipment (both capital and technical means) is given. This type of cyclical underemployment also occurs in countries exporting primary products, when external demand falls. Its magnitude is a direct function of the importance of foreign trade in any particular country, as well as of the relation between foreign trade and the country's domestic economy. Disguised underemployment will be the greater, the more important is the subsistence sector, which generally absorbs the excess labour and which serves as shock-absorber for the cyclical fluctuations of external demand. Visible unemployment will be greater, on the other hand, the less important is the subsistence sector of the economy.

The other two types of underemployment, which are much more important in underdeveloped economies, are mainly due to lack of productive equipment. Structural underemployment, or, as it is generally called, hidden underemployment, is a chronic feature in the primary producing sectors of such backward economies. Paradoxically, it becomes more acute

[1] For example, in Mexico, although real wages in specific branches of production have fallen, the average income, in real terms, of wage-earners seems to have risen owing to the shift from less productive to more productive occupations. Cf. D. López Rosado and J. F. Noyola Vázquez, 'Los salarios reales en México, 1939–1950', *El Trimestre Económico*, Vol. XVIII, April/June 1951.

[2] *Essays in the Theory of Employment*, 2nd edition, London, 1947, p. 62.

with the introduction of new techniques in primary production, when the other sectors of the economy fail to keep step and expansion is uneven. This type of underemployment is reflected in a desire to work, at existing wage rates, on the part of thousands of—mostly agricultural—workers and of housewives, who lack regular employment during the greater part of the year's normal working time. This constitutes a serious loss of human resources.[1]

The remaining type of underemployment which occurs in primary economies in process of development, is one which we shall call underemployment of expansion, because it arises in times not of depression, but of economic growth. It is due to the failure of capital and of most complementary means of production to increase at the same rate as the supply of labour in secondary and tertiary activities. This type of underemployment is accentuated by deficit financing of development programmes and the resulting inflation, which intensifies the cityward migration of agricultural workers and thereby unduly swells the supply of labour in face of a limited supply of other complementary means of production. These workers then find themselves under the necessity to engage in activities of very low productivity. They become, for instance, pedlars of all kinds of goods and services requiring little or no capital outfit, such as vendors of fruit, *chickle* and cigars, lottery tickets, newspapers, or else car washers, bootblacks, porters, waiters, and shop assistants. The remarkable feature of this type of underemployment is that it is continuously nourished by the vast reserves of hidden underemployment in rural areas. Underemployment of expansion is much less in evidence in the modern cities of the great industrial countries, though it increases even there in periods of rapid growth.

[1] Professor Moisés T. de la Peña was one of the first economists to draw attention to the loss of resources occasioned by this kind of underemployment, which he called 'rural leisure'. One of the present authors has analysed this problem in 'Una hipótesis sobre el sistema económico de México', *El Trimestre Económico*, March 1951, and, more fully, in *Estabilidad de Cambios, el Cilco y el Desarrollo Económico*, México, 1951.

The problem of underemployment in backward economies may be represented graphically as follows :

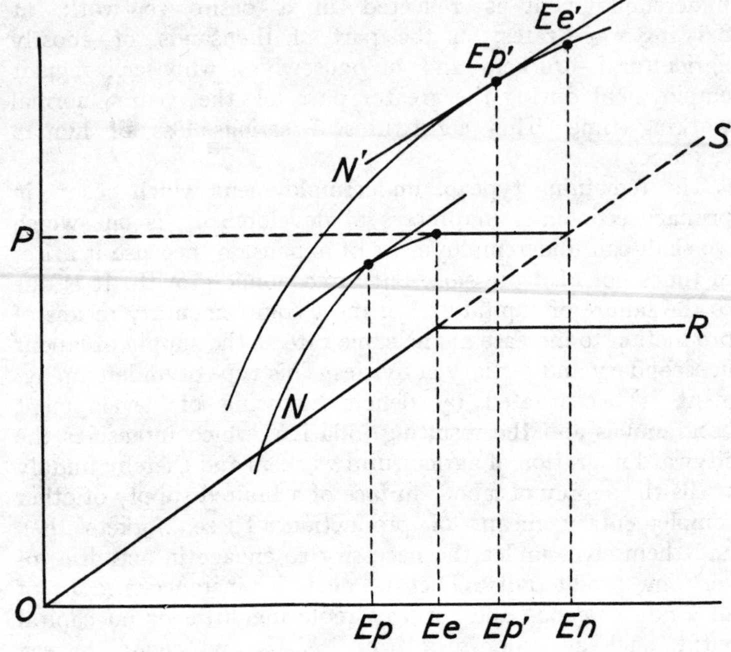

N=**National product.** *E*=**level of Employment.** *N*=*f* (*E*).

Let us assume that the employed labour force is *OEn*. The production curve *N* expresses the national product obtained with given productive equipment at different levels of employment. Beyond *OP*, no matter how much the labour force increases, total output will increase no more. The given productive resources, other than labour, have reached their maximum productivity and the national product can be increased only if new productive equipment is added and we pass to a new production curve *N′*.

The nominal employment level *En* is a situation in which there is hidden underemployment, and where the marginal productivity of the factor labour equals zero ; indeed, it equals zero anywhere beyond the effective employment level *Ee*, where the national product ceases to increase. If OS represents the average wage rate, then productive employment Ep is that where marginal productivity equals the real wage rate. Beyond the point of effective employment, Ee, a greater quantity of factor labour no longer yields any increment to total output, total wages R become stationary—in other words, the wage curve becomes discontinuous, since there can be no real remuneration for zero productivity, and a national product of equal size will now have to be apportioned to a greater number of workers. Underemployment is $OEn - OEp$.

When productive equipment increases, the production curve is displaced to N', hidden underemployment disappears and, by and large, nominal employment En will coincide with effective employment Ee'. Productive employment will have risen to Ep', on the assumption of constant average wage rates;[1] there still remains a residue of underemployment $OEn - OEp'$, which will be absorbed in productive employment in the measure in which availability of complementary resources (fixed and circulating capital, organization, technical knowledge) increases.

Let En be the nominal volume of employment, Ep productive employment (where the marginal productivity of labour equals the real wage rate), and Ec 'full employment', defined as a situation in which there is neither underemployment nor unemployment (productive equipment and effective demand are adequate, there is a sufficiency of complementary resources, the productivity of labour is at its maximum and optimum). The following definitions then hold: $En > Ep < Ec =$ underemployment; $En = Ep = Ec =$ full employment; $En = Ep < Ec =$ unemployment; and $En < Ep > Ec =$ overfull employment.[2]

From the above analysis it follows that a positive policy to combat underemployment (disguised, hidden or due to expansion) in underdeveloped economies requires a stream of

[1] If average wage rates increase, the argument is substantially the same, although the new level of productive employment will be somewhat lower.

[2] We speak of overfull employment when, at a given size and productivity of the labour force, there is full employment and a rise in the demand for investment goods. Cf. B. Ohlin, *The Problem of Employment Stabilization* (New York, 1949).

investment expenditure at a rate and of a composition adequate for the absorption of the net annual underemployment which arises at the very time when the average productivity of the factor labour increases through greater supplies of capital goods, raw materials and complementary resources (including training and technical education). This is the way to turn investment programmes into powerful weapons of employment policy.

The necessary rate of investment expenditure must not be determined simply as a function of aggregate demand and of its distribution among consumption and other needs; it is essential to consider, above all, the investment's net generation of productive employment and to avoid loss of real production through underutilization of existing human resources. The net contribution of the newly created employment to the national product must be the greatest possible, in terms of the difference between the value of gross product and the monetary cost occasioned by the increase in productive activity during the period of the planned investment.

The process of shifting labour units from a position of underemployment to more productive activities requires the incentive of higher rewards. Such a rise is difficult to achieve when prices are constant or even falling, but is encouraged when prices are allowed to rise moderately, so that marginal profits exceed marginal production costs. In such a situation, aggregate demand for merchandise will be in excess of current production (if we assume constancy of the reserves of gold and foreign exchange, of the levels of foreign credits and domestic stocks, and if we further assume the absence of suppressed inflation); consequently, the demand for labour will increase. In time, the available supply of labour will be used up, the scarcity of labour will, in turn, become a stimulus to the rationalization of methods of production. In this manner, labour will be shifted from less productive into more productive occupations, and the national product will grow.

This paper must not be concluded without stressing the dangers inherent in a policy of large productive investments, which are indispensable for combating underemployment in backward economies. These dangers include maldistribution of the profits conditioned by rising prices, the probable loss of gold and foreign exchange reserves with resulting disequilibrium in the balance of payments, and finally distortion in the composition of national investment. The kind of investment policy outlined above must be accompanied by various restrictive and selective measures of monetary, credit and fiscal policy (the more so since inflation accentuates underemployment of expansion), as well as by exchange and foreign trade controls.

Summing up, the most effective remedy for underemployment is a policy which combines an adequate rate of well-balanced investment with a moderate rise in prices, at levels of full productive employment, growing national output and rising real *per capita* incomes.

THE FACTOR-PROPORTIONS PROBLEM IN UNDERDEVELOPED AREAS*

by **R. S. Eckaus**

THE CONCEPTS 'STRUCTURAL DISEQUILIBRIUM', 'OVERPOPULATION', 'technological unemployment' and 'underemployment' appear frequently in the literature on underdeveloped areas and there is considerable discussion of the comparative desirability for use in such areas of relatively labour-intensive or capital-intensive techniques. This paper is intended to help clarify some of the underlying issues and to begin to provide a theoretical basis for their analysis.

Many of the underdeveloped areas of the world have large agrarian populations in which there is either persistent open unemployment or in which the marginal productivity of the working force is so low that it is commonly believed that withdrawal of a sizable fraction would not significantly affect output. This seems to be the case to varying degrees for much of Asia and the Middle East. Other countries, such as Italy, show persistent urban as well as rural unemployment or underemployment. It is a common feature of the unemployment in these countries that it fails to respond to fiscal policy measures designed to increase employment by stimulating effective demand. Use of conventional income-generating techniques appears in fact to create inflationary pressures and balance-of-payments difficulties long before full employment is approached.

This interpretation of the condition of many underdeveloped areas has led to the formulation of a number of alternative explanatory hypotheses which are presented in Section I.

* *The American Economic Review*, September 1955. Reprinted by permission of the American Economic Association and the author. The author wishes to express his gratitude to the Center for International Studies, under whose auspices he did the work upon which this paper is based, to the seminar group of the Center for criticism and encouragement and especially to F. M. Bator and P. N. Rosenstein-Rodan. He is also indebted to P. A. Samuelson and R. Solow for their interest. An Italian translation of this article appeared in *L'Industria*, November 1955.

One of these hypotheses appears, at this stage of investigation, to be particularly fruitful in casting light on some of the outstanding characteristics of underdeveloped areas and is elaborated in Section II. Two approaches to the problems of empirical testing of the hypotheses are outlined in Section III.

The hypotheses presented below suggest that the unemployment difficulties of underdeveloped areas are not basically due to lack of effective demand but stem from 'market imperfections', limited opportunities for technical substitution of factors and inappropriate factor endowments.[1] The techniques of analysis of factor-market imperfections are well known.[2] The implications of limited technical substitutability of factors were first analysed by Abraham Wald[3] and more recently by the linear programming techniques.[4] Further development of the theoretical analysis in this paper consists mainly of an elaboration of geometrical techniques, which are used to apply the theory specifically to the problems of underdeveloped areas.

I. The Factor-proportions Hypotheses

The analysis which follows has grown out of the suggestion by C. P. Kindleberger that underdeveloped areas such as Italy are characterized by 'structural disequilibrium at the factor level'. This concept, formulated by Kindleberger and E. Despres, is identified as follows:

Disequilibrium at the factor level may arise either because a single factor receives different returns in different uses or because

[1] The hypotheses and analysis have come to be known at the Center for International Studies, Massachusetts Institute of Technology, as the 'factor-proportions' problem.

[2] E.g., Joan Robinson, *Essays in the Theory of Employment*, 2nd ed. (Oxford, 1947), ch. 2.

[3] A. Wald, 'Über einige Gleichungssysteme der mathematischen Okonomie', *Zeitschr. f. Nationalokon.*, Dec. 1936, VII, 636–70; cf. also, W. L. Valk, *Production, Pricing and Employment in the Static State* (London, 1937), p. 58.

[4] E.g., R. Dorfman, *Application of Linear Programming to the Theory of the Firm* (Berkeley, U.S.A., 1951). In his paper 'Full Employment and Fixed Coefficients of Production' (*Quarterly Journal of Economics*, Feb. 1955, pp. 23-44), M. Fukuoka also relates the assumption of fixed coefficients in production to the problem of unemployment.

the price relationships among factors are out of line with factor availabilities.[1]

This suggestion has been the starting point for two types of explanation of unemployment or underemployment in underdeveloped areas. The first type assumes that available technology would permit full use of the working force at some set of relative prices and finds the source of unemployment in various types of 'imperfections' in the price system. The second type suggests that there are limitations in the existing technology or the structure of demand which lead to a redundancy of labour in densely populated, underdeveloped areas. The two types of hypotheses are combined in Section II to obtain a more general analysis.

The Market Imperfections Hypotheses

In the accompanying figure the vertical axis represents the rate of real wages and the horizontal axis the amount of labour. The curves DD' and SS' represent the aggregate supply and demand relations for a typical industry if factor markets are competitive. Under competitive conditions the wage rate would settle at E.[2]

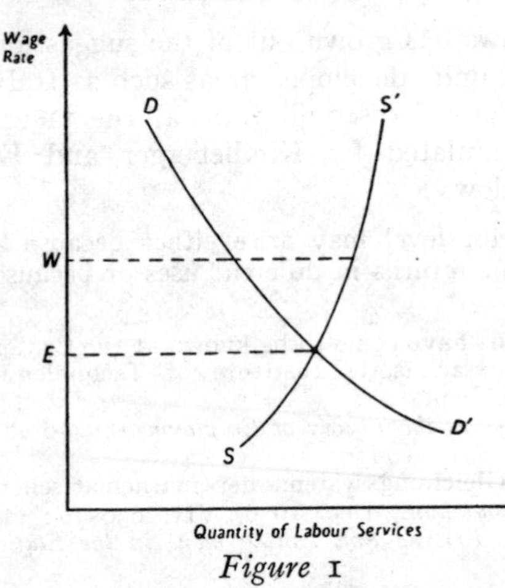

Figure 1

Suppose, however, that trade union pressures, immobility of labour, government social legislation or other factor-market imperfections maintain the wage rate at W rather than allowing it to fall to E. The effective labour supply curve would be WS'. At the higher wage rate the demand for labour would not absorb all the labour available and it could be said, as

[1] C. P. Kindleberger and E. Despres, 'The Mechanism for Adjustment in International Payments—The Lessons of Post-war Experience', *The American Economic Review*, Proceedings, May 1952.

[2] Fixed supply and demand curves such as those in Figure 1, suppose, of course, constant resources, technology and consumer tastes.

Kindleberger does, that, *ceteris paribus*, the wage rate does not represent factor endowments.

To isolate the influence of various types of imperfections let us now consider a case in which factor mobility, or lack of it, is not important and continue to confine the analysis to a closed economy. If the system had become adjusted to a particular complex of rigidities there would be no need for factor mobility in the absence of changes in techniques or tastes.[1]

The comparative use of the factors of production, depending as it does on the factor-price ratios and technology, would, however, reflect the 'true availability' of labour only if wages were kept at *E* in Figure 1. If wages are kept at *W* there is an 'artificially' high ratio of the price of labour to the price of capital. Since we are explicitly assuming that factor substitution is, in fact, possible, a structure of production may result with a higher capital-labour ratio than otherwise. If the diagram were representative of large parts of an economy, as output increased full employment of the given labour force would require the use of more capital than if the structure of production were adjusted to a lower labour-capital price ratio, unless the substitution effects were offset by increasing returns to scale. In a country in which capital was scarce and unemployment of considerable magnitude, the attempt to achieve full employment by use of relatively capital-intensive investment would be more likely to lead to inflation and balance-of-payments difficulties, short of full employment, than if more labour-intensive techniques were used.

The development of social policy in economically underdeveloped areas frequently proceeds more rapidly than economic growth. Imitation of the techniques of more advanced countries is not confined to technology. Elaborate social security legislation and aggressive government-encouraged union movements are often found in densely populated, low *per capita* income countries which are just on the threshold of

[1] 'If effective demand always moved up and down in the same well-worn channels, a supply of each type of labour would always be ready waiting to meet demand for it, when effective demand expanded, and the question of mobility would not arise.' Joan Robinson, op. cit., p. 30.

economic advancement. There is little or no scope for such devices for raising wages except in the relatively more advanced and well-organized sectors. Therefore, new industrial projects may face the prospect of wage rates quite different from those prevailing in the handicraft and agrarian sectors and thus may be compelled to use different factor proportions. These considerations suggest that the foregoing analysis may be quite relevant for underdeveloped areas.

The next step in the analysis is to abandon the assumptions of constant technology and consumer tastes and to investigate the effects of changes in the composition of demand for goods and factors due to such influences as changes in methods of production or in the directions or levels of demand as a result of changes in tastes or foreign competition. In this second case, as the level of aggregate effective demand rises, goods will be demanded in different proportions than formerly and the location and magnitudes of the demand for factors of production will shift. If labour is not mobile, or if it takes considerable wage increases to shift it, then factor disequilibrium such as depicted in Figure 1 for the preceding case of constant tastes and technology would develop in certain industries. An increase in the level of effective demand would push other industries to the limits of capacity relatively quickly in this second case. Money wages and prices would begin to rise, not uniformly but in the 'bottleneck' sectors, prior to the achievement of general full employment. New investment in these sections would tend to increase still further the substitution of capital for labour while offsetting tendencies in the relatively stagnant sectors would work slowly, if at all. The balance of payments under the pressure of growing domestic inflationary pressures and increased demand for capital imports would tend also to develop deficits at an earlier stage in the expansion of national income. This could all be superimposed upon and could aggravate the 'factor disequilibrium' previously discussed. It would be distinguishable, however, as there would be evidence of excess capacity and stranded capital-goods resources indicating an original misallocation or a structural shift.

There is at least superficial evidence to suggest that the factors stressed in this hypothesis may be operative in some underdeveloped countries. For example, although Italy has a persistent unemployment of about 2 million in a population of around 47 million, there are also some sectors of the Italian economy, such as shipbuilding, in which there is persistent unused physical capital plant and equipment. Moreover, we would expect that in underdeveloped areas the working force would be even more bound by tradition, reluctance to change location and barriers to social as well as physical movement than is the case in more advanced, industrialized countries; this would also contribute to the problems created by structural change.

Closely related to this second hypothesis is an explanation which locates the source of factor disequilibrium in barriers to the entry of new firms into profitable industries whose expansion is limited by various types of monopolistic restrictions. This and the other types of 'imperfections' could aggravate the 'factor disequilibrium'.

One further related hypothesis remains to be considered here.[1] Suppose that, whatever the actual characteristics of the production function and degree of technical substitutability of factors, businessmen believe that they face a production function with constant coefficients, i.e., no factor substitution is possible. Indian businessmen, for example, may believe that the 'American way' of producing is the best and only way and that this always involves high ratios of capital to labour. Plant engineers accustomed to emulating 'Western' technology may not be sensitive to the range of choice actually available in manufacturing processes and may impose unnecessary technical constraints on managers in underdeveloped countries. Thus in Figure 2, although the solid lines, x_1, x_2 . . . may represent the real contours of the production function, businessmen may regard the dashed lines x'_1, x'_2 . . . as the ones along which they must move.

In this case the expansion path P would be independent of the factor-price ratios, and, therefore, of the supply curve of labour such as indicated in Figure I. Expansion of effective demand would tend to run into

[1] I am indebted to F. M. Bator for the suggestion of this case.

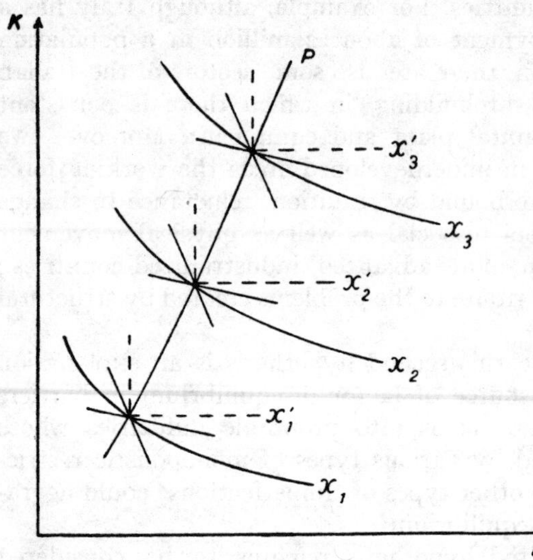

Figure 2

the limits imposed by capital capacity prior to the achievement of full employment with consequent inflationary tendencies and balance-of-payments difficulties. This could take place even if Figure 2 were not characteristic of all sectors of industry.

The Technological Restraints Hypothesis

It is fairly common for observers to report finding modern, capital-intensive equipment and techniques used in underdeveloped areas where relative factor prices would suggest the use of more labour-intensive techniques. I should now like to suggest that the use of the 'modern' techniques is not necessarily irrational emulation but the result of real limitations in the technological choices available, and that this, in turn, is a major source of labour-employment problems in underdeveloped areas. At this point the exposition will be oversimplified to indicate in stark outline the nature of the argument. In the next section the hypothesis will be combined with some of the market-imperfections hypotheses in an attempt to describe some of the major characteristics of underdeveloped and overpopulated areas by the use of a relatively simple theoretical framework.

The basic assumptions of the following analysis are: (1) in large sectors of an economy there are only a few alternative processes which can be utilized; (2) these processes are relatively capital-intensive.[1] There have been frequent comments which describe certain features of underdeveloped and overpopulated areas as essentially the result of limited variability in the coefficients of production. An example of this kind of comment is the frequently observed 'underemployment' in agriculture, where this is taken to mean that, with agricultural techniques remaining unchanged, withdrawal of farm labour would not reduce output.

The Case of One Good, Two Factors and One Process. In the first, most simple case to be considered, suppose that only one good is produced in the economy, national product, which requires two factors, capital and labour.[2] Assume also that only one process can be used to produce national product, i.e., that the factors must be used in fixed proportions. This situation is represented in Figure 3, where the heavy black line represents national output, x_1 of 1 unit; the lighter lines represent higher outputs. Quite irrespective of relative factor prices, points *a*, *b*, *c*, etc., represent the combinations of factors which will be used to produce output and the slope of the line joining these points is equal to the constant, capital-labour ratio.

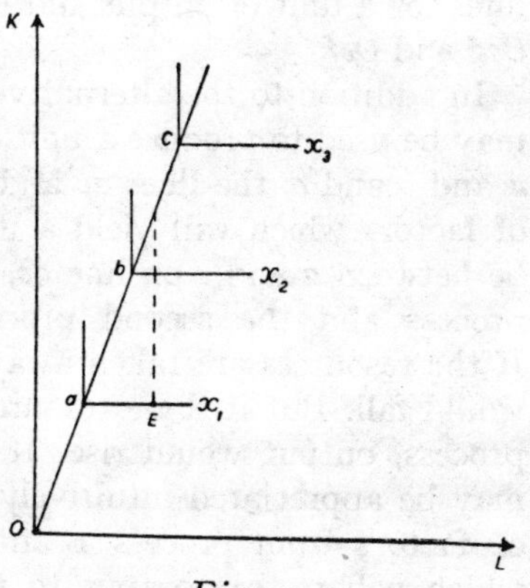

Figure 3

Only when the factors of production are actually available in proportions equal to the fixed capital-labour ratio is there the possibility that both can simultaneously be fully utilized. If the actual factor endowment is off the line *Oabc*, for example, at point *E*, there must inevitably be some unemployment of labour which is not amenable to any fiscal or monetary policy

[1] A production 'process' is a way of combining different factors of production whose *proportions* are determined by technology, although the *scale* of production and thus the absolute quantities of the factors used may be freely variable.

[2] Confining the analysis to only two factors is not essential but highly convenient for geometrical demonstrations.

for its alleviation. Labour is a redundant factor and only by increasing capital stock in the amount indicated by the length of the dashed line can the unemployment be eliminated.[1] Conventional compensatory fiscal policy would, in this case, only result in inflationary pressures. The persistent open and 'disguised' unemployment in underdeveloped countries may be at least partially of this kind.

Two or More Processes. Suppose now that a second and a third relatively more labour-intensive process is developed for the production of the same good, national output, so that three processes are now available. This is represented in Figure 4 by the existence of two more right-angled constant-product lines for a unit of output and two additional expansion paths, *Ocd* and *Oef*.

In addition to the alternative combinations of factors which may be used to produce a unit of output represented by points *a* and *c* and *e*, the lines *ac* and *ce* also represent combinations of factors which will yield a unit of output. It is possible to be between *a* and *c* on line *ac*, for example, by using the first process and the second process in different combinations. If the resources are taken away from the first process, output would fall. But if these resources are then used in the second process, output would rise. It can be shown rigorously[2] and may be appreciated intuitively that there is some withdrawal of factors from process 1 and subsequent use in process 2 which will restore output to the unit level. Correspondingly the line *bd* represents combinations of process 1 and process 2 and of the two factors capital and labour which are optimal for the production of the x_2 level of output.[3]

In this second case where several processes are available the proportions in which the two factors can be used are not confined to either the expansion path of the first process or

[1] I recognize that it is stretching a definition considerably to call redundant factors 'unemployed'. However, since it is specifically the hypothesis of this paper that the labour called 'unemployed' or 'underemployed' in underdeveloped areas is redundant, I shall, with this warning, use the terms interchangeably.

[2] Cf. Dorfman, op. cit., pp. 39–41.

[3] It can be seen by drawing a line from *a* to *e* that, for any output, any combination involving processes 1 and 3 would require more of at least one factor than a combination of processes 2 and 3.

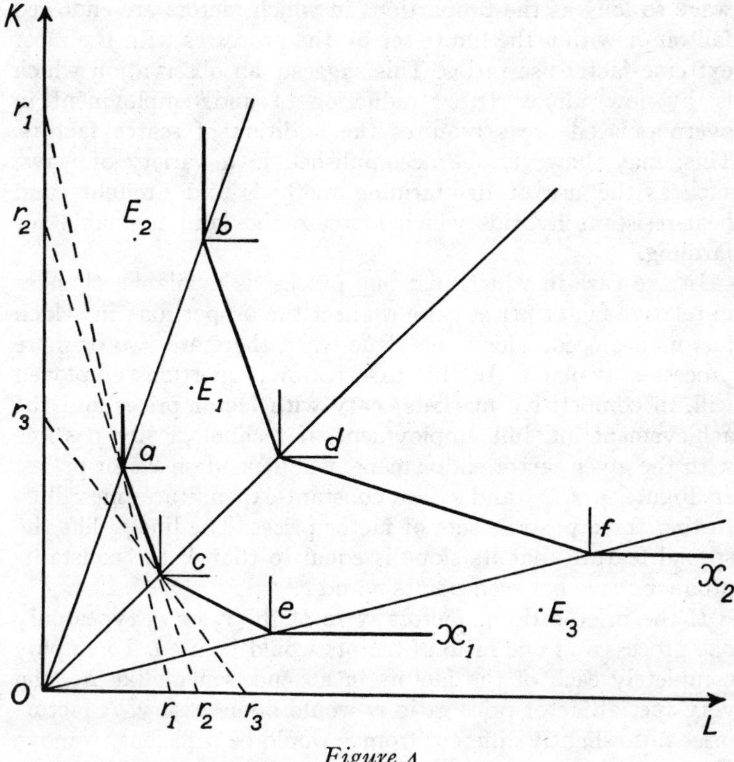

Figure 4

the expansion path of the second process, or both, but may be any place within the area bounded by *Oab* and *Oef*. Thus the factor endowment E_1, while inevitably implying some unemployment of labour when only the first process was available, can now be fully utilized by using the first process on a smaller scale and switching some of the capital to the second process. If, however, the factor endowment should be outside the area bounded by the two expansion paths, at E_2 or E_3, for example, structural unemployment of capital capacity or of labour would ensue in exactly the same manner as in the preceding case of one process, regardless of factor-price ratios or fiscal policy.

If more than two processes are available to the economy, full employment of all factors will be *possible* at a nonzero wage so long as the proportions in which factors are endowed fall on or within the limits set by the processes with the most extreme factor-use ratios. This suggests an observation which is, by now, almost trite : reduction of underemployment in overpopulated areas requires the addition of scarce factors. This, may, however, be accomplished in a variety of ways, such as the use of dry-farming methods and drought- and heat-resistant hybrids which increase the land available for farming.

In the case in which just one process is available, changes in relative factor prices cannot affect the proportions in which factors are used. This is not true when there are two or more processes available. In this case factor proportions employed will, in competitive markets, vary with factor prices and the achievement of full employment, if technologically possible with the given factor endowment, will depend on factor prices. In Figure 4, r_1, r_2 and r_3 are constant-expenditure lines illustrating three possible sets of factor prices. The line r_2 has the special feature that its slope is equal to that of the constant-product curve between points a and c.[1]

If the price ratio of factors were of the r_1 or r_3 types only one process and one ratio of factors would be used. To employ completely each of the factors in an endowment like E_1, the very special factor-price ratio r_2 would be necessary. A factor-price ratio slightly different from r_2 would be sufficient to move factor-use ratios away from E_1 to one of the isoquant vertices. Moreover, having reached a vertex of an isoquant it would be possible for large changes in relative factor prices to occur without leading to factor substitution.

Two Goods and Two Factors. An interesting question is whether the restriction of the analysis to only a single good is responsible for the character of the conclusion. By use of an Edgeworth-Bowley type box diagram we can continue to have the advantage of graphic techniques without loss of simplicity and extend the analysis to the case of two goods.

Let us now assume that we have two goods x_1 and x_2, each of which can be produced by two, fixed-proportions processes,

[1] Constant expenditure lines r_4 and r_5 could be drawn analogously to r_2, and r_1, with a slope equal to that of ce, and less than that of ce respectively.

and that constant returns to scale prevail ;[1] only two factors, capital, K, and labour, L, are used. Figure 5a shows a few of the infinity of equal-product lines which could be drawn for different outputs of the two goods. The solid lines refer to product 1, the dashed lines to product 2. In Figure 5b, these isoquants are used to construct a box diagram. The dimensions of each side of the box represent the total amount of factors available. Any point within the box simultaneously represents four quantities: the amount of capital and the amount of labour used in producing x_1 which is determined by measurement from the lower left-hand corner, and the amount of capital and the amount of labour used in the x_2 industry, measured from upper right-hand corner.

Figure 5b provides the basis for the derivation of the 'efficiency locus' for the two goods x_1 and x_2. If production takes place at any point off this locus, it is possible by recombination of factors to produce more of one good without diminishing the output of the other. If along the efficiency locus corresponding amounts of the two goods are read off and plotted on a chart as in Figure 5c, the transformation or production-possibility curve between x_1 and x_2 is obtained.

To locate a point on the efficiency locus we must specify a

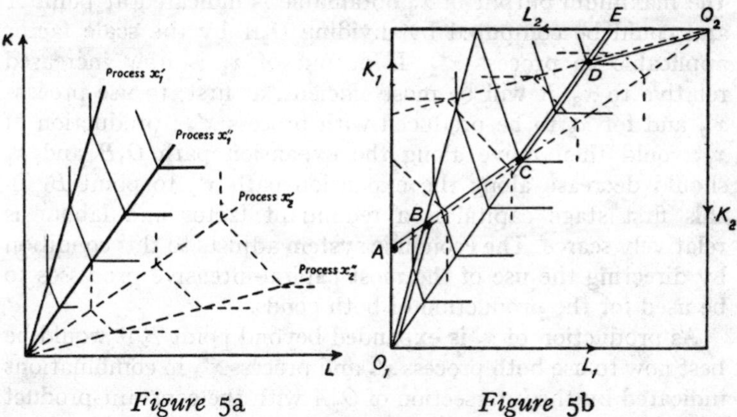

Figure 5a *Figure* 5b

[1] The assumption of constant returns to scale is, of course, maintained not because it is considered the best description of reality but for its analytical convenience. Some comments on the effects on the analysis of dropping this assumption are made below, pp. 367-8.

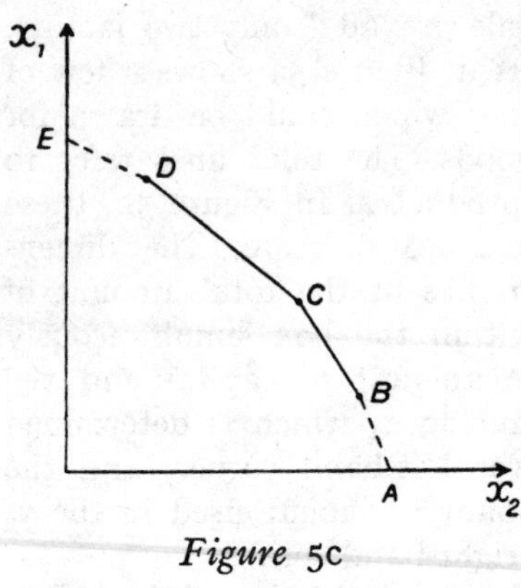

Figure 5c

particular amount of x_1 to be produced and find the maximum of x_2 which can simultaneously be produced. Graphically, we must move along the specified x_1 isoquant crossing x_2 equal-product lines until we reach the highest x_2 isoquant obtainable. The optimum positions achieved will thus be located at tangencies of the x_1 and x_2 equal-product lines where the lines just touch without crossing. Since, in the present case, each equal-product line is made up of segments of straight lines, the optimal positions will be corner tangencies. By repetition of this maximizing process for a series of points the entire efficiency locus can be determined.

Since in the present case the efficiency locus for the two goods is a rather complicated succession of line segments we shall trace it out carefully. Starting at O_1, zero output of x_1, the maximum output of x_2 obtainable is indicated at point A and could be computed by dividing O_2A by the scale factor applicable to process x'_2. If output of x_1 is now increased relative to x_2, it will be most efficient, at first, to use process x'_1 and for x_2 to be produced with process x'_2; production of x_1 would then move along the expansion path O_1B and x_2 should decrease along the expansion path x'_2 to point B. In this first stage capital is a redundant factor and labour is relatively scarce. The economic system adjusts to this condition by directing the use of the most capital-intensive processes to be used for the production of both goods.

As production of x_1 is expanded beyond point B it would be best now to use both process x'_1 and process x''_1 in combinations indicated by the intersection of O_2A with the constant-product lines for commodity x_1 as long as these intersections lie between the expansion paths of x'_1 and x''_1; production of x_2 should continue to be by means of process x'_2 alone, however. This second stage is indicated by the points on the segment BC

which belong to both the combination of x'_1 and x''_1 and process x'_2. By tracing along an x_1 isoquant between B and C it can be seen that shifting to the expansion path O_2A makes possible a larger production of x_2 for the particular output of x_1 than if we had remained on the path O_1B. As production of x_1 is expanded in this stage and production of x_2 is decreased, capital becomes more scarce relative to labour due to the relatively high labour-capital ratio of the resources released by the decrease in production of x_2.

In the third stage, as output of x_1 is farther increased, it is most efficient to use only process x''_1. But now for any given output of x_1, the maximum amount of x_2 can be obtained by use of the more labour-intensive process x''_2 in combination with process x'_2. The third stage on the efficiency locus is indicated by line CD.

Finally, still further expansion of production x_1 continues to be best done along the expansion path of process x''_1 until, at point E, x_1 is being produced to the complete exclusion of x_2. In this fourth and final stage the output of x_2 should be produced only by process x''_2.

Only in the fourth stage and the first stage of the efficiency locus would optimum allocation imply some unemployment of one of the factors. In the first stage the unemployment of capital for different outputs of x_1 and x_2 is indicated by the vertical distance between lines AB and O_1B. In the final stage the unemployment of labour is measured by the horizontal distance between lines DE and DO_2.

Actually the occurrence and qualitative significance of any of the stages depends on both technology and factor endowments. If process x''_1 were relatively more labour-intensive than is shown, its expansion path would pivot to the right and stage 2 in Figure 5b would be prolonged. As common sense would suggest, development of a sufficiently labour-intensive process for x_1 could cause stages three and four to disappear entirely and with them the possibility that there could be an 'optimal' configuration which involved unemployment of labour. A similar effect would result from a decrease in the amount of labour endowment. This could be depicted by squeezing together the left- and right-hand sides of the box in Figure 5b. Increasing the labour supply would mean stretching the box horizontally. This would not only increase the range of outputs associated with stage 4 but also, if pushed far enough, first eliminate stage 1, the capital unemployment stage, and then stage 2.

The points *ABCDE* on the technical transformation curve in Figure 5c correspond to the similarly lettered points on the efficiency locus in Figure 5b.[1] At first when only a little x_1 is produced and, relatively, a lot of x_2, we should move along the segment *AB* using process x'_1 and x'_2. Unemployment of capital associated with this segment on Figure 5b will be reduced as we approach *B*. Relative labour scarcity is limiting along this segment and the slope of the line segment *AB* will depend on the ratio of the labour inputs of output of x_2 to x_1. The relative labour intensity of process x'_2 compared to process x'_1 as drawn on Figure 5a accounts for the steepness of the segment.

The line segment *ED* on Figure 5c has an exactly analogous justification to that for the segment *AB*. Labour unemployment will be reduced as *D* is approached from point *E*. Capital is the only scarce factor and the relative capital intensity of process x''_1 as compared to process x''_2 accounts for the flatness of *ED*.

Point *C* is located conveniently relative to points *B* and *D*. More of x_1 is produced at *C* than at *B*, though not so much more as produced at point *D*. Likewise less x_2 is produced at *C* than at *B* though not as much less at *D*. The segments *BC* and *CD* will be straight lines as can be verified by noting in Figure 5b that, due to the assumption of constant returns to scale in all processes, there must be a constant ratio between changes in output of x_2 along the line O_2A between *C* and *B*, for example, and changes in output of x_1.

It was pointed out with regard to the efficiency locus in Figure 5b that changes in factor endowment and technology could shorten, extend or even completely eliminate various stages of the efficiency locus. This applies also to the separate

[1] In the constant-returns-to-scale case, only relative factor endowments are important in determining the *shape* of the transformation curve. If the absolute factor endowments were changed while relative factor endowments remain constant, it would amount to sliding the north-east and south-west vertices of the box on the connecting diagonal.

segments of the technical transformation curve. The technical transformation curve of Figure 5c illustrates all the possible stages which could be produced by this simple case, from unemployment of capital to unemployment of labour. It should not be presumed that this range of possibilities will actually exist in a particular system at any one time. Rather, it is the hypothesis of this paper that technology and factor endowments in underdeveloped areas are such that a segment like *DE*, in which labour is redundant, is important in their transformation curves.

To demonstrate the importance of demand conditions for employment when the conditions assumed in the present hypothesis exist, we shall draw a transformation curve in Figure 6 consisting only of stage *CD*, along which there is full employment of both capital and labour, and the labour-redundant stage *DE*. This can be envisaged as the result of a high rate of population growth which has stretched the labour axis very far. We can now see that actual achievement of full employment depends on the relative demands for the two goods. Market baskets whose composition falls along *CD* will allow full employment ; along *DE* labour will be redundant. A geometrical demonstration which is suggestive, though lacking in rigour, can be given. Suppose that the lines i_1 and i_2 represent two different possibilities for the community's indifference curve for the two goods. Only in the case in which the indifference curve is tangent along *CD* will optimal output imply full employment. The community must face a conflict in goals between full employment and maximum value of output if i_2 is in fact its indifference curve.[1] Extending the

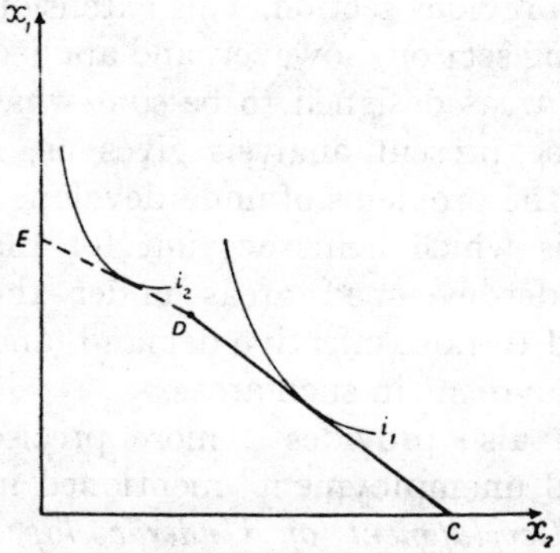

Figure 6

[1] A major qualification to this analysis, still on the static level, is the possibility that the shape and position of the community indifference curves might not be independent of the particular processes or combinations of processes which are used. To handle this difficulty it would be necessary to determine the shifts in income distribution which result from changes in factor prices and to explore the differentials in tastes of the recipients of the different types of income.

analysis to include many goods would widen the range within which factor endowments could vary without unemployment of one or more factors resulting. There would, however, still be no guarantee that the composition of goods demanded would always hit on a full-employment point.

It may also be observed that if it is possible to buy and sell in foreign trade at price ratios between the slopes of CD and DE, full employment would again be possible though not necessary. To determine whether or not it would result, it would be necessary to know the reciprocal demands for exports and imports.

It would be possible to elaborate this model now by investigating the implications for the analysis of market imperfections such as were considered in the previous section. This extension will be postponed to the following section, however, and applied to a model of underdeveloped areas designed to be somewhat more realistic. As it stands the present analysis gives us, I believe, important insight into the problems of underdeveloped areas. It presents a hypothesis which helps account for the inflationary tendencies of underdeveloped areas under the impact of programmes designed to raise effective demand, and for the stubbornness of unemployment in such areas.

The analysis of this section also provides a more precise definition for the 'technological unemployment' mentioned in *Measures for the Economic Development of Underdeveloped Countries.*[1] Technological unemployment may be a real problem for underdeveloped areas if it is defined, as in this section, as redundant labour arising from resource and technological restraints and the structure of demand.

II. A Model of Underdeveloped and Overpopulated Areas[2]

Though the analysis of the previous section is suggestive, it is hard to believe that all of the unemployment and underemployment in underdeveloped areas represents literally useless labour. Moreover, the assumption of only a few alternative

[1] United Nations, Department of Economic Affairs (New York, 1951).

[2] I am particularly indebted to P. N. Rosenstein-Rodan for discussion of the issues raised in this section.

processes and a quite limited range for substitution of factors does not seem to fit well the technological characteristics of a number of important industries, as, for example, agriculture. I shall attempt therefore to move towards greater realism by use of a two-sector model (one section with fixed, and one with variable coefficients of production), and investigation of the effects of market imperfections in such a system. To the assumption of limited opportunities for substitution in some industries is added the hypothesis that in many other industries there is a considerable range of variability in the proportions in which factors can be used.

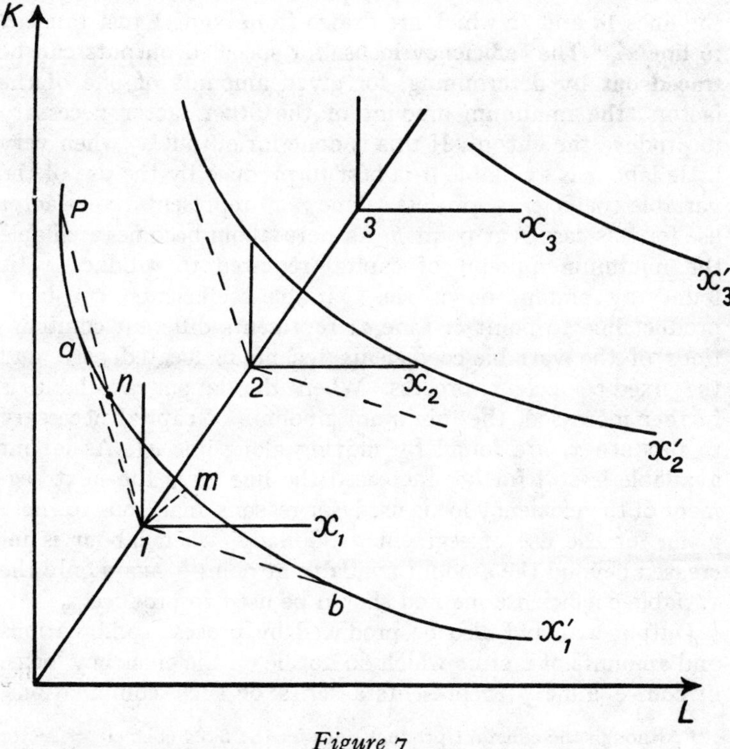

Figure 7

It will be useful to initiate the discussion under the assumption that each of the two sectors produce the same product. Suppose that in Figure 7 the constant-product lines of the fixed-coefficient industry are represented by the lines x_1, x_2, ...[1] and the constant-product lines of the variable coefficient industry by the lines x'_1, x'_2 . . . .

The output x_1 could be produced by the factor combination and technique represented by point 1 or any of the factor combinations using the variable-proportions technique represented by the line x'_1. Moreover, following the reasoning on page 356 above, it is also possible to produce x_1 by simultaneously using both the fixed-coefficients and variable-coefficients techniques. All of the lines which could be drawn from point 1 to line x'_1 represent a *combination* of methods which would produce output x_1; all such lines fall between the lines 1*a* and 1*b* which are drawn from point 1 just tangent to line x'_1.[2] The 'efficiency locus' for specified outputs can be traced out by determining, for given amounts of one of the factors, the minimum amount of the other factor necessary to produce the output. If this is done for output x_1 when very little labour is available it is best to produce by the use of the variable-coefficients process alone; a representative factor use for this case is at point *p*. As more labour becomes available the minimum amount of capital required to produce x_1 is found by sliding down the variable-coefficients constant-product line to point *a*. Line *a*1 represents different combinations of the variable-coefficients technique located at *a* and the fixed-coefficient process. When the labour available is further increased, the minimum amounts of capital necessary to produce x_1 are found by moving along line *a*1. As labour available is still further increased the line 1*b* is the next segment of the efficiency locus used, for reasons analogous to those given for the use of segment *a*1. Finally, when labour is increased beyond the amount available at point *b*, again only the variable-coefficients method should be used to produce x_1.

Output x_1 could also be produced by process combinations and amounts of factors which do not lie on the efficiency locus, of course. Line *p*1 represents a series of such combinations,

[1] Although the constant-product lines for the fixed-coefficients sector are drawn in Figure 7 as if only one process is available, the demonstration is perfectly general and its implications are applicable when more than one process is available for the fixed-coefficient industry.

[2] I am indebted to R. Solow for the criticism of a previous paper which led to this formulation.

using in varying proportions the variable-coefficients techniques located at p or n and the fixed-coefficient process located at point 1. Any combination of methods along $pn1$, however, would result in higher costs for x_1 than a method found on the efficiency locus; methods along $pn1$ could also be used to produce larger amounts than x_1. Of course, many lines like $pn1$ could be drawn between $a1$ and the vertical portion of the fixed-coefficient x_1 isoproduct line and, analogously, between $1b$ and the horizontal portion of the fixed-coefficient isoproduct line. Lines like $1m$, of which many could also be drawn, represent combinations of methods which would also produce x_1, but require more of *both* labour and capital than points on the efficiency locus. The boundaries of lines such as $1m$ are the vertical and horizontal portions of the fixed-coefficients x_1 isoproduct line.

Figure 7 embodies the constant-returns-to-scale assumption for both the fixed-coefficients and variable-coefficients method. This is not necessarily the most realistic or relevant assumption, however, nor does the relative position of the two types of curves, or the shape of the variable-coefficients isoquants necessarily correspond closely to reality. It is useful to recognize other, special cases which may have important empirical significance. In Figure 7, for example, only the extremes of the isoproduct curves of the variable-coefficients technique were a part of the efficiency locus for any particular output, and, as drawn, relatively little substitution was possible at such extremes. It would, of course, be possible to draw figures in which the 'efficient' isoproduct ridge lines follow the variable-coefficients lines so as to allow substitution of factors over a considerable range.

The effect of divergent rates of return to scale on the shape and slope of the constant-product ridge lines is illustrated in Figure 8 for one possible set of relations. In the fixed-coefficients process it is assumed that there are increasing returns to scale (shown by decreasing distances between x_1, x_2, x_3, along any ray from the origin). In the variable-coefficients method constant returns to scale are the rule (shown by constant distances between x'_1, x'_2, x'_3, along a ray from the origin). In this example, the efficient isoproduct lines change their shape as output is increased. For output x_1 only the variable-

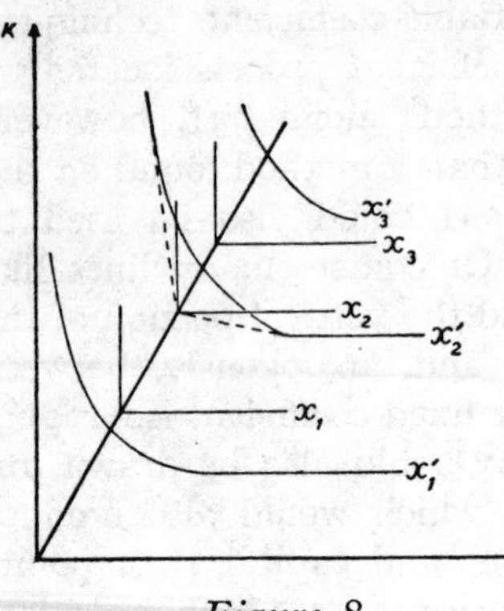

Figure 8

coefficients constant-product line is relevant. For output x_2 the 'efficient' isoproduct ridge line involves use of both the fixed- and variable-coefficient techniques. Finally, for output x_3, only the fixed-coefficient technique is 'efficient' and the ridge lines involving the variable-coefficient method necessarily have a positive slope.

Figure 8 provides the formal basis for some useful deductions. Changes in factor prices which might at one scale of output induce shifts in the proportions in which factors are used, may not induce such shifts at another scale of output or may only produce smaller shifts. Likewise techniques of production not feasible at one scale of production may become mandatory for efficiency at another scale.

In Figures 6, 7 and 8 it is particularly clear that in order for the system to travel along its most efficient production isoquant it is necessary that factor prices be flexible. Factor-price rigidities would make parts of the efficient constant-product lines unattainable for profit-maximizing businessmen.

We can now go rapidly through an analysis of the two-sector model hypothesis assuming that each sector produces a different commodity. The geometrical representation of this, using the box diagram technique introduced in the previous section, is provided by Figure 9a. The assumption that for x_1 only two alternative processes are available is maintained for convenience; the resulting production-possibility curves for x_1 are shown by the solid lines. The assumption of variable coefficients in the production of x_2 is limited to the sector between its ridge lines because at these ridge lines the marginal productivity of one of the factors becomes zero and further input of this factor would have no effect on output.[1]

[1] It is assumed that there is no disposal problem and, thus, that the production isoquants do not bend back on themselves.

The production functions for x_1 and x_2 are reproduced in the box diagram in Figure 9b: the dimensions of the box are determined by the factor endowments.[1] Using this box diagram we can trace out the efficiency locus for the two products by repeatingly asking the question, 'For a given amount of x_1 what is the maximum amount of x_2 which can be produced?' In the process of tracing out the efficiency locus, the transformation curve can be drawn for the two goods.

Starting at O_1, zero output of x_1, the maximum amount of x_2 producible is given by O_2A. If the output of x_1 is increased relative to x_2, it would be most efficient at first to use process x'_1 for x_1 and to produce x_2 by travelling along its most capital-intensive ridge line, O_2A. This represents optimal behaviour up to point B. In this stage although both products are being produced capital is a redundant factor. This results in spite of the variability of coefficients in production of x_2 because outside the upper ridge line of x_2 capital has zero marginal productivity. Stage I is represented on the transformation curve in Figure 9c as segment AB.

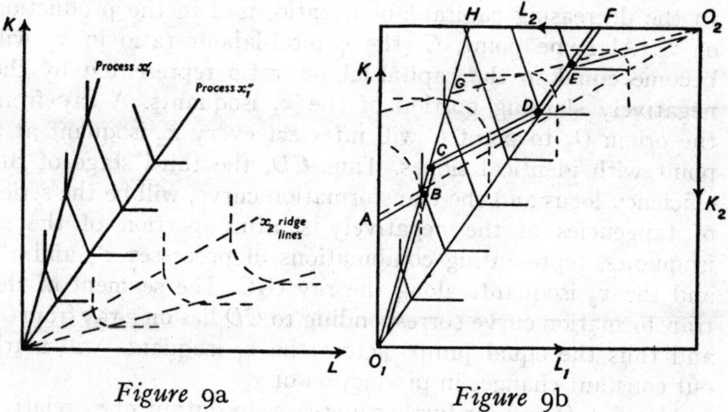

Figure 9a *Figure* 9b

The efficiency locus from B to C is traced out by finding the succession of points at which the x_1 constant-product curves touch the highest x_2 constant-product curves. In this stage process x'_1 will be used for x_1 and a varying combination

[1] Again only the ratio of the factor endowments is important as long as constant returns to scale is assumed.

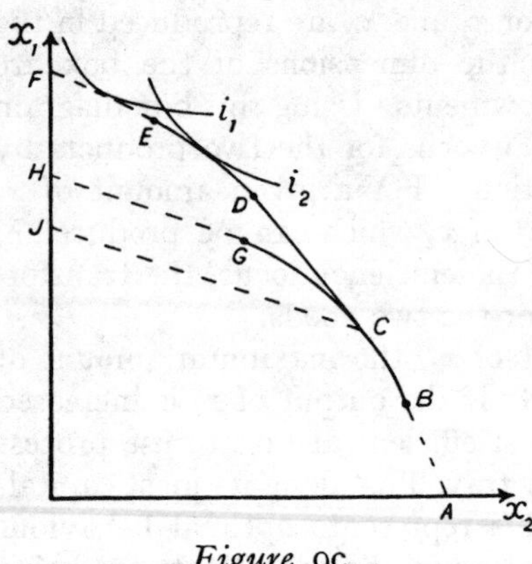

Figure 9c

of factors for x_2. The segment of the transformation curve for this stage, BC, will be curved as equal increases in production of x_1 along x'_1 will not result in constant changes in output of x_2. Only along rays from the origin O_2 will equal distances imply equal differences in output of x_2. BC will be concave to the origin as is 'normal' for transformation curves; graphically it can be seen that smaller and smaller changes along x'_1 are needed in order to move across equal changes in output of x_2. As production moves from B to C the points at which x'_1 corners touch the x_2 isoquants will be characterized by smaller and smaller slopes on the x_2 isoquants, corresponding to the decreasing capital-labour ratio used in the production of x_2. At some point, C, the capital-labour ratio in x_2 will become equal to the capital-labour ratio represented by the negatively slanting portion of the x_1 isoquants. A ray from the origin O_2 to point C will intersect every x_2 isoquant at a point with identical slopes. Thus CD, the third stage of the efficiency locus and the transformation curve, will be the series of tangencies of the negatively slanting portion of the x_1 isoquants, representing combinations of processes x'_1 and x''_1 and the x_2 isoquants along the ray O_2C. The segment of the transformation curve corresponding to CD lies on a ray from O_2 and thus the equal jumps across the x_1 isoquants will mark out constant changes in production of x_2.

At point D and for further increases in output of x_1 relative to x_2 it would be best to use only process x''_1 for production of x_1. The segment of the transformation curve, DE, corresponding to DE on the efficiency locus, is curved for reasons similar to those which created the curvature of segment BC.

The final stage of the efficiency locus is the labour unemployment stage. The marginal productivity of labour has fallen to zero in the x_2 sector and in a perfect factor market wages would fall to zero. *EF* represents this final stage on the transformation curve in Figure 9c.

ABCDEF in Figure 9c is the full transformation curve for this case. There are now curved as well as straight-line segments, and the kinks characteristic of the previous transformation curves have disappeared.[1]

In Figure 9b, as in Figure 5b, it is possible to visualize the effects of structural changes by altering the shape and position of the production isoquants for each product and the dimensions of the box.

The box diagram approach helps to clarify the implication of the differences in substitutability in the fixed-coefficient and variable-coefficient sectors. It is clear that the outputs at which one or another factor becomes redundant will be determined by the limits of substitution in the variable-coefficients sector and the most extreme labour- and capital-intensive processes in the fixed-coefficient sector, not by the discontinuities of the latter sector. These have other important effects, however.

Suppose that the respective demands for output are such that a large part of the available capital is drawn into the capital-intensive and fixed-coefficient sector. The amount of labour which can be absorbed in these sectors is dependent on the amount of capital available. Since capital is a scarce factor, labour employment opportunities in this sector are limited by its availability rather than by demand for output. The relatively plentiful labour supply is then pushed into the variable-coefficient sector and absorbed there as long as the marginal value productivity of labour is higher than the wages it receives.

In this case, as in the models of the preceding sections, unemployment is not due to lack of effective demand and as a result cannot be relieved by conventional contracyclical economic policy designed to stimulate spending. If employment opportunities in the fixed-coefficient sectors were limited by capital scarcity or some other resource bottleneck, an increase in demand rather than stimulating additional output would

[1] Being off the efficiency curve, it may be noted, is like being on an isoquant $1m$ in the single-good case. Cf. Figure 7 above.

only create inflationary pressures. Likewise, in the variable-coefficient sectors if the marginal productivity of labour were zero, the first effects of an increase in demand for output would be an increase in prices without an increase in production. If more of the scarce factors were made available to the fixed-coefficient sectors, more labour could then be employed and would be used, if there were an effective demand for its output. Additional amounts of the scarce factors in the variable-coefficients sector would also increase labour productivity and output if demand were adequate.

It is possible in this case of two sectors, one of fixed and one of variable coefficients, for a divergence to exist between the full-employment output and the output with maximum value, just as in the case of fixed-coefficient processes for each of two goods, as depicted in Figure 6 above. This could result even if there were no market imperfections. If, in Figure 9c, the community indifference curves were like i_1 rather than i_2 so that the tangency occurred in the capital-scarcity, labour-surplus stage, the divergence could exist. On the other hand, community-indifference curves shaped like i_2 would mean that it would be possible for full-employment output and maximum-value output to be identical. This demonstration is subject to the same qualifications applied to the one-good case.

Without empirical knowledge, it is not possible to evaluate certainly the relative importance of each of the stages of the transformation curve 9c. However, according to the hypothesis advanced here the transformation curve for underdeveloped areas would consist mainly of the high labour-intensity and labour-unemployment segments such as *DE* and *EF*.

We have thus far in this section assumed the existence of competitive markets and profit-maximizing entrepreneurs. We have shown that, even under such assumptions, technology, factor endowments and final demands may combine in ways which make it very difficult for underdeveloped areas to solve their problems of unemployment and underemployment. It is possible now to broaden the analysis by combining it with the analysis of the effects of market imperfections discussed in Section I to determine what further problems are created when some of the assumptions of competition are dropped.

Behind the transformation curve lie many fine adjustments as factors are shifted from one industry to another and recombined in varying proportions to obtain the maximum output from one industry for given outputs of the other industry. It has been assumed in deriving the transformation curve that the necessary adjustments would be accomplished as they would be in a perfect factor market. But flexibility within wide limits is required to achieve every possible position on a transformation locus such as that in Figure 9c. When imperfections and rigidities of various types obstruct the movements of factors and prices, the system will not be able to achieve its optimum transformation curve but will instead do no better than to move along some other, less than optimal curve. Limited factor-price flexibility may be quite serious when at least one good is produced with fixed-coefficient processes. If rigid factor prices render a relatively labour-intensive process unprofitable, the only alternative process may involve a big jump to a quite capital-intensive process as well as a drastic obstacle to substitution in the variable-coefficients process.

Since we are interested in the effect of imperfections in the factor markets, it will be useful to distinguish transformation curves which assume perfect adjustments in the factor markets; these will be called 'technical transformation curves'. Transformation curves which take into account market imperfections will be different from the technical transformation curves; these latter relations will be designated 'market transformation curves'.[1] Different types of market imperfections will create different types of shifts away from the technical transformation curve, so there is not one market transformation curve for each technical transformation curve but many.

It may help to approximate reality to assume that factor-price ratios in the variable-coefficients sector are relatively more flexible than those in the fixed-coefficients sector. This

[1] The effect of factor-market imperfections in shifting the market transformation curve inside the technical transformation curve has been pointed out and analysed for international trade by G. Haberler, 'Some Problems in the Pure Theory of International Trade', *The Economic Journal*, June 1950, LX, 223–40 and by P. Samuelson, 'Evaluation of Real National Income', *Oxford Economic Papers*, Jan. 1950, II (N.S.), 18–19 for welfare economics; others have probably also noted the effect.

might result from differential strength of union organization or susceptibility to government wage controls. Suppose, for example, that by means of union pressures or minimum wage legislation real wages of labour were maintained so that in the fixed-coefficients sector the labour-capital price ratio was set above that represented by the slope of the constant product curve combining processes x'_1 and x''_1 in Figure 9b ; the factor-price ratio in the variable-coefficients sector may still be assumed to vary freely. The cost-minimizing combination of factors is determined for any particular output at the point at which the production-possibility schedule for that output touches the lowest expenditure line. If the production-possibility schedule has any slope at this point, it is a condition of equilibrium that this slope be equal to the factor-price ratio which determines the slope of the expenditure line. As a result under the present assumptions process x''_1 would never be used. It would always be more profitable to use process x'_1 alone in producing x_1. The transformation curve would be *ABCGH* in Figure 9c ; this is below the technical transformation curve and has a much longer range of unemployment. If both sectors were characterized by such high, inflexible factor-price ratios, the economy's transformation curve would approach *ABCJ*.[1]

Barriers to the movement of factors would have the effect of moving the market transformation curve even further inside the technical transformation curve and increasing the range over which a factor is redundant.

Thus imperfections in factor markets have several undesirable effects. They reduce the amount of goods available and create a wider range of combinations of goods over which labour may become unemployed, depending on the structure of final demand.

Although the effects of rigid wages on the transformation curve of the economy are clear, welfare judgements as to the results of removal of the factor-price rigidities are subject to the same qualifications as in the previous case. Much depends

[1] Barriers to capital movement created by monopoly may create situations analogous to those described above resulting from labour-market imperfections.

on the effects of a change in methods on the income distribution, and, via income distribution, on community preferences.

III. Empirical Verification

The analysis above is based on hypotheses which can be tested empirically and which deserve to be given factual content. Empirical testing requires measurement of the proportions in which productive factors can be and are actually used. Essentially the objective of such research would be an investigation of production functions.

Although the concept of the production function has been familiar for some time, its empirical investigation has, as is common, been neglected with important noteworthy exceptions. In this connexion it should be noted that even though it is sometimes presented as an analysis of productive processes and its terminology is taken from the theory of production, input-output analysis, as it now stands, does not reveal the technologies actually in use in an economy. For this purpose a much higher degree of disaggregation would be necessary than is currently practiced or appears feasible. Interindustry flows may strongly reflect historical incidents by which certain technical processes are concentrated in a particular sector which subcontracts for other sectors. Or, if similar technical processes are widely used, the interindustry flows in a particular year may reflect different cyclical patterns in industry; one industry producing at its capacity may subcontract to another industry which has equipment capable of performing the necessary operations and is cyclically depressed.[1] Studies of capital coefficients made for input-output tables do indicate, however, a method which can be used for a factor-proportions study.[2]

The objective of the process analysis approach newly developed at the Rand Corporation is exactly the empirical determination of production functions. The emphasis of the process-

[1] This point is made with force by H. Markowitz in *Process Analysis of the Metal Working Industries*, The Rand Corporation (Santa Monica, 1953), pp. 7–8.

[2] Especially the studies made by the Inter-Industry Analysis Branch of the Office of Chief Economist, Bureau of Mines, U. S. Department of Interior.

analysis approach in establishing all the alternatives on a production-possibility schedule, which is essential for programming, is somewhat different from a factor-proportions study. For the latter study not only the range of possibilities but the relative frequencies of their use and dynamic considerations involved in choice are important. The methods of process analysis can also be used for a factor-proportions study, however.

For the study of factor proportions two general approaches seem to be available. The first, suggested by input-output studies of capital coefficients and which will be called the 'product analysis' method, involves a census in each plant studied of the amounts of each type of factor of production used in the expansion of the output of a particular product. The second method, based on classifications of technical processes, requires the determination of the combinations of factors actually used by firms to perform certain standardized 'tasks'.

These approaches to the factor-proportions study are not necessarily logically separate, nor should they always be completely different in application. The great advantage of process analysis in precise identification of outputs can compensate for the weakness of product analysis where multiproduct plants are involved. The advantage of product analysis in inclusion of all contributing inputs can be important when using the process-analysis approach where it is difficult to isolate the contributions of all inputs. Thus, it is important in particular cases to have in mind a method combining both the product and process analyses.

The application of product analysis can be made in two ways: (1) By abstracting the data required from the engineering plans which are prepared when a new investment is undertaken and which list the construction, equipment, labour and materials required for the operation of the plant. Accounting records of new investment expenses could also supply part of the necessary information. (2) By means of 'factor inventories' of existing plants to provide for these plants the information which the investment plan analysis provides for new expansions. No easy and automatic application of product analysis techniques is possible in the face of problems such as those raised by multiproduct firms and the measurement of the expansion of capacity. These problems can often be overcome, I believe, to make this a fruitful method.

Process analysis is based on the conception that all productive activity can be divided into separate technical processes with similar outputs whose inputs can be identified and compared. Process analysis thus provides another logically satisfactory approach to study of factor-proportions. The process-analysis approach can moreover provide the basis for a comparison of factor-proportions by final products, and thus for an independent check of factor-proportions computed by the product-analysis method. This could be achieved by determining the appropriate physical processes and levels of activity necessary for the output of a particular final product and aggregating their factor inputs. The procedure just described is, in fact, that actually used in modern engineering practice in plant and equipment design and layout.

The disadvantage of the process-analysis approach, however, stemming from the kinds of information which would be generally available, I believe, occurs precisely where the product-analysis method is strong. The information for the process-analysis approach must come from the records of inputs to particular processes and these records, because of the purposes for which they are kept, will seldom be sufficiently detailed and comprehensive as to the inputs involved in a process. As a result it will often be necessary in using the process-analysis approach to estimate the contributions of 'indirect' inputs to the processes studied.

A major source of information for the application of the process-analysis approach may be the time cards kept by many firms. These cards list for each worker the time which he takes at each type of machine which he uses to perform the operations on the particular piece. These cards would have the labour inputs and machines specified for particular tasks and often contain other useful data as well. The job sheets which accompany production orders are also sources of information as they list the time per unit and in total required by each type of machine and process to finish a particular item.

Conclusions

In this paper a number of different hypotheses have been developed and combined for the purpose of explaining outstanding features of some underdeveloped areas: the persistence of unemployment and underemployment, the coexistence of 'modern' capital-intensive techniques and methods using a great deal of labour and little capital, and large differentials in factor returns in different sectors. I have suggested that to a considerable degree these conditions may be the result of a few characteristic conditions: factor-market imperfections, and limited technical substitutability of factors, with divergences between the proportions in which goods are demanded and in which they can be supplied with full use of available factors.

Factor-market imperfections which limit factor mobility create employment problems in underemployed areas with low *per capita* incomes and limited capital resources which are not different in kind but are much different in degree from those existing in the more advanced countries.

When the proportions in which factors can be combined are variable without limit, i.e., with decreasing but always positive marginal returns to labour, additional labour can always produce additional output. If the technical substitutability of factors is limited, as is suggested here, the possibility of labour redundancy arises. Even if there are some sectors in which labour always has a positive marginal product there may be a divergence between maximum value output and full employment output if there is insufficient demand for the output of these sectors. These possibilities are again more important for the underdeveloped areas whose resource endowments are often not suited to the factor proportions dictated by the technological leadership of advanced countries. Differences in income distribution and the range of products may also make limited technical substitutability a more pressing problem in underdeveloped than in advanced areas.

6. MODELS OF DEVELOPMENT

THE MECHANICS OF ECONOMIC DEVELOPMENT*

by **H. W. Singer**

IN WHAT FOLLOWS, WE SHALL CONSIDER SOME OF THE important relations in development planning for underdeveloped countries, first (Sections I, II and III) with the help of a numerical illustration (hopefully thought of as reasonably realistic) and then (Section IV) with the help of a more general model of the type made familiar by the work of Domar, Harrod and Hicks. It is hoped that this approach will help toward an understanding of some of the problems involved in development planning, and their mutual interrelation.

I

The model on page 382 shows in its top part the typical structure of an underdeveloped economy.

The 'model scheme' assumes that 70 per cent of the population is in the agricultural sector; that the share of agriculture in the total 'national' income is 40 per cent; that the ratio of agricultural *per capita* income to average *per capita* income is 57 per cent. It is of considerable interest to note that in 1799–1860, when the U.S. *per capita* national income was $216 of 1926 purchasing power, 72·8 per cent of the population was in agriculture, agriculture accounted for 39·3 per cent of the total national income, and the ratio of *per capita* incomes in agriculture to the average was 54 per cent.[1] These figures come remarkably close to those assumed in the scale model.

* *The Indian Economic Review,* August 1952. Reprinted by permission of the editor of the *Indian Economic Review* and the author. The author is a member of the U. N. Secretariat, but the views expressed in this article are his personal views and not necessarily those of the United Nations Organization.

[1] Robert F. Martin, 'National Income in the U.S., 1799–1938', National Industrial Conference Board, New York, 1939; quoted by Simon Kuznets, 'National Income Estimates for the U.S. prior to 1870', *Journal of Economic History,* Spring 1952.

MODEL SCHEME

1,000 persons at $100 each = total 'national' income $100,000

AGRICULTURE		NON-AGRICULTURE
700 persons at $57 each = $40,000		300 persons at $200 each = $60,000

Natural increase each year 12·5 persons = 1·25%

70% in agriculture		30% outside agriculture
+ 8·75 persons		+ 3·75 persons
− 8·75 persons	*Transfer from Agriculture: 'Industrialization'*	+ 8·75 persons
0 persons		+ 12·50 persons

DEVELOPMENT OUTLINE

A. 'INDUSTRIALIZATION' (Transfer)
Cost: $4,000 per worker transferred
= $1,600 per person transferred
(8·75 persons) = $14,000 (Yield 17%)
Increased annual net output = $2,333

(Capital/Income Ratio 6 : 1)

B. AGRICULTURAL INVESTMENT
Cost: $4,800
Benefit: 3% of agricultural production (Yield: 25%) = $1,200

(Capital/Income Ratio 4 : 1)

C. PROVISION OF ADDITIONAL CAPITAL FOR 3·75 PERSONS OUTSIDE AGRICULTURE ($800 per person)
Cost: $3,000
Benefit: $750

(Capital/Income Ratio 4 : 1)

TOTAL COST (A + B + C): $21,800
'Naturally available' .. $ 6,000
Deficit .. $15,800
(Increase at rate of 1¼%)

TOTAL BENEFIT: $4,283 per annum of which $3,033 is increase *per capita*.

Development becomes self-supporting in			Disposition of *per capita* increase	
	Years		*New Development*	*Increase in Consumption*
Case I	13	(11)	$1,500 (50%)	$1,500
Case II	50	(27)	$ 600 (20%)	$2,400
Case III	never	(67)	$ 180 (6%)	$2,820

We consider a group of 1,000 persons in an underdeveloped community, and assign to this community a *per capita* income of $100 each at current prices. As far as national income figures can be relied upon, this would represent a community which could be considered as about average for the underdeveloped parts of the world. The total 'national' income of the group would then be $100,000. We are not concerned here with the difficulties of accurate measurement of national income, or of their meaning, in underdeveloped communities. We shall merely assume that a satisfactory way has been found of measuring incomes. We shall leave it open whether the figure represents a measurement of economic welfare, of material resources or only of resources entering into the market economy. Either definition will do as long as it is consistently kept in mind.

We next divide our group into an agricultural sector and a non-agricultural sector. It is one of the characteristics of underdeveloped communities that 60–80 per cent of the population are engaged in agriculture. We assume 70 per cent in agriculture and 30 per cent outside. This is a proportion which seems to be pretty closely correlated with the income levels assumed.

Next, the model assigns a *per capita* income of $57 to the 700 persons in the agricultural sector, and $200 to the non-agricultural sector. The available statistics—for what they are worth—seem to be remarkably unanimous in determining *per capita* income in the agricultural sector of underdeveloped economies as around 55-60 per cent of the average *per capita* income.[1]

In view of the small size of the non-agricultural sector, the assignment of 57 per cent of the average *per capita* figure to the agricultural sector carries with it the corollary of twice the national average in the non-agricultural sector.[2]

[1] It is remarkable that this relation also applies to more developed countries. In the U.S., income per head in agriculture in 1930 was 59 per cent of the average national income, in the U.K. 63 per cent. In Sweden, it was 58 per cent in 1920, but this seemed to have dropped to 40 per cent in 1930 (figures taken from E.M. Ojala : *Agriculture and Economic Progress*, Oxford University Press, London 1952, Table li).

[2] This latter figure is, of course, higher than the corresponding figures for the U.S., U.K. and Sweden, since the non-agricultural sector is much larger there. In none of these three countries did non-agricultural income approach twice the national average, although Sweden in 1870 came fairly close to that ratio. (loc. cit.)

A high ratio of average income in the non-agricultural sector to the national average is in accordance with observed facts and general impressions.

In considering the assumed *per capita* income levels in the agricultural sector and the non-agricultural sector, it may be useful to recall again that income is not necessarily used here as a measure of relative welfare in the two sectors.

It follows for our model—and for reality if our assumptions are realistic—that national income originating in agriculture accounts for only 40 per cent of the total national income, even though the bulk of the population is engaged in the agricultural sector. Thus, it is only with reference to employment and not with reference to national income that agriculture can, in strict truth, be described as the 'basic' activity in underdeveloped countries. This point is worth making since reports of missions and similar documents abound with statements that improvements in agriculture are in some sense 'more important' than non-agricultural improvements, since agriculture is the 'basic activity'.

So much for the present structure of our underdeveloped group. Economic development for this group will mean a structural change. The proportion of population in agriculture will have to fall, and the non-agricultural sector will have to expand. It may be noted that for our present purposes *it is entirely irrelevant* whether this structural change is considered as the 'purpose' or 'objective' of economic development, or as its consequence. Whether we start off with industrialization, with agricultural development, or in whatever way, rising income levels will have to be accompanied by a corresponding change in structure : i.e., a relative shrinkage of the agricultural sector. If a 70 : 30 ratio of agriculture is typical of underdeveloped countries, something like a 20 : 80 or 15 : 85 ratio is typical of countries at a high state of economic development, which are assumed to be closed systems (or after allowance has been made for surpluses of exports or imports of agricultural products).

The speed or rate of economic development may then be described by the rate at which the 70 : 30 ratio in economic structure is approximated to the 20 : 80 ratio which represents ultimate equilibrium at a high level of development.

A convenient assumption for an economy in a fairly rapid process of economic development is to assume that the agricultural population will remain constant in absolute numbers, and that the change in structure is brought about by a concentration of the natural increase in population in the non-agricultural sector. This assumption has been satisfied with a fair degree of approximation in a number of countries going through a process of development in an area of settled population.[1]

Thus, over long periods of British, Swedish, Russian and Japanese development, the agricultural population remained approximately constant in absolute size. This assumption of constant absolute size of the agricultural population has been incorporated in our model. It should be emphasized, however, that this represents fairly rapid economic development.[2]

The model could be adjusted to any other slower rate of development. Thus, it could be assumed that one-third or one-half of the natural increase in population goes into agriculture, or that the rate of increase in the non-agricultural sector is twice or three times or five times that in the agricultural sector, etc.

In our model, we assume an increase in population by 1·25 per cent per annum. This is the estimated actual figure in the underdeveloped world as a whole. Contrary to a general impression, there is no clear-cut evidence that the population in the underdeveloped world as a whole increases significantly faster than in the more developed parts.[3] The model population of 1,000 will thus increase by 12·5 in the first year.

In accordance with our assumption, the agricultural population remains at 700, and the total increase of 12½ persons is added to the 300 persons in the non-agricultural sector, resulting in a rate of growth of about 4 per cent per annum in the

[1] Excluding such countries as the U.S., Canada, Australia, etc., where development was associated with new settlement, and agriculture and non-agriculture expanded together.

[2] Although it would take 108 years on this assumption for a 70 : 30 ratio to be converted into a 20 : 80 ratio, assuming a rate of population increase over the whole period of 1¼ per cent per annum.

[3] The contrary impression may be due largely to a fixation on a few areas (often islands) of rapid population growth, such as Puerto Rico, Ceylon and others. It may also partly be due to comparison with the low birth-rate of industrialized countries in the nineteen-thirties.

non-agricultural sector. The structural ratio on this assumption is changed from 70:30 to 69·1:30·9, approximately. If the rate of population increase should slacken in the course of economic development, the resulting degree of structural change each year would be correspondingly less.

The increase in the non-agricultural sector of 12·5 persons may be divided up into 3·75 persons representing the natural increase of population in the non-agricultural sector,[1] and of 8·75 persons representing the transfer of the natural increase of population in the agricultural sector from that sector to the non-agricultural sector. This distinction between the two increments in the non-agricultural sector may or may not be considered relevant in a numerical model approach. One could either assume that the increase from whatever source has to be provided with new capital on standards identical to both groups, or else one may assume different standards. For instance, in our model we consider the two increments separately. We shall assume that the natural increase of population in the non-agricultural sector (the 3·75 persons) is fitted into the non-agricultural sector at prevailing standards of productivity and capital equipment, whereas the 8·75 persons, representing transfer from agriculture, are the labour spearhead of a more advanced technology amounting to some 'deepening' in the non-agricultural sector.

II

We are now in a position to consider a Development Outline for our underdeveloped community. The community is faced with three tasks:

(*a*) to equip the 8·75 persons transferred from the agricultural to the non-agricultural sector in such a manner that they can become the spearhead of an improved technology. This transfer may be called, for short, 'industrialization', provided that we remain conscious of the fact that it includes transfer to commercial, financial, personal services, etc.;

(*b*) to increase agricultural production, with the constant number of persons employed in agriculture, sufficiently to provide food for the increased population in the non-agricultural

[1] Assuming that the natural rate of increase in population is the same in the agricultural and non-agricultural sectors.

sector, and also to provide for such increases in consumption as are part of the development programme;

(*c*) to provide for the natural increase of population in the non-agricultural sector at prevailing standards.

We shall consider these three steps in turn.

(*a*) The cost and results of 'industrialization' will depend on the specific circumstances of the individual country. The cost may best be estimated as a dollar investment per person transferred or per worker. Cost per worker will be high where the proportion of public utilities and heavy industries included in the development programme is high, and also where large-scale units of production at advanced standards of technology are provided. Some years ago, the cost of providing additional employments of a non-agricultural type was frequently estimated to be $2,500 per worker transferred, or $1,000 per person transferred. For our present purposes, this figure would have to be somewhat increased, partly because of the rise in prices since then, partly because a community at a standard of $100 national income *per capita* would have to include in a long-range development programme a high proportion of capital-intensive basic services and utilities. The standard of technologies will partly depend on what technologies are available, and since technological research is centred in capital-rich countries, and since capital goods will have to be largely imported, it follows that the standard of technology will have to be more advanced than what would naturally correspond to the circumstances of the underdeveloped group. It may be noted that overpopulation, while it makes 'industrialization' more necessary, also tends to make it cheaper, provided that the right kind of labour-intensive technologies are at the disposal of the underdeveloped countries. Hence, it is true only in a restricted sense that 'overpopulation' is an obstacle to economic development.

We shall assume a cost of $4,000 per worker transferred, or $1,600 per person transferred. This would provide at present prices for a reasonable proportion of such capital-intensive installations as large-scale irrigation, power and railways, while at the same time assuming a modest standard of technology and leaning towards smaller scale and lighter industries, as well as towards commercial and personal services. It makes some slight allowance for housing provision and urban community services, but would still involve considerable strain in that respect.

On the basis of this assumption, the transfer of 8·75 persons would cost our underdeveloped community $14,000 per annum or 14 per cent of the 'national' income of $100,000.

What yield can be expected from this investment of $14,000 on 'industrialization'? At this point, we shall have to discard the economist's bias in favour of assuming a high 'marginal productivity' in underdeveloped countries. In underdeveloped countries, it is rarely possible simply to add a piece of directly productive equipment, and at the same time observe the *ceteris paribus* of marginal productivity. Basic services, such as power, transport, etc., are already overstrained and it is not possible to add to the load without also including in the investment an extension of basic services itself (or else taking away services from other enterprises thus again diminishing true social marginal productivity). Thus, although marginal productivity in underdeveloped countries may be assumed to be high, in view of the universal shortage of capital, in fact it is an irrelevant concept. The relevant concept is the productivity of the complete 'package' of directly productive capital equipment *plus* that required to produce components or complementary goods, *plus* the provision of basic services required for the new investment. If related to this whole 'package', productivity may come out quite low, as has been the experience (often unanticipated) of many investments in underdeveloped countries. On the other hand, as investment proceeds and becomes cumulative, the productivity of investment begins to increase again, as economies of linkage and scale come into operation.

In our model, since we assume a poor community, in its early stages of development, undertaking an all-round investment programme we will have to assume fairly low productivity (or its converse, a high capital/income ratio). We shall assume a productivity of 17 per cent, equivalent to a capital/income ratio of 6 : 1.[1]

[1] In view of some of the subsequent argument, it may be useful to add here that this capital/income ratio is based on the assumption of orthodox forms of investment; i.e., exclusive of special utilization of unemployed and underemployed labour for direct capital formation, or other unorthodox forms of investment.

On this assumption, the investment of $14,000 will yield an annual net income of $2,333, or 2·3 per cent of the initial 'national' income.

(*b*) The agricultural investment target can be derived from the rate of structural change. Since the total population increases by 1¼ per cent per annum, while the agricultural population remains constant, it follows that agricultural productivity (output per person) must increase by at least 1¼ per cent per annum if food supplies are to be maintained.[1]

This 1¼ per cent increase in productivity is, however, in the nature of a minimum. In practice, agricultural productivity will have to be increased by more. In the first place, it is not enough to *produce* 1¼ per cent of more food; it is also necessary to *transfer* it to the non-agricultural sector. In fact, transfer of food must increase by at least 4 per cent per annum if food supplies in the non-agricultural sector are to be maintained. In practice, in order to increase the transfer of food by 4 per cent it will be necessary to increase the productivity by more than 1¼ per cent, since farmers will not normally transfer their total increase in food production. They will want to consume some of it themselves. The supply curve of farmers in underdeveloped countries is notoriously inelastic or even backward rising. Furthermore, in the process of economic development, it will be necessary to provide for at least a moderate increase in consumption in the non-agricultural sector. Short of strong-arm methods, some kind of incentive will have to be given both to farmers themselves and to the population in the non-agricultural sector. Assuming that consumption *per capita* is to be increased by at least 1 per cent per annum—a small improvement—and assuming that farmers will transfer one-half of their increased production, it follows that the increase in agricultural productivity must be at least 3 per cent. Since present agricultural output is $40,000 in our model community, an increase of $1,200 must be achieved. This is the agricultural target, consistent with the general development outline.

How much will it cost to achieve this increase of $1,200 per annum in agricultural production? Again, circumstances differ.

[1] In underdeveloped countries, food supplies may often be considered as representative, for practical purposes, of consumption in general.

In this case, overpopulated countries may find it more expensive to increase agricultural output than countries with a plentiful supply of land. In nearly all underdeveloped countries, opportunities exist for raising agricultural output by comparatively cheap methods, such as improved seeds, local irrigation, better rotation, better tools, etc. Assuming that such opportunities exist and are systematically used, it has been estimated that a yield of 25 per cent (or a capital/income ratio of 4 : 1) would be possible in agricultural investment.[1]

If we accept this estimate, it would be possible to achieve the required increase of $1,200 per annum in the agricultural sector by a capital investment of $4,800. It should be understood, however, that this is based on optimistic assumptions, and in some countries at all stages, and in most countries at some stages, it may be more expensive to achieve this agricultural target.

(*c*) We have next to consider the cost of providing for the natural increase of population in the non-agricultural sector. We shall assume that no attempt is made to provide the natural increase of population with a more advanced technology than that corresponding to the present level of the group under review. This means that 3·75 persons representing the natural increase in the non-agricultural sectors should be equipped with sufficient capital to produce $200 *per capita* per annum. The capital/income ratio presently obtaining in the non-agricultural sector is assumed to be 4 : 1. This corresponds to a net yield of 25 per cent per annum. This assumption seems to fit in with the scattered data available as to net yield outside agriculture in underdeveloped countries. It assumes a lower capital/income ratio than in the case of a more advanced technology, because of a higher proportion of personal services, commercial activities and very small scale enterprise—all of them containing, in underdeveloped countries, an element of underemployment or disguised unemployment. On the other hand, the yield is assumed to be somewhat lower (or the capital/income ratio somewhat higher) than in more developed countries. The reason for this is the strain on public services,

[1] *Measures for the Economic Development of Underdeveloped Countries*, a report by a group of experts appointed by the Secretary-General of the United Nations, New York, May 1951, page 76, table 2.

lack of external economies, lower managerial standards, less reliable flows of raw materials and difficulties in skilled labour supply. The absence of a technology suitable to the abundance of labour and shortage of capital also makes the capital income ratio higher than it otherwise would be.

If the above assumption of yield of 25 per cent is correct, it would take an investment of $800 for each of the 3·75 persons representing the increase in population to be fitted into the non-agricultural sector. This results in a total investment of $3,000 and an increase in annual net income by $750.

III

We are now in a position to consider the aggregate cost and benefits of the outlined development programme, and assess its feasibility in relation to the available resources. The total cost of the development programme is $21,800. Of this, $14,000 represents the cost of 'industrialization', $4,800 represents the cost of agricultural development, and $3,000 represents the cost of providing for the natural increase of population in the non-agricultural sector.

The benefits from this investment add up to a $4,283 increase in net income per annum. This represents an increase in the total 'national' income of 4·3 per cent. When allowance is made for the increase in population, the increase in *per capita* income is 3 per cent. This is a fairly rapid rate of increase, partly because of the assumed rapid rate of structural change, and partly because of the assumed increase in the rate of consumption as a necessary accompaniment of the structural change assumed. The figure of 3 per cent increase in *per capita* national income could be reduced if milder assumptions were made in both these respects.

The total cost of $21,800 represents 22 per cent of the assumed national income. This is a rate of investment which, at low income levels, has been occasionally achieved under special conditions,[1] but clearly cannot be assumed to be financed by voluntary savings, even if supplemented by the

[1] Thus rates of investment exceeding 20 per cent have been estimated for early stages of Japanese, Russian and perhaps also British economic development.

moderate budget surpluses possible by fiscal techniques practicable in underdeveloped countries. Nor can it be expected that the mild degree of inflation which would still be compatible with the execution of a rational development programme, could result in 'forced savings' of anything like this degree.

If we assume that net savings available for new investment of a *per capita* income level of $100 are no more than 6 per cent, it follows that only $6,000 out of the $21,800 required would be available for the financing of this development outline. (Six per cent net savings at this income level represents the present state of affairs in underdeveloped countries; the assumption that all these net savings are available for the financing of a development programme represents a considerable improvement over what is now actually achieved.) Our underdeveloped group is, therefore, faced with a deficit of $15,800 in the financing of its development programme.

The conclusion at which we have thus arrived is that a community of the type considered in the model cannot finance a programme of rapid economic development through capital investment from its presently available domestic resources. Unless we admit defeat at this point, there are four possible approaches:

(1) The first would be to reduce the cost of the development programme by lowering the capital/income ratio (or increasing the yield per unit of capital employed). This would require adoption of labour-intensive technology, and possibly unorthodox forms of investment based on utilization of the unemployed and underemployed labour of our underdeveloped group.

(2) A second approach would be to increase net savings through attempts at reducing consumption below the initial level of $94 *per capita* assumed to be voluntarily accepted with the existing distribution of income.

(3) The third approach would be to reduce the rate of population increase. This would, in our model, reduce capital requirements in three ways: (*a*) less people would have to be transferred out of agriculture, in order to keep agricultural population constant in size; (*b*) accordingly, the increase in food production would have to be less, and thus the agricultural investment programme could be cut, and (*c*) natural increase of population in the non-agricultural sector would

be smaller. Thus, in our model, total expenditure on the development programme would decline exactly in proportion to the rate of increase in population.

(4) Finally, it would be possible to carry out the development programme if the domestic resources of the group are supplemented from outside.

The first three cases are perhaps more conveniently summarized in the more general form of 'dynamic equation' of the Domar-Harrod type rather than in a numerical model. This is done in the last section of this article. Before doing so, however, the fourth case may be illustrated with the help of the lower section of the Model Scheme on page 382.

If we assume that the total deficit of $15,800 in the initial year, and the deficits in subsequent years, are covered by an influx of foreign capital, the questions arising—all of them related—are : For how long has the influx of foreign capital to continue until development can be financed from domestic resources ? What will be the resulting final capital debt ? What balance of payments surplus will the receiving country have to achieve to repay the debt initially incurred ?

Obviously the answers to these questions depend largely on the disposition of the increments in output achieved in the course of economic development. In the limiting case, if the whole increase is consumed and net savings remain at $6,000 annually, the problem is clearly insoluble. Since requirements will gradually increase with the increase in aggregate population, the deficit will increase, the period over which foreign capital is required will be infinite, and the final debt burden will be infinite.[1]

The Model Scheme on page 382 incorporates three different assumptions about the disposition of the *per capita* increase in income. In the first instance, (I), a high marginal rate of savings of 50 per cent has been assumed; in the second instance, (II), a still high marginal rate of savings of 20 per cent; in the third instance, (III), it has been assumed that the marginal rate of savings is no higher than the average rate of savings, i.e. 6 per cent. The Model Scheme shows that in the first

[1] Or at least it will last until the structure of the economy has been changed to the 20/10 ratio between agriculture and non-agriculture which has been defined as the structure of a mature economy.

instance, development becomes self-supporting in 13 years; in the second instance, 50 years; in the third instance, never at all. The last conclusion is rather interesting: since the total cost of the development programme increases by 1¼ per cent each year, i.e. by $197 in the first year and cumulatively more in subsequent years, it follows that a constant increase in savings by $180 each year will be as useless for achieving self-promoting development as no savings at all.

It will also be noted that a reduction in the marginal rate of savings from 50 per cent to 20 per cent will increase the period over which the influx of foreign capital is required (and thus the ultimate capital debt) not twice but fourfold. This shows that the final debt burden is highly elastic in respect of marginal rates of savings. A little austerity now will save a lot of austerity later.

The Model thus illustrates the strategic role of marginal rates of savings. Present incomes of underdeveloped countries are so low that there are fairly strict limits to the volume of savings out of *present* incomes. The main hope for increased savings rests in saving a high proportion of the *increments* in income arising in the course of economic development. This also indicates the importance of giving priority in development programmes to those kind of projects in which a high proportion of the benefits can be recaptured for new investment. Simple benefit/cost calculations are only part of the story.

A simple calculation from the Model will show that if the marginal rate of savings is as high as 50 per cent—i.e., if consumption *per capita* increases at the rate of 1½ per cent, while income *per capita* increases at the rate of 3 per cent—the total influx of foreign capital required over a period of 13 years will be approximately $100,000. Assuming that this debt carries an average interest burden of 8 per cent, but that no amortization is required, the repayment burden would be $8,000 per annum. This would represent approximately 5 per cent of the national income at the moment when development has become self-supporting, and a falling proportion after that as the national income continues to increase. Over the average of 30 years after development has become self-supporting, the repayment burden would amount to 3 per cent of the national income. Since the underdeveloped countries as a whole export about 20 per cent of their estimated national income, the initial repayment burden would require additional exports amounting to about one-quarter of present 'normal' exports falling to an export surplus of around 15 per cent over the average of the first 30 years of self-supporting development. These figures would, of course, be increased if the initial capital debt had to be repaid as well as serviced, but the initial burden of repayment would be compensated by the subsequent reduction in interest charges.

These figures in proportion do not look unfeasible, but it should be remembered that they are based on an extraordinarily high rate of marginal savings, viz. 50 per cent.

If the marginal rate of savings is 20 per cent (Case II), the required total influx of capital would amount to $400,000 and the repayment burden after 50 years, when development becomes self-supporting, will be over 8 per cent of the national income, even without repayment. In view of the large capital debt, repayment would add heavily to the annual burden. Thus in the second case, the influx of foreign capital would not only have to be long sustained, but it would also either presuppose a heavily export-oriented economic development, or else create balance-of-payments troubles (unless, of course, the repayment burden is lightened through waivers, grants-in-aid or defaults).

In Case III, with the marginal rate of savings no higher than the average rate of savings, obviously, since the deficit increases each year by more than the assumed increment to savings of $180 per annum, development will never become self-supporting.

The above calculations are made on the assumption of a constant absolute increment to net savings, equal to 50 per cent, 20 per cent, and 6 per cent respectively, of the initial increase in *per capita* incomes. This may be a somewhat pessimistic assumption, in view of the fact that national income *per capita* increases over the period contemplated by 3 per cent per annum. In spite of the fact that recent research seems to have shown that the income schedule of a rising propensity to save does not seem to hold over periods beyond trade cycles, it may be hopefully assumed that the annual increment to savings will also rise by 3 per cent per annum. In that case, of course, the period when development becomes self-supporting will be shortened, and the ultimate repayment burden correspondingly less. The results, on this assumption, are also shown in the Model Scheme on page 382, in brackets.

It will be noted that if the increment in savings is assumed to rise by 3 per cent per annum, development becomes self-supporting even in the third case when marginal savings are assumed to be only 6 per cent. In that case, even though additional savings fail to meet additional costs of development in the first years, they ultimately make self-supporting development possible, since they rise at the rate of 3 per cent per annum, whereas the cost of development only increases at the rate of $1\frac{1}{4}$ per cent per annum. Even so, 67 years are required for development to become self-supporting, and the ultimate capital debt would be very high. However, if national income doubles every 15 years, the total national income in 60 years would be around \$1·6 million (instead of the present \$100,000), and the resulting repayment burden would not necessarily be very high. It is not so much a high repayment burden, but rather the very long period of time over which the capital influx would have to be steadily maintained, which makes this approach to economic development seem unfeasible.

IV

We may now try to look at this problem in a more general fashion. A very simple, almost tautological, equation can be constructed which links D, the rate of economic development (defined as growth of *per capita* income and assumed to be proportionate to growth of *per capita* capital) with the rate of net savings (s), the productivity of new investment per unit of capital (p)[1], and the rate of annual increase of population (r). The equation reads as follows : $D = sp - r$.

This equation can be used to answer four different questions, and it provides a surprising amount of insight into the mechanics of development.

1. Given the rate of net savings, productivity and population increase—what is the possible rate of development ?

[1] (p) also represents the inverted capital/income ratio previously mentioned.

2. Given the target rate of economic development, and given the productivity of capital and rate of population increase—what net savings are necessary to support the stipulated rate of development ?

3. Given the stipulated rate of economic development, and given the rate of savings and of productivity, what rate of population increase can be supported ?

4. Given the stipulated rate of economic development, and given the rate of savings and population increase—what must be the productivity of new investment per unit of capital employed ? The answer to this last question is of particular interest.

The answer to all these questions can be obtained by substituting parameters in the equation.

In illustrating the answers to be obtained, we shall stipulate a rate of economic development of 2 per cent annual increase in *per capita* income; a rate of net savings of 6 per cent of net national income; a rate of population increase of 1¼ per cent; and a capital/income ratio for normal investment of 5 : 1.[1]

The answer to Question 1 is as follows. *With 6 per cent net savings, a capital/income ratio of 5 : 1 and a rate of population increase of 1¼ per cent, no improvement in the national* per capita *income, and no economic development by means of investment is possible.* The economy is a stationary economy. Since the estimated parameters for savings, population increase and capital/income ratio are believed to be fairly realistic, the equation would seem to explain the absence of spontaneous development in so many underdeveloped countries at very low income levels.

2. The answer to Question 2. *With a stipulated rate of development of 2 per cent per annum, a capital/income ratio of 5 : 1 and a rate of population increase of 1¼ per cent, a rate of net savings of 16¼ per cent is necessary, to make possible the stipulated rate of development.* This rate of savings is about three times the rate actually observed in underdeveloped countries.

[1] The assumptions correspond fairly closely to those underlying the table on page 76 of a U.N. report by a group of experts, *Measures for the Economic Development of Underdeveloped Countries*, U.N. Department of Economic Affairs, New York, May 1951.

3. Answer to Question 3. *With a stipulated rate of development of 2 per cent, a rate of net savings of 6 per cent and a capital/income ratio of 5 : 1, no increase in population can be supported.* Development at the stipulated rate would only be possible in a society of stationary population.

4. Answer to Question 4. *With a stipulated rate of economic development of 2 per cent per annum, a rate of net savings of 6 per cent and population increasing at the rate of 1¼ per cent per annum, the productivity of investment per unit of capital would have to be 54 per cent* (*or a capital/income ratio of less than 2 : 1*). If the normal productivity of investment is 20 per cent (or the capital/income ratio 5 : 1) this means that the stipulated rate of economic development can only be sustained if technologies can be found using little more than one-third the amount of capital per unit of output than orthodox capital investment.

The last result gives us the crux of the problem. Assuming that the yield of capital is only 20 per cent and that the technology is fixed at a capital/income ratio of 5 : 1, no economic progress by investment is possible, unless output can be increased by direct utilization of unemployed and underemployed manpower and natural resources with no, or practically no, further application of capital. Alternatively, the whole technology of all new investment must be diluted in the direction of labour intensity; the equation indicates the degree to which such dilution will be necessary.

There is yet another approach: If the required yield per unit of capital is 54 per cent, but the annual yield is only 20 per cent, it might still be possible to sustain the stipulated rate of economic development, provided that an increase in output 1·7 times that achieved by *new* investment can be achieved by increasing the productivity of *existing* capital. Since the annual increase in output is 3¼ per cent (2 per cent *per capita* and 1¼ per cent increase in population), and since the increase in output is assumed to be associated with a corresponding increase in the amount of capital, i.e. by 3¼ per cent per annum, it follows that a further increase in output of 1·7 times as much again can only be obtained by increasing the productivity of existing capital by (1·7 × 3·25 per cent) or 5·525 per cent. *The stipulated rate of development can be sustained if in addition* *to normal investment, the productivity of existing capital is at the same time increased by a little over $5\frac{1}{2}$ per cent per annum.* Studies of the cotton textile industries in Latin-American countries, among other studies, have shown the scope for improvement in the productivity of existing capital.[1]

A last word may be indicated about the r (rate of population increase) in the equation ($D = sp - r$). It will be noted that in the equation r appears as a negative factor, with a *minus* sign. This must not be interpreted as 'proof' of the view that 'population is an obstacle to economic development'. If the r—the rate of population increase—appears as a negative factor, this does by no means exclude the possibility that a high r may have such an effect on s or p that the net effect of an increased r may not be as negative as the formula seems to show, and may even be positive. The effect on s is not likely to be especially helpful, but the relation between r and p is a different kettle of fish. A state of overpopulation—the result of a high previous r—as well as a high current rate of increase in population—a high current r—provides not only a challenge but also an opportunity. An opportunity, that is, so to adjust the technology of new investment that p—increased output per unit of capital—rises; and also so to increase the productivity of existing capital by the application of additional labour that p is again increased.

[1] *Labour Productivity of the Cotton Textile Industry in Five Latin-American Countries*, United Nations Publications, Sale No.: 1951 : II. G. 2.

ECONOMIC DEVELOPMENT WITH UNLIMITED SUPPLIES OF LABOUR*

by **W. Arthur Lewis**

THIS ESSAY IS WRITTEN IN THE CLASSICAL TRADITION, MAKING the classical assumption, and asking the classical question. The classics, from Smith to Marx, all assumed, or argued, that an unlimited supply of labour was available at subsistence wages. They then enquired how production grows through time. They found the answer in capital accumulation, which they explained in terms of their analysis of the distribution of income. Classical systems thus determined simultaneously income distribution and income growth, with the relative prices of commodities as a minor by-product.

Interest in prices and in income distribution survived into the neo-classical era, but labour ceased to be unlimited in supply, and the formal model of economic analysis was no longer expected to explain the expansion of the system through time. These changes of assumption and of interest served well enough in the European parts of the world, where labour was indeed limited in supply, and where for the next half century it looked as if economic expansion could indeed be assumed to be automatic. On the other hand over the greater part of Asia labour is unlimited in supply, and economic expansion certainly cannot be taken for granted. Asia's problems, however, attracted very few economists during the neo-classical era (even the Asian economists themselves absorbed the assumptions and pre-occupations of European economics) and hardly any progress has been made for nearly a century with the kind of economics which would throw light upon the problems of countries with surplus populations.

When Keynes's *General Theory* appeared, it was thought at first that this was the book which would illuminate the problems of countries with surplus labour, since it assumed an unlimited supply of labour at the current price, and also,

* *The Manchester School*, May 1954. Reprinted by permission of *The Manchester School* and the author.

in its final pages, made a few remarks on secular economic expansion. Further reflection, however, revealed that Keynes's book assumed not only that labour is unlimited in supply, but also, and more fundamentally, that land and capital are unlimited in supply—more fundamentally both in the short-run sense that once the monetary tap is turned the real limit to expansion is not physical resources but the limited supply of labour, and also in the long-run sense that secular expansion is embarrassed not by a shortage but by a superfluity of saving. Given the Keynesian remedies the neo-classical system comes into its own again. Hence, from the point of view of countries with surplus labour, Keynesianism is only a footnote to neo-classicism—albeit a long, important and fascinating footnote. The student of such economies has therefore to work right back to the classical economists before he finds an analytical framework into which he can relevantly fit his problems.

The purpose of this essay is thus to see what can be made of the classical framework in solving problems of distribution, accumulation, and growth, first in a closed and then in an open economy. It is not primarily an essay in the history of economic doctrine, and will not therefore spend time on individual writers, inquiring what they meant, or assessing its validity or truth. Our purpose is rather to bring their framework up-to-date, in the light of modern knowledge, and to see how far it then helps us to understand the contemporary problems of large areas of the earth.

The Closed Economy

We have to begin by elaborating the assumption of an unlimited supply of labour, and by establishing that it is a useful assumption. We are not arguing, let it be repeated, that this assumption should be made for all areas of the world. It is obviously not true of the United Kingdom, or of North-west Europe. It is not true either of some of the countries usually now lumped together as underdeveloped; for example there is an acute shortage of male labour in some parts of Africa and of Latin America. On the other hand it is obviously the relevant assumption for the economies of Egypt, of India, or of Jamaica. Our present task is not to supersede neo-classical economics, but merely to elaborate a different framework for those countries which the neo-classical (and Keynesian) assumptions do not fit.

In the first place, an unlimited supply of labour may be said to exist in those countries where population is so large relatively to capital and natural resources, that there are large sectors of the economy where the marginal productivity of labour is negligible, zero, or even negative. Several writers have drawn attention to the existence of such 'disguised' unemployment in the agricultural sector, demonstrating in each case that the family holding is so small that if some members of the family obtained other employment the remaining members could cultivate the holding just as well (of course they would have to work harder : the argument includes the proposition that they would be willing to work harder in these circumstances). The phenomenon is not, however, by any means confined to the countryside. Another large sector to which it applies is the whole range of casual jobs—the workers on the docks, the young men who rush forward asking to carry your bag as you appear, the jobbing gardener, and the like. These occupations usually have a multiple of the number they need, each of them earning very small sums from occasional employment ; frequently their number could be halved without reducing output in this sector. Petty retail trading is also exactly of this type ; it is enormously expanded in over-populated economies ; each trader makes only a few sales ; markets are crowded with stalls, and if the number of stalls were greatly reduced the consumers would be no whit worse off—they might even be better off, since retail margins might fall. Twenty years ago one could not write these sentences without having to stop and explain why in these circumstances, the casual labourers do not bid their earnings down to zero, or why the farmers' product is not similarly all eaten up in rent, but these propositions present no terrors to contemporary economists.

A little more explanation has to be given of those cases where the workers are not self-employed, but are working for wages, since it is harder to believe that employers will pay wages exceeding marginal productivity. The most important of these sectors is domestic service, which is usually even more inflated in overpopulated countries than is petty trading (in Barbados 16 per cent of the population is in domestic service). The reason is that in overpopulated countries the code of ethical behaviour so shapes itself that it becomes good form for each person to offer as much employment as he can. The line between employees and dependents is very thinly drawn. Social prestige requires people to have servants, and the grand seigneur may have to keep a whole army of retainers who are really little more than a burden upon his purse. This is found not only in domestic service, but in every sector of employment. Most businesses in underdeveloped countries employ a large number of 'messengers', whose contribution is almost negligible ; you see them sitting outside office doors, or hanging around in the courtyard. And even in the severest slump the agricultural or commercial employer is expected to keep his labour force somehow or other—it would be immoral to turn them out, for how would they eat, in countries where the only form of unemployment assistance is the charity of relatives ? So it comes about that even in the sectors where people are working for wages, and above all the domestic sector, marginal productivity may be negligible or even zero.

Whether marginal productivity is zero or negligible is not. however, of fundamental importance to our analysis. The price of labour, in these economies, is a wage at the subsistence level (we define this later). The supply of labour is therefore 'unlimited' so long as the supply of labour at this price exceeds the demand. In this situation, new industries can be created, or old industries expanded without limit at the existing wage ; or, to put it more exactly, shortage of labour is no limit to the creation of new sources of employment. If we cease to ask whether the marginal productivity of labour is negligible and ask instead only the question from what sectors would additional labour be available if new industries were created offering employment at subsistence wages, the answer becomes even more comprehensive. For we have then not only the farmers, the casuals, the petty traders and the retainers (domestic and commercial), but we have also three other classes from which to choose.

First of all, there are the wives and daughters of the household. The employment of women outside the household depends upon a great number of factors, religious and conventional, and is certainly not exclusively a matter of employment opportunities. There are, however, a number of countries where the current limit is for practical purposes only employment opportunities. This is true, for example, even inside the United Kingdom. The proportion of women gainfully employed in the U.K. varies enormously from one region to another according to employment opportunities for women. For example, in 1939 whereas there were 52 women gainfully employed for every 100 men in Lancashire, there were only 15 women gainfully employed for every 100 men in South Wales. Similarly in the Gold Coast, although there is an acute shortage of male labour, any industry which offered good employment to women would be besieged with applications. The transfer of women's work from the household to commercial employment is one of the most notable features of economic development. It is not by any means all gain, but the gain is substantial because most of the things which women otherwise do in the household can in fact be done much better or more cheaply outside, thanks to the large-scale economies of specialization, and also to the use of capital (grinding grain, fetching water from the river, making cloth, making clothes, cooking the midday meal, teaching children, nursing the sick, etc.). One of the surest ways of increasing the national income is therefore to create new sources of employment for women outside the home.

The second source of labour for expanding industries is the increase in the population resulting from the excess of births over deaths. This source is important in any dynamic analysis of how capital accumulation can occur, and employment can increase, without any increase in real wages. It was therefore a cornerstone of Ricardo's system. Strictly speaking, population increase is not relevant either to the classical analysis, or to the analysis which follows in this article, unless it can be shown that the increase of population is caused by economic development and would not otherwise be so large. The proof of this proposition was supplied to the classical economists by the Malthusian law of population. There is already an enormous literature of the genus: 'What Malthus *Really* Meant', into which we need not enter. Modern population theory has advanced a little by analysing separately the effects of economic development upon the birth rate, and its effects on the death rate. Of the former, we know little. There is no evidence that the birth rate ever rises with economic development. In Western Europe it has fallen during the last eighty years. We are not quite sure why ; we suspect that it was for reasons associated with development, and we hope that the same thing may happen in the rest of the world as development spreads. Of the death rate we are more certain. It comes down with development from around 40 to around 12 per thousand ; in the first stage because better communications and trade eliminate death from local famines ; in the second stage because better public health facilities banish the great epidemic diseases of plague, smallpox, cholera, malaria, yellow fever (and eventually tuberculosis) ; and in the third stage because widespread facilities for treating the sick snatch from the jaws of death many who would otherwise perish in infancy or in their prime. Because the effect of development on the death rate is so swift and certain, while its effect on the birth rate is unsure and retarded, we can say for certain that the immediate effect of economic development is to cause the population to grow ; after some decades it begins to grow (we hope) less rapidly. Hence in any society where the death rate is around 40 per thousand, the effect of economic development will be to generate an increase in the supply of labour.

Marx offered a third source of labour to add to the reserve army, namely the unemployment generated by increasing efficiency. Ricardo had admitted that the creation of machinery could reduce employment. Marx seized upon the argument, and in effect generalized it, for into the pit of unemployment he threw not only those displaced by machinery, but also the self-employed and petty capitalists who could not compete with larger capitalists of increasing size, enjoying the benefits of the economies of scale. Nowadays we reject this argument on empirical grounds. It is clear that the effect of capital accumulation in the past has been to reduce the size of the reserve army, and not to increase it, so we have lost interest in arguments about what is 'theoretically' possible.

When we take account of all the sources we have now listed —the farmers, the casuals, the petty traders, the retainers (domestic and commercial), women in the household, and population growth—it is clear enough that there can be in an overpopulated economy an enormous expansion of new industries or new employment opportunities without any shortage of unskilled labour becoming apparent in the labour market. From the point of view of the effect of economic development on wages, the supply of labour is practically unlimited.

This applies only to unskilled labour. There may at any time be a shortage of skilled workers of any grade—ranging from masons, electricians or welders to engineers, biologists or administrators. Skilled labour may be the bottleneck in expansion, just like capital or land. Skilled labour, however, is only what Marshall might have called a 'quasi-bottleneck', if he had not had so nice a sense of elegant language. For it is only a very temporary bottleneck, in the sense that if the capital is available for development, the capitalists or their government will soon provide the facilities for training more skilled people. The real bottlenecks to expansion are therefore capital and natural resources, and we can proceed on the assumption that so long as these are available the necessary skills will be provided as well, though perhaps with some time lag.

If unlimited labour is available, while capital is scarce, we know from the Law of Variable Proportions that the capital should not be spread thinly over all the labour. Only so much labour should be used with capital as will reduce the marginal productivity of labour to zero. In practice, however, labour is not available at a zero wage. Capital will therefore be applied only up to the point where the marginal productivity of labour equals the current wage. This is illustrated in Figure 1. The horizontal axis measures the quantity of labour, and the vertical axis its marginal product. There is a fixed amount of capital. *OW* is the current wage.

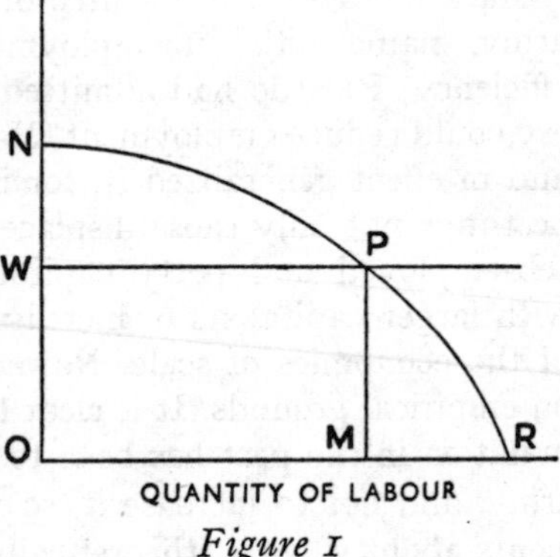

Figure 1

If the marginal product of labour were zero outside the capitalist sector, *OR* ought to be employed. But it will pay to employ only *OM* in the capitalist sector. *WNP* is the capitalists' surplus. *OWPM* goes in wages to workers in the capitalist sector, while workers outside this sector (i.e. beyond *M*) earn what they can in the subsistence sector of the economy.

The analysis requires further elaboration. In the first place, after what we have said earlier on about some employers in these economies keeping retainers, it may seem strange to be arguing now that labour will be employed up to the point where the wage equals the marginal productivity. Nevertheless, this is probably the right assumption to make when we are set upon analysing the expansion of the capitalist sector of the economy. For the type of capitalist who brings about economic expansion is not the same as the type of employer who treats his employees like retainers. He is more commercially minded, and more conscious of efficiency, cost and profitability. Hence, if our interest is in an expanding capitalist sector, the assumption of profit maximization is probably a fair approximation to the truth.

Next, we note the use of the terms 'capitalist' sector and 'subsistence' sector. The capitalist sector is that part of the economy which uses reproducible capital, and pays capitalists for the use thereof. (This coincides with Smith's definition of the productive workers, who are those who work with capital and whose product can therefore be sold at a price above their wages.) We can think, if we like, of capitalists hiring out their capital to peasants ; in which case, there being by definition an unlimited number of peasants, only some will get capital, and these will have to pay for its use a price which leaves them only subsistence earnings. More usually, however, the use of capital is controlled by capitalists, who hire the services of labour. The classical analysis was therefore conducted on the assumption that capital was used for hiring people. It does not make any difference to the argument, and for convenience we will follow this usage. The subsistence sector is by difference all that part of the economy which is not using reproducible capital. Output per head is lower in this sector than in the capitalist sector, because it is not fructified by capital (this is why it was called 'unproductive';

the distinction between productive and unproductive had nothing to do with whether the work yielded utility, as some neo-classicists have scornfully but erroneously asserted). As more capital becomes available more workers can be drawn into the capitalist from the subsistence sector, and their output per head rises as they move from the one sector to the other.

Thirdly we take account of the fact that the capitalist sector, like the subsistence sector, can also be subdivided. What we have is not one island of expanding capitalist employment, surrounded by a vast sea of subsistence workers, but rather a number of such tiny islands. This is very typical of countries in their early stages of development. We find a few industries highly capitalized, such as mining or electric power, side by side with the most primitive techniques ; a few high class shops, surrounded by masses of old style traders ; a few highly capitalized plantations, surrounded by a sea of peasants. But we find the same contrasts also outside their economic life. There are one or two modern towns, with the finest architecture, water supplies, communications and the like, into which people drift from other towns and villages which might almost belong to another planet. There is the same contrast even between people ; between the few highly westernized, trousered, natives, educated in western universities, speaking western languages, and glorying in Beethoven, Mill, Marx or Einstein, and the great mass of their countrymen who live in quite other worlds. Capital and new ideas are not thinly diffused throughout the economy ; they are highly concentrated at a number of points, from which they spread outwards.

Though the capitalized sector can be subdivided into islands, it remains a single sector because of the effect of competition in tending to equalize the earnings on capital. The competitive principle does not demand that the same amount of capital per person be employed on each 'island', or that average profit per unit of capital be the same, but only that the marginal profit be the same. Thus, even if marginal profits were the same all round, islands which yield diminishing returns may be more profitable than others, the earliest capitalists having cornered the vantage points. But in any case marginal profits are not the same all round. In backward economies knowledge is one of the scarcest goods. Capitalists have experience of certain types of investment, say of trading or plantation agriculture, and not of other types, say of manufacturing, and they stick to what they know. So the economy is frequently lopsided in the sense that there is excessive investment in some parts and underinvestment in others. Also, financial institutions are more highly developed for some purposes than for others—capital can be got cheaply for trade, but not for house building or for peasant agriculture, for instance. Even in a very highly developed economy the tendency for capital to flow evenly through the economy is very weak; in a backward economy it hardly exists. Inevitably what one gets are very heavily developed patches of the economy, surrounded by economic darkness.

Next we must say something about the wage level. The wage which the expanding capitalist sector has to pay is determined by what people can earn outside that sector. The classical economists used to think of the wage as being determined by what is required for subsistence consumption, and this may be the right solution in some cases. However, in economies where the majority of the people are peasant farmers, working on their own land, we have a more objective index, for the minimum at which labour can be had is now set by the average product of the farmer; men will not leave the family farm to seek employment if the wage is worth less than they would be able to consume if they remained at home. This objective standard, alas, disappears again if the farmers have to pay rent, for their net earnings will then depend upon the amount of rent they have to pay, and in overpopulated countries the rent will probably be adjusted so as to leave them just enough for a conventional level of subsistence. It is not, however, of great importance to the argument whether earnings in the subsistence sector are determined objectively by the level of peasant productivity, or subjectively in terms of a conventional standard of living. Whatever the mechanism, the result is an unlimited supply of labour for which this is the minimum level of earnings.

The fact that the wage level in the capitalist sector depends upon earnings in the subsistence sector is sometimes of immense political importance, since its effect is that capitalists have a direct interest in holding down the productivity of the subsistence workers. Thus, the owners of plantations have no interest in seeing knowledge of new techniques or new seeds conveyed to the peasants, and if they are influential in the government, they will not be found using their influence to expand the facilities for agricultural extension. They will not support proposals for land settlement, and are often instead to be found engaged in turning the peasants off their lands. (Cf. Marx on 'Primary Accumulation'.) This is one of the worst features of imperialism, for instance. The imperialists invest capital and hire workers; it is to their advantage to keep wages low, and even in those cases where they do not actually go out of their way to impoverish the subsistence economy, they will at least very seldom be found doing anything to make it more productive. In actual fact the record of every imperial power in Africa in modern times is one of impoverishing the subsistence economy, either by taking away the people's land, or by demanding forced labour in the capitalist sector, or by imposing taxes to drive people to work for capitalist employers. Compared with what they have spent on providing facilities for European agriculture or mining, their expenditure on the improvement of African agriculture has been negligible. The failure of imperialism to raise living standards is not wholly to be attributed to self interest, but there are many places where it can be traced directly to the effects of having imperial capital invested in agriculture or in mining.

Earnings in the subsistence sector set a floor to wages in the capitalist sector, but in practice wages have to be higher than this, and there is usually a gap of 30 per cent or more between capitalist wages and subsistence earnings. This gap may be explained in several ways. Part of the difference is illusory, because of the higher cost of living in the capitalist sector. This may be due to the capitalist sector being concentrated in congested towns, so that rents and transport costs are higher. All the same, there is also usually a substantial difference in real wages. This may be required because of the psychological cost of transferring from the easy going way of life of the subsistence sector to the more regimented and urbanized environment of the capitalist sector. Or it may be a recognition of the fact that even the unskilled worker is of more use to the capitalist sector after he has been there for some time than is the raw recruit from the country. Or it may itself represent a difference in conventional standards, workers in the capitalist sector acquiring tastes and a social prestige which have conventionally to be recognized by higher real wages. That this last may be the explanation is suggested by cases where the capitalist workers organize themselves into trade unions and strive to protect or increase their differential. But the differential exists even where there are no unions.

The effect of this gap is shown diagrammatically in Figure 2, which is drawn on the same basis as Figure 1. *OS* now represents subsistence earnings, and *OW* the capitalist wage (real not money). To borrow an analogy from the sea, the frontier of competition between capitalist and subsistence labour now appears not as a beach but as a cliff.

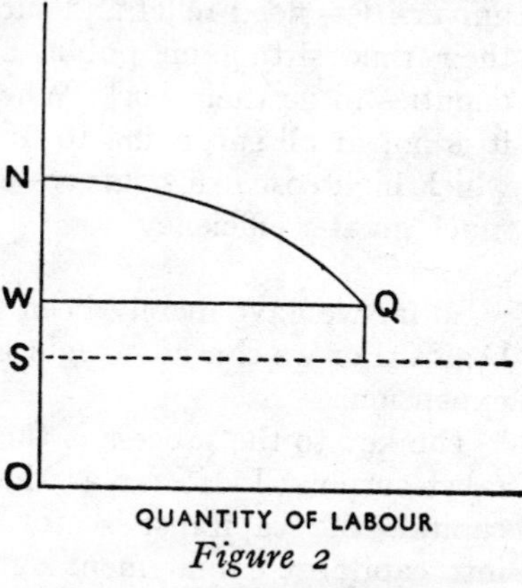

Figure 2

This phenomenon of a gap between the earnings of competing suppliers is found even in the most advanced economies. Much of the difference between the earnings of different classes of the population (grades of skill, of education, of responsibility or of prestige) can be described only in these terms. Neither is the phenomenon confined to labour. We know of course that two firms in a competitive market need not have the same average profits if one has some superiority to the other; we reflect this difference in rents, and ask only that marginal rates of profit should be the same. We know also that marginal rates will not be the same if ignorance prevails—this point we have mentioned earlier. What is often puzzling in a competitive industry is to find a difference in marginal profits, or marginal costs, without ignorance, and yet without the more efficient firm driving its rivals out of business. It is as if the more efficient says: 'I could compete with you, but I won't', which is also what subsistence labour says when it does not transfer to capitalist employment unless real wages are substantially higher. The more efficient firm, instead of competing wherever its real costs are marginally less than its rivals, establishes for itself superior standards of remuneration. It pays its workers more and lavishes welfare services, scholarships and pensions upon them. It demands a higher rate on its marginal investments; where its competitors would be satisfied with 10 per cent, it demands 20 per cent, to keep up its average record. It goes in for prestige expenditure, contributing to hospitals, universities, flood relief and such. Its highest executives spend their time sitting on public committees, and have to have deputies to do their work. When all this is taken into account it is not at all surprising to find a competitive equilibrium in which high cost firms survive easily side by side with firms of much greater efficiency.

So far we have merely been setting the stage. Now the play begins. For we can now begin to trace the process of economic expansion.

The key to the process is the use which is made of the capitalist surplus. In so far as this is reinvested in creating new capital, the capitalist sector expands, taking more people into capitalist employment out of the subsistence sector. The surplus is then larger still, capital formation is still greater, and so the process continues until the labour surplus disappears.

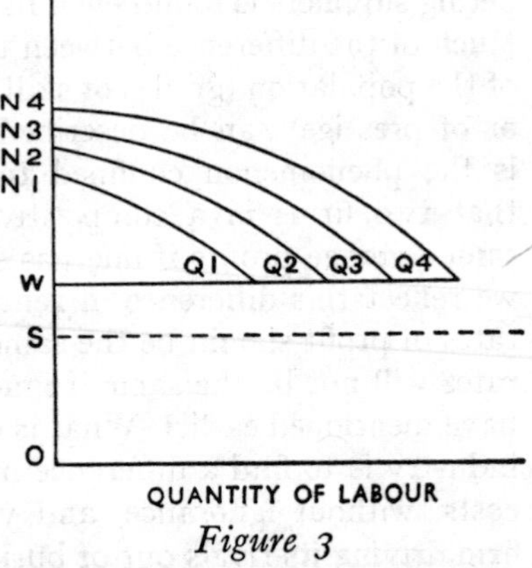

Figure 3

OS is as before average subsistence earnings, and *OW* the capitalist wage. WN_1Q_1 represents the surplus in the initial stage. Since some of this is reinvested, the amount of fixed capital increases. Hence the schedule of the marginal productivity of labour is now raised throughout, to the level of N_2Q_2. Both the surplus and capitalist employment are now larger. Further reinvestment raises the schedule of the marginal productivity of labour to N_3Q_3. And the process continues so long as there is surplus labour.

Various comments are needed in elaboration. First, as to the relationship between capital, technical progress, and productivity. In theory it should be possible to distinguish between the growth of capital and the growth of technical knowledge, but in practice it is neither possible nor necessary for this analysis. As a matter of statistical analysis, differentiating the effects of capital and of knowledge in any industry is straightforward if the product is homogeneous through time, if the physical inputs are also unchanged (in kind) and if the relative prices of the inputs have remained constant. But when we try to do it for any industry in practice we usually find that the product has changed, the inputs have changed and relative prices have changed, so that we get any number of indices of technical progress from the same data, according to the assumptions and the type of index number which we use. In any case, for the purpose of this analysis it is unnecessary to distinguish between capital formation and the growth of knowledge within the capitalist sector. Growth of technical knowledge outside the capitalist sector would be fundamentally important, since it would raise the level of wages, and so reduce the capitalist surplus. But inside the capitalist sector knowledge and capital work in the same direction, to raise the surplus and to increase employment. They also work together. The application of new technical knowledge usually requires new investment, and whether the new knowledge is capital-saving (and thus equivalent to an increase in capital) or labour-saving (and thus equivalent to an increase in the marginal productivity of labour) makes no difference to our diagram. Capital and technical knowledge also work together in the sense that in economies where techniques are stagnant savings are not so readily applied to increasing productive capital; in such economies it is more usual to use savings for building pyramids, churches, and other such durable consumer goods. Accordingly, in this analysis the growth of productive capital and the growth of technical knowledge are treated as a single phenomenon (just as we earlier decided that we could treat the growth of the supply of skilled labour and the growth of capital as a single phenomenon in long-run analysis).

Next we must consider more closely the capitalist surplus. Malthus wanted to know what the capitalists would do with this ever-growing surplus ; surely this would be an embarrassing glut of commodities ? Ricardo replied that there would be no glut ; what the capitalists did not consume themselves, they would use for paying the wages of workers to create more fixed capital (this is a free interpretation, since the classical economists associated the expansion of employment with an increase of circulating rather than of fixed capital). This new fixed capital would then in the next stage make possible the employment of more people in the capitalist sector. Malthus persisted ; why should the capitalists produce more capital to produce a larger surplus which could only be used for producing still more capital and so *ad infinitum* ? To this Marx supplied one answer : capitalists have a passion for accumulating capital. Ricardo supplied another : if they don't want to accumulate, they will consume instead of saving ; provided there is no propensity to hoard, there will be no glut. Employment in the next stage will not be as big as it would have been if they had created more fixed capital and so brought more workers into the capitalist sector, but so long as there is no hoarding it makes no difference to the current level of employment whether capitalists decide to consume or to save. Malthus then raised another question ; suppose that the capitalists do save and invest without hoarding, surely the fact that capital is growing more rapidly than consumption must so lower the rate of profit on capital that there comes a point when they decide that it is not worth while to invest ? This Ricardo replied, is impossible ; since the supply of labour is unlimited, you can always find employment for any amount of capital. This is absolutely correct, for his model ; in the neo-classical model capital grows faster than labour, and so one has to ask whether the rate of profit will not fall, but in the classical model the unlimited supply of labour means that the capital/labour ratio, and therefore the rate of surplus, can be held constant for any quantity of capital (i.e. unlimited 'widening' is possible). The only fly in the ointment is that there may develop a shortage of natural resources, so that though the capitalists get any amount of labour at a constant wage, they have to pay ever rising rents to landlords. This was what worried Ricardo; it was important to him to distinguish that part of the surplus which goes to landlords from that part which goes to capitalists, since he believed that economic development inevitably increases the relative scarcity of land. We are not so certain of this as he was. Certainly development increases the rent of urban sites fantastically, but its effect on rural rents depends on the rate of technical progress in agriculture, which Malthus and Ricardo both gravely underestimated. If we assume technical progress in agriculture, no hoarding, and unlimited labour at a constant wage, the rate of profit on capital cannot fall. On the contrary it must increase, since all the benefit of technical progress in the capitalist sector accrues to the capitalists.

Marx's interest in the surplus was ethical as well as scientific. He regarded it as robbery of the workers. His descendants are less certain of this. The surplus, after all, is only partly consumed; the other part is used for capital formation. As for the part which is consumed, some of it is a genuine payment for service rendered—for managerial or entrepreneurial services, as well as for the services of public administrators, whether these are paid salaries out of taxes, or whether they live off their rents or *rentes* while performing unpaid public duties as magistrates, lord-lieutenants, or the like. Even in the U.S.S.R. all these functionaries are paid out of the surplus, and handsomely paid too. It is arguable that these services are overpaid; this is why we have progressive taxation, and it is also one of the more dubious arguments for nationalization (more dubious because the functionaries of public corporations have to be paid the market rate if the economy is only partially nationalized). But it is not arguable that all this part of the surplus (i.e. the part consumed) morally belongs to the workers, in any sense. As for the part which is used for capital formation, the experience of the U.S.S.R. is that this is increased, and not reduced, by transforming the ownership of capital. Expropriation deprives the capitalists of control over this part of the surplus, and of the right to consume this part at some later date, but it does nothing whatever to transfer this part of the surplus to the workers. Marx's emotional approach was a natural reaction to the classical writers, who sometimes in unguarded moments wrote as if the capitalist surplus and its increase were all that counted in the national income (cf. Ricardo, who called it 'the net revenue' of production). All this, however, is by the way ; for our present interest is not in ethical questions, but in how the model works.

The central problem in the theory of economic development is to understand the process by which a community which was previously saving and investing 4 or 5 per cent of its national income or less, converts itself into an economy where voluntary saving is running at about 12 to 15 per cent of national income or more. This is the central problem because the central fact of economic development is rapid capital accumulation (including knowledge and skills with capital). We cannot explain any 'industrial' revolution (as the economic historians pretend to do) until we can explain why saving increased relatively to national income.

It is possible that the explanation is simply that some psychological change occurs which causes people to be more thrifty. This, however, is not a plausible explanation. We are interested not in the people in general, but only say in the 10 per cent of them with the largest incomes, who in countries with surplus labour receive up to 40 per cent of the national income (nearer 30 per cent in more developed countries). The remaining 90 per cent of the people never manage to save a significant fraction of their incomes. The important question is why does the top 10 per cent save more? The reason may be because they decide to consume less, but this reason does not square with the facts. There is no evidence of a fall in personal consumption by the top 10 per cent at a time when industrial revolutions are occurring. It is also possible that, though they do not save any more, the top 10 per cent spend less of their income on durable consumer goods (tombs, country houses, temples) and more on productive capital. Certainly, if one compares different civilizations this is a striking difference in the disposition of income. Civilizations in which there is a rapid growth of technical knowledge or expansion of other opportunities present more profitable outlets for investment than do technologically stagnant civilizations, and tempt capital into productive channels rather than into the building of monuments. But if one takes a country only over the course of the hundred years during which it undergoes a revolution in the rate of capital formation, there is no noticeable change in this regard. Certainly, judging by the novels, the top 10 per cent in England were not spending noticeably less on durable consumer goods in 1800 than they were in 1700.

Much the most plausible explanation is that people save more because they have more to save. This is not to say merely that the national income per head is larger, since there is no clear evidence that the proportion of the national income saved increases with national income per head—at any rate our fragmentary evidence for the United Kingdom and for the United States suggests that this is not so. The explanation is much more likely to be that saving increases relatively to the national income because the incomes of the savers increase relatively to the national income. The central fact of economic development is that the distribution of incomes is altered in favour of the saving class.

Practically all saving is done by people who receive profits or rents. Workers' savings are very small. The middle-classes save a little, but in practically every community the savings of the middle-classes out of their salaries are of little consequence for productive investment. Most members of the middle-class are engaged in the perpetual struggle to keep up with the Jones's; if they manage to save enough to buy the house in which they live, they are doing well. They may save to educate their children, or to subsist in their old age, but this saving is virtually offset by the savings being used up for the same purposes. Insurance is the middle-class's favourite form of saving in modern societies, yet in the U.K., where the habit is extremely well developed, the annual net increase in insurance funds from all classes, rich, middle, and poor is less than 1½ per cent of the national income. It is doubtful if the wage and salary classes ever anywhere save as much as 3 per cent of the national income, net (possible exception: Japan). If we are interested in savings, we must concentrate attention upon profits and rents.

For our purpose it does not matter whether profits are distributed or undistributed; the major source of savings is profits, and if we find that savings are increasing as a proportion of the national income, we may take it for granted that this is because the share of profits in the national income is increasing. (As a refinement, for highly taxed communities, we should say profits net of taxes upon profits, whether personal income or corporate taxes.) Our problem then becomes what are the circumstances in which the share of profits in the national income increases ?

The modified classical model which we are using here has the virtue of answering the question. In the beginning, the national income consists almost entirely of subsistence income. Abstracting from population growth and assuming that the marginal product of labour is zero, this subsistence income remains constant throughout the expansion, since by definition labour can be yielded up to the expanding capitalist sector without reducing subsistence output. The process therefore increases the capitalist surplus and the income of capitalist employees, taken together, as a proportion of the national income. It is possible to imagine conditions in which the surplus nevertheless does not increase relatively to national income. This requires that capitalist employment should expand relatively much faster than the surplus, so that within the capitalist sector gross margins or profit plus rent are falling sharply relatively to wages. We know that this does not happen. Even if gross margins were constant, profits in our model would be increasing relatively to national income. But gross margins are not likely to be constant in our model, which assumes that practically the whole benefit of capital accumulation and of technical progress goes into the surplus ; because real wages are constant, all that the workers get out of the expansion is that more of them are employed at a wage above the subsistence earnings. The model says, in effect, that if unlimited supplies of labour are available at a constant real wage, and if any part of profits is reinvested in productive capacity, profits will grow continuously relatively to the national income, and capital formation will also grow relatively to the national income.

The model also covers the case of a technical revolution. Some historians have suggested that the capital for the British Industrial Revolution came out of profits made possible by a spate of inventions occurring together. This is extremely hard to fit into the neo-classical model, since it involves the assumption that these inventions raised the marginal productivity of capital more than they raised the marginal productivity of labour, a proposition which it is hard to establish in any economy where labour is scarce. (If we do not make this assumption, other incomes rise just as fast as profits, and investment does not increase relatively to national income.) On the other hand the suggestion fits beautifully into the modified classical model, since in this model practically the whole benefit of inventions goes into the surplus, and becomes available for further capital accumulation.

This model also helps us to face squarely the nature of the economic problem of backward countries. If we ask, 'Why do they save so little?', the truthful answer is not 'Because they are so poor', as we might be tempted to conclude from the path-breaking and praiseworthy correlations of Mr Colin Clark. The truthful answer is 'Because their capitalist sector is so small' (remembering that 'capitalist' here does not mean private capitalist, but would apply equally to state capitalist). If they had a larger capitalist sector, profits would be a greater part of their national income, and saving and investment would also be relatively larger. (The state capitalist can accumulate capital even faster than the private capitalist, since he can use for the purpose not only the profits of the capitalist sector, but also what he can force or tax out of the subsistence sector.)

Another point which we must note is that though the increase of the capitalist sector involves an increase in the inequality of incomes, as between capitalists and the rest, mere inequality of income is not enough to ensure a high level of saving. In point of fact the inequality of income is *greater* in overpopulated underdeveloped countries than it is in advanced industrial nations, for the simple reason that agricultural rents are so high in the former. Eighteenth century British economists took it for granted that the landlord class is given to prodigal consumption rather than to productive investment, and this is certainly true of landlords in underdeveloped countries. Hence, given two countries of equal incomes, in which distribution is more unequal in one than in the other, savings may be greater where distribution is more equal if profits are higher relatively to rents. It is the inequality which goes with profits that favours capital formation, and not the inequality which goes with rents. Correspondingly, it is very hard to argue that these countries cannot afford to save more, when 40 per cent or so of the national income is going to the top 10 per cent, and so much of rent incomes is squandered.

Behind this analysis also lies the sociological problem of the emergence of a capitalist class, that is to say of a group of men who think in terms of investing capital productively. The dominant classes in backward economies—landlords, traders, moneylenders, priests, soldiers, princes—do not normally think in these terms. What causes a society to grow a capitalist class is a very difficult question, to which probably, there is no general answer. Most countries seem to begin by importing their capitalists from abroad; and in these days many (e.g. U.S.S.R., India) are growing a class of state capitalists who, for political reasons of one sort or another, are determined to create capital rapidly on public account. As for indigenous private capitalists, their emergence is probably bound up with the emergence of new opportunities, especially something that widens the market, associated with some new technique which greatly increases the productivity of labour if labour and capital are used together. Once a capitalist sector has emerged, it is only a matter of time before it becomes sizeable. If very little technical progress is occurring, the surplus will grow only slowly. But if for one reason or another the opportunities for using capital productively increase rapidly, the surplus will also grow rapidly, and the capitalist class with it.

In our model so far capital is created only out of profits earned. In the real world, however, capitalists also create capital as a result of a net increase in the supply of money—especially bank credit. We have now also to take account of this.

In the neo-classical model capital can be created only by withdrawing resources from producing consumer goods. In our model, however, there is surplus labour, and if (as we shall assume) its marginal productivity is zero, and if, also, capital can be created by labour without withdrawing scarce land and capital from other uses, then capital can be created without reducing the output of consumer goods. This second proviso is important, since if we need capital or land to make capital the results in our model are the same as the results in the neo-classical model, despite the fact that there is surplus labour. However, in practice the proviso is often fulfilled. Food cannot be grown without land, but roads, viaducts, irrigation channels and buildings can be created by human labour with hardly any capital to speak of—witness the Pyramids, or the marvellous railway tunnels built in the mid-nineteenth century almost with bare hands. Even in modern industrial countries constructional activity, which lends itself to hand labour, is as much as 50 or 60 per cent of gross fixed investment, so it is not difficult to think of labour creating capital without using any but the simplest tools. The classical economists were not wrong in thinking of lack of circulating capital as being a more serious obstacle to expansion in their world than lack of fixed capital. In the analysis which follows in this section we assume that surplus labour cannot be used to make consumer goods without using up more land or capital, but can be used to make capital goods without using any scarce factors.

If a community is short of capital, and has idle resources which can be set to creating capital, it seems very desirable on the face of the matter that this should be done, even if it means creating extra money to finance the extra employment. There is no loss of other output while the new capital is being made, and when it comes into use it will raise output and employment in just the same way as would capital financed not by credit creation but out of profits. The difference between profit-financed and credit-financed capital is not in the ultimate effects on output, but in the immediate effects on prices and on the distribution of income.

Before we come to the effects on prices, however, we should pause a moment to notice what happens to the output of consumer goods in this model and the others while credit-financed capital is being created, but before it begins to be used. In the neo-classical model an increase in capital formation has to be accompanied by a corresponding fall in the output of consumer goods, since scarce resources can do one or the other. In the Keynesian model an increase in capital formation also increases the output of consumer goods, and if the multiplier exceeds 2, the output of consumer goods increases even more than capital formation. In our model capital formation goes up, but the output of consumer goods is not immediately affected. This is one of those crucial cases where it is important to be certain that one is using the right model when it comes to giving advice on economic policy.

In our model, if surplus labour is put to capital formation and paid out of new money, prices rise, because the stream of money purchases is swollen while the output of consumer goods is for the time being constant. What is happening is that the fixed amount of consumer goods is being redistributed, towards the workers newly employed, away from the rest of the community (this is where the lack of circulating capital comes into the picture). This process is not 'forced saving' in the useful sense of that term. In the neo-classical model the output of consumer goods is reduced, forcing the community as a whole to save. In our model, however, consumer-goods output is not at any time reduced ; there is a forced redistribution of consumption, but not forced saving. And, of course, as soon as the capital goods begin to yield output, consumption begins to rise.

This inflationary process does not go on for ever ; it comes to an end when voluntary savings increase to a level where they are equal to the inflated level of investment. Since savings are a function of profits, this means that the inflation continues until profits increase so much relatively to the national income that capitalists can now finance the higher rate of investment out of their profits without any further recourse to monetary expansion. Essentially equilibrium is secured by raising the ratio of profits to the national income. The equilibrator need not however be profits ; it might equally be government receipts, if there is a structure of taxes such that the ratio of government receipts to the national income rises automatically as the national income rises. This seems to be just about what happened in the U.S.S.R. In the crucial years when the economy was being transformed from a 5 per cent to a (probably) 20 per cent net saver, there was a tremendous inflation of prices (apparently prices rose about 700 per cent in a decade), but the inflationary profits largely went to the government in the form of turnover tax, and by the end of the decade a new equilibrium was in sight.

It is not, however, always a simple matter to raise profits relatively to national income simply by turning on the monetary tap. The simplest and most extreme model of an inflation would be to assume that when the capitalists finance capital formation by creating credit, the money all comes back to them in the very next round in the form of an increase in their profits. In such a model profits, voluntary savings and capital formation can be raised to any desired level in a very short time, with only a small increase in prices. Something like this may well apply in the U.S.S.R. In real terms, however, this implies that there has been a fall in the share of the national income received by other people, including a fall in their real consumption, since they have had to release consumer goods for the previously unemployed who are now engaged in capital formation. It may be the farmers who are worse off, this showing itself in the prices of manufactures rising relatively to farm prices. Or it may be the workers in the capitalist sector who are worse off, because farm prices and the prices of manufactures rise faster than their wages. Or the blow may be falling upon salaried workers, pensioners, landlords or creditors. Now in the real world none of these classes will take this lying down. In the U.S.S.R., where the intention was that the capital formation should be at the expense of the farmers, it led in the end to organized violence on both sides. In our model it is hard to get away with it at the expense of the workers, since the wage in the capitalist sector must stand at a certain minimum level above subsistence earnings if labour is to be available. Generally, what happens as prices rise is that new contracts have to be made to take account of rising price levels. Some classes get caught, but only temporarily.

Now, if one pursued this argument logically, it would lead to the conclusion that equilibrium could never be reached—at any rate, so long as the banking system is content to supply all 'legitimate' demands for money. If none of the other classes can be soaked, it seems impossible for profits to rise relatively to the national income for more than a temporary space, and it therefore seems impossible to reach an equilibrium level of savings equal to the new level of investment. The inflation, once begun, goes on for ever. This, however, is not possible for another reason, namely the fact that the real national income is not fixed, but rising, as a result of the capital formation. Therefore all that is required is that capitalists' real incomes rise faster than other people's. Beyond the first year or two, when the additional consumer goods begin to appear, it is not necessary for any class to reduce its consumption. By the time the process of recontracting has begun, output has also begun to rise, and it is therefore possible to reach a *modus vivendi*.

We can give an exact description of this equilibrium in our modified classical model. In this model the average subsistence real income is given, and so also therefore is the real wage in the capitalist sector. It is not possible, by inflation or otherwise, to reach a new equilibrium in which the capitalist surplus has increased at the expense of either of these. If, therefore, the capitalists begin to finance capital formation out of credit, they lower the real incomes of the others only temporarily. Wages would then be chasing prices continuously but for the fact that, since output is growing all the time, profits are growing all the time. Hence the part of the investment which is financed out of credit is diminishing all the time, until equilibrium is reached. For example, suppose that an investment of £100 a year yields £20 a year profit, of which £10 a year is saved. Then, if capitalists invest an extra £100 a year, all of which in the first year is financed out of credit, by the eleventh year profits will be £200 a year greater, savings will be £100 a year greater and there will be no further monetary pressure on prices. All that will remain from the episode is that there will be £1,000 more useful productive capital at work than there would have if the credit creation had not taken place.

Thus we have two simple models marking the extreme cases. In the first, all the credit created comes back to the capitalists at once as profits (or to the state capitalist as taxes). Equilibrium is then reached easily, with the capitalists gaining at the expense of all others. In the other model the capitalists can only gain temporarily ; equilibrium then takes much longer to reach, but it is reached eventually. In the first case we need only an expansion of money income ; but in the second case it is the expansion of real income which eventually brings the capitalists the required proportion of the national income.

The fact that capital formation increases real output must also be borne in mind in the analysis of the effects of credit creation upon prices. The inflations which loom most in our minds are those which occur in war-time, when resources are being withdrawn from producing consumer goods. If the supply of money is increasing while the output of goods is falling, anything can happen to prices. Inflation for the purpose of capital formation, however, is a very different kettle of fish. For it results in increasing consumer-goods output, and this results in falling prices if the quantity of money is held constant.

Perhaps it may be as well to illustrate a simple case. Suppose that £100 is invested every year, in the first instance by creating credit, and that each investment yields £30 a year in its second year and after. Suppose that it costs nothing to reap the yield; the price of £30 charged for the product being pure rent derived from its scarcity (investment in an irrigation works is a nearly perfect illustration). Then, if we use the Keynesian formula for a demand inflation, and assume the multiplier to be 2, money income will rise to an equilibrium level of + £200 a year. Output, however, will begin to increase by + £30 a year from the second year onward. By the eighth year output will have increased by + £210, while money income will have increased only by slightly less than + £200. Thereafter prices will be below the initial level, and will fall continuously. The alleged precision of this analysis is of course subject to all the usual objections against applying multiplier analysis to inflationary conditions, namely the instability of the propensity to consume, the effect of secondary investment, and the dangers of cost inflation. But though the precision is spurious, the result is nevertheless real. Inflation for purposes of capital formation is self-destructive. Prices begin to rise, but are sooner or later overtaken by rising output, and may, in the last state, end up lower than they were at the beginning.

We may now sum up this section. Capital formation is financed not only out of profits but also out of an expansion of credit. This speeds up the growth of capital, and the growth of real income. It also results in some redistribution of the national income, either temporarily or permanently, according to the assumptions one makes—in the model we are using, the redistribution is only temporary. It also prevents prices from falling, as they otherwise would (if money is constant and output rising), and it may drive prices up substantially if (as in our model) the distribution of income cannot be altered permanently by monetary measures, since prices will then continue to rise until real output has risen enough to effect the required redistribution. Thereafter prices fall further, since inflation raises prices while capital is being created, but the increased output which then results brings them down again.

One point remains. We have seen that if new money is used to finance capital formation the rise of prices eventually peters out, as savings grow into equilibrium with investment; and reverses itself, as the output of consumer goods begins to pour out. The new equilibrium, however, may take a long time to reach, and if also the flow of new money is substantial the resulting rise of prices may strike fear into the hearts of the public. People do not panic if prices rise for two or three years; but after that they may begin to lose confidence in money, and it may become necessary to call a drastic halt. This is the most important practical limitation on the extent to which capital formation can be financed in this way. This is why the banking authorities have always tended to alternate short periods of easy credit with sharp periods of restriction. Bank credit moves three steps up and one step down instead of moving up continuously. This also brings us to the threshold of the trade cycle. If capital were financed exclusively out of profits, and if there were also no hoarding, capital formation would proceed steadily. It is mainly the existence of an elastic credit system which makes the trade cycle an integral part of the mechanism of economic development in an unplanned economy. It is not necessary, however, for us to enter into analysis of the cycle since in this respect the model we are using does not yield results different from those of other models.

We have said very little so far about the activities of government, since our basic model uses only capitalists, their employees, and subsistence producers. Governments affect the process of capital accumulation in many ways, however, and not least by the inflations into which they run. Many governments in backward countries are also currently anxious to use surplus manpower for capital formation, and as there is a great deal that can be done with labour and a few tools (roads, irrigation, river walls, schools and so on), it is useful to say something on the subject. We shall therefore in this section analyse the effect of inflation-financed government formation of capital, and thereby also give ourselves the chance to recapitulate the analysis of the previous section.

The results, it will be remembered, lie within two extremes. At one extreme all the money spent by the government comes back to it in taxes, and this is accepted by all classes. In this case, prices rise very little. At the other extreme, all classes refuse to accept a redistribution between themselves and the government. In this case prices tend to rise continuously, except that rising output (as a result of the capital formed) sooner or later catches up with prices and brings them down again. Rising output will also increase the government's 'normal' share of the national income, and all monetary pressure will cease when the 'normal' share has risen to the level of the inflated share which it was trying to get.

These results give us the questions we must ask. (1) What part of marginal income returns automatically to the government? (2) What effect does inflation have upon the various classes? And (3) What effect has government capital formation upon output?

(One other point must be remembered. In all this analysis so far we have assumed a closed economy. In an open economy inflation plays havoc with the balance of payments. We have therefore to assume that the government has strict control over foreign transactions. This assumption holds for some backward economies; others would get into an awful mess if they launched upon inflationary finance.)

It is not possible that all the money spent by the government should come back to it in the first round, since this would presume that the government took 100 per cent of marginal income. If the government takes any part of marginal income, some of the money will come back to it; but even the Keynesian multiplier will not bring it all back unless taxation is the only leakage (i.e. there is no saving). The larger the government's share of marginal incomes, the more it will get back, the quicker it will get it, and the smaller will be the effect on prices.

Since the second world war a number of governments of modern industrial states seem to be taking around 40 to 50 per cent of marginal incomes in taxation, and this is one of the major reasons why their price levels have not risen more, despite heavy pressure on resources for capital formation, defence, etc. In backward countries, however, governments take only a very small part of marginal incomes. The best placed governments from this point of view are those in countries where output is concentrated in a few large units (mines, plantations) and therefore easily taxed, or where foreign trade is a large part of the national income, and is thus easily reached by import and export duties. One of the worst off is India, with a large part of its output produced by subsistence producers and small scale units, hard to reach, and with less than 10 per cent of national income passing in foreign trade. In many cases, marginal taxation is less than average taxation, for when money incomes rise, the government continues to charge the same prices for railway travel or for stamps, and hesitates to raise land taxes on the peasants, with the result that money incomes rise faster than government receipts. No government should consider deficit financing without assuring itself that a large part of increases in money income will automatically come back to itself. By contrast, the U.S.S.R., with its very high rate of turnover tax, automatically mops up surplus funds injected into the system, before they are able to generate much demand inflation *via* the multiplier process.

The next question is the effect of inflation upon the distribution of income. The surplus money raises prices, some more than others. The government will probably try to prevent prices from rising, but will succeed better with some than with others. It is easy to apply price control to large-scale enterprises, but very hard to prevent the farmers from raising food prices, or the petty traders from making big margins. From the point of view of capital formation, the best thing that can happen is for the surplus money to roll into the pockets of people who will reinvest it productively. The merchant classes would probably use it mainly for speculation in those commodities that are getting scarce. The middle-classes would mainly buy big American cars with it, or go on trips to Europe, wangling the foreign exchange somehow. The peasants ought to use it to improve their farms, but probably most would use it only to pay off debt, or to buy more land. There is really only one class that is pretty certain to reinvest its profits productively, and that is the class of industrialists. The effects of an inflation on secondary capital formation therefore depend first on how large the industrial class is, and secondly on whether the benefit goes largely to this class. In countries which have only a small industrial class, inflation leads mainly to speculation in commodities and in land, and to the hoarding of foreign exchange. But in any country which has a substantial industrialist class, with the passion this class has for ruling over bigger and better factories, even the most frightening inflations (e.g. Germany from 1919) leave behind a substantial increase in capital formation. (Have we hit here upon some deep psychological instinct which drives the industrialist to use his wealth more creatively than others ? Probably not. It is just that his job is of the kind where passion for success results in capital formation. The peasant farmer wants to have more land, not more capital on his land [unless he is a modern capitalist farmer] so his passion is dissipated merely in changes in the price and distribution of land. The merchant wants to have a wider margin, or a quicker turnover, neither of which increases fixed capital. The banker wants more deposits. Only the industrialist's passion drives towards using profits to create a bigger empire of bricks and steel.) It follows that it is in industrial communities that inflations are most helpful to capital formation ; whereas in countries where the industrial class is negligible there is nothing to show for the inflation when it is over, except the original investment which started it off. We should also note that many governments do not like the fact that inflation enables industrialists to earn the extra profits with which they create fixed capital, since this results in an increase of private fortunes. They therefore do all they can to prevent the inflation from increasing the profits of industrialists. More especially, they clamp down on industrial prices, which are also from the administrative point of view the easiest prices to control. Since it is the industrialist class which saves most, the result is to exacerbate the inflation. It would be much sounder to pursue policies which would result in the profits of industrialists rising more rapidly than other incomes, and then to tax these profits away, either immediately, or at death.

Inflation continues to be generated so long as the community is not willing to hold an amount equal to the increased investment expenditure. It is not therefore enough that savings should increase to this extent, for if these savings are used for additional investment the initial gap still remains. The gap is closed only if the savings are hoarded, or used to buy government bonds, so that the government can now finance its investments by borrowing, instead of by creating new money. Hence in practice, if the government wishes the inflation to be ended without reducing its investment, it must find means of bringing into its coffers as much in taxes or in loans as it is spending. If it is failing to do this, the inflation will continue ; it is then better that it should continue because capitalists are spending their profits on further capital formation than because other classes are chasing a limited output of consumer goods ; but if it is desired to end inflation as soon as possible, all classes should be encouraged to invest in government bonds rather than to spend in other ways.

Finally we come to the relation between capital and output. If the intention is to finance capital formation by creating credit, the best objects for such a policy are those which yield a large income quickly. To finance school building by creating credit is asking for trouble. On the other hand, there are a lot of agricultural programmes (water supplies, fertilizers, seed farms, extension) where quick and substantial results may be expected from modest expenditure. If there are idle resources available for capital formation it is foolish not to use them simply because of technical or political difficulties in raising taxes. But it would be equally foolish to use them on programmes which take a long time to give a small result, when there are others which could give a large result quickly.

We may sum up as follows. If labour is abundant and physical resources scarce, the primary effect on output is exactly the same whether the government creates capital out of taxation or out of credit creation : the output of consumer goods is unchanged, but is redistributed. Hence credit creation must be seen primarily as an alternative to taxation, which is worth the troubles it brings only if trying to raise taxes would bring even more troubles. Credit creation has however one further lead upon taxation in that if it also redistributes income towards the industrial class (if there is an industrial class), it will speed up capital formation out of profits. If it is impossible to increase taxation, and the alternative is between creating capital out of credit, and not creating it at all, the choice one has then to make is between stable prices or rising output. There is no simple formula for making this choice. In some communities any further inflation of prices would ruin their fragile social or political equilibrium ; in others this equilibrium will be destroyed if there is not a sharp increase in output in the near future ; and in still others the equilibrium will be ruined either way.

We may now resume our analysis. We have seen that if unlimited labour is available at a constant real wage, the capitalist surplus will rise continuously, and annual investment will be a rising proportion of the national income. Needless to say, this cannot go on for ever.

The process must stop when capital accumulation has caught up with population, so that there is no longer surplus labour. But it may stop before that. It may stop of course for any number of reasons which are outside our system of analysis, ranging from earthquake or bubonic plague to social revolution. But it may also stop for the economic reason that, although there is a labour surplus, real wages may nevertheless rise so high as to reduce capitalists' profits to the level at which profits are all consumed and there is no net investment.

This may happen for one of four reasons. First, if capital accumulation is proceeding faster than population growth, and is therefore reducing absolutely the number of people in the subsistence sector, the average product per man in that sector rises automatically, not because production alters, but because there are fewer mouths to share the product. After a while the change actually becomes noticeable, and the capitalist wage begins to be forced up. Secondly, the increase in the size of the capitalist sector relatively to the subsistence sector may turn the terms of trade against the capitalist sector (if they are producing different things) and so force the capitalists to pay workers a higher percentage of their product, in order to keep their real income constant. Thirdly, the subsistence sector may also become more productive in the technical sense. For example, it may begin to imitate the techniques of the capitalist sector ; the peasants may get hold of some of the new seeds, or hear about the new fertilizers or rotations. They may also benefit directly from some of the capitalist investments, e.g., in irrigation works, in transport facilities, or in electricity. Anything which raises the productivity of the subsistence sector (average person) will raise real wages in the capitalist sector, and will therefore reduce the capitalist surplus and the rate of capital accumulation, unless it at the same time more than correspondingly moves the terms of trade against the subsistence sector. Alternatively, even if the productivity of the capitalist sector is unchanged, the workers in the capitalist sector may imitate the capitalist way of life, and may thus need more to live on. The subsistence level is only a conventional idea, and conventions change. The effect of this would be to widen the gap between earnings in the subsistence sector, and wages in the capitalist sector. This is hard to do, if labour is abundant, but it may be achieved by a combination of trade union pressure and capitalist conscience. If it is achieved, it will reduce the capitalist surplus, and also the rate of capital accumulation.

The most interesting of these possibilities is that the terms of trade may move against the capitalist sector. This assumes that the capitalist and subsistence sectors are producing different things. In practice this is a question of the relationship between industry and agriculture. If the capitalists are investing in plantation agriculture side by side with their investment in industry, we can think of the capitalist sector as self-contained. The expansion of this sector does not then generate any demand for anything produced in the subsistence sector, and there are therefore no terms of trade to upset the picture we have drawn. To bring the terms of trade in, the simplest assumption to make is that the subsistence sector consists of peasants producing food, while the capitalist sector produces everything else.

Now if the capitalist sector produces no food, its expansion increases the demand for food, raises the price of food in terms of capitalist products, and so reduces profits. This is one of the senses in which industrialization is dependent upon agricultural improvement ; it is not profitable to produce a growing volume of manufactures unless agricultural production is growing simultaneously. This is also why industrial and agrarian revolutions always go together, and why economies in which agriculture is stagnant do not show industrial development. Hence, if we postulate that the capitalist sector is not producing food, we must either postulate that the subsistence sector is increasing its output, or else conclude that the expansion of the capitalist sector will be brought to an end through adverse terms of trade eating into profits. (Ricardo's problem of increasing rents is first cousin to this conclusion ; he worried about rents increasing *inside* the capitalist sector, whereas we are dealing with rents *outside* the sector.)

On the other hand, if we assume that the subsistence sector is producing more food, while we escape the Scylla of adverse terms of trade we may be caught by the Charybdis of real wages rising because the subsistence sector is more productive. We escape both Scylla and Charybdis if rising productivity in the subsistence sector is more than offset by improving terms of trade. However, if the subsistence sector is producing food, the elasticity of demand for which is less than unity, increases in productivity will be more than offset by reductions in price. A rise in the productivity of the subsistence sector hurts the capitalist sector if there is no trade between the two, or if the demand of the capitalist sector for the subsistence sector's product is elastic. On the assumptions we have made, a rise in food productivity benefits the capitalist sector. Nevertheless, when we take rising demand into account, it is not at all unlikely that the price of food will not fall as fast as productivity increases, and this will force the capitalists to pay out a larger part of their product as wages.

If there is no hope of prices falling as fast as productivity increases (because demand is increasing), the capitalists' next best move is to prevent the farmer from getting all his extra production. In Japan this was achieved by raising rents against the farmers, and by taxing them more heavily, so that a large part of the rapid increase in productivity which occurred (between 1880 and 1910 it doubled) was taken away from the farmers and used for capital formation ; at the same time the holding down of the farmers' income itself held down wages, to the advantage of profits in the capitalist sector. Much the same happened in the U.S.S.R., where farm incomes per head were held down, in spite of farm mechanization and the considerable release of labour to the towns ; this was done jointly by raising the prices of manufactures relatively to farm products, and also by levying heavy taxes upon the collective farms.

This also defines for us the case in which it is true to say that it is agriculture which finances industrialization. If the capitalist sector is self-contained, its expansion is in no way dependent upon the peasants. The surplus is wholly 'at the expense' of the workers in the capitalist sector. But if the capitalist sector depends upon the peasants for food, it is essential to get the peasants to produce more, while if at the same time they can be prevented from enjoying the full fruit of their extra production, wages can be reduced relatively to the capitalist surplus. By contrast a state which is ruled by peasants may be happy and prosperous, but it is not likely to show such a rapid accumulation of capital. (E.g., will China and the U.S.S.R. diverge in this respect ?)

We conclude, therefore, that the expansion of the capitalist sector may be stopped because the price of subsistence goods rises, or because the price is not falling as fast as subsistence productivity per head is rising, or because capitalist workers raise their standard of what they need for subsistence. Any of these would raise wages relatively to the surplus. If none of these processes is enough to stop capital accumulation, the capitalist sector will continue to expand until there is no surplus labour left. This can happen even if population is growing. For example, if it takes 3 per cent of annual income invested to employ 1 per cent more people, an annual net investment of 12 per cent can cope with as much as a 4 per cent increase in population. But population in Western Europe at the relevant times grew only by 1 per cent or so per annum (which is also the present rate of growth in India), and rates of growth exceeding $2\frac{1}{2}$ per cent per annum are even now rather rare. We cannot say that capital will always grow faster than labour (it obviously has not done so in Asia), but we can say that if conditions are favourable for the capitalist surplus to grow more rapidly than population, there must come a day when capital accumulation has caught up with labour supply. Ricardo and Malthus did not provide for this in their models, because they overestimated the rate of growth of population. Marx did not provide for it either, because he had persuaded himself that capital accumulation increases unemployment instead of reducing it. (He has a curious model in which the short-run effect of accumulation is to reduce unemployment, raise wages and thus provoke a crisis, while the long-run effect is to increase the reserve army of unemployed.) Of the classical economists only Adam Smith saw clearly that capital accumulation would eventually create a shortage of labour, and raise wages above the subsistence level.

When the labour surplus disappears our model of the closed economy no longer holds. Wages are no longer tied to a subsistence level. Adam Smith thought they would then depend upon the degree of monopoly (a doctrine which was re-presented in the 1930s as one of the novelties of modern economic analysis). The neo-classicists invented the doctrine of marginal productivity. The problem is not yet solved to anyone's satisfaction, except in static models which take no account of capital accumulation and of technical progress. It is, however, outside the terms of reference of this essay and we will not pursue it here.

Our task is not, however, finished. In the classical world all countries have surplus labour. In the neo-classical world labour is scarce in all countries. In the real world, however, countries which achieve labour scarcity continue to be surrounded by others which have abundant labour. Instead of concentrating on one country, and examining the expansion of its capitalist sector, we now have to see this country as part of the expanding capitalist sector of the world economy as a whole, and to enquire how the distribution of income inside the country and its rate of capital accumulation, are affected by the fact that there is abundant labour available elsewhere at a subsistence wage.

The Open Economy

When capital accumulation catches up with the labour supply, wages begin to rise above the subsistence level, and the capitalist surplus is adversely affected. However, if there is still surplus labour in other countries, the capitalists can avoid this in one of two ways, by encouraging immigration or by exporting their capital to countries where there is still abundant labour at a subsistence wage. We must examine each of these in turn.

Let us first clear out of the way the effects of the immigration of skilled workers, since our main concern is with an abundant immigration of unskilled workers released by the subsistence sectors of other countries. It is theoretically possible that the immigration of skilled workers may reduce the demand for the services of native unskilled workers, but this is most unlikely. More probably it will make possible new investments and industries which were not possible before, and will thus increase the demand for all kinds of labour, relatively to its supply.

We must also get out of the way relatively small immigrations. If 100,000 Puerto Ricans emigrate to the United States every year, the effect on U.S. wages is negligible. U.S. wages are not pulled down to the Puerto Rican level; it is Puerto Rican wages which are then pulled up to the U.S. level.

Mass immigration is quite a different kettle of fish. If there were free immigration from India and China to the U.S.A., the wage level of the U.S.A. would certainly be pulled down towards the Indian and Chinese levels. In fact in a competitive model the U.S. wage could exceed the Asian wage only by an amount covering migration costs plus the 'cliff' to which we have already referred. The result is the same whether one assumes increasing or diminishing returns to labour. Wages are constant at subsistence level plus. All the benefit of increasing returns goes into the capitalist surplus.

This is one of the reasons why, in every country where the wage level is relatively high, the trade unions are bitterly hostile to immigration, except of people in special categories, and take steps to have it restricted. The result is that real wages are higher than they would otherwise be, while profits, capital resources, and total output are smaller than they would otherwise be.

The export of capital is therefore a much easier way out for the capitalists, since trade unions are quick to restrict immigration, but much slower in bringing the export of capital under control.

The effect of exporting capital is to reduce the creation of fixed capital at home, and therefore to reduce the demand for labour. Labour will still be required to create the capital (e.g. to make machines for export), but domestic labour will no longer be required to work with the capital, as it would also be if the capital were invested at home.

This, however, is only one side of the picture, for the capital may be used in foreign countries in ways which raise the standard of living of the capital-exporting country (and so offset wholly or partly the first effect), or in ways which lower it (thus aggravating the first effect). The result depends on the type of competition which there is between the capital-exporting and the capital-importing countries.

Let us assume, to begin with, that there is no competition, and even no trade. Both countries are self-sufficient. Wages however are rising in country *A*, while labour is abundant in country *B*. *A's* capitalists therefore invest their capital in *B*. Trade returns show first the export surplus from *A*, representing the transfer of capital, and later the import surplus representing the return home of dividends. There is no effect on the workers in *A* other than that their wages cease to rise, as they would have if the capital were invested instead at home. If *A's* resources and *B's* resources are exactly the same, wages cannot rise in *A* until capital accumulation in *B* has wiped out *B's* labour surplus.

Now in the real world the resources of two countries are not exactly alike, and it cannot be taken for granted that it will be more profitable to invest in *B* if profits are falling in *A* (which also cannot be taken for granted). The profitability of investing in a country depends upon its natural resources, upon its human material, and upon the amount of capital already invested there.

The most productive investments are those which are made to open up rich, easily accessible natural resources, such as fertile soil, ores, coal or oil. This is the principal reason why most of the capital exported in the last hundred years went to the Americas and to Australasia rather than to India or to China, where the known resources were already being used. In the well developed parts of the world (in the resource sense) the main opportunity for productive investment lies in improving techniques—these countries are well (even over-) developed in the resource sense, but underdeveloped in their techniques. It is profitable to use capital to introduce new techniques, but this is not as profitable as using capital to make available both new techniques and also new resources. This also explains why the United Kingdom rapidly became a capital-exporting country (the limits of its natural resources were soon reached), whereas the United States is very late in reaching this stage, since its natural resources are so extensive that capital investment at home is still very profitable even though wages are very high.

Productivity depends also on the human material. Even though the genetic composition of peoples may be much the same, as far as potential productivity may be concerned, their cultural inheritance is very different. Differences in literacy, forms of government, attitudes to work, and social relations generally may make a big difference to productivity. Capitalists naturally find it more profitable and safer to invest in countries where the atmosphere is capitalist than they do in widely different cultures.

But this is not all. For the productivity of investment in *B* depends not only upon *B's* natural resources and its human institutions, but also upon the efficiency of all other industries whose services the new investment would require to use. This depends partly upon how highly capitalized these other industries are. The productivity of one investment depends upon other investments having been made before. Hence it may be more profitable to invest capital in countries which already have a lot of capital than to invest it in a new country. If this were always so, no capital would be exported, and the gap between wages in the surplus (labour) and non-surplus countries would not diminish but would widen. In practice capital export is small, and the gap does widen, and we cannot at all exclude the possibility that there is a natural tendency for capital to flow towards the capitalized, and to shun the uncapitalized.

If we could assume that there is a natural tendency for the rate of profit to fall in a closed economy, we could say that however low the rate may be in other countries, the rate in the closed economy must ultimately fall towards the level elsewhere, after which capital export must begin. Practically all the best known economists of every school, in every century, have affirmed that such a tendency exists, though their reasons have varied widely. The most notable exception is Marshall, who gave the right answer, which is that increasing capital per head tends to lower the yield of capital, while increasing technical knowledge tends to raise it. Thus, said Marshall, the yield fell from 10 per cent in the Middle Ages to 3 per cent in the middle of the eighteenth century—a long period of slow technical growth—after which the decline was arrested by the great increase in opportunities for using capital. This being so, the natural tendency for the yield of capital to fall is nothing but a popular myth. The yield may fall or it may not ; we cannot foretell.

We get a different answer, however, if we turn from the rate of profit on capital in general to the rate in particular lines of investment. In any particular line the possibilities of further expansion are soon exhausted, or at any rate greatly reduced. All industries develop on a logistic pattern, growing fairly slowly at first, then rapidly, and later on growing again quite slowly. Hence the investors in any particular line sooner or later come to a point where there is not much more scope for investment in that line at home. It is open to them to put their accumulating profits into quite different industries. But there is also the temptation to stick to the field in which they have specialized knowledge, and to use their profits to take the industry into new countries.

What brings about the exportation of capital is not inevitably falling home profits, or rising wages at home, but simply the fact that foreign countries having different resources unutilized in different degrees there are some profitable opportunities for investment abroad. This is not even dependent on capital accumulation having caught up with surplus labour at home; for even if there is still surplus labour at home, available at subsistence wages, investment opportunities abroad may be more profitable. Many capitalists residing in surplus labour countries invest their capital in England or the United States.

We must therefore beware of saying that a country will begin to export capital as soon as capital accumulation at home catches up with labour supply. All the same, countries do export capital, and we can say that if labour is scarce in those countries, the effect is to reduce the demand for labour in those countries and thus to prevent wages from rising as much as they otherwise would.

Let us now assume that the two countries do not compete, but trade with each other. There are two variants of this case. One where the two countries produce only one good, but a different good in each. Here wage levels are not determined in relation to each other. In the second case, each country produces two or more goods, one of which is common to both, and is the good produced in the subsistence sector.

Suppose that in the first case country *A* produces wheat, and country *B* produces peanuts. Relative prices are determined solely by supply and demand. Assume that a capitalist sector develops in *A*, applying new techniques to wheat production. At first it may get unlimited labour at an average wage in wheat related to average subsistence wheat production. In due course, however, the surplus is eliminated and wheat wages start to rise. If the capitalist techniques which fructified wheat production are equally applicable to peanuts, it will pay to export capital to *B*, where unlimited labour is available at a wage related to average subsistence output of peanuts.

As in the case discussed before, wages in *A* will be held down by the profitability of investing capital in *B*. A new element, however enters into consideration, because of the effects of investment on the terms of trade. When capital is being invested in *A*, and raising the output of wheat, the price of peanuts will rise relatively. Hence the capitalist workers in *A* as well as subsistence workers in *A* will be worse off in terms of peanuts, though earning the same real wage in wheat. And the workers in *B* will be better off in terms of wheat, while earning the same in peanuts. When capital is invested in *B* the opposite happens: the terms of trade are moved against the *B* workers in favour of the *A* workers.

The moral is that capital export may benefit the workers on balance if it is applied to increasing the supply of things they import. For example, in the Britain of 1850 exclusive investment at home in the cotton industry, while tending to raise wages, might also still more have depressed the terms of trade against the cotton industry.

When we pass to the second case, the result is the same, except that the terms of trade are now determinate. Assume that both countries produce food, but do not trade in it. Country *A* also produces steel, and country *B* also produces rubber. If *B* can release unlimited supplies of labour from subsistence food production, wages in *B* will equal average (not marginal) product in food (abstracting from the difference between subsistence and capitalist wages). In *A* also the wage cannot fall below productivity in the food industry. We may simplify by assuming in the first instance that labour is the sole factor of production and that one day's labour

in *A* produces 3 food or 3 steel
in *B* ,, 1 ,, or 1 rubber.

Earnings in *A* will then be three times earnings in *B* (the difference in food productivity). And the rate of exchange will be 1 food = 1 steel = 1 rubber. Suppose now that productivity increases in *B's* rubber industry only, so that one day's labour produces instead 3 rubber. This is excellent for the workers in *A*, since 1 steel will now buy 3 rubber. But it will do the workers in *B* no good whatsoever (except in so far as they purchase rubber), since their wage will continue to be 1 food. If on the other hand the subsistence economy became more productive, wages would rise correspondingly. Suppose that 1 day's labour in *B* now produced 3 food or 1 rubber, wages would be as high in *B* as in *A*, and the price of rubber would now be 1 rubber = 3 steel. Workers in *A* are benefited if productivity in *B* increases in what they buy, and are worse off if productivity in *B* increases in *B's* subsistence sector. Workers in *B* are benefited only if productivity increases in their subsistence sector ; all other increases in productivity are lost in the terms of trade.

We have here the key to the question why tropical produce is so cheap. Take for example the case of sugar. This is an industry in which productivity is extremely high by any biological standard. It is also an industry in which output per acre has about trebled over the course of the last 75 years, a rate of growth of productivity which is unparalleled by any other major industry in the world—certainly not by the wheat industry. Nevertheless workers in the sugar industry continue to walk barefooted and to live in shacks, while workers in wheat enjoy among the highest living standards in the world. The reason is that wages in the sugar industry are related to the fact that the subsistence sectors of tropical economies are able to release however many workers the sugar industry may want, at wages which are low, because tropical food production per head is low. However vastly productive the sugar industry may become, the benefit accrues chiefly to industrial purchasers in the form of lower prices for sugar. (The capitalists who invest in sugar do not come into the argument because their earnings are determined not by productivity in sugar but by the general rate of profit on capital ; this is why our leaving capital out of this and subsequent analysis of the effects of changing productivity upon wages and the terms of trade simplifies the analysis without significantly affecting its results.) To raise the price of sugar, you must increase the productivity of the tropical subsistence food economies. Now the contribution of the temperate world to the tropical world, whether in capital or in knowledge, has in the main been confined to the commercial crops for export, where the benefit mainly accrues to the temperate world in lower prices. The prices of tropical commercial crops will always permit only subsistence wages until, for a change, capital and knowledge are put at the disposal of the subsistence producers to increase the productivity of tropical food production for home consumption.

The analysis applies to all tropical commercial products of which an unlimited supply can be produced because unlimited natural resources exist, in relation to demand—e.g. land of suitable quality. It does not apply where natural resources of a particular kind are scarce. For example, the lands suitable for cultivating sugar or peanuts are very extensive. But mineral-bearing lands, or lands with just the right suitability for cocoa, are relatively scarce. Hence the price of a mineral, or of cocoa, may rise to any level consistent with demand. If the lands are owned by capitalists, employing workers, this will make little difference to their wages. But if these scarce lands are owned by peasants, the peasants may of course become rich. In general the peasants have got little out of their mineral-bearing lands, especially when these have been expropriated by imperial governments (or declared to be Crown property) and sold to foreign capitalists for a song. Cocoa is the only case (a doubtful one) where it seems that a world scarcity of suitable land may now permanently bring to the peasants earnings higher than they could obtain from subsistence food production.

This is not to say that the tropical countries gain *nothing* from having foreign capital invested in commercial production for export. They gain an additional source of employment, and of taxation. The accumulation of fixed capital in their midst also brings nearer the day when the demand for labour will catch up with the supply (though even this will not raise wages in any one tropical country until they start to rise in all, since capital would otherwise merely transfer itself to the countries where there is still a surplus). What they do not gain is rising real wages; the whole benefit of increasing productivity in the commercial sector goes to the foreign consumer, at least in the early stages. In the latest stages they may also gain if their peasants imitate the capitalist techniques, so that subsistence productivity rises; or if the continual increase in the output of commercial crops moves the terms of trade in favour of subsistence food production; either of these changes would react upon real wages (see pages 431-5), but would do so effectively only when the changes have extended throughout the tropical world.

In the next case we assume that the two countries can produce the same things, and trade with each other. *A* is the country where labour is scarce, *B* the country where unlimited labour is available in the subsistence (food) sector. Using the classical framework for the Law of Comparative Costs we write that one day's labour

in *A* produces 3 food or 3 cotton manufactures
in *B* ,, 2 ,, or 1 ,, ,,

This, of course, gives the wrong answer to the question 'who should specialize in which', since we have written the average instead of the marginal products. We can assume that these coincide in *A*, and also in cotton manufacture in *B*. Then we should write, in marginal terms,

in *A* produces 3 food or 3 cotton manufactures
in *B* ,, 0 ,, or 1 ,, ,,

B should specialize in cotton manufacture and import food. In practice, however, wages will be 2 food in *B* and between 3 food and 6 food in *A*, at which levels it will be 'cheaper' for *B* to export food and import cotton.

This divergence between the actual and what it ought to be is the most serious difference which the existence of surplus labour makes to the neo-classical theory of international trade. It has caught out many economists, who have wrongly advised underdeveloped countries on the basis of current money costs, instead of lifting the veil to see what lies beneath. It has also caught out many countries which have allowed (or been forced to allow) their industries to be destroyed by cheap foreign imports, with the sole effect of increasing the size of the labour surplus, when the national income would have been increased if the domestic industries had instead been protected against imports. The fault is not that of the Law of Comparative Costs, which remains valid if written in real marginal terms, but of those who have forgotten that money costs are entirely misleading in economies where there is surplus labour at the ruling wage.

Of course if labour is a free good but the two industries use some scarce resource, such as land or capital, the comparison has to be made not in terms of labour cost but in terms of the scarce resource. Thus, even though labour is unemployed, it may be more economic to use capital to increase the production of food than to use it in creating new manufacturing industries. Adam Smith was as usual on the ball; this was the substance of his argument that a tariff could not raise the national income even if it increased employment, since it would simply be diverting capital from more to less productive uses. (The Keynesian model doesn't help, since it assumes unlimited capital as well as unemployment.) All the same, there may be cases where it is more economic to use capital to create new industries, rather than to fructify old ones, and where this is nevertheless not the most profitable thing to do, in the financial sense, because labour has to be paid a wage when its marginal productivity is really zero. Moreover, many manufacturing activities do not in fact use any other scarce resource but labour. The handicraft and cottage industries especially, which may provide employment for up to 10 per cent of the people in backward countries, use no capital resources to speak of. Yet these are the very first industries to be destroyed by cheap imports of manufactures (e.g. the havoc wrought to the Indian cotton industry in the first half of the nineteenth century).

The Law of Comparative Costs, rightly applied, enables us to predict the pattern of international trade. We can say that those countries which have inadequate agricultural resources in relation to their populations (e.g. India, Japan, Egypt, Great Britain, Jamaica) must live by importing agricultural products and exporting manufactures; metal manufactures if they have the coal and ores (India, Great Britain) and light manufactures if they have not (Japan, Egypt, Jamaica). Correspondingly countries which are rich in agricultural land (U.S.A., Argentina), should be net exporters of agricultural products at relatively good terms of trade. Currently this pattern is distorted by the divergence between money and real costs. But if world population continues to grow at its current rate, this pattern must emerge in due course, unless there are revolutionary developments in agricultural science.

Let us, however, continue to examine this case, assuming that no distortion is taking place. As before *A* is developed while *B* has surplus labour in food. Suppose that one day's labour

in *A* produces 5 food or 5 cotton manufactures
in *B* ,, 1 ,, or 3 ,, ,, (average).

B ought to specialize in cotton, and will actually do so. Wages and prices are determinate. The wage in *B* will be 1 food, the price of cotton will be 1 cotton equals $\frac{1}{3}$ food, the wage in *A* will be 5 food, and *A* will get all the benefit of the exchange. Suppose now that productivity increases in *B's* cotton industry. *B's* wage is unchanged, and the whole benefit accrues to *A*. But if productivity increases in *B's* food industry (the average rising say from 1 to 2) *B's* wage will rise (from 1 food to 2 food). *A's* wage will still be 5 food, but cotton will now be dearer (1 cotton equals $\frac{2}{3}$ food), to the advantage of *B* and disadvantage of *A*. (*B's* wage is determinate because there is unlimited labour available at a subsistence wage; and all the benefit of the exchange goes to *A* because *B* is producing both commodities.)

It is time to say a word about the effect of increasing the subsistence productivity in countries with surplus labour. The analysis is the same as we made for the closed economy (pages 431-5), except that we must now think of the world as a whole as the closed economy. We must also think of the commercial sector of these economies as being a part of the world capitalist sector.

Then, if the world capitalist sector is not dependent on the peasants for food, even to feed its plantation and mining labourers in the surplus countries, an increase in the productivity of the peasants must raise wages against the capitalists. To have this effect, however, productivity must rise in all these countries, otherwise the capitalists will simply transfer from those countries where subsistence productivity has risen to those where it has not.

If, on the other hand, we assume that the capitalists need the peasants' food, and that the demand for food is inelastic, then increased productivity reduces the price of food even more, and so reduces the share of capitalist workers in the capitalist product. This again assumes that the changes are world-wide; if one country raises its productivity, the price of food will not fall; wages will rise in that country, and capitalists will move elsewhere. However, even if the price of food falls, the peasants eat most of their output, and will still be better off. For example, suppose a peasant produces 100 food, eats 80 food, and sells 20 food for 20 manufactures. Suppose now that his productivity increases to 200, reducing the price of food by more than half, say to 0·4. The peasant can now have 30 manufactures, costing 75 food, and still eat 125 food instead of 80. The standard of living in the surplus countries is thus raised nearer to that of the advanced countries, but the terms of trade move against both the food and the commercial products of the surplus countries (would move in favour of the commercial products if the elasticity of demand for food were 1·0 or more).

In practice, food production in tropical countries with surplus labour is only a small part of world food production (Asia and Africa together produce less than 20 per cent of the world's food). Hence increases in food productivity in the tropics could not reduce the price of food *pari passu*. Real wages would therefore rise, and the terms of trade would move in favour of tropical commercial products. This would hurt labour in the industrial countries in so far as it was buying such products, and benefit it in so far as tropical countries were competing in industrial production.

This brings us finally to the case where the two countries *A* and *B* produce competing goods to sell in third markets. This need not detain us long. If capital is exported in ways which raise subsistence productivity in the capital-importing country, the workers in the capital-exporting country will benefit, since the wages of their rivals will be raised. If, however, it is exported to increase productivity in the exporting sector of the capital-importing country, the workers in the capital-exporting country will be doubly hit, first by the reduced capital accumulation at home, and then again by the fall in their rivals' prices.

We may conclude as follows. Capital export tends to reduce wages in capital-exporting countries. This is wholly or partly offset if the capital is applied to cheapening the things which the workers import, or to raising wage costs in countries which compete in third markets (by raising productivity in their subsistence sectors). The reduction in wages is however aggravated if the capital is invested in ways which raise the cost of imports (by increasing productivity in subsistence sectors), or which increase the productivity of competing exports.

We have also seen that capital-importing countries with surplus labour do not gain an increase in real wages from having foreign capital invested in them, unless this capital results in increased productivity in the commodities they produce for their own consumption.

Summary

We may summarize this article as follows :

1. In many economies an unlimited supply of labour is available at a subsistence wage. This was the classical model. The neo-classical model (including the Keynesian) when applied to such economies gives erroneous results.

2. The main sources from which workers come as economic development proceeds are subsistence agriculture, casual labour, petty trade, domestic service, wives and daughters in the household, and the increase of population. In most but not all of these sectors, if the country is overpopulated relatively to its natural resources, the marginal productivity of labour is negligible, zero, or even negative.

3. The subsistence wage at which this surplus labour is available for employment may be determined by a conventional view of the minimum required for subsistence ; or it may be equal to the average product per man in subsistence agriculture, plus a margin.

4. In such an economy employment expands in a capitalist sector as capital formation occurs.

5. Capital formation and technical progress result not in raising wages, but in raising the share of profits in the national income.

6. The reason why savings are low in an undeveloped economy relatively to national income is not that the people are poor, but that capitalist profits are low relatively to national income. As the capitalist sector expands, profits grow relatively, and an increasing proportion of national income is re-invested.

7. Capital is formed not only out of profits but also out of credit creation. The real cost of capital created by inflation is zero in this model, and this capital is just as useful as what is created in more respectable fashion (i.e. out of profits).

8. Inflation for the purpose of getting hold of resources for war may be cumulative ; but inflation for the purpose of

creating productive capital is self-destructive. Prices rise as the capital is created, and fall again as its output reaches the market.

9. The capitalist sector cannot expand in these ways indefinitely, since capital accumulation can proceed faster than population can grow. When the surplus is exhausted, wages begin to rise above the subsistence level.

10. The country is still, however, surrounded by other countries which have surplus labour. Accordingly as soon as its wages begin to rise, mass immigration and the export of capital operate to check the rise.

11. Mass immigration of unskilled labour might even raise output per head, but its effect would be to keep wages in all countries near the subsistence level of the poorest countries.

12. The export of capital reduces capital formation at home, and so keeps wages down. This is offset if the capital export cheapens the things which workers import, or raises wage costs in competing countries. But it is aggravated if the capital export raises the cost of imports or reduces costs in competing countries.

13. The importation of foreign capital does not raise real wages in countries which have surplus labour, unless the capital results in increased productivity in the commodities which they produce for their own consumption.

14. The main reason why tropical *commercial* produce is so cheap, in terms of the standard of living it affords, is the inefficiency of tropical *food* production per man. Practically all the benefit of increasing efficiency in export industries goes to the foreign consumer ; whereas raising efficiency in subsistence food production would automatically make commercial produce dearer.

15. The Law of Comparative Costs is just as valid in countries with surplus labour as it is in others. But whereas in the latter it is a valid foundation of arguments for free trade, in the former it is an equally valid foundation of arguments for protection.

THE ROLE OF INDUSTRIALIZATION IN DEVELOPMENT PROGRAMMES*

by **Hollis B. Chenery**

INDUSTRIALIZATION IS THE MAIN HOPE OF MOST POOR COUNTRIES trying to increase their levels of income. It is also the most controversial aspect of the problem of economic development. Attempts to apply general economic principles to this field have usually proven inconclusive. This result has been due to an incomplete theoretical formulation of the problem as well as to inadequate data. In most cases there remains a wide margin of disagreement between the advocates of international specialization and investment in primary production on the one hand and the proponents of 'balanced growth' and industrialization on the other.

Most of the participants in this controversy would probably accept the proposition that the primary aim of a developing country is to secure the greatest increase in its income (total or *per capita*) from its available resources in the long run. The main problem lies in evaluating the amount of scarce resources which will actually be required by alternative types of production. For a number of reasons, the price system, which makes this evaluation fairly accurate in more highly developed economies, is often a rather unreliable guide to the desirability of investment in an underdeveloped economy. Even when corrections have been made for the more obvious defects in prices, such as tariffs and subsidies, there remain two sets of factors which make a partial equilibrium analysis based on existing prices very difficult: (1) the existence of structural disequilibrium in the use of factors of production, with labour commonly underemployed and capital and foreign exchange rationed; and (2) the interconnectedness of

* *The American Economic Review*, May 1955. Reprinted by permission of the American Economic Association and the author. This paper is based on a study of Resource Allocation in Development Programmes which was made possible by a grant from the Stanford Committee for Research in the Social Sciences.

productive sectors, as a result of which investment in one may make investment in others more profitable—often called 'external economies'.[1]

Both of these factors are particularly important in evaluating industrial investments. Less than half of the total use of primary factors takes place directly in the average sector producing an industrial commodity; the remainder is scattered throughout the economy in the sectors producing raw materials, producer services, and other industrial commodities. In contrast, most of the requirements of capital, labour, raw materials, and foreign exchange for agricultural and mineral production and services occur directly in the producing sector. It is therefore possible to take account of the existence of structural disequilibrium fairly well in evaluating non-industrial investments, but both the existing disequilibrium and the effects of future investment complicate judgements on industrial investment.

The present paper will investigate the influence of these two factors—structural disequilibrium and external economies—on the optimum amount and composition of industrial investment in a development programme. Such an analysis can only be made in the context of a general equilibrium model because intersectoral relations are the essence of the problem. The empirical background for the model is taken from an overall study of the Italian economy[2] and of the development programmes for Southern Italy.[3]

The paper consists of three parts. The first summarizes the essential features of the model and the method of application.

[1] The distinction between these 'pecuniary' external economies and the more traditional 'technological' external economies has been pointed out by Scitovsky in 'Two Concepts of External Economies', *The Journal of Political Economy*, April 1954 (reprinted here, pp. 295-308). Rosenstein-Rodan was among the first to analyse this factor in 'Problems of Industrialization of Eastern and South-Eastern Europe', *The Economic Journal*, 1943, pp. 202–11 (reprinted here, pp. 245-55).

[2] Preliminary results have been published in H. B. Chenery, P. G. Clark, and V. Cao Pinna, *The Structure and Growth of the Italian Economy* (Rome : U. S. Mutual Security Agency, 1953).

[3] Empirical data for the analysis of development programmes within the framework of a regional input-output model is being collected by the Input-Output Unit of the Italian government and the Association for the Industrialization of Southern Italy, to which the author is a consultant.

The second part shows the effect on industrial investment of variation in three key factors reflecting the factor endowments of a given area : the labour supply, the availability of foreign exchange, and the rate of growth. The third part shows the difference between an optimum programme which takes into account external economies and one which does not. It also tries to shed some light on the general problem of investment priorities.

I. A Model of Economic Development

General Characteristics. In order to throw light on the problems I have just outlined, the analytical model must include the following elements : (1) the use of capital, labour, and purchased materials and services in each type of production ; (2) the foreign exchange cost of possible imports ; (3) the foreign demand for possible exports ; (4) restrictions on the commodity composition of any increase in national income ; (5) availability of labour, foreign exchange, investment funds, and other scarce resources.

The statistical basis for such an analysis is provided by an input-output table, augmented by studies of consumer demand, export demand, etc. The solution to the problem involves choice between domestic production and imports, between production for the home market and exports, and maximization of output within the given restraints. The analytical technique, therefore, must be the more general one of linear programming, which in this case is a straightforward extension of input-output methods.

The purpose of the investment programme is to secure a specified increase in national income with a minimum use of investment funds, subject to limitations on the composition of national income, export demand, labour supply, and foreign exchange availability. In the case of Southern Italy, investment funds are variable through subsidies from the central government, and total investment is therefore variable within limits. In other cases, the maximum growth achievable from a given rate of saving could be estimated by varying the time period of the analysis.

The several restrictions in the model are incorporated in the solution in various ways :

1. The division of national income between consumption and investment is taken as fixed. Consumption is assumed to be a function of *per capita* income only, as described below. All elements in final demand are therefore determined by the assumed increase in national income.

2. Total investment must equal savings plus the excess of imports over exports, summed over the time period involved (ten years). We are not concerned with the time path of production during the period, however, but only with the flow of goods and services at its end. If necessary, the amount of investment included in final demand may be modified in a successive approximation.

3. The excess of imports over exports must correspond to the required amount of external investment funds determined by the solution. Solutions must be determined for several possible levels of the trade deficit to meet this condition.

4. The price of labour must be such that total demand does not exceed the total supply.

The size of the model used represents a compromise between the need for sufficient detail to illustrate the interdependence actually existing among productive sectors and the necessity to hold down costs of computation. Since the interconnexions among the industrial sectors are the most significant, the test model contains nine industrial sectors, two sectors of primary production, and three service sectors. Five export sectors have been distinguished, while imports are possible in ten of the fourteen sectors. This model represents a considerable aggregation of the original Italian input-output study, which contained sixty sectors, and of the matrix for Southern Italy, which contained twenty-eight sectors.

Elements in the Model. The following paragraphs will indicate the conceptual nature of the various elements in the model. For present purposes, it is sufficient to consider the numerical data as fairly realistic estimates of the parameters involved. The input coefficients and consumption estimates result from extensive statistical investigations, while most of the other relations are based on scantier evidence or (where indicated) on pure hypothesis.

1. *Total Requirements.* As the model is formulated, a specific set of final consumption levels for the several commodity

groups is taken as the goal of the investment programme. These requirements can in most cases be satisfied from either production or imports. The Gross National Product in the target year will equal the total of these final demands less the import surplus. To simplify the analysis, I assume that capacity in the base year is fully utilized and that in no case will it be efficient to shut down existing production. Present production (net of inter-industry use) can then be subtracted from the given final demands to determine the total requirements by sector to be supplied from either increased production (requiring new investment) or imports. These two sets of estimates are shown in Table 3 on page 458.

Final demand consists of government consumption, private consumption, investment, and exports. (The estimates of final demand were made in Italy by the collaborating groups noted above. They were taken as data for the present test, with the exception of some exports, which were allowed to vary as explained below.) The magnitude of investment was based on the estimated sum of domestic savings and the import surplus (as indicated above) while government consumption was projected from past trends; the composition of both was kept unchanged. A more detailed study was made of private consumption. Consumption estimates for some seventy commodity groups were based on population growth and income elasticities related to prospective increases in *per capita* incomes. They were then aggregated to the present number of sectors.

2. *Production Possibilities*. Each of the commodity groups in the model represents an aggregation of many subgroups. For this test, I have secured average input coefficients through aggregating the intersectoral flows into fourteen groups. I have retained the variation in capital/output ratios within each sector, however, by arranging the subsectors in the order of their capital intensity and assuming that their output will be required in fixed proportions. On this assumption, it will be economical to produce those commodities within each sector which have low direct capital requirements and import those having higher capital requirements, since the indirect capital use within each major sector is assumed to be the same for all subsectors. (If this assumption is not made, the number of sectors must be increased.)

For the linear programming model, the alternative ways of satisfying the given requirements in sectors where imports are possible consist of mixtures of domestic production and imports. The input requirements for domestic production are given in Table 1, and the capital and labour requirements in Table 2A. Some allowance must be made in using minimum investment as a test of efficiency for the fact that capital goods have different degrees of durability. This was done here in the case of land reclamation and other agricultural construction through reducing the capital requirement by the estimated present value of the capital stock twenty-five years hence. An alternative would be to treat capital consumption as a separate input. The assumed variation in capital coefficients within each sector is largely hypothetical, as are the labour coefficients. The capital coefficients in industry were based on a sample of some seventy-five investment projects which were actually undertaken in the past few years. Imports are assumed to require one unit of foreign exchange in each sector except agriculture (assumed to require 1·25).

The choice between domestic production and imports is made by comparing the marginal direct and indirect use of capital in domestic production with the domestic price of imports. This procedure results in a decrease in the proportion of requirements in each sector which is imported as the price of foreign exchange rises.

3. *Exports.* The assumed demand functions for exports are given in Table 2B. The optimum level of exports in each sector will be that at which the marginal (direct and indirect) cost of producing exports is equal to the domestic value of the marginal revenue from increased exports. This optimum level will increase for higher prices of foreign exchange.

Solution. The techniques of solving linear programming problems need not concern us here, but the concepts are useful. In the present case it was possible to take advantage of the fact that the matrix of input coefficients can be made almost triangular—i.e., the interdependence is almost all in one direction, as shown in Table 1. This characteristic makes it possible to solve the problem without inverting the matrix of coefficients, which saves on solution time and also makes it easy to handle the demand functions for exports which have been assumed.

Table 1 : *Input Coefficients*[1]

Sector	I	II	III	IV	V	VI	VII	VIII	IX	X	XI	XII	XIII	XIV
I. Clothing ..	+·917	—	—	·001	·001	—	—	—	—	—	—	—	—	—
II. Textiles ..	·254	+·615	·001	·003	·016	—	—	·001	—	—	·008	—	·001	—
III. Construction..	—	—	+·819	·013	·011	—	·010	—	—	—	·004	—	·001	—
IV. Mechanical ..	·003	—	·063	+·897	·012	—	·001	—	—	—	·001	—	—	—
V. Other industries ..	·005	·001	·033	·037	+·857	·001	·003	—	·037	—	·008	—	·001	—
VI. Food	·027	·001	—	—	·001	+·873	·001	·021	—	·006	·023	·001	·002	—
VII. Metallurgy ..	·001	—	·081	·221	·018	·004	+·515	—	—	—	·011	—	—	—
VIII. Agriculture ..	·003	·138	·002	—	·149	·430	·002	+·899	·011	—	·023	·005	·001	·001
IX. Transport ..	·001	·005	·011	·011	·049	·021	·017	·022	+·966	·032	·012	·151	—	—
X. Petroleum ..	·002	·008	·027	·017	·010	·005	·019	·004	·253	+·987	·015	·011	·003	·018
XI. Chemicals ..	·018	·059	·042	·017	·089	·006	·050	·023	·002	·013	+·691	·032	—	·001
XII. Mining ..	·001	·005	·058	·003	·002	·004	·055	·001	·048	·211	·071	+·995	—	·035
XIII. Services ..	·357	·168	·043	·141	·193	·192	·007	·169	·027	·084	·132	·067	+·957	·010
XIV. Power.. ..	·001	·007	·005	·009	·004	·003	·049	·002	·038	—	·035	·013	·005	+·994

[1] Per unit of output (in value terms).

The concept of 'shadow price' plays a key role in the solution. It measures the total use of scarce resources in the economy to produce a given commodity. In the present case shadow prices are expressed in terms of investment cost. The shadow prices of other basic factors whose supply is limited—foreign exchange and labour—are measured by their opportunity costs. Given the prices of these resources, the shadow price of

Table 2A : Capital and Labour Coefficients

Sector	Labour/Output Coefficient[1]	Average Capital/Output[2] Coefficient
I. *E* Clothing Export	1·00	·5
I. Clothing ..	1·00	·2+·1*d*
II. *E* Textile Export..	·50	·65
II. Textile	·50	·5+·275*d*
III. Construction ..	1·80	·45
IV. *E* Mechanical Export ..	·65	·87
IV. Mechanical ..	·65	·5+·75*d*
V. Other Industry	·90	·2+·9*d*
VI. *E* Food Export ..	·15	·58
VI. Food	·15	·33+·25*d*
VII. Metallurgy ..	·50	·6+·9*d*
VIII. Agriculture ..	0	2·0+·833*d*
IX. Transportation	·50	3·86
X. Petroleum ..	·15	·72
XI. *E* Chemical Export	·35	·75
XI. Chemical ..	·35	·38+*d*
XII. Mining	·45	—6·796+10*d*+1·578*d*
XIII. Services.. ..	3·00	·58
XIV. Power	·20	3·0

each commodity consists of its direct capital cost plus the sum of all its inputs multiplied by their shadow prices. The optimum solution is reached by comparing the cost of securing each commodity by alternative methods with the value given by its shadow price. This method is well suited to handle alternative production techniques when such data are known.

The usual method of solving a linear programming problem involves fixing the resource availabilities and output require-

[1] In 1,000 employees per billion lira of output.

[2] Where *d* is the ratio of domestic production to total requirements in each sector.

ments and determining the optimum combination of activities which corresponds to these limitations. In the present case it has proved useful to examine the implications of varying levels of availability of foreign exchange and labour. I have therefore assumed several combinations of the prices of labour and foreign exchange and determined the use of these resources corresponding to the assumed prices. The results can be plotted in a

Table 2B: Assumed Demand for Exports

Sector	Export Level[1]
I. *E* Clothing	200 (1 — *P*)
II. *E* Textiles	300 (1 — *P*)
IV. *E* Mechanical	600 (1 — *P*)
VI. *E* Food	2,000 (1·1 — *P*)
XI. *E* Chemical	200 (1 — *P*)

Table 3: Total Requirements by Sector

Sector	Final Demand[2]	Total Requirements[3]
I. Clothing	278	162
II. Textiles	195	191
III. Construction	447	280
IV. Mechanical	427	383
V. Other industries	163	144
VI. Food	1,308	443
VII. Metallurgy	36	31
VIII. Agriculture	639	98
IX. Transport	70	24
X. Petroleum	225	168
XI. Chemicals	132	149
XII. Mining	63	68
XIII. Services	148	40
XIV. Power	59	22
Total	4,190	2,203

[1] Where *P* is the price in foreign currency. All functions are purely hypothetical.

[2] Including 416 billion of exports for which the demand is taken as given.

[3] Final demand less domestic production in excess of inter-industry demand in the base year; i.e., the excess of projected total demand over net domestic availabilities in the base year. Total requirements are equal to the increase in GNP plus the excess of imports over exports.

graph, as in Figure 2 on page 463, from which it is possible to determine the optimum prices corresponding to any levels of foreign exchange and labour. These prices in turn determine the activities used and investment in each sector.

For each set of parameters, we have made several trials with varying prices of foreign exchange, holding the other parameters constant.[1] The results of these trials are shown in Table 4. Each one represents the solution requiring the minimum investment under the stated assumptions as to the values of the parameters. In the first three trials, an interpolation has been made at a constant deficit of 284, which was estimated to be the average amount of external resources necessary to achieve the desired increase in GNP within a ten-year period.

II. Key Factors in Industrial Development

I will now investigate the effects of differences in resource endowments, factor proportions, savings levels, and other basic factors on the optimum patterns of economic development. The hypothesis underlying this study is that industrialization may play a very diverse role in different types of country. Where structural disequilibrium exists, it is almost impossible to determine from the price system the true weight which should be given to these factors in investment decisions.

Variation in the underlying structural factors is reflected in a formal model through differing values of some of the parameters. Here I will analyse effects of variation in the parameters related to three basic characteristics of developing economies: (1) factor proportions; (2) availability of foreign exchange; (3) the rate of growth.

Factor Proportions. The optimum pattern of economic development obviously varies widely with the endowment of available economic resources. Individual mineral resources, specific types of agricultural land, etc., are reflected in the capital requirements of individual sectors and determine the desirability of specific types of primary production. They require little comment. The relative abundance of larger categories of economic factors—aggregate natural resources, labour, and

[1] All the calculations on the aggregated model were made by Kenneth Kretschmer.

Table 4: Results of Trial Solutions

	A1	A2	A3	A4	A5	B1	B2	B3	C1	C2	C3	D1	D2	D3	E
Price of foreign exchange	2·7	2·8	2·9	3·0	2·84[1]	3·0	3·3	3·5	3·5	3·8	3·719[1]	2·7	3·0		3·60
Price of labour	0	0	0	0	0	·3	·3	·3	·6	·6	·6	0	0		0
Requirements[2]	1·0	1·0	1·0	1·0	1·0	1·0	1·0	1·0	1·0	1·0	1·0	·5	·5		1·0
Exports	686	714	739	766	725	597	680	737	582	666	643	686	766		651
Imports	1,163	1,062	944	832	1,009	1,278	964	739	1,208	823	927	861	629		926
Trade deficit	477	348	205	66	284	681	284	2	626	158	284	175	−137		276
Increase in GNP	1,391	1,524	1,672	1,812	1,590	1,150	1,553	1,834	1,187	1,652	1,527	953	1,051		1,598
Investment in:															
Industry	1,436	1,600	1,789	1,959	1,685	1,063	1,494	1,824	1,023	1,468	1,348	1,033	1,448		1,629
Agriculture	389	519	676	838	589	376	840	1,231	625	1,289	1,110	293	637		789
Services	669	717	772	818	742	579	720	818	592	746	704	436	555		740
Total	2,494	2,836	3,238	3,615	3,016	2,019	3,054	3,874	2,240	3,503	3,162	1,736	2,640		3,158
Total labour[3]	2,839	3,042	3,270	3,473	3,145	2,346	2,929	3,347	2,298	2,923	2,755	1,914	2,423		3,001
Ratio of investment to increase in GNP ..	1·793	1·861	1·937	1·994	1·895	1·755	1·966	2·112	1·887	2·120	2·057	1·850	2·513		1·976

[1] Interpolated.
[2] Fraction of requirements sector given in Table 3.
[3] Excluding labour in agriculture.

investment funds—is subject to more general analysis. The most significant relationship is that between population or labour force as a whole and natural resources plus capital stock. It is often suggested that in the 'overpopulated' areas, where pressure on the developed resources—primarily agricultural—is high, industrialization is more desirable than in countries where a shift of the labour force from agriculture to industry (without investment or technological improvement) would cause a significant fall in agricultural output.

Population pressure may affect several parameters in the model. In the first place, it means that there will be a fairly unlimited supply of labour available for non-agricultural employment. This labour is not a free good because—at least in part—it must be moved to towns, housed, and trained. In our system, this means that labour will have a shadow price or capital cost greater than zero but in all probability considerably less than the actual wage rate. In other cases, the opportunity cost of labour may equal or exceed its wage.

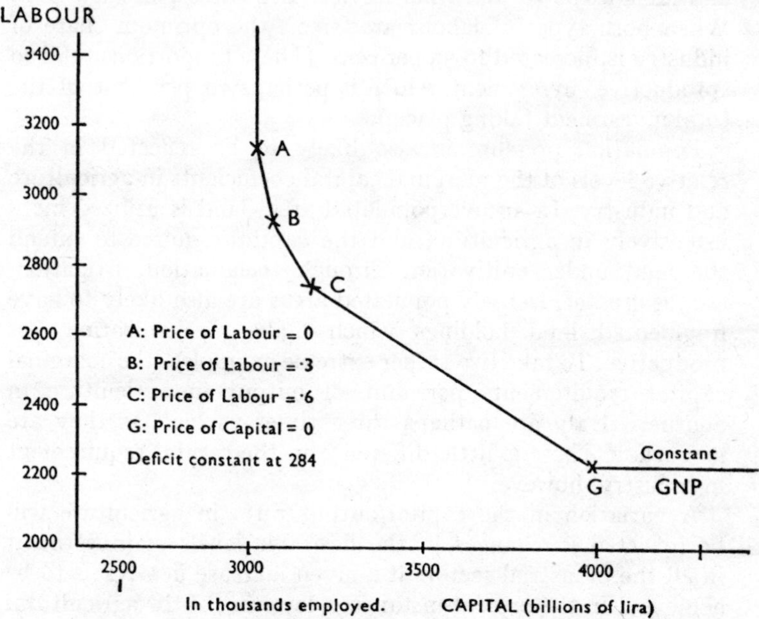

Figure 1. Substitution between Capital and Labour

The overall possibility of substituting labour for capital with fixed input coefficients is shown in Figure 1. Point *C* corresponds roughly to existing wage rates in Southern Italy, while point *A* represents the optimum solution with labour as a free good. The variation in total capital requirements corresponding to this change in the use of labour is not large—about 5 per cent—because the composition of imports and exports is the only factor which has been allowed to vary; techniques of production and the composition of final demand have been kept constant.

This variation in the optimum investment pattern takes place largely in the industrial sector. When the price of non-agricultural labour is taken at approximately the existing wage rate (no opportunity cost is assigned to agricultural labour, on the theory that even the most successful investment programme will leave it in surplus supply), the fraction of total investment going into industry in the optimum programme is 43 per cent. ('Industry' includes mining and manufacturing and excludes power and other services. See Table 4 on page 460.) When both types of labour are 'free', the optimum share of industry is increased to 55 per cent. (These proportions refer to 'productive' investment, which is perhaps 70 per cent of the total investment taking place.)

Population pressure is also likely to be reflected in the relative levels of the marginal capital coefficients in agriculture and industry. In an overpopulated area, land is utilized more intensively in agriculture, and the capital required to extend the land under cultivation through reclamation, irrigation, etc., is greater. Densely populated areas are also likely to have fragmented land holdings which make mechanization less productive. To take two rather extreme examples, the marginal capital requirements per unit of output in agriculture in Southern Italy are perhaps three times as high as they are in Turkey. There is little difference in the capital requirement in industry, however.

A variation in the capital/output ratio in agriculture will be reflected in changes in the desirable levels of investment in all the industrial sectors if a given increase in GNP is to be achieved. In the present instance, a lowering of the agricultural capital coefficient by about 15 per cent produced a decrease in the share of investment going to industry of about 20 per cent. Only the food-processing industries increased their output. These particular values of course depend on the variability of capital coefficients within agriculture and industry.

Both of these aspects of the factor proportions problem thus appear to be quite significant in determining the role to be given to industrial investment. The importance of the 'employment ratio' may be overstressed in actual practice, however, when it is divorced from the overall test of increasing national income.

Availability of Foreign Exchange. The ability of a country to secure foreign exchange is another key factor in determining the desirable extent of industrial development. Industrialization consists primarily in the substitution of domestic production of manufactured goods for imports. The choice between domestic production and imports should be based on the scarce

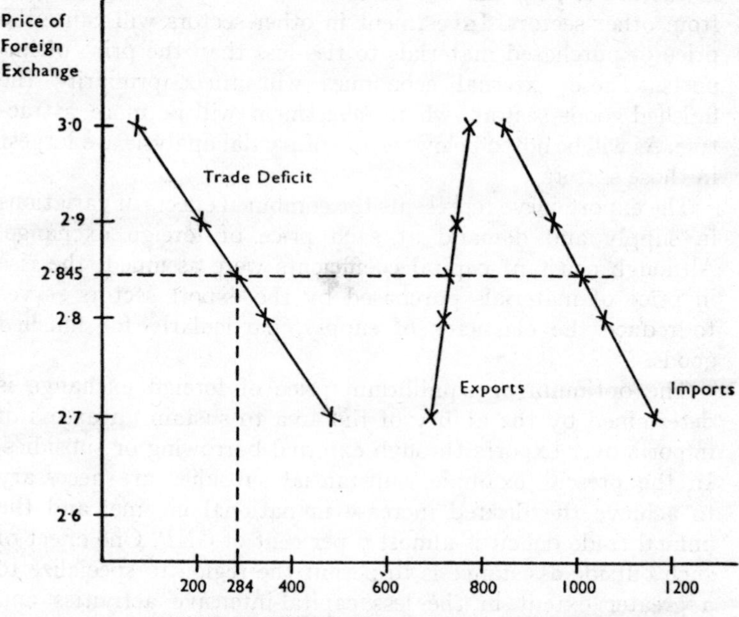

Figure 2. Effect of the Price of Foreign Exchange on the Trade Deficit

resources required by each alternative. In a linear programming model, this decision is based on the shadow price of foreign exchange, which is determined by the opportunity cost of domestic production in the marginal importing and exporting sectors. In equilibrium, the price of foreign exchange becomes the reciprocal of the marginal productivity of investment in these sectors.

The effect of changes in the price of foreign exchange on imports and exports is shown in Figure 2. The import curve represents the total demand of the economy for imports, taking account of optimum readjustments in domestic production at each price of foreign exchange.

The effect on the investment decision in any sector of a rise in the price of foreign exchange will be determined by three factors: (1) the rise in the price of imports of the commodity produced; (2) the variation in direct capital and labour costs in the sector; (3) the rise in the cost of materials purchased from other sectors. Investment in other sectors will cause the price of purchased materials to rise less than the price of imports. These external economies will affect primarily the finished-goods sectors, where investment will be more attractive. As will be noted below, errors of partial analysis are largest in those sectors.

The export curve represents the combined effects of variations in supply and demand at each price of foreign exchange. Although constant capital coefficients were assumed, the rise in price of materials purchased by the export sectors serves to reduce the elasticity of supply, particularly for finished goods.

The optimum or equilibrium price of foreign exchange is determined by the ability of the area to sustain an excess of imports over exports through external borrowing or subsidies. In the present example, substantial subsidies are necessary to achieve the desired increase in national income, and the annual trade deficit is almost 7 per cent of GNP. One effect of such outside assistance is to permit the region to specialize to a greater extent in the less capital-intensive activities and secure a given increase in regional income with a somewhat smaller use of capital. Since many branches of industry are less capital intensive than agriculture in the present model, a higher deficit results in a greater proportion of investment going to industry. In other countries, the opposite result might well occur, however.

Since the equilibrium price of foreign exchange determines the limits to which investment should be carried in each sector where exports and imports are possible, it is the most crucial parameter in formulating a development programme. If too low a value is used, for example, the trade deficit will be larger than can be financed and emergency measures to stimulate exports or reduce imports will have to be taken. These will lead to investment at lower rates of productivity than would be the case if the proper exchange rate had been used throughout the programme. The resulting increase in total cost of the programme is illustrated in Section III (page 467).

The Rate of Growth. The rate of growth affects the pattern of investment in two different ways. In the first place, foreign exchange earnings are fairly independent of the rate of growth. Except for improvements in technology or possible economies of scale in export production arising from a larger domestic market, foreign exchange earnings depend on the exchange rate and the elasticity of foreign demand for such exports.

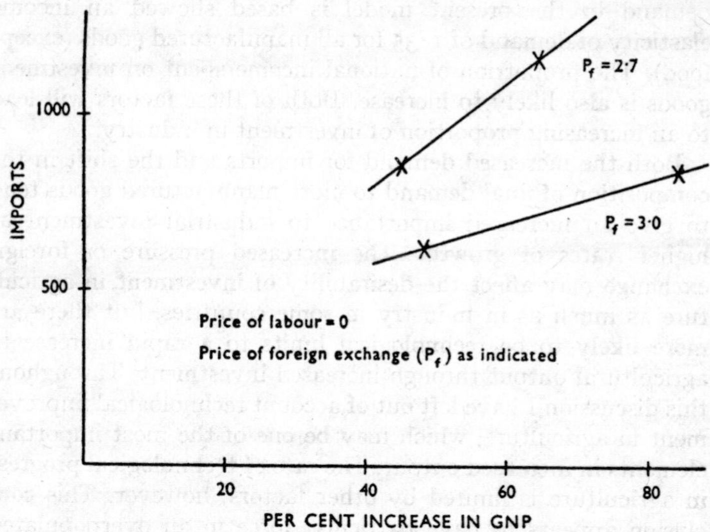

Figure 3. *Effect of Growth on Import Requirements*

Imports, however, will increase with the rate of growth unless the exchange rate is changed, as shown in Figure 3. Even if foreign borrowing depends to some extent on the growth in national income, there will be a tendency for the net deficit to be greater at higher rates of growth.

In order to limit the trade deficit of foreign exchange availabilities a higher price must be given to foreign exchange. In the present example, an increase in the rate of growth by 10 per cent would have increased the exchange rate needed to maintain a constant deficit by 2 per cent. The marginal productivity of investment would fall by the same amount. Although this effect is not significant for small variations, when the growth rate is greatly accelerated it may become quite important. Higher growth rates lead to a greater need for self-sufficiency unless export demand is highly elastic.

The rate of growth will also act on the composition of investment through its effects on final demand. As *per capita* incomes increase, the proportion of income spent on manufactured consumer goods of all kinds may be expected to increase. The study of consumption in Southern Italy on which the final demand in the present model is based showed an income elasticity of demand of 1·35 for all manufactured goods (except food). The proportion of national income spent on investment goods is also likely to increase. Both of these factors will lead to an increasing proportion of investment in industry.

Both the increased demand for imports and the shift in the composition of final demand to more manufactured goods tend to give an increased importance to industrial investment at higher rates of growth. The increased pressure on foreign exchange may affect the desirability of investment in agriculture as much as in industry in some countries, but there are more likely to be technological limits to a rapid increase in agricultural output through increased investment. Throughout this discussion I have left out of account technological improvement in agriculture, which may be one of the most important elements in increased output. The rate of technological progress in agriculture is limited by other factors, however. This conclusion appears to have particular force in an overpopulated area like Southern Italy, where a further increase in the rate of growth in the agricultural sector can only be secured at very high capital/output ratios.

III. Structural Interdependence and Investment Priorities

The preceding section has illustrated the way in which the decisions affecting industrialization depend on resource availabilities and investment in requirements in all sectors. The interdependence among sectors introduces errors into any method of making investment decisions based only on the characteristics of single sectors or projects. I shall now try to analyse these errors and suggest methods of improving partial methods from the experience gained in solving a general equilibrium model.

Errors in Partial Analysis. Partial analysis uses the same general test for investment allocation as does linear programming: the marginal productivity of investments included in the programme should be greater than those which are excluded. The marginal productivity may not be equal in each sector because of limitations on the commodity composition of output even though a perfect price system would bring about such equality. With either method, an optimum programme satisfying the various resource limitations can only be arrived at by trial and error. There are various routes by which the final solution can be reached, but a convenient method in both cases is to assume a marginal productivity of investment, to exclude projects falling below this figure, and then to see whether investment funds have been exhausted and other limitations satisfied. In the partial analysis it is possible to take account of some errors in the price system, such as the existence of a tariff on imports of the product, but not of the indirect effects of such errors on the price of purchased materials.[1]

As has been pointed out earlier, the partial analysis is subject to two general types of error arising out of interconnectedness: inability to determine how much of a given commodity will be

[1] A suggested method using partial sector analysis has been given in my 'Application of Investment Criteria', *Quarterly Journal of Economics*, February 1953, pp. 76–96.

required and the omission of external economies due to investment in other sectors. The first type of error is probably of greater quantitative significance. To measure it would require a comparison of the output forecasts which would be made in ignorance of the input-output pattern with the results of the present model. These errors would be small for finished goods and larger for intermediate products and producer services. Since the latter sectors have higher capital coefficients, the errors in estimating investment requirements would be greater than those in forecasting output. They cannot be measured here for lack of a basis of comparison, however.

The second type of error—omission of external economies—can be isolated by assuming the same knowledge of the interdependence of output in both cases and the use of constant current prices in determining which commodities shall be domestically produced and which imported. The partial method would therefore assume a constant ratio of value-added to total output in each trial. To compare this method to the linear programming model, I have made a solution corresponding approximately to trial A5 in Table 4 in that the increase in GNP is almost the same (see trial E, Table 4). The differences between these two solutions show the magnitude and also the nature of the errors in the partial method.

In terms of the overall test of capital requirements (labour being assumed free in this trial), the difference of about 115 billion lira (corrected for the difference in GNP) is not large—about 4 per cent of total investment requirements. If we limit the comparison to the marginal cases in which external economies have some significance, however, this difference is much more important.

The best indication of the inefficiency of the partial method is the fact that the marginal productivity of investment (the reciprocal of the price of foreign exchange) with the partial method is much lower—28 per cent as compared with 35 per cent for linear programming. This difference results from the fact that external economies are not taken into account and underinvestment in some sectors results. In other sectors, investment must be pushed to lower levels of productivity to secure the same increase in GNP. There will be underinvestment in the sectors which purchase a large amount from other sectors, as in the production of finished goods. Textile production in the present case was 40 per cent lower with the partial method than with linear programming. Conversely, there will be overinvestment in primary production and basic industries to compensate for the first error ; agriculture is 30 per cent higher with the partial method.

Regardless of the values of the various parameters, there will be this systematic bias in favour of primary production and basic industries and against finished goods when external economies are ignored. These biases also extend to the export sectors.

Planning Industrial Development. To improve on partial analysis, some of the effects of structural interdependence must be taken into account. The methodology which has been used here may be helpful even when all the elements are not known. This method takes advantage of the fact that interdependence in the economy is not general, but is largely 'one way'. The demand for basic materials depends on the demand for finished goods ; the demand for minerals and agricultural products depends on the first two categories ; and, finally, the demand for fuels, power, transport, and producer services depends on all of the others. The extent of this one-way interdependence in the Italian economy is shown in Table 1 ; less than 5 per cent of the interindustry flows occur to the right of the diagonal when the sectors are arranged in such a way as to minimize such circular interdependence. To compute output requirements we should start with the sectors at the top of the list, while to trace out the effects of external economies on prices we should start at the bottom.

A procedure which will introduce some of the elements of a general equilibrium analysis into the usual sector approach is the following :

1. Divide the economy into as many sectors as can be managed and arrange them in the order of maximum one-way interdependence as indicated in Table 1.

2. Within each sector, rank projects according to their marginal return on investment, using expected prices and correcting for tariffs, subsidies, etc., where possible.

3. Estimate the final demands in the economy which would result from the increase in income expected from the investment programme.

4. Using an assumed marginal productivity of investment, exclude projects in each sector which have lower returns, wherever there is the alternative of importing. Include all export projects which exceed this rate of return. Start at the bottom of the list in making this estimate (with services and primary production) and revise the cost of purchased materials where possible on the basis of previous decisions as to imports or domestic production.

5. Starting at the top of the list of sectors, compute the required output in each from the final demand and the estimated use in preceding sectors. Compute imports, exports, and the payments deficit.

6. Revise the size of the programme downward if the available investment funds have been exceeded. Revise the productivity of investment downward if the trade deficit is excessive. Repeat the calculation until limits on investment, foreign exchange, and other resources are satisfied.

It would require a paper much longer than the present one to explore the practical problems involved in each of these steps. They will vary greatly depending on the type of information available. One great advantage of using such a framework for investment analysis, however, is that it can incorporate whatever fragmentary information is available from a variety of sources—engineering studies, demand analyses, import statistics, etc.

IV. Conclusion

The role of industrialization in economic development cannot be evaluated by looking only at individual sectors. This paper has explored the ways in which our judgements may be modified by looking at the total effects of an investment programme. To make this investigation, I have had to abandon the *ceteris paribus* assumptions of partial equilibrium analysis and work with a general equilibrium system. Although some of the parameters are estimated from very inadequate evidence, the most important elements—the input coefficients

—are the most reliable. Few of the above conclusions would have been changed by large deviations in the other parameters.

Knowledge of structural interdependence is particularly important in the industrial sectors of the economy. The external economies which occur in these sectors provide the justification for investment in 'social overhead' facilities and in much of primary production. The desired level of output in each industrial sector depends on developments in the others. We have seen that factor proportions, comparative advantage, and the rate of growth all affect the amount and type of industrial investment which is desirable. My main result, therefore, has been to stress the need for overall analysis in planning industrial development.

THE APPEAL OF CONFISCATION IN ECONOMIC DEVELOPMENT*

by **M. Bronfenbrenner**

'What's mine is mine, and what's yours is mine too.'

Apocryphal Communist Proverb

THE APPEAL OF CONFISCATION IN FINANCING ECONOMIC development is not 'pure propaganda' in the sense of economic fallacy. It must be taken seriously, not shrugged off by easy analogies to 'a shot in the arm' or 'the goose that laid the golden eggs'. For confiscation of capital has not killed the goose that laid the golden eggs in the Soviet Union, in China, or in the other 'people's democracies'. It seems rather to have been an important device permitting these countries to develop and industrialize rapidly, while other countries, in which the influence of Western ethics has been stronger, are lagging behind. It is questionable whether the lagging countries can be expected permanently to eschew the device of confiscating capital under their control unless capital is made available to them from abroad in large amounts at attractive terms; it is likewise questionable whether such largesse is in the economic interest of the lending countries.

The issue we discuss is not whether confiscation can be justified by some accepted or conventional Occidental standard of morals or propriety, but merely whether it brings the pragmatic results desired, namely economic development without sacrifice to the scale of living of the mass of the population. It will be our contention that confiscation has done so, is doing so, and will continue to do so, by shifting income to developmental investment from capitalists' consumption, from transfer abroad, and from unproductive 'investment' like luxury housing. Therein lies the appeal of confiscation, although it is argued persuasively on the other side in

* *Economic Development and Cultural Change,* Vol. III, No. 3, April 1955. Reprinted by permission of the University of Chicago Press and the author.

developed countries that these accomplishments require totalitarian dictatorship for their realization and that development is not worth this price.

Historical demonstration of the effects of confiscation past and present requires data from developing and developed economies on both sides of the Iron Curtain, which are not yet available in reliable form, and which may never become available at all. As an admittedly inferior substitute for historical data, I propose to 'illustrate' the power of confiscation by hypothetical models of an underdeveloped overpopulated economy. The salient characteristics of this economy I shall seek to render fairly realistic for a large group of countries, but there will be others for which the model will remain completely meaningless. (The reader with time to spare may spend some of it in creating an alternative which will fit both Greenland and India, both Puerto Rico and Outer Mongolia.) The model will be sufficiently simple to remain within the bounds of primary school arithmetic. This limitation of technique will prevent consideration of bottlenecks, cyclical oscillations, balance-of-payments problems, structural relations between economic sectors, and other important effects which have been treated formally in more elaborate applications of 'process analysis' to economic development.[1]

Model I. Our hypothetical economy has a net national and personal income of 100, after depreciation and before direct taxes. Income, both before and after taxes, is divided between service income[2] and property income in the proportion of 85

[1] For three such applications, see: J. J. Polak, 'Balance of Payments Problems of Countries Reconstructing with the Help of Foreign Loans', *Quarterly Journal of Economics*, LVII (February 1943), 208–40; reprinted in American Economic Association, *Readings in the Theory of International Trade*; H. W. Singer, 'The Mechanics of Economic Development', *The Indian Economic Review* (August 1952), reprinted in the present volume, pp. 381-99; Trygve Haavelmo, *A Study in the Theory of Economic Evolution* (Amsterdam, 1954).

[2] 'Service income' includes both compensation of employees and gross profits of proprietors of unincorporated enterprises. Its recipients include, along with the proletariat and peasantry, the bulk of those bourgeois segments classified in Mainland China as 'petty' or 'national'.

to 15.[1] While tax progression may be on the statute books, it plays no significant role in modifying either the functional or the personal distribution of income.[2] (Throughout this study, the reader is invited to substitute his own estimates when mine appear imaginative or fantastic.)

[1] This property share is too high for areas in which population is scanty and land rent low. It is probably too low for densely populated areas with rich agricultural or mining land. A few statistical estimates, given below, are the best available, but refer to countries in which the property share may be lower than it is in the bulk of the underdeveloped world.

Continent and Country	Percentage Distribution of Income			
	Employee Compensation	Unincorporated Enterprises	Property Income	Transfer Payments
Africa				
Northern Rhodesia (1949)	63·6	32·7	1·4	2·3
Southern Rhodesia (1949)	55·4	33·0	8·1	3·5
Asia				
Ceylon (1951) . .	74·7	13·1	5·5	6·6
Japan (1949) . .	46·8	49·7	1·9	1·6
North America				
Puerto Rico (1948–9)	52·7	39·1		8·2
South America				
Peru (1947)	44·4	36·0	13·1	6·5

Sources: For Ceylon, unpublished data of the Central Bank of Ceylon, made available to the writer by the courtesy of Professor Theodore Morgan; for other countries, United Nations Statistical Office, 'National Income and Its Distribution in Underdeveloped Countries', *United Nations Statistical Papers*, Series E, No. 3 (New York, 1951), p. 18.

[2] One or more of the three following reasons often explains the disappointing results of progressive taxation in underdeveloped countries: (1) the extremely limited number of technically competent administration and enforcement officials; (2) the susceptibility of underpaid and overworked civil servants to direct or indirect corruption; and (3) class systems which render it improper for the mere tax-office clerk to question the returns or statements of wealthy merchants or landowners who are his social superiors.

Of the assumed property share of 15, one-third, or 5, comprises net saving (above depreciation of capital).[1] I ignore net savings out of service income as unimportant quantitatively. Of the total net savings of 5, 40 per cent (or 2) takes forms available for domestic economic development, either as capital goods or as 'social overhead capital'. The remainder (or 3) is dissipated in foreign investments, inventories, or residential housing of a luxury or semi-luxury variety.[2] Population is growing at the rate of 1·5 per cent a year. Aggregate net income is growing at the rate of 1·7 per cent a year. This last figure is compounded of a 15 per cent return on developmental investment (including a substantial write-up for external economies), a 60 per cent return on population growth (where any figure under 100 per cent indicates 'diminishing returns'), and a flat 0·5 per cent for 'entrepreneurship' or innovation, including particularly the introduction of methods already in vogue in other countries.[3]

[1] Gross saving (and investment) percentages would of course be much larger. An estimate by the United Nations Economic Commission for Latin America, for example, concludes that 14 per cent of the total income of this area entered into gross savings in 1953, but that this savings coefficient was 'barely sufficient for an annual *per capita* growth of 0·9 per cent'. *International Co-operation in a Latin American Development Policy* (New York, 1954).

[2] Dissipation in hoards, or in bidding up the values of land and other existing assets, may also exist. I do not consider it here because such dissipation can be counteracted with relative ease by deficit financing on the part of the government. Dissipation such as is listed in the text requires diversion of real goods from developmental investment to exports, inventories, or residential construction.

[3] For two independent estimates, one more sanguine than ours and one less so, consider the following running quotation from Joseph J. Spengler, 'Demographic Patterns', in Harold F. Williamson and John A. Buttrick (eds.), *Economic Development: Principles and Patterns* (New York, 1954), pp. 77 f.:

'The movement of aggregate income is dominated by: (1) equipment or income-producing wealth; (2) technical and related forms of progress; and (3) the magnitude of the labour force. With factors (2) and (3) constant, a 1 per cent increase in the amount of "capital" in use will be accompanied by an increase of 0·25 to 0·35 per cent in aggregate net income. With factors (1) and (2) constant, a 1 per cent increase in the labour force will be accompanied by an income increase of 0·65 to 0·75 per cent. On the basis of these estimates and of growth actually recorded in various national incomes, the forces included under (2) have been increasing net incomes in advanced countries something like 1 per cent per year.

'Somewhat similar results were obtained by E. C. Olson in a study

With population growing at 1·5 per cent per year and aggregate income at 1·7 per cent, the annual growth rate of *per capita* income is only, to a first approximation, 0·2 per cent.[1] If there is no change in the income distribution, *per capita* service income also grows at this same rate (0·2 per cent per year). This is near-stagnation, which widens annually the developmental gap separating this economy from the advanced countries of the Western World.

These figures are summarized and presented as Table I. This table has been expanded to include the results of 5, 10, and 20 years of growth compounded according to the assumptions which we have made.

Table I : The Status Quo : Economic Stagnation

Line No.	Units	Current	After 5 years	After 10 years	After 20 years
1. Real income ..	Absolute	100·0	108·8	118·4	140·1
2. Service income ..	,,	85·0	92·5	100·6	119·1
3. Property income	,,	15·0	16·3	17·8	21·0
4. Saving ratio ..	Per cent	5·0	5·0	5·0	5·0
5. Developmental investment ratio	,,	2·0	2·0	2·0	2·0
6. Population growth rate	,,	1·5	1·5	1·5	1·5
7. Aggregate income growth rate ..	,,	1·7	1·7	1·7	1·7
8. *Per capita* income growth rate	,,	0·2	0·2	0·2	0·2
9. *Per capita* income	Index No.	100·0	101·0	102·0	104·1
10. *Per capita* service income	,,	85·0	85·9	86·7	88·5

Notes : (Line 7) = ·15 (Line 5) + ·60 (Line 6) + 0·5
(Line 8) = (Line 7) − (Line 6) (Approximation)

based on international comparisons. He found that a 1 per cent increase in the employed population was accompanied by only about 0·25 per cent increase in the national income ; and that 1 per cent increases, respectively, in the total amounts of energy and livestock used, were accompanied by increases of about 0·5 and 0·25 per cent in the national income.'

[1] The United Nations Economic Commission for Asia and the Far East (ECAFE) is more pessimistic. With population growing at 1·5 per cent per annum, ECAFE estimates 6 to 7 per cent net investment to be required for maintenance of existing *per capita* income under East Asian conditions. 'Some Financial Aspects of Development Programmes in Asian Countries', *Economic Bulletin for Asia and the Far East* (Jan.–June 1952), pp. 1 f.

Model II. 'Comes the Revolution.' It may indeed be a social revolution, with or without substantial violence and destruction. It may be a capital levy at rates close to 100 per cent. It may be 'nationalization', with compensation wiped out by rapid inflation.[1] At any rate, all capital goods which yield incomes become State property. Certain consumer durable goods which can be converted to income-yielding uses, or sold abroad for capital imports, also become State property. All income from this property goes to the State, none to the former property owners, even though they may retain the bare legal title to certain of the assets. None of the income from property is paid to the service-income classes directly; there is no immediate redistribution or 'social dividend' in this model. Because of the absence of redistribution I call this model 'Confiscation, Russian Style', with special reference to the period of the first four Five-Year Plans, although the figures I shall use cannot be applied realistically to actual Soviet experience.[2]

More precisely, let us suppose that two-thirds of what had previously been property income (or 10 per cent of the total national income), is used by the State for development purposes broadly conceived, i.e., including not only capital goods but also 'social overhead capital'. The other third of what had previously been property income (or 5 per cent of the total national income) is dissipated by additional 'non-productive' government expenditures[3] (public buildings, armaments, military and police personnel, etc.), or into symbolic compensation for the former property-owners. The five per cent leakage also includes income which would have been earned by private

[1] 'Nationalization' with approximately full compensation, on the British model, will not in itself bring about the increases in saving and investment which are postulated below.

[2] A critic has suggested that they might have been realistic for a Soviet Union which had succeeded in remaining neutral during World War II, or located in a world free from major wars.

[3] There is much to be said for rehabilitation of the classical economists' distinction between productive and non-productive activities, the former contributing to the maintenance or expansion of the level of economic development and the latter not. We must grant the distinction to be invalid in terms of the creation of utilities, and it is inaccurate to identify this distinction, as the classical economists did, with the distinction between the production of goods and the production of services. Cf. Paul Baran, 'Economic Progress and Economic Surplus', *Science and Society*, VII (Fall 1953), pp. 290–300.

parties but which is not earned under public ownership, either because of damage during revolutionary upheaval or because of inefficient allocation by the public authorities. Income created by conversion of nationalized consumer durables (e.g., crops grown on former hunting preserves or golf courses) will be a deduction from the leakage, as will income acquired from foreign sale of other nationalized durables like jewelry and art objects.

An important point in this discussion of leakages is often misunderstood, both by Socialists and by their opponents. The Socialist need not deny the technical superiority of private gain to public interest in allocating land and capital to their most productive uses, although he usually feels compelled to do so, sometimes with reason. Neither need the Socialist deny, as he often does, the involuntary social service performed by the landlord, capitalist, or entrepreneur who makes the more efficient allocation. The Socialist need deny only that this service is worth 10, 15, or 25 per cent of the national income of a poor country, a far less plausible proposition. The Socialist can be compared in this respect to a shabby-genteel buyer of a shabby-genteel used car, who should deny only that the new model is worth to him its 50 per cent extra cost but who insists on assuaging his ego with verbiage about 'they don't make them this good any more'.

Returning to our theoretical scheme: Let the current year be one in which 'normalcy' has been restored after the Revolution. The aggregate income growth rate under public control has fallen to 12·5 per cent of the developmental investment rate plus 55 per cent of the population growth rate plus an improvement or innovation factor of 0·4 per cent. The corresponding figures in Model I were 15, 60, and 0·5 respectively. The reductions are further allowances, over and beyond the five per cent leakage, for the presumably greater efficiency of private over social entrepreneurship. As for population, its rate of growth begins to increase, partially in anticipation of better days to come and partly in response to improvements as they are achieved. Over five years the (geometric) mean growth rate is 1·55 per cent, over 10 years 1·60 per cent, over 20 years 1·65 per cent, with an eventual asymptote at 1·75 per cent.[1] Nevertheless, comparing Model II with Model I, we see immediately a higher growth rate of *per capita* income, which is caused by diversion of the bulk of property income to development purposes.[2] *Per capita* service income keeps pace, despite the absence of direct redistribution, and rises at once above the near-stagnation of the status quo. Diversion of property income to developmental investment has triumphed over both the Malthusian bogey of overpopulation and the Brozenian bogey of 'Fabian' entrepreneurship.[3] The triumph is only on paper and is derived from arbitrary figures, but in selecting these figures I have attempted 'leaning to one side' against the appeal of confiscation, and can imagine no realistic assumptions leading to contrary qualitative conclusions in societies whose income distributions include high property

[1] A growth rate of 1·50 per cent in the current year, rising by 0·02 per cent per year until 1·60 per cent is reached in year 5, then by 0·01 per cent per year until 1·75 per cent is reached in year 25, will yield geometric means close to those in the text.

[2] A query from a cynical critic at this point remains unanswered: Can any government but a totalitarian dictatorship devote 10 per cent of its national income to developmental investment year after year without being voted out of office by the partisans of Santa Claus here and now? An American survey of actual Soviet experience underlines the criticism. 'It may be inferred . . . that Soviet industrial growth was as rapid as it was *because of*, rather than *despite*, the existence of central planning and authoritarian control. It seems doubtful that the amount and pattern of Soviet investment would ever be duplicated in an essentially consumer-oriented market economy. . . . Such a level and pattern of investment, and the rapid economic growth which results, could only be accomplished by an economic system designed to fulfil the wishes of central planners. Resources must be directed, despite the needs and desires of households, predominantly into machines which produce machines (and weapons) rather than into machines which produce consumers' goods and services, including housing.' Franklyn D. Holzman, 'Soviet Economic Growth', *World Politics*, VII, No. 1 (October 1954), p. 144.

[3] Yale Brozen has become the most articulate professional spokesman in America for those economists and business leaders who consider private entrepreneurship an indispensable ingredient in economic development over the long period. His position is summarized in his essay, 'Entrepreneurship and Technological Change', in Williamson and Buttrick, op. cit., pp. 196–236, and this in turn is summarized in a one-sentence quotation from W. T. Easterbrook (ibid., p. 224): 'The straightest, perhaps the only, road to social security is via entrepreneurial security.'

An interesting and suggestive classification of entrepreneurship into 'innovating', 'imitative', 'Fabian', and 'drone' varieties, due to Clarence Danhof, is used by Brozen, ibid., p. 205.

shares which are not ploughed back into economic development. Table II, summarizing these results, is presented immediately below.

Table II : Confiscation, Russian Style

Line No.	Units	Current	After 5 years	After 10 years	After 20 years
1. Real income ..	Absolute	100·0	113·1	128·4	166·1
2. Service income	,,	85·0	96·2	109·1	141·2
3. Property income	,,	0·0	0·0	0·0	0·0
4. Saving ratio ..	Per cent	10·0	10·0	10·0	10·0
5. Development investment ratio	,,	10·0	10·0	10·0	10·0
6. Population growth rate	,,	1·50	1·55	1·60	1·65
7. Aggregate income growth rate ..	,,	2·48	2·50	2·53	2·57
8. *Per capita* income growth rate ..	,,	0·98	0·95	0·93	0·92
9. *Per capita* income	Index No.	100·0	104·9	119·7	120·1
10. *Per capita* service income	,,	85·0	89·1	93·3	102·1

Notes : (Line 7) = ·125 (Line 5) + ·55 (Line 6) + 0·40
(Line 8) = (Line 7) – (Line 6) (Approximation)
(Line 6) and (Line 7) are geometric means over the respective time periods.

Model III. A lower rate of growth after the 'Revolution', but higher personal incomes during the earlier years of development, can be obtained by diverting part of what was formerly property income for consumption purposes. In the third model, one-third of property income (5 per cent of national income, 6 per cent of service income) is redistributed to the recipients of service income, as for example by increases in industrial real wages or by replacement of high agricultural land rents by lower agricultural land taxes. Property income, in this third model, has therefore been divided into three equal parts : developmental investments, leakages, and transfers to service income. This disposal of the proceeds of confiscation to include transfers to service income I call 'Chinese style', although the figures bear no intentional quantitative similarity to actual developments in Mainland China.[1]

The other assumptions of Model II are retained here, with the results presented as Table III. All the unfavourable features of Model II are retained; the leakages, the inefficiencies in resource allocation, the slowing of innovation, the increased population growth rate. Another 'unfavourable' feature has been added, from the developmental point of view: redistribution of income from savers to spenders. Nevertheless, growth is more rapid than under Model I, as measured either by aggregate or *per capita* income. Growth is slower than under the 'Russian-style' confiscation of Model II, but it reaches the common people more rapidly, due to the redistribution feature. (Comparing Tables I and III, no great divergence can be seen

Table III: Confiscation, Chinese Style

Line No.	Units	Current	After 5 years	After 10 years	After 20 years
1. Real income ..	Absolute	100·0	109·8	120·8	146·6
2. Service income ..	,,	90·0	98·8	108·7	131·9
3. Property income .	,,	0·0	0·0	0·0	0·0
4. Saving ratio ..	Per cent	5·0	5·0	5·0	5·0
5. Developmental investment ratio .	,,	5·0	5·0	5·0	5·0
6. Population growth rate	,,	1·50	1·55	1·60	1·65
7. Aggregate income growth	,,	1·86	1·88	1·91	1·93
8. *Per capita* income growth rate ..	,,	0·36	0·33	0·31	0·28
9. *Per capita* income	Index No.	100·0	101·7	103·4	105·8
10. *Per capita* service income	,,	90·0	91·5	93·1	95·2

Notes: (Line 7) = ·125 (Line 5) + ·55 (Line 6) + 0·40
(Line 8) = (Line 7) − (Line 6) (Approximation)
(Line 6) and (Line 7) are geometric means over the respective time periods.

[1] It is conceivable that Russian practice after Stalin's death may be shifting closer to this model than to Model II.

in the course of income *per capita*. The divergence in service income *per capita*, the more significant item for the masses, is attributable almost entirely to redistribution on the basis of these arbitrary figures.)

Choice as between Models II and III depends upon the preferences of revolutionary societies, and still more of revolutionary leaders. Time preferences are important, and likewise the choice between high growth rates and income redistribution. As this is written (1954–5), Model III seems to exercise the greater fascination for the underdeveloped world.

Neither of the confiscation models, it should be noted, forces the common people to finance development themselves in terms of lower real incomes at any time, although the attainment of higher real incomes may be postponed in the interests of capital accumulation. Comparing either model with the status quo, it is difficult to see how any could prefer the latter, unless he be an adherent of morality *ruat coelum* or of Professor Ayres' 'Divine Right of Capital'. The popular appeal of confiscation appears to require less economic explanation than does the democratic resistance thereto.

Confiscation of capitalist property and property income is credited with no significant part in the economic development of Western Europe, North America, Australasia, or Japan. If our models possess any verisimilitude, this seems strange at first glance. Yet there are a number of reasons which combined to make the developing Western world safe for the capitalist in the nineteenth century, which cannot be relied upon to make the developing remainder of the world equally safe for his biological or spiritual progeny in the twentieth century. Some of these considerations relate directly to certain of the figures of our models; others involve social issues which we have been unable to reduce to numerical form. I list eight factors; no historical instance rested significantly on all eight, and no one of the eight applied significantly to all the economies which developed early.[1]

[1] The development of this section was assisted significantly by Benjamin Higgins' paper on 'Economic Development of Underdeveloped Areas, Past and Present', (*Land Economics*, August 1955) and by the criticisms by several friends of an earlier draft of the present essay.

1. Highly important, except in the Japanese case, was the the high social mobility which prevailed in the developing countries. In most cases, the period of rapid development seems to have been an age of 'three generations from shirt-sleeves to shirt-sleeves'. More significantly, it was an age in which entrepreneurship in developmental activity was a promising route from the bottom to the top of the social ladder. A large part of the population saw its future, or its descendants' future, in entrepreneurship and thereafter in property-ownership, however extravagant these visions became in the event. As a result, neither egalitarianism nor confiscation could hold great popular appeal over long periods. Social mobility in an upward direction is exceptional in the underdeveloped communities of today, and such mobility as exists appears to exercise little influence on the political and economic attitudes of the people.

2. Expropriation, moreover, has seldom had in the advanced capitalist countries the aid of xenophobia which it has in much of the present-day underdeveloped world. Most of the capital in the Western countries was held by native citizens, if we except specie hoards in Italian, Jewish, or Levantine hands. These native citizens were not, like the *compradores* of China, the agents of foreign interests. When capital was foreign-held, the owners tended to be similar to native citizens in race, religion, and general mores. Ownership of capital was not associated with overbearing foreigners prejudiced against 'the natives' on racial or religious grounds. Such prejudice and overbearingness as existed was primarily in the opposite direction most of the time, as witness the history of European Jewry. The contrast with present-day Asia, Africa, or Latin America need not be dwelt on further.

3. In the eighteenth and nineteenth centuries there was little of the self-conscious haste that infuses the two-to-ten-year plans of today. (Japan under the Meiji Emperor was a partial exception, as was Germany under Bismarck.) There was implicit confidence that development would come in time, by Adam Smith's 'invisible hand', and relative unconcern about the precise date. The United States, for example, waited for 100 years after independence as a satisfied raw material producer, before challenging British primacy in manufacturing

on the world market. During the same period, American enterprisers extended railroads ahead of their traffic and built factories beyond the market capacity for their outputs, relying on the next decade or generation (plus tariffs or subsidies, but not central planning) to justify their rashness. The underdeveloped countries of today, precisely because they have been left behind for a century or more, want to catch up in a hurry, and have no faith in market forces or private enterprise to achieve in 1950 what they did not achieve in 1850 or 1900.

4. In our Model I, only 13 per cent of property income is reinvested in domestic economic development. The appeal of confiscation would be less if this figure were higher. The figure given is probably too high for much of the present underdeveloped world. But it would have been too low for New England, Yorkshire, or the Ruhr Valley, during their periods of expansion. For these regions rose to economic greatness when the Calvinistic heritage dominated their religious scene, although Calvin himself had long passed away. The Calvinist heritage meant, in the nineteenth century as well as the sixteenth and seventeenth, that high incomes were justified, if at all, by high saving and investment, and that luxurious consumption was frowned upon as abuse of divine stewardship. Delhi and Versailles might have exercised the same 'demonstration effect' upon developing Boston and Manchester—lowering investment and disturbing the balance of payments—which Paris and Hollywood exercise on developing Latin America today. But they did not, and private capital justified itself by its works. In the present underdeveloped world, however, the drive of wealthy businessmen 'to accumulate capital and expand their enterprises is continuously counteracted by the urgent desire (or social compulsion) to imitate in their living habits the socially dominant "old families", to prove by their conspicuous outlays that they are socially (and therefore also politically) not inferior to their aristocratic partners in the socially ruling coalition'[1]. Or, as the matter is summed up by Spengler, production dominated consumption in the developing West of the eighteenth and nineteenth centuries, while

[1] Paul A. Baran, 'National Economic Planning', in B. F. Haley (ed.), *Survey of Contemporary Economics*, Vol. II (Homewood, Illinois, 1952), p. 378.

consumption is tending to dominate production in the underdeveloped countries of the twentieth century.[1]

5. Conversely, eighteenth- and nineteenth-century governments were less adequately equipped to execute economic development projects than the Iron and Bamboo Curtain governments of the twentieth century. To hand over property or property income to the typical Stuart, Bourbon, or Romanoff monarch or minister would have wasted the returns and the principal as well. More chaos than progress would have resulted from State Socialism under Charles II, Louis XV, or Nicholas II. Leakages would have absorbed 100 per cent of the property income. Aesop's fable of the goose and the golden eggs would have applied. The classical economists were platitudinously right in listing the security of private property as a requisite for economic progress.[2] But as John Stuart Mill himself seems to have foreseen, this doctrine can no longer be applied without modification.[3] Although many a government of a modern underdeveloped country follows the ineffective Stuart-Bourbon-Romanoff pattern, there is usually a good chance that its revolutionary successor will not. In weighing the feasibility of a Socialist alternative to a stagnant capitalism, the present character of the existing non-Socialist government (viz. the Kuomintang of Chiang Kai-shek) should often be given less weight than the anticipated character of its Socialist rival (in this case, the Chinese Communist Party).

6. Confiscation of capitalist property and its income may have played no great part in the economic development of the Western world,[4] but other forms of confiscation were not

[1] Joseph J. Spengler, op. cit., p. 96.

[2] See, e.g., John Stuart Mill, *Principles of Political Economy* (ed. W. J. Ashley) (London, 1909), pp. 881 f.

[3] Ibid., pp. 204–11, including a famous passage (p. 208) :
'If, therefore, the choice were to be made between Communism with all its chances, and the present state of society with all its sufferings and injustices ; if the institution of private property necessarily carried with it as a consequence, that the produce of labour should be apportioned as we now see it, almost in an inverse ratio to the labour . . . if this or Communism were the alternative, all the difficulties, great or small, of Communism would be but as dust in the balance.'

[4] Although Americans, for example, should not forget the wholesale debt repudiations of the Midwestern and South Central States following the Panic of 1837.

avoided. The natural resources of America, Canada, Australia, New Zealand, South Africa were confiscated from aboriginal tribes. Individual and communal rights of the English peasantry were confiscated piecemeal over the three or four centuries of the enclosure movement. Feudal baronies in France and ecclesiastical properties in England, rice subventions of Japanese *samurai*, were all confiscated by the State and converted largely to private developmental uses as incidents of the French Revolution, the English Reformation, and the Westernization of Japan. So great was the loot of Bengal that Premier Nehru can speak, with no more than pardonable patriotic exaggeration, of the British industrial revolution of the eighteenth century being financed through the proceeds of confiscated Indian capital.[1] One is reminded of Karl Marx on 'The Genesis of the Industrial Capitalist': 'If money . . . comes into the world with a congenital blood-stain on one cheek, capital comes dripping from head to foot, from every pore, with blood and dirt.'[2]

7. With such exceptions as have been mentioned, the legitimacy of private property rights, acquired through purchase or bequest, has been recognized throughout the Western world throughout the period of Western economic development. It has become too fundamental a part of the Western legal system to succumb to immediate frontal assault. But under the impact of international collectivist ideologies, the 'legitimacy' concept of property rights is following the 'legitimacy' concept of royal sovereignty into the discard in country after country, where it has become less firmly and honourably established. This is particularly true when, as in such cases as the *zamindari* of India, or the oil concessions of Iran, 'legitimate' ownership rights are traceable to questionable transactions in a relatively recent past.

8. Some developed countries (Japan being perhaps the best example) accumulated the bulk of the capital for their development from the masses of the people. In Japan this was done by keeping the peasants at the subsistence level through

[1] Jawaharlal Nehru, *The Discovery of India* (New York: John Day, 1946), p. 296 f., citing also Brooks Adams, *The Law of Civilization and Decay*.

[2] Karl Marx, *Capital*, Vol. I (Chicago, 1906), p. 834.

increasing land taxes (which were shifted generally to the tenant farmers),[1] and holding real wages down through inflation and monopsonistic labour market practices. But the peasants and workers of most underdeveloped countries have become too well enlightened by Leftist leaders, and have come to possess too much military and political strength, for such alternatives to confiscation to be widely effective in raising capital in the latter half of the twentieth century.[2]

Confiscation of property and property income runs counter to Western notions of economic morality. More important, it runs counter to Western economic interests. For when property is expropriated, foreign property will usually be expropriated earlier and on less considerate terms than domestic.[3] Western nations are therefore doubly concerned with the appeal of confiscation in underdeveloped countries. If, as I believe, the appeal of confiscation makes economic sense, it will probably increase with time. The question arises : How should Western policy meet the ideological and the practical threats to Western interests ?

The optimum solution, from the Western point of view, would be a reformist, voluntary 'democratic alternative', which would provide growth rates comparable to those of our Models II and III without the concomitant expropriation of

[1] Shifting of land taxes to tenants implies a situation in which landlords were not exacting maximum rentals from tenants before the taxes were imposed or increased. The feudal landlords in Japan prior to the Meiji Restoration were far from economic men, and probably failed in many cases to collect the full rental value of their properties.

[2] The principal exception to this generalization is found where the Government forces crop deliveries at low fixed prices, and then resells them at higher market prices, the profit going largely for development purposes. (Thailand and Burma, for example, gain large revenues from this system of rice marketing.) If the analysis in the text is correct, such regressive taxation of the peasantry will not continue politically feasible for many years after the peasants are informed (as they are being informed) of the economic significance of the two-price policies.

[3] There are many exceptions to this general statement (e.g., Yugoslavia under Marshal Tito), usually involving political relations between the expropriating country and the homelands of the foreign investors.

foreign and domestic property.[1] Many such 'democratic alternatives' may be found on paper: taxation (other than capital levies), increased saving by propertied classes, 'mobilizing' this saving for development purposes, and so on. Efforts in these directions are laudable, and nothing said here should be interpreted in their disparagement. However, I shall make the pessimistic assumption in the remainder of this paper that, for much of the underdeveloped world, any 'democratic' or 'voluntary' alternative is too little and comes too late—that it is, in other words, Utopian—so that the appeal of confiscation must be answered by suppression of revolutionary movements and/or through sweetening of the *status quo* through economic aid from Western sources.

The traditional way of dealing with backward peoples' disregard of advanced Western concepts of property rights has been suppression, and the traditional mechanism of suppression has been a species of the genus 'imperialism'. The precepts of Western business etiquette and the interests of Western economic adventurers were enforced simultaneously upon the 'lesser breeds without the Law'. Offending countries became colonies, dependencies, protectorates, satellites, 'spheres of influence', or were otherwise disciplined. This was 'gunboat diplomacy'. But the gunboat diplomacy species of imperialism has passed with its prophet, Rudyard Kipling. There will doubtless remain for some time areas in which one or another Power finds an aerial version of gunboat diplomacy effective in enforcing the economic proprieties in the interests of its influential citizens. (Kenya in Africa and Guatemala in Central America come to mind, in the context of the middle 1950s.) But such areas are apparently shrinking rather than expanding, and gunboat diplomacy has come not always to pay even where it still works. That is to say, the enmities which it creates are becoming more widespread and therefore more costly to combat around the globe and in the long run than is justified

[1] Critics have suggested another optimum solution, from the Western point of view: the indefinite renunciation of economic development by the 'backward' two-thirds of the world's population. This is (almost) certainly wrong. Almost any development short of autarchy creates customers and suppliers for the rest of the world faster than it creates competitors—special cases to the contrary notwithstanding.

by the value of the capital it preserves in the limited area still open to its use. A country forcibly restrained from expropriating property income this year may go 'behind the Curtain' in the next. Or its example will be used to move some other country Leftward (or Eastward, as the case may be).

Imperialistic repression of confiscation now operates generally in disguise, as a necessary concession to world-wide nationalistic aspirations. Its usual present form is the supply of military assistance to maintain in power governments in underdeveloped countries which can be trusted not to confiscate foreign property, however little may be said for them on other grounds and however little support they may be able to generate among their subjects. But many of the objections to gunboat diplomacy apparently apply with almost equal force to this successor. It too often fails, outside the military orbit of some Western power. And when it succeeds, it too may not be worth its cost in the long run, when the regime maintained in power is a stench in its neighbours' nostrils and the method of maintenance alienates these neighbours politically and economically.

The expectation of rewards for good behaviour, in the form of future foreign loans and investments, seems already much more efficacious in forestalling expropriation than is the fear of punishment or the bolstering of 'friendly' governments by military aid. When a country stands to lose more in future aid by confiscating private capital within its control than it stands to gain from the value of the capital at stake, it usually exercises a seemly caution and restraint in dealing with private interests affiliated with sources of potential largesse. But the hope or the promise of reward must be substantial, plausible, and contemporary. Crumbs from the table will not do, nor pie in the sky when you die. Here lies the rub, for those benevolent global planners in the United States and the international agencies who hope to forestall confiscatory financing indefinitely by a spate of kind words and a few billion dollars spread thinly in time and space over the underdeveloped world.

Once the loans and investments are made, moreover, their expansion cannot end easily. Capital sunk at long term in a foreign land is, like a wife and children, a hostage to fortune. (In this case, a hostage to expropriation.) The hostage may be safeguarded by additional capital, or promises thereof. When made, these additional loans and investments become ransoms to expropriation. Like other ransoms, they must be large and they must eventually be delivered. Unlike other ransoms, each payment becomes another hostage to be ransomed. As the total hostage of capital increases, the greater the temptation it presents to the confiscator, and the greater the ransom required for its continued protection. The greater becomes the value of existing foreign investment required continuously to safeguard it against expropriation.[1]

The attempt by the West to bribe or buy its way out of confiscation of its investments in the underdeveloped countries may yet become the white man's burden of the twentieth century. It is costly enough in the present, to taxpayers in the advanced countries and to victims of inflation and material shortages. What is more alarming is that each instalment paid on the cost will increase rather than decrease the cost of each subsequent instalment, with no upper bound in sight until the borrowing country has achieved development at a rate satisfactory to its leaders.

In these circumstances, my own suggestion is for withdrawal, for 'economic neo-isolation' of the developed from the underdeveloped world. It is less a suggestion for a new policy, in fact, than a franker and more brutal recognition of the nature of present Western policy, and for undeceiving the underdeveloped countries regarding prospects for early relaxation.

Capital remains scarce, despite gloomy forecasts of its superfluity in 'mature economies'. It remains scarce for purely domestic uses both civil and military.[2] Capital being scarce, the advanced countries give first priority to their domestic needs, and distribute it for development in the rest of the world only on a cautious and niggardly scale. They make it available abroad—in quantity, that is to say—only at going rates of interest, and under acceptable guarantees against not only expropriation but also freezing of interest, profits, and principal repayments.

[1] In this discussion I consider the absolute volume of new investment, not its proportion to the national income of the investing country.

[2] I need not face the issue here as to whether the scarcity would survive reduction of Western defence expenditures to the level of the 1920s.

Neo-isolation, as I see it, is little beyond explicit recognition of the facts if I see them aright, and a resulting limitation of government (and government-guaranteed) development loans within the same quantitative limits as the charitable grants typified by the American Point Four programme, however meagre and unsatisfactory these limits may seem to developing countries. Neo-isolation, if adopted as formal policy, would mean saying (as against hinting) to the governments of the underdeveloped countries: 'We appreciate and sympathize with your desire for economic progress. Therefore we recognize the appeal of expropriation in financing economic development, if not to yourselves then to your successors in office. We recognize as well the economic soundness of confiscation, from your point of view. We therefore feel it unsafe to lend you appreciably more than we can afford to present you free of charge. We are unwilling to assume a financial "white man's burden" of ransoming an increasing volume of existing loans and investments from confiscation by an increasing volume of new ones. If private individuals and international associations are more venturesome, well and good, but we are unwilling to underwrite their ventures.'

Such bluntness and brutality would lead to an immediate disadvantage to the West. It would accelerate, by decades if not by generations, the evil day of expropriation of existing Western assets in many countries, although (if the previous argument is correct) it would reduce total Western losses from the expropriation process. Neo-isolation would also raise delicate questions of relations with expropriating governments, and questions of possible domestic compensation to the owners of the confiscated foreign assets. These questions involve details which must be worked out differently in each case, but certain general rules may apply and may be useful:

1. Diplomatic relations with confiscating governments should not be broken off.

2. No more favourable treatment should be demanded for Western nationals in the event of confiscation than is given to citizens of the confiscating country. (If more favourable treatment is offered, without pressure, there is no reason for non-acceptance.) Equality of treatment should ordinarily be striven for; it cannot always be achieved.

3. Domestic compensation for victims of foreign expropriation should neither be promised nor ruled out wholesale. Amounts to be paid should be estimated on the merits of individual cases, with consideration for (*a*) the manner in which the property was acquired, (*b*) the historical and reproduction cost of the assets confiscated, (*c*) the record of the claimant's relations with the government and people of the confiscating country prior to confiscation, and (*d*) the returns already paid prior to confiscation. If guarantees of domestic compensation are made to enterprisers of particular foreign projects, they should be conditional upon satisfactory performance on points (*a*) and (*c*) above, upon application of the 'prudent investment' principle under point (*b*), and upon moderation under point (*d*). Compensation should not be paid for unrealized capital gains from speculation in real estate or in inventories.

Underdeveloped areas are not all alike. There are many in which our pessimistic models do not apply. There are many in which a 'democratic alternative' to both stagnation and confiscation is in actual operation. There is no uniform treadmill which one may call 'The Political Economy of Backwardness'.[1] For this reason among others, there are many countries in which confiscation is not a near-term problem. In these countries, a defeatist neo-isolation policy should not be applied. It is not in fact being applied there ; statistical analysis shows Western aid concentrated in such countries, to an extent otherwise incomprehensibly disproportionate.[2]

[1] For an opposite view, cf. Paul A. Baran, 'On the Political Economy of Backwardness', reprinted in the present volume, pp. 75-92, as well as other writings already cited in this essay. Baran is more right than wrong in his neo-Marxian analyses. His writings are a welcome antidote to the Pollyanna pronunciamentos of some official agencies and the unfounded confidence in 'pragmatism' (or 'muddling through') of the remainder. Baran suffers nevertheless from the oversimplification of identifying every backward area with every other, with the Poland of the inter-war 'Colonels' Clique' as the possible archetype.

[2] Concentration of Western loans and investments in areas where confiscation is not threatened may conceivably, if the results are favourable, exercise some degree of contagion on the remainder of the underdeveloped world, and reduce somewhat the general threat of confiscation.

What are the underdeveloped areas to which neo-isolation is inappropriate? There would appear to be five major categories in which large-scale international lending for development purposes seems appropriate, and in most of which it is in fact being carried on.

1. Isolation would be mistaken, first of all, in areas which, while technically underdeveloped, have already attained high living standards and rapid social mobility upwards. Here confiscation exercises no more appeal than it did on the nineteenth-century American frontier. These are the areas *par excellence* of successful 'democratic alternatives' to both stagnation and expropriation. Alaska, Labrador, and perhaps Brazil provide examples. Illustrations from Asia, from Africa, or from heavily populated regions generally are difficult if not impossible to find.

2. At the other end of the scale, isolation need not be applied in those areas in which there is nothing worth confiscating, i.e. in which there is neither property income nor luxury consumption on any scale. Libya, Afghanistan, and Nepal are examples. Loans and investments here may or may not be productive, but they will probably be safe from expropriation unless these countries are taken over by Communist aggression, unless the investments themselves create a leisure class as target for expropriation, or unless the burden of interest charges and principal repayments is set too high for the countries to meet while still developing at reasonable rates.

3. Isolation should not apply, thirdly, where the yield of capital is high enough to satisfy simultaneously the demands of foreign investors and the aspirations of domestic political leaders. Regions rich in natural resources, particularly petroleum, fall into this category: Saudi Arabia in the Middle East, Venezuela in South America, Brunei on the island of Borneo. Paradoxically, this category also includes many of the 'new democracies', where confiscation has already occurred and a rapid growth rate has already been attained. A foreign loan to the Soviet Union, which expropriated all pre-1917 foreign investments in Russia, would be a safer economic proposition than a foreign loan to, let us say, Cambodia, in which confiscation of Western assets has never been permitted. Reluctance or refusal to consider investment in loans to socialist

states is ascribable more readily to resentment of the past than to timorousness for the future.

4. Isolation is also ill-advised in areas where expropriation of property is ruled out by the fundamental law of a Western Power close enough to exercise effective supervision—tinged with imperialism, if you will. Puerto Rico and Cuba are cases in point here. In other areas, such as Portugal, political control seems safely in the hands of the propertied classes and their religious allies for the next generation or two, and expropriation does not loom presently as a significant political possibility.

5. The final exception pertains to instances of particularly close racial, religious, or cultural ties between developing countries and foreign sources of capital, which assuage the conflicts of interest that might otherwise occur. It would be difficult to imagine Israel, for example, defaulting on its obligations to Western Jewish communities while it retains its independence, or New Zealand defaulting on obligations to creditors in Great Britain.

But these are after all little more than exceptions. They do not disturb seriously my general anticipation of an increasing appeal of confiscation in economic growth, until the bulk of world development is financed by State expropriation of the property share of the national income. Neither do they disturb seriously my general recommendation of continued economic isolation and withdrawal from most of the non-Socialist underdeveloped world as the 'least worst' policy for Western capitalism in the face of the threat implied in the appeal of confiscation. These defeatist conclusions apply particularly in Asia, where the direct influence of the Russian and Chinese expropriations is greatest, and where counter-pressures from the West can least easily be brought to bear.

INDEX